BESTSELLING BOOK SERIES

Creating Web Pages A
Desk Reference For D

B

2008

The Many Technologies Packed into a Web Page

26x 7/13

Blogs & Online Services
(Book II)

HTML/XHTML
(Book VI)

JavaScript
(Book VIII)

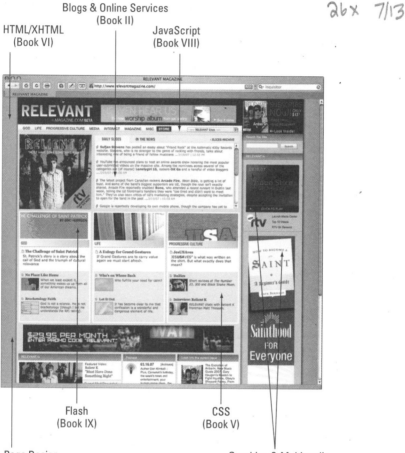

Flash
(Book IX)

CSS
(Book V)

Page Design
(Book I)

Graphics & Multimedia
(Book VII)

Dissecting an HTML Element

Element (or tag)

Start tag

End tag

`<a href="index.html">Home</a>`

Attribute

Attribute value

Content

For Dummies: Bestselling Book Series for Beginners

Creating Web Pages All-in-One Desk Reference For Dummies®

Cheat Sheet

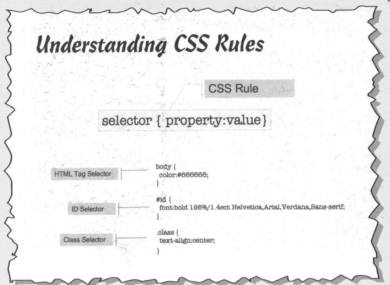

Understanding CSS Rules

CSS Rule

selector { property:value }

HTML Tag Selector
```
body {
  color:#666666;
}
```

ID Selector
```
#id {
  font:bold 195%/1.4em Helvetica,Arial,Verdana,Sans-serif;
}
```

Class Selector
```
.class {
  text-align:center;
}
```

Ten (or So) Really Useful (and Free) Web Sites

Site	Use When You Need To . . .
Stock.xchng (www.sxc.hu)	Download free quality stock photos
www.morguefile.com/	Download more free quality stock photos
www.dafont.com	Download free fonts
Open Source Web Design (www.oswd.org)	Download free design templates
www.colourlovers.com	Get color palettes for your site
Typetester (typetester.maratz.com)	Compare fonts side-by-side to use on your site
www.browsershots.com	Test your page design in different browsers
iCapture (www.danvine.com/icapture)	See what your page design looks like in Mac OS X Safari
www.gliffy.com	Create flowcharts and other diagrams for your site
www.flashkit.com	Download free Flash source files and resources
www.dynamicdrive.com	Download free JavaScript scripts

Wiley, the Wiley Publishing logo, For Dummies, the Dummies Man logo, the For Dummies Bestselling Book Series logo and all related trade dress are trademarks or registered trademarks of John Wiley & Sons, Inc. and/or its affiliates. All other trademarks are property of their respective owners.

Copyright © 2007 Wiley Publishing, Inc. All rights reserved. Item 9629-1.

For more information about Wiley Publishing, call 1-800-762-2974.

For Dummies: Bestselling Book Series for Beginners

Creating Web Pages
ALL-IN-ONE DESK REFERENCE

FOR

DUMMIES®

3RD EDITION

SAN DIEGO PUBLIC LIBRARY
OCEAN BEACH

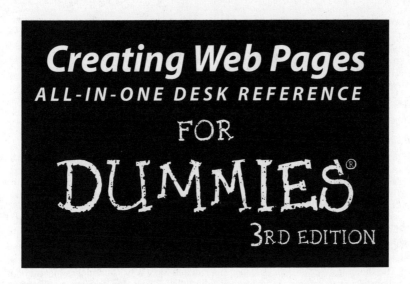

Creating Web Pages
ALL-IN-ONE DESK REFERENCE
FOR
DUMMIES®
3RD EDITION

by Richard Wagner and Richard Mansfield

APR 2 1 2008

SAN DIEGO PUBLIC LIBRARY
OCEAN BEACH

BICENTENNIAL
1807
WILEY
2007
BICENTENNIAL

Wiley Publishing, Inc.

Creating Web Pages All-in-One Desk Reference For Dummies®, 3rd Edition
Published by
Wiley Publishing, Inc.
111 River Street
Hoboken, NJ 07030-5774
www.wiley.com

Copyright © 2007 by Wiley Publishing, Inc., Indianapolis, Indiana

Published by Wiley Publishing, Inc., Indianapolis, Indiana

Published simultaneously in Canada

No part of this publication may be reproduced, stored in a retrieval system or transmitted in any form or by any means, electronic, mechanical, photocopying, recording, scanning or otherwise, except as permitted under Sections 107 or 108 of the 1976 United States Copyright Act, without either the prior written permission of the Publisher, or authorization through payment of the appropriate per-copy fee to the Copyright Clearance Center, 222 Rosewood Drive, Danvers, MA 01923, (978) 750-8400, fax (978) 646-8600. Requests to the Publisher for permission should be addressed to the Legal Department, Wiley Publishing, Inc., 10475 Crosspoint Blvd., Indianapolis, IN 46256, (317) 572-3447, fax (317) 572-4355, or online at http://www.wiley.com/go/permissions.

Trademarks: Wiley, the Wiley Publishing logo, For Dummies, the Dummies Man logo, A Reference for the Rest of Us!, The Dummies Way, Dummies Daily, The Fun and Easy Way, Dummies.com, and related trade dress are trademarks or registered trademarks of John Wiley & Sons, Inc. and/or its affiliates in the United States and other countries, and may not be used without written permission. All other trademarks are the property of their respective owners. Wiley Publishing, Inc., is not associated with any product or vendor mentioned in this book.

LIMIT OF LIABILITY/DISCLAIMER OF WARRANTY: THE PUBLISHER AND THE AUTHOR MAKE NO REPRESENTATIONS OR WARRANTIES WITH RESPECT TO THE ACCURACY OR COMPLETENESS OF THE CONTENTS OF THIS WORK AND SPECIFICALLY DISCLAIM ALL WARRANTIES, INCLUDING WITHOUT LIMITATION WARRANTIES OF FITNESS FOR A PARTICULAR PURPOSE. NO WARRANTY MAY BE CREATED OR EXTENDED BY SALES OR PROMOTIONAL MATERIALS. THE ADVICE AND STRATEGIES CONTAINED HEREIN MAY NOT BE SUITABLE FOR EVERY SITUATION. THIS WORK IS SOLD WITH THE UNDERSTANDING THAT THE PUBLISHER IS NOT ENGAGED IN RENDERING LEGAL, ACCOUNTING, OR OTHER PROFESSIONAL SERVICES. IF PROFESSIONAL ASSISTANCE IS REQUIRED, THE SERVICES OF A COMPETENT PROFESSIONAL PERSON SHOULD BE SOUGHT. NEITHER THE PUBLISHER NOR THE AUTHOR SHALL BE LIABLE FOR DAMAGES ARISING HEREFROM. THE FACT THAT AN ORGANIZATION OR WEBSITE IS REFERRED TO IN THIS WORK AS A CITATION AND/OR A POTENTIAL SOURCE OF FURTHER INFORMATION DOES NOT MEAN THAT THE AUTHOR OR THE PUBLISHER ENDORSES THE INFORMATION THE ORGANIZATION OR WEBSITE MAY PROVIDE OR RECOMMENDATIONS IT MAY MAKE. FURTHER, READERS SHOULD BE AWARE THAT INTERNET WEBSITES LISTED IN THIS WORK MAY HAVE CHANGED OR DISAPPEARED BETWEEN WHEN THIS WORK WAS WRITTEN AND WHEN IT IS READ.

For general information on our other products and services, please contact our Customer Care Department within the U.S. at 800-762-2974, outside the U.S. at 317-572-3993, or fax 317-572-4002.

For technical support, please visit www.wiley.com/techsupport.

Wiley also publishes its books in a variety of electronic formats. Some content that appears in print may not be available in electronic books.

Library of Congress Control Number: 2007926387

ISBN: 978-0-470-09629-1

Manufactured in the United States of America

10 9 8 7 6 5 4 3 2 1

WILEY

About the Authors

Richard Wagner is an experienced Web designer, the inventor of the NetObjects ScriptBuilder Web tool, and the former vice president of product development for NetObjects. A versatile writer with a wide range of interests, he is also the author of *XSLT For Dummies*, *C.S. Lewis & Narnia For Dummies* (both published by Wiley), and many others. His online home is at Digitalwalk.net.

Richard Mansfield's recent titles include *CSS Web Design For Dummies* (Wiley), *Office 2003 Application Development All-in-One Desk Reference For Dummies* (Wiley), *Visual Basic .NET Power Tools*, with Evangelos Petroutsos (Sybex), and *The Savvy Guide to Digital Music* (SAMS). From 1981 through 1987, he was the editor of *COMPUTE!* magazine. Richard has written hundreds of magazine articles and two columns. He began writing books full time in 1991 and has written a total of 40 books. Of those, four became bestsellers: *Machine Language for Beginners* and *The Second Book of Machine Language* (both from COMPUTE! Books), *The Visual Guide to Visual Basic*, and *Visual Basic Power Toolkit,* with Evangelos Petroutsos (both from Ventana). Overall, his books have sold more than 500,000 copies worldwide and have been translated into 12 languages.

Dedication

From Richard Mansfield: To my agent, Matt Wagner.

Authors' Acknowledgments

From Richard Wagner: I was thankful for working with a superior editorial team at Wiley during the production of this book. My sincere thanks to Nicole Sholly, for her flawless management of this project. Thanks also to Elizabeth Kuball, for her attention to detail and keen editing eye. Danilo Celic brought to the book a strong technical insight that ensured an overall consistency in quality and coverage. Many thanks also go to Steve Hayes, for his steady hand on the project, as well as my agent, Matt Wagner. Finally, a special thanks goes to my wife, Kimberly, and our three boys. I've got the best "home field advantage" of any author.

From Richard Mansfield: I'd like to thank all the good people at Wiley for their assistance with this book. Gratitude, in particular, goes to Nicole Sholly for her helpful explanations and thoughtful comments. In addition, I thank Rebecca Whitney and Teresa Artman, the copy editors, and Danilo Celic, the technical editor, for their contributions to the book's quality.

Publisher's Acknowledgments

We're proud of this book; please send us your comments through our online registration form located at www.dummies.com/register/.

Some of the people who helped bring this book to market include the following:

Acquisitions, Editorial, and Media Development

Project Editor: Nicole Sholly

Senior Acquisitions Editor: Steve Hayes

Copy Editors: Rebecca Whitney, Teresa Artman

Technical Editor: Danilo Celic

Editorial Manager: Kevin Kirschner

Media Development and Quality Assurance: Angela Denny, Kate Jenkins, Steven Kudirka, Kit Malone

Media Development Coordinator: Jenny Swisher

Media Project Supervisor: Laura Moss-Hollister

Editorial Assistant: Amanda Foxworth

Sr. Editorial Assistant: Cherie Case

Cartoons: Rich Tennant (www.the5thwave.com)

Composition Services

Project Coordinator: Heather Kolter

Layout and Graphics: Claudia Bell, Carrie A. Foster, Denny Hager, Stephanie D. Jumper, Heather Ryan, Ronald Terry, Christine Williams

Proofreaders: Aptara, John Greenough

Indexer: Aptara

Anniversary Logo Design: Richard Pacifico

Publishing and Editorial for Technology Dummies

Richard Swadley, Vice President and Executive Group Publisher

Andy Cummings, Vice President and Publisher

Mary Bednarek, Executive Acquisitions Director

Mary C. Corder, Editorial Director

Publishing for Consumer Dummies

Diane Graves Steele, Vice President and Publisher

Joyce Pepple, Acquisitions Director

Composition Services

Gerry Fahey, Vice President of Production Services

Debbie Stailey, Director of Composition Services

Contents at a Glance

Table of Contents

Introduction

*I*f you're interested in creating a Web site, chances are that you've at least seen the terms *HTML, XHTML, CSS, JavaScript,* and *Flash* floating around. Maybe your friends talk about their blogs or MySpace pages and you don't know whether you should do the same or dive into using a more powerful tool, like Adobe Dreamweaver or Microsoft Expression Web.

However, unless you're a professional Web designer, you might be a bit unsure of — and maybe even a little intimidated by — figuring out where to start. You have to know which of these technologies is important to know about and which ones can be left to the techie-geek crowd. What's more, you need to know the *least* amount of information you need to have in order to create a decent Web site.

Along the way, you may occasionally need to dig into the code of your Web page and understand what's going on behind the scenes. However, when possible, you'll probably want to use Dreamweaver or Expression Web to handle most of that lower-level coding for you.

If these sorts of issues ring true for you, you have the right book in hand.

About This Book

In *Creating Web Pages All-in-One Desk Reference For Dummies,* 3rd Edition, we take you on a tour around the World Wide Web. The ten minibooks packed inside these pages cover all the "required" technologies that you need to know about to create Web pages. Here are some tasks that we show you how to do in this reference book:

✦ Create attractive, professional-looking Web pages.

✦ Enjoy some of the most popular Web services, including MySpace, eBay, Blogger, and Google Pages.

✦ Use Adobe Dreamweaver or Microsoft Expression Web to create Web sites.

✦ Make sense of HTML code.

✦ Use Cascading Style Sheets (CSS) to style your Web site.

✦ Use graphics and multimedia effectively.

✦ Make your pages interactive, by adding JavaScript scripts.

✦ Use Adobe Flash to add animated Flash movies to your site.

Foolish Assumptions

In *Creating Web Pages All-in-One Desk Reference For Dummies,* 3rd Edition, we don't assume that you already know to create a Web page or that you're familiar with the technologies we cover, such as HTML, Cascading Style Sheets, and JavaScript. However, we assume that you have surfed the Web and know what a Web site is. We also assume that you have a working knowledge of either a Windows or Mac computer and have used Microsoft Word or a similar word processing program.

Conventions Used in This Book

By *conventions*, we simply mean a set of rules we use in this book to present information to you consistently:

✦ **Screen shots:** Some of the browsers and Web site software that we cover in this book run on both the Microsoft Windows and Mac OS X platforms. The screen shots in this book feature both the Mac and Windows versions, but all the instructions are for both operating systems.

✦ **Special formatting:** When you see a term *italicized,* look for its definition, which is included so that you know what words mean in the context of Web site design and creation. Web site addresses and e-mail addresses appear in monofont so that they stand out from regular text. Code appears in its own font, set off from the rest of the text, like this:

```
<p class="normalPara">
It's a <em>brave</em> new world.
</p>
```

✦ **HTML terminology:** A Web page is created by using HTML, which is a *markup programming language* used for organizing and displaying the information you present. HTML is composed of many *elements,* such as a p (paragraph) that looks like this:

```
<p>Here is a paragraph</p>
```

The <p> is the *start tag,* and the </p> is the *end tag.* The text between them is the *content.* The entire piece of code is referred to as the p *element,* or *tag.* The terms are synonymous.

✦ **HTML and XHTML:** In Book VI, you explore what HTML and XHTML (Extensible HTML) are and how the technologies differ from each other. However, for the rest of the book, when we speak of HTML, we speak in a generic sense and are speaking of both HTML and XHTML in the discussion.

What You Don't Have to Read

We structured this book modularly: It's designed so that you can easily find just the information you need and so that you don't have to read anything that doesn't pertain to your task at hand. We include sidebars here and there throughout the book that contain interesting information that isn't necessarily integral to the discussion at hand; feel free to skip over them. You also don't have to read the Technical Stuff icons, which parse out ubertechie tidbits (which might or might not be your cup of tea).

How This Book Is Organized

Creating Web Pages All-in-One Desk Reference For Dummies, 3rd Edition, is split into nine minibooks. You don't have to read the book sequentially, you don't have to look at every minibook, you certainly don't have to read every chapter, and you don't even have to read all the sections in any particular chapter. (Of course, you can if you want to; the book is a good read.) And, the table of contents and the index can help you quickly find whatever information you need. In this section, we briefly describe the topics that each minibook contains.

Book 1: Web and Page Design

Start off right by exploring proven Web page design principles. Book I covers such topics as organizing an effective site, designing with white space, using the rule of thirds, and avoiding the nine most common Web site mistakes.

Book II: Online Services

Some of the hottest names on the Web are online services that you can use to create a presence on the Web. In this minibook, we show you how to create a MySpace page, a blog on Blogger, and a full Web site using Google Pages. Finally, we wrap up by showing you how to sell goods online through eBay.

Book III: Microsoft Expression Web

Expression Web is the flagship Web design tool from Microsoft. This integrated Web site design and authoring environment sports a visual page designer. In Book III, we walk you through the steps required to design, create, and publish a Web site by using Expression Web.

Book IV: Dreamweaver

Available for both Windows and Mac, Dreamweaver has long been the industry standard Web design software package. Book IV introduces you to the key features of Dreamweaver and shows you how to quickly become productive in using it.

Book V: Cascading Style Sheets

We don't think it's an overstatement to say that Cascading Style Sheets (or CSS, for short) is an essential technology to understand and work with as you begin to create Web sites. CSS helps revolutionize the way you structure a Web site by separating your page's content from the formatting rules you create. That may not sound like a big deal, but it makes your job as a Web site creator *much* easier. In this minibook, you discover the power of this technology by exploring all its major features, including inheritance, selectors, and cascades.

Book VI: HTML/XHTML

Web pages are written in the special tag-based languages HTML (short for Hypertext Markup Language) or XHTML (Extensible HTML). Dreamweaver and Expression Web generally do a good job of hiding the complex HTML code from you in their visual environments. However, in some cases, you can't avoid peeking "under the hood." Book VI comes in handy to help you know what's going on in the midst of the source code.

Book VII: Graphics and Multimedia

Graphics can make or break your Web site design. Book VII shows you how best to obtain images, optimize them, and explore other important graphics techniques, such as hotspots, image maps, and rollovers.

Book VIII: Scripting

In this minibook, you discover the world of JavaScript. Using JavaScript, you can write scripts for your Web pages to make them interactive and respond to user events (button clicks, for example). We introduce you to the key concepts you need to know to be productive with scripting and then show you how to seamlessly add scripts into your Web page and make them work.

Book IX: Flash

A Flash movie is by far the most important add-in to a Web page. In fact, Flash movies are so widespread and popular that some sites are written entirely by using Flash. With Flash, you can add interactivity and animation that goes far beyond what HTML and JavaScript can do by themselves. In this minibook, you discover how to be productive in the Flash authoring environment and how to create basic movies.

About the CD

The CD included with this book comes packed with several useful Windows and Mac applications and Web links to many more applications for instant downloading. You can use these software tools to help you in creating your Web pages.

Icons Used in This Book

Dummies books are known for using helpful icons that point you in the direction of useful information. This section briefly describes the icons used in this book.

The Tip icon points out helpful information or key techniques that can save you time and effort.

The Remember icon is used to point out something particularly important in the text to help you in your understanding of the technology.

The Warning icon is synonymous with saying "Hey, you — be careful!" When you see this icon, pay attention and proceed with caution.

This icon denotes nearby techie information. If you're not feeling very technical, you can skip this info.

Where to Go from Here

You can begin by starting out with Book I. Or, if you want to dive into a specific topic right away, consider any of these jumping-off points:

- ✦ To create an immediate Web presence, check out Book II.
- ✦ To create cool, well-designed pages, check out Book I, Chapter 2.
- ✦ To master style sheets, take a look at Book V.
- ✦ To find out the basics of creating an HTML document, check out Book VI, Chapter 1.
- ✦ To gain a working knowledge of the HTML source code, check out Books V, VI, and VIII.
- ✦ To create interactive Web sites, go to Books VIII and IX.

Book I

Web & Page Design

The 5th Wave   By Rich Tennant

RURAL WEB DESIGN

©RICHTENNANT

"What you want to do, is balance the image of the pick-up truck sittin' behind your home page, with a busted washing machine in the foreground."

Contents at a Glance

Chapter 1: Getting Started with Your Web Site

In This Chapter

↙ Getting to know the lingo for creating Web sites

↙ Understanding how a Web site is published

↙ Discovering Web sites that work and ones that don't

*P*erhaps you created a simple Web site in the past and are now ready for the next step.

Or, maybe you always wanted to build your first site but don't know the first place to start.

Either way, in this chapter, we outfit you with the basics you need to get you on the road to achieving the goals, purposes, hopes, dreams, imaginings, and hankerings that you have for your Web site. (The "hankerings" part may be difficult to pull off, but we'll do our best.)

In this chapter, we introduce you to all of the important terms, technologies, and tools that you use along the way.

Knowing the Lingo and the Basics

Anytime you start doing something new, one challenge is picking up the lingo. The Web has so many new terms floating about every day that you can easily pick up some terms, but you might find that other, more techie concepts or technologies go right over your head. So, here's a crash course to make sure that we're all on the same page.

Navigating the Web

A *Web site* is a collection of pages, usually formatted in HTML (Hypertext Markup Language), that contains text, graphics, and multimedia elements, such as Flash, audio, or video files. The main page of a site is known as a *home page,* which links to other documents in the site by using hyperlinks. All these pages are stored on a *Web server,* which is the name for a computer that hosts the site.

A variety of sites are on the Web, including

✦ Corporate sites

✦ Personal home pages

✦ Blogs

✦ MySpace profiles

✦ Special-interest sites

Every Web site has a unique address, known as a *URL* (Uniform Resource Locator). A URL looks like

```
http://www.cnn.com

http://www.myspace.com/everestdude

http://www.digitalwalk.net/index.html
```

The main part of the URL (`cnn.com`, `digitalwalk.net`) is known as a *domain name.*

A user enters the URL in a browser, such as Microsoft Internet Explorer. The browser sends the request across the Internet, and through the magic of Disney Imagineering, it winds up at the doorsteps of the Web server. (Okay, although the underlying technology is magical, Mickey Mouse has nothing to do with it.) The Web server then responds by sending the requested page back to the browser.

The Web server is often hosted by an Internet service provider (ISP) or Web hosting provider. Some providers are free, but generally most of the more reliable ones charge a fee for their services. Fortunately, intense competition has driven down the monthly fees to generally be the equivalent of three or four grande cappuccinos (our preferred form of currency).

If you have the right Internet connection (such as a T1 line), you can host a Web site on your own computer. Most cable and DSL customers, however, are prohibited from doing this.

Creating and publishing a Web site

When you create a Web site, you work with HTML (Hypertext Markup Language) documents. The HTML tag-based programming language is used for presenting information. It intermixes content with instructions for how and where to present it on the page.

These pages, which have a .html or .htm extension, look different depending on the software you use to view them. When you view an HTML document in a text editor like Notepad, you see a bunch of weird-looking code, as shown in Figure 1-1. However, a browser knows what all these instructions mean and can then *render* (a fancy word for processing and displaying) the document in all its visual glory, as shown in Figure 1-2.

Creating Web pages: The alternatives

When you create a presence on the Web, you can either put on a geek hat and write the HTML code for your Web site or let a piece of software (such as Dreamweaver) or an online service (such as MySpace) do this work for you. Most of these solutions allow you to work inside a visual environment to design your pages. Figure 1-3 shows you the visual editor inside Dreamweaver.

Because everyone's needs are different and can evolve over time, we show you all these alternatives in this book. Book II walks you through the online alternatives, such as MySpace and Blogger. Books III and IV show you how to work with the two major Web site builders that you can install on your computer. And, Book VI gives you the lowdown on how to successfully work with HTML code without getting a migraine.

Figure 1-1:
HTML documents can look intimidating "under the hood."

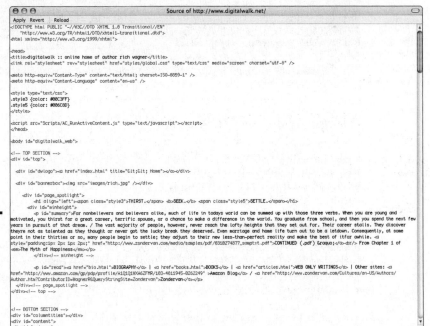

Figure 1-2:
HTML
documents,
however,
can look
visually
attractive
when
viewed in a
browser.

Adding graphics and other media files

If you're used to working with Microsoft Word or other word processors, you've probably added a graphical image to a document. When you perform this action in Word, it embeds a copy of the graphic from its original file into the document. Therefore, if you were to e-mail the file to a friend, the image would be displayed on your friend's computer when the document is opened.

In contrast, although HTML documents display graphics, video, and other media as content, this media is never stored inside the HTML file itself. Instead, the HTML document links to external image files or Flash media. Therefore, the Web site includes not only HTML documents but also any other media file that you add to your page layout.

The other common types of files you work with include

✦ Cascading Style Sheets (`.css`); see Book V

✦ Graphics (`.jpg`, `.gif`, and `.png`); see Book VII

✦ JavaScript files (`.js`); see Book VIII

✦ Flash movies (`.swf`); see Book IX

Publishing your site

When you're done creating your Web site, you *publish* your files to your Web site hosting server. If you're creating the pages on your own computer, publishing involves uploading all the HTML, graphic, and other media files. When the files have been successfully added to the Web server, the Web site is considered *live,* or open for all the world to see.

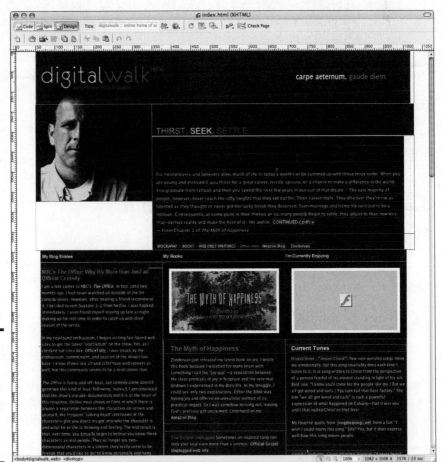

Figure 1-3:
Dream-
weaver
enables
you to work
with HTML
documents
visually.

Browsing the browsers

The software that we all use to navigate the Web is a *browser,* and you can choose from a few:

✔ **Microsoft Internet Explorer** is now the dominant browser; roughly 7 in 10 people use it as their main entryway to the World Wide Web.

✔ **Firefox**, a free open source browser, has emerged as the number-two browser. It not only works on all major platforms (Windows, Mac, and Linux) but also has an amazing number of free extensions that you can add to it, to greatly enhance your browsing experience. We have to recommend one extension in particular as an essential part of your Web site building toolkit. The Web Developer toolbar provides an amazing number of capabilities that help you test the design and functionality of your Web pages. To download Firefox and extensions, visit www.mozilla.org.

✔ **Safari**, the dominant browser on the Mac platform, is included as part of the Mac OS X operating system.

✔ **Opera** (www.opera.com) is a commercially available browser that sports powerful functionality.

No matter which browser you prefer, you should have at least two or three browsers installed on your computer that you can use for testing your Web site. Each browser has idiosyncrasies that can occasionally affect your page design. Having these on hand helps you catch the problem before your visitors do!

Rich, for example, works with Safari to test his pages initially, and then later checks it against Firefox for Mac. However, before publishing, he crosschecks his pages on Internet Explorer and Firefox for Windows.

Surf and Study: Discovering What Works and What Doesn't

Before you begin creating your Web site, we recommend that you spend some time surfing to various Web sites. Rather than browse the site, however, *study* it. Consider each of these issues:

✦ **Identify what you like and dislike about the design of the site.** If you like it, jot down styling concepts you want to emulate. If you dislike it, make sure to avoid these mistakes yourself. (See Chapter 2 of this mini-book for more on design strategy.)

✦ **Consider the overall "tone" of the site.** Does the site look overly formal or informal? Professional or amateurish? You should set a tone for your site and make sure that your content, design, color, and font selection all work together in support of it.

✦ **Look for the overall messaging of the site.** What's being communicated through the design, graphics, and text of the home page? Is there a single theme? Are you getting mixed messages? Is it successful? For your Web site, develop a consistent, coherent theme or message and then create the site around it.

✦ **Check out the site's navigation.** Can you easily find the information you're looking for? Can you get lost in the site? You should develop a site that's easy to navigate. (See Chapter 3 of this minibook for more on site organization.)

✦ **Identify the technologies being used.** When you come across an effect or interactive feature that you really like, dive under the hood and identify the technology that the site is using to pull off the effect.

To do so, right-click the page and choose View Source from the pop-up menu, a feature that's available in most browsers. Inside the HTML source, you can find all the nitty-gritty details of the technology behind the scenes. Be sure to read Book VI first, to help you navigate your way through the source.

When you come across a site you really like, don't blatantly copy its design or actual files. Instead, use other sites as inspirations to spawn your own creative ideas.

If you get into a rut trying to find interesting Web sites to explore, we recommend checking out www.coolhomepages.com and www.cssbeauty.com/gallery. Both sites feature a gallery of well-designed sites that can inspire you.

If you feel intimidated by the high level of expertise necessary to pull off a good Web site design, don't sweat it. Most of these sites are created by design professionals. The idea is to learn from their designs and techniques, not to try to copy or compete with them.

Chapter 2: Best Practices in Web Design

In This Chapter

✔ Keeping your design simple

✔ Maintaining consistency

✔ Applying the rule of thirds to your site design

✔ Avoiding the nine most common site design problems

Because the Web is a visual medium, the design of your Web site can be as important as the content you offer on your site. If your design is tacky, amateurish, and annoying, visitors might not treat you seriously or might hit the Back button before you can cry out "But I tried!"

Therefore, even before we get into the specifics of how to create a Web site, we spend some time talking about how to design it. In this chapter, we explore several proven design principles that you should understand. In addition, we also talk about what not to do — those errors that you should avoid from the start.

Applying Three Proven Design Principles to Your Site

Back in the mid-1990s, the Web was filled with sites that were dense with information. They were functional, but they often looked liked they had been designed by a trash compactor — smashing as much content inside the page as possible. However, sometime over the past decade, the world of design caught up with the Web.

In Chapter 1 of this minibook, we recommend that you begin by spending some time analyzing other well-designed sites. If you find several candidates, we're willing to bet that, in spite of their visual differences, they employ many of the same proven design principles. Here are several to consider.

Simplicity: Less is more

If the past century has stressed any single aesthetic principle, it is that less is more. You see it in glass-box architecture, Hemingway's sparse sentences, minimalist painting — and, indeed, throughout the Web.

You would expect contemporary design in a Web page devoted to one of today's most respected fashion houses. Armani (www.armani.com) delivers, as you can see in Figure 2-1.

Figure 2-1:
Armani's clean, elegant design sense pervades his Web site.

This figure show how minimal content can create a highly effective Web page: one photo, one menu, five icons, and some nearly transparent text scrolling across the photo. Note the use of few words here. Most of the page is, in fact, white space (discussed in the next section).

A second example of minimalist design is Google (www.google.com). The popular search engine's home page is famous for its refusal to include anything considered unnecessary.

Consider the opposite extreme — the Web site of a major news outlet, such as the BBC (news.bbc.co.uk), as shown in Figure 2-2. An Armani-like site wouldn't make any sense, but the site aims to keep the overall design as simple as possible, in spite of the complexity of information it's presenting. This site generally displays three columns plus a side panel of links; dozens of stories, many photos, and headline links are all displayed at once.

The reality is, however, that most of us aren't Armani, Google, or the BBC. We can't get by with just placing a couple words here or there on the page and living with a minimalist design. But we don't need to deal with the constant flood of content of a news service. Our aim, therefore, should be to strike a balance by following the age-old advice to *keep it simple*.

Figure 2-2:
The BBC News site aims to present a wealth of information in a simple manner.

Here are some ideas to consider:

✦ **Have a center point of focus, particularly for your home page.** Your primary focus — the thing that catches a visitor's eye first — should have considerable punch. Make it big, sharp, and forceful. By contrast, other elements of the page can tend toward the paler, softer-focused, and smaller. In other words, the majority of your page should be visually gentle, with one main exception.

✦ **Include lots of white space, and also try to simplify the organization of the page.** We discuss using white space in the next section.

✦ **Go easy on the overall number of links.**

✦ **Use two or three columns.**

✦ **Give the visitor a simple, obvious pathway down through your page.** Don't make them flit around because your page is confusing and complex.

✦ **Consider putting your main symbol (whether an image or a headline) in a vibrant color.**

Avoiding background noise

One of the most important parts of a page to follow the *keep it simple* rule is your background. It should be a single color (often white, gray, or black) or a gradual gradient (a gradual blend from one color or shade to another) that doesn't compete visually with the content of your page. Nothing is more annoying to visitors than having bright colors or flashing images in the background.

Keeping things clean with white space

White space, also called *negative space,* is a design term that refers to regions that are empty of text or graphics. It doesn't necessarily mean that the space is colored white. Empty areas can be any color or even a gradient (a visual transition between colors). For example, the white space shown in Figure 2-1 is colored black. White space serves several purposes:

✦ **Increase readability:** Text on computer screens can be more difficult to read than paper. Give your viewers plenty of white space, to make the content more readable.

✦ **Keep things clean:** Viewers aren't overwhelmed with the feeling that they must buckle down and work to get through all the information you're cramming into their view.

✦ **Emphasize your content:** When your page is less crowded, each image and paragraph has greater value and doesn't compete with the others.

✦ **Free you for an effective design:** By using more white space, you have greater freedom to move items around, which helps build an effective design.

Consider, for example, `Deepblue.com`, the site for a Web design firm (see Figure 2-3). As you can see, its home page is very clean, containing a minimal amount of information surrounded by lots of white space.

Being consistent across the site

Although the home page of a site often has a page layout that's different from the rest of the pages, the overall site design should be consistent in terms of colors, fonts, font sizes, margins, and other elements.

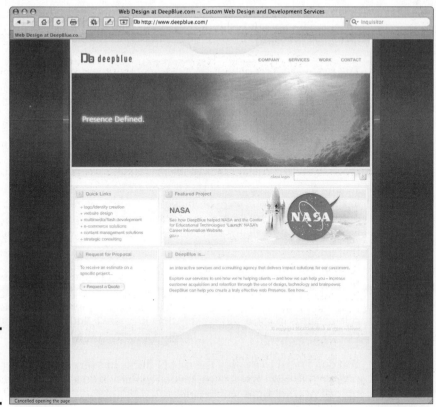

Figure 2-3:
A generous
use of white
space.

Several technologies are available that can help you simplify this task. First, the Cascading Style Sheets (CSS) technology allows you to set styles and formatting rules for your site in one location and attach every page of your site to those rules. We cover CSS fully in Book V.

Understanding the Rule of Thirds

Growing up, we had a "rule of thirds" that we always followed around the dinner table. After we quickly scarfed down two helpings of the meal, our rule was that the first person to ask for thirds could eat the remainder of the food portions. However, that rule of thirds became unfashionable after our pants no longer fit around out waistlines.

Several years ago, we discovered a design principle of the same name. Although it may not help your waistline, this rule helps you create a well-designed Web site.

The *rule of thirds* is one of the most persistent and pervasive tenets of Western art: This rule has been employed successfully by everyone from brilliant Greek sculptors to contemporary greeting card designers, with good reason. When an image or a page is divided into thirds vertically and horizontally and objects are positioned on those lines, the image is simply more pleasing to the eye. (For an example, check out Figure 2-6, coming up in the "Tweaking your page design with the rule of thirds" section.)

When you apply the rule of thirds to your Web site, the main subject is rarely in the center of your page or image. Too much symmetry makes for a bad overall composition. In addition, you avoid centering the horizon line — that is, equal amounts of sky and land — which would divide the visual in the middle horizontally.

Therefore, as you design a page, we recommend experimenting. Move elements around. Tweak your original ideas and see what happens. When you feel pretty good about a page, pull back to take a dispassionate look at it with the rule of thirds in mind. More likely than not, you'll find that adjusting your page design with the rule of thirds in mind improves the look of your Web page.

You don't need to employ the rule of thirds in every last photograph you take or Web page you design. If you regularly follow this rule of composition, though, your designs will benefit.

Tweaking your page design with the rule of thirds

Consider how a page design can be modified by following the rule of thirds. To start, you need a focal point. Like any good painting or photograph, your Web pages benefit from having an object that's the main topic or the most prominent visual element — whatever the viewer is supposed to notice first.

Figure 2-4 illustrates a Web page displayed in an abstract way to highlight its primary zones: some text (gray blocks), some bold text (the dark block), and headlines (black bars). Overall, this isn't a bad design because it has variety and is also balanced. Note that it's not symmetrical: It's balanced. That's an important difference.

However, Figure 2-4 lacks a focal point. Nothing really punchy or extraordinary exists on the page to draw the viewer's attention. Remember that a focal point stands out from the rest of the page. It can even be as simple as an unusual shape — something that doesn't match the other shapes on the page, as shown in Figure 2-5.

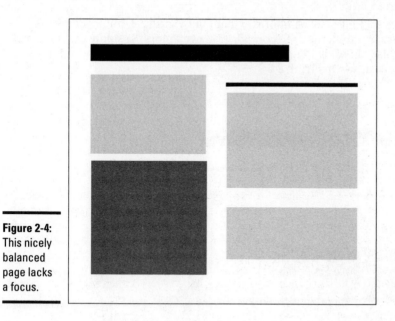

Figure 2-4:
This nicely
balanced
page lacks
a focus.

Figure 2-5:
A new
shape
provides a
focus.

Figure 2-5 looks like an improvement over Figure 2-4, but invoking the rule of thirds can strengthen the composition even more. To apply the rule, draw imaginary lines dividing your Web page into thirds vertically and horizontally, as shown in Figure 2-6.

Figure 2-6:
Divide your image or Web page into nine imaginary zones.

Place straight lines (walls and horizons, for example) along any of these lines.

The points in which these lines intersect are the best places to put your focus: the subject of the picture. The four spots where the lines intersect are *hotspots.* Figure 2-7 is a further improvement to the design with the dancer now moved to a hotspot.

Next, we move the focal point to one of the other hotspots. You see that it looks good in those locations as well. Remember that you have four hotspots to experiment with. In Figure 2-8, the dancer is positioned in the upper left hotspot. Also notice that the dancer has been reversed from her position in Figure 2-7; now, she dances *into* the page shown in Figure 2-8.

When you have *motion* in your composition (an arrow, a dancer, or anything that points or "moves"), good design emphasizes ensuring that the motion moves into — not out of — your page. The focal point is the first thing the viewer sees, and it should lead the eye into the page.

Figure 2-7:
The focal
point is
moved onto
a hotspot.

Figure 2-8:
The dancer
looks good
in this other
hotspot.

Balancing the rule of thirds with the background

When tinkering with object focus placement according to the rule of thirds, pay attention to the background you use. You can see that the design shown in Figure 2-9 isn't nearly as successful as the one in Figure 2-8 even though the dancer is positioned on a hotspot. With this design, the focal point is swallowed by the dark background.

Figure 2-9:
The focal point is swallowed by the dark background.

Another rule of good composition is that you should violate white space: That is, move a focal point so that it isn't framed or sunk into its background but instead pokes into the surrounding white space. In Figures 2-7 and 2-8, the dancer leaps out of the background into the white space. That's the better choice.

Of all these page designs, Figure 2-7 is arguably the best. It's the most balanced because the dancer counteracts the weight of the large headline at the top of the page. The final choice is, of course, up to you.

Background image positioning

You should also employ rule of thirds hotspots with your background images. You might be tempted to center the background image shown in Figure 2-10, thinking that the page is balanced if the background image is in the middle. Although that's true, also remember that balance should be combined with interest, and unity combined with variety.

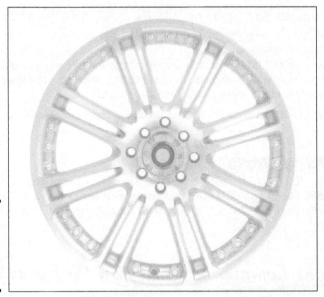

Figure 2-10:
Avoid
centering a
symmetrical
background.

When you move your background over to a rule of thirds hotspot, you maintain balance while adding interest to your composition.

With that in mind, we try moving around the background image from Figure 2-10. Notice the overall improvement in Figure 2-11. The background now radiates from the hotspot, not from the center.

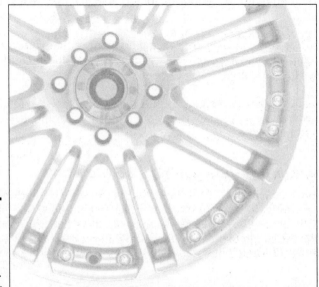

Figure 2-11:
Move the
background
for a better
composition.

Photoshop plug-ins

While Adobe Photoshop has no built-in feature to help you employ the rule of thirds, powerretouche.com offers some helpful *plug-ins* (third-party components that can add functionality), which you can add into Photoshop for this purpose.

Finessing graphics

Using the rule of thirds applies to more than the overall design on your page. For added visual appeal, remember to apply it with the graphics that you add to the page. See Book VII, Chapter 1 for applying the rule of thirds to your graphics.

Avoiding Eight Common Web Design Problems

As you consider the good design principles we discuss in this chapter, we also want to tell you about the "bad stuff," the common mistakes that Web designers often make. Sometimes these problems occur from the start, and sometimes they creep in slowly as you update and modify your site over time.

Clutter eats your site alive

Clutter makes visitors uncomfortable and gives them the impression that your site is disorganized. Avoid it. You want your site easy for visitors to get the information that they're looking for, not feel like they're lost in a Dharma experiment.

Unless you're adding a blog or personal home page that you're using as your digital dumping grounds, ditch useless content that doesn't add anything to your goals for your site.

If you have a tendency to create a cluttered design, take the reins and throw out everything possible. Then throw out even more, or move items to pages deeper within the site.

Overwhelming your visitors at the start

This error sometimes results from being so enthusiastic about what's on your site that you overwhelm your visitors by throwing everything at them on the home page. Determine what's most essential and highlight it, but be disciplined enough to place other content on other pages. As long as you have a good navigation scheme (see Chapter 3 of this minibook), you'll be fine.

Confusion comes with complexity

Visitors make instant decisions the moment they arrive on your site. If they're confused or annoyed, they click the Back button and never return. If you can't simplify by eliminating clutter (see the "Clutter eats your site alive" section), you have to employ your design skills to clarify by design.

Divide your page into logical areas, to make clear what goes with what. Traditionally, horizontal and vertical lines were used to fence off various areas on a Web page, just like newspapers continue to do now. However, contemporary Web design often eliminates lines in favor of bars of color zones in the background, multimedia areas (audio and animation using Flash, for example), navigation bars, and other visually distinct areas. Figure 2-12 illustrates how a variety of textures, colors, and multimedia zones can separate content into recognizable categories.

Figure 2-12: The page is organized with zones of texture, color, and animation.

Mixing and matching design ideas never works

Avoid creating a Web design that mixes and matches various styles, no matter how strong they are by themselves. Instead, use a visual theme that's coherent and organized and helps give you a unique identity. Whether it's the *New York Times* famous gothic typeface, Martha Stewart's beloved pale aquamarine, or the NBC peacock, visual themes are indispensable in identifying a person or organization.

By carefully selecting graphics, font typefaces, and colors that work together and match your tone and messaging, you can create a design that holds together visually and gives your site personality.

For deciding which colors work well together, we recommend checking out `www.colorschemer.com/schemes` and `www.colourlovers.com`.

For comparing and contrasting font typefaces, check out `typetester.maratz.com`.

Extreme symmetry is a yawner

As we mention in the rule-of-thirds discussion earlier in the chapter, a major graphical design rule — for magazine ads, interior decorating, photography, Web pages, and many other fields — is to avoid using extreme symmetry. Simply, don't position the *focus* (the main item) of your page or photo smack dab in the center. If a lit Christmas tree is the focus of a snapshot, don't have the tree right in the middle of the picture. If you're photographing the sea, don't have the horizon line where water meets sky in the middle of your shot.

The problem with symmetry is that it removes quite a bit of the life, the subtle conflict, that is necessary for successful contemporary design. It's the visual equivalent of the newspaper story "People Strolled through the Park Yesterday."

From the Dept. of Redundancy Dept.: Self-linking pages

Avoid linking to the same page in your Web site. If, for example, you display a common navigation bar at the top of each page, make sure to highlight the link for the current page through special formatting. This effect helps visitors easily identify their location in the Web site visually. At the same time, disable that link so that nothing happens if the user clicks it. Self-linked pages confuse people.

Forgetting about the visitor

Some site design errors result from an inadequate site navigation structure. You might recall from the earlier section "Overwhelming your visitors at the start" that you should resist the urge to put all your eggs in the home page basket. Divide what you're selling into categories and create separate pages (or whole groups of pages) for those categories.

Double-check navigation. Having links to pages that don't exist is sloppy. Ask outsiders unfamiliar with your site to see whether they can quickly and intuitively locate precisely what they're after. Although a Search feature can be helpful, your customer should ideally be able to click visual cues — icons, photos, and navigation bars — to locate subcategories, such as Antique Quilts or Under–$200 Quilts. For example, if your major categories group products by cost, even something as simple as four tabs with $, $$, $$$, and $$$$ symbols on them can assist visitors. Then, when they click one of these selections, perhaps they'll find their chosen cost group further divided by tabs indicating age, size, color, or whatever. The idea is to let them get to their particular wishes — perhaps the page displaying your second-most-expensive, large, blue quilts — with only two or three mouse clicks.

Negligence is like moldy bread

Don't work hard creating your Web site and then forget about it and let it waste away. Just as successful stores continually keep themselves up to date, you need to do the same with your Web site. Follow these tips:

✦ **Update your blog or news section.** If you have a blog or What's New section, be sure to regularly post new information. At minimum, even if you don't add new material, be sure to take off content that's outdated.

✦ **Keep your copyright date current.** Few things date your site more than an old copyright date at the bottom of the page. If visitors see a two-year-old date on your site, they assume that you've stopped updating it.

✦ **Check links.** Periodically test both internal and external links you provide. Delete broken links or update them to the new URLs.

Insecurity makes people nervous

You wouldn't enjoy shopping at a nasty store where suspicious characters are peeking over your shoulder as you enter your PIN code, or are stuffing copies of your Visa charge receipt into their pockets. Likewise, if you're selling goods on eBay or directly on your Web site, you must reassure your customers on the Internet that you're trustworthy and will provide secure financial transactions.

Chapter 3: Organizing and Navigating Your Web Site

In This Chapter

✔ Deciding between random or sequential access

✔ Combining structures

✔ Navigating via bars

*W*e've always thought that a well-organized Web site is much like a GPS for your automobile. A road map or atlas throws all the possible routes and destinations at you, leaving you all alone to figure out where you are and how to best get there. A GPS, on the other hand, gives you just the facts you need at your exact location to successfully navigate to your intended destination.

In much the same way, your Web site needs to be GPS-enabled, so to speak. Visitors should feel like they're navigating your Web site with a GPS in hand rather than simply being tossed a road atlas. They need to be able to intuitively locate the content that they're looking for without bombarding them with every possible option.

In this chapter, you explore the important concepts to consider as you organize your site.

Creating a Site Hierarchy

Web sites usually have a logical, tree-like hierarchy to them. A home page branches out into four to six section pages, some of which might have subpages or even subsections under them. Larger sites might have several of these subsections, whereas smaller sites might have little beyond the original section pages.

When you organize your site as a tree-like structure, some branches quickly and easily fall into place. However, other pages might take much more work before you can figure out exactly where they fall into place.

As you organize your site, make sure that you put on a visitor's hat and look at the overall structure like a newcomer would. As the creator of the site, you have the "inside scoop" and understand the various interrelationships that exist among the content. However, be aware of how this content logically fits together to the uninformed.

To organize your site structure, follow these steps:

1. **Make a flat list of all the pages you want to add to your Web site.**

   If you have an existing site, don't automatically reuse the same hierarchy. Start from scratch this time around and see where you end up.

2. **Put the pages into broad topical groups.**

   Organize the pages into various groups that naturally fit together.

   For example, a small consulting firm that sells goods and services might have 30 pages that the owners want to include on their site. The pages might naturally fall under just five distinctive topics, such as News, About Us, Services, Portfolio, and Products.

   Avoid using too many groups because they turn into the main sections of your site. You should be able to organize your site into five to eight clearly defined and distinct topical categories.

3. **Label the group with a prosaic name that clearly and effectively describes it.**

   These group names will be the names of your Level 2 pages (just under the home page) that you will want to include on the navigation menu of the site. (See the next section for more about navigation menus.)

   Avoid being too clever, abstract, vague, or generic in your labeling. You simply want a term that can people can intuitively understand without having to think much about it. For example, if you're selling cars, label it Cars, not Automatic Transport Vehicles or Your New Transportation Device.

4. **Identify subgroups within each broad group.**

   Check to see whether your topics can be further subdivided. If so, group them together and name the subgroup according to the conventions described in Step 3.

   If you have a really large Web site, you can repeat this step as needed. However, work to limit the number of tiers on your site structure to three under the home page. When visitors have to plunge much deeper than that, they easily get lost.

5. **Go through each page on your site and identify pages that must be linked directly from the home page, even if the link doesn't neatly fit within the hierarchy you established.**

   Web sites normally function best when you have a well-defined site organization, but never be so rigid that you hurt the site's usefulness.

   Analyze each of the pages you identified and determine their overall importance. If they're *very* important, you might want to move them to a separate first-level category. Or, if not, there are various places on the home page that you can highlight these special pages, even if they don't work being on the main navigation menu.

6. **Create each of the pages in the software package you're using.**

   If you're using Expression Web, flip over to Book III. Or, if you're using Dreamweaver, you can find what you're looking for in Book IV.

When you finish organizing your Web site hierarchy, we recommend getting a friend or person off the street to look it over and provide feedback. (We find that the cappuccino bribe is particularly effective.)

Navigating Your Site with a Navigation Menu

Web site design goes beyond the page layout, colors and fonts, and other visual elements. Your design should also encompass the organization of your site.

Sites almost always display a *navigation menu* (or *menu bar*), which is a set of graphical or textual links to the major sections of your site. Although the home page might have its own navigation scheme, the rest of the Web site usually has a common navigation bar found at one of two locations on each page:

✦ A horizontal menu bar is located at the top of the page, usually under a banner or logo.

✦ A vertical menu bar is placed along the left side.

Whichever main navigation you decide to use, a text-only menu bar is traditionally placed at the bottom of the page, to eliminate the need to scroll up to change pages. In Book VII, Chapter 4, we show you how to create a navigation menu bar with rollovers.

Figure 3-1 illustrates a travel site where the home page is essentially just one large navigation bar. The user has no trouble understanding how to use this site or how to navigate it.

When you move to any of the other pages of the site, these same links are placed on a menu bar, as shown in Figure 3-2.

Notice that the page shown in Figure 3-2 uses a horizontal menu for top-level navigation and a vertical menu for navigation within that section.

You can create a navigation menu manually. Even better, Dreamweaver and Expression Web offer features that create navigation menus for you.

Figure 3-1: With an uncluttered home page, a visitor understands how to navigate your site.

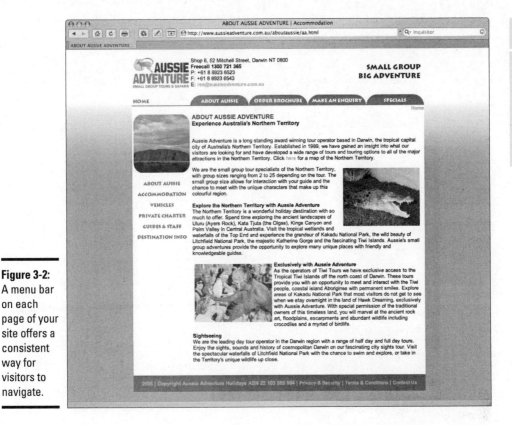

Figure 3-2:
A menu bar
on each
page of your
site offers a
consistent
way for
visitors to
navigate.

Book II

Online Services

The 5th Wave   By Rich Tennant

Hang on! I keep entering a search for "squishy red orb next to the lungs," and this dumb browser keeps taking me to sites for rubber balls, Silly Putty, and chew toys.

Contents at a Glance

Chapter 1: Creating Your Own Space on MySpace

In This Chapter

✔ **Introducing the MySpace experience**

✔ **Creating your MySpace profile**

✔ **Personalizing your MySpace profile**

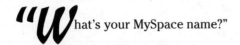**W**hat's your MySpace name?"

Given the explosive popularity of MySpace.com, chances are high that someone has asked you that question. Perhaps you don't know what MySpace is. Perhaps you visited the site but weren't sure how to create your own profile. Regardless of your reasons, this chapter will help get you into the most popular social networking site on the planet.

In this chapter, we begin by telling you about the social networking phenomenon. After that, we guide you through the process of setting up a profile that's tailored for your personality.

Going Social with MySpace

MySpace is a social networking Web site that provides a personal Web site (a *profile*), an interactive network of friends, blogs, photos, videos, and music. Think of MySpace as the Internet equivalent of the local neighborhood hangout spot. People chat, associate with a group of buddies, play their music, and share their snapshots.

MySpace has always been closely associated with music. Bands, both signed and unsigned, regularly use MySpace as a place to promote their music. Major artists have used MySpace as a platform for introducing new albums. In fact, go to www.myspace.com/*yourfavoritebandname*, and you're likely to find a MySpace profile. Some analysts even believe that MySpace is as significant to the music world as MTV was back in the 1980s.

Making sure that your kids are safe at MySpace

Child safety has increasingly been a concern among many with MySpace because the potential for predators is very real. So, if you're a teen or the parent of teenagers, you must be sure to seriously consider the safety issue and take appropriate precautions. Here are some issues to be aware of:

✔ You must be at least 14 years old to register for a MySpace account. A teen who is 14 or 15 automatically receives a private profile, which limits the amount of personal information that can be shared. However, because kids sometimes lie about their ages, parents of teens should be responsible enough to ensure that their children's profiles match their actual ages.

✔ Users over 16 years can choose how many personal details they want to make public to everyone and determine the information available only to their friends.

✔ Users over 18 can't add users under 16 as friends.

Be sure to check out the MySpace safety tips and tips for parents at `www.myspace.com/Modules/Common/Pages/SafetyTips.aspx`. Even better, the user-driven site `www.myspacesafetytips.com` provides a place for information posting and feedback among MySpace users and parents.

Given its friend-and-music focus, the popularity of MySpace has primarily come from teens and twentysomethings. Adults over 35 years old may find MySpace useful too as a place to network, connect with old friends, or simply hang their hat somewhere on the Web.

Having said that, although MySpace users are of all ages, at its heart, MySpace is, quite frankly, about *all things youth.* As a result, if you're an adult and discover that you feel too old for MySpace, skip over to Chapters 2 and 3 of this minibook. In those chapters, we show you two other ways to get an online presence.

MySpace isn't the only social networking site out there. Other popular social networking sites include Bebo.com, Friendster.com, and Facebook.com.

Setting Up a MySpace Profile

Your personal space on MySpace is known as a *profile,* where you provide personal details about who you are, what music you like, and what your interests are, for example. In this section, we walk you through the steps to set up your own profile.

1. **Go to www.myspace.com.**

You see the MySpace home page, shown in Figure 1-1.

2. **Click the Sign Up! button to get started.**

The form displayed in Figure 1-2 asks for basic information about who you are.

3. **Fill in the form labeled Join MySpace Here, and be sure to read and then agree to the terms of service and the privacy policy.**

Click the Sign Up button to continue. After you do, the Upload Some Photos! page is displayed (see Figure 1-3).

4. **Click the Choose File button and locate an image of yourself that you want to use in your profile. Then click the Upload button.**

Or, if you prefer not to upload a photo now, click the Skip for Now link.

Book II
Chapter 1

Creating Your Own
Space on MySpace

Click here to create a profile.

Figure 1-1:
The
MySpace
home page.

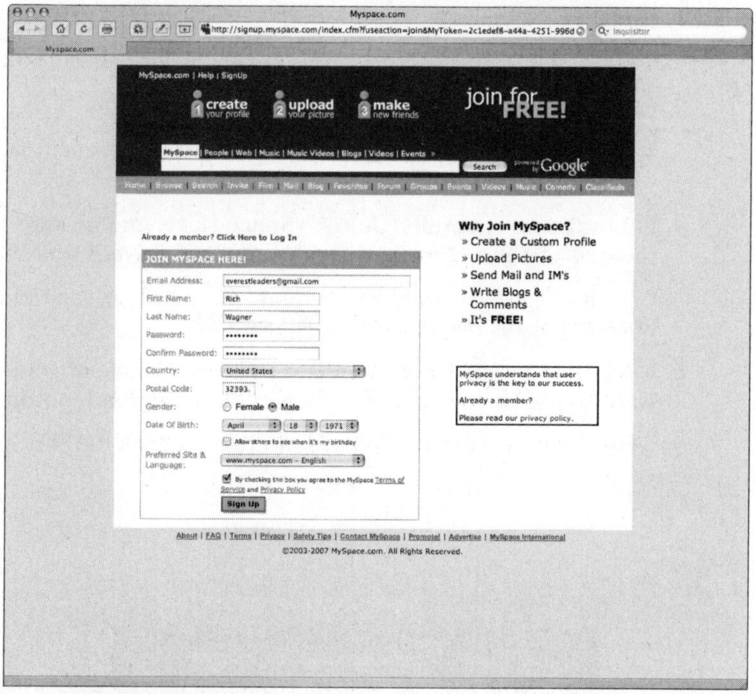

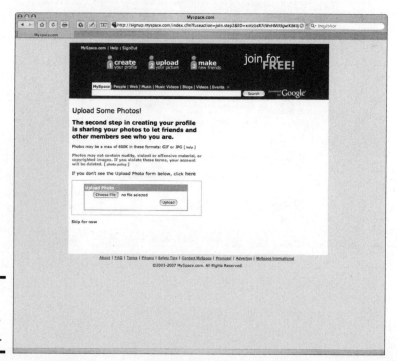

Figure 1-2:
Signing
up for
MySpace.

Figure 1-3:
Uploading
pictures for
your profile.

The Invite Friends to Your Space! page is displayed. (See Figure 1-4.)

5. **In the space provided, enter the e-mail addresses of friends and other people you want to socialize with on MySpace.**

   You can use the boxes to customize the e-mail message they receive. Click Invite to continue.

   If you don't want to invite anyone now, click the Skip for Now link.

   After you do this, your basic profile is created for you, as shown in Figure 1-5.

6. **Click the Verify Your Email Address! link.**

   MySpace needs to confirm your e-mail address, so follow the instructions to do that.

7. **Click the Pick Your MySpace Name/URL! link.**

   Figure 1-6 shows you the page that's displayed.

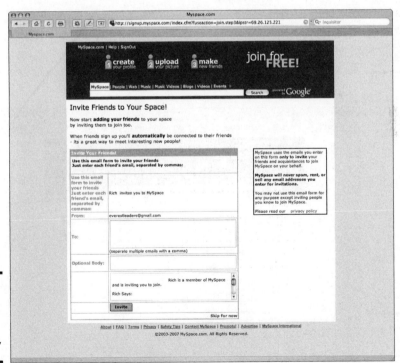

Figure 1-4: Let friends know that you "MySpace."

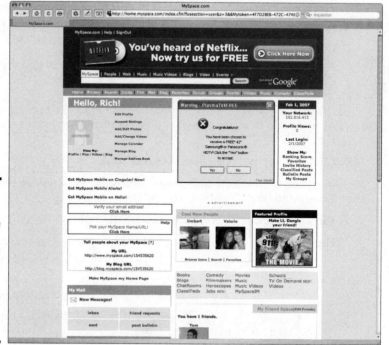

Figure 1-5: If you look between the ads, you may be able to just make out one author's MySpace profile.

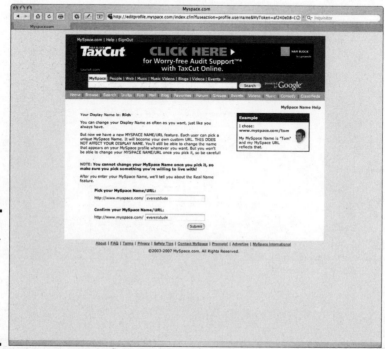

Figure 1-6: Picking your unique, one-of-a-kind, and exclusive MySpace name.

Each MySpace user picks a unique name to have associated with her profile. Your name can be the same as your Display Name, but it doesn't need to be. The name you choose is the way to access your profile on MySpace: `www.myspace.com/`*YourMySpaceName*.

As the text on the site indicates, choose your name carefully. After you pick a name, you cannot change it.

8. Enter the MySpace Name you want and click the Submit button.

If you select a name that has already been chosen, you're asked to select again.

After you finish this process, MySpace gives you a chance to enter your real name. This information isn't made visible as part of your profile, but is used only when someone is looking specifically for you.

**Book II
Chapter 1**

**Creating Your Own
Space on MySpace**

Enter your name and click Submit or click the Skip link.

Be sure to read the sidebar "Making sure that your kids are safe at MySpace," earlier in this chapter, as you consider adding your personal data.

A summary page appears (see Figure 1-7) after you complete this task.

Now that your basic profile is up and running, it's time to spice it up and give it some personality.

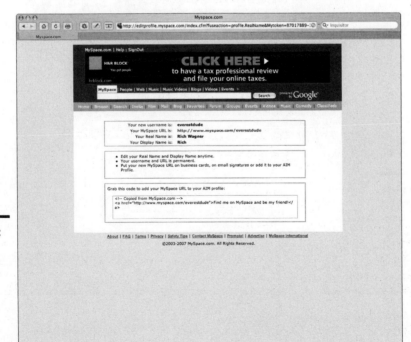

Figure 1-7:
He did it!
One of the
authors is
now a
MySpace
member.
His life is
complete!

9. **Return to your profile by going to your MySpace URL (www.myspace.com/*YourMySpaceName*).**

10. **Click the Edit Profile link that's in the main information box, beside the photo area.**

A No Photo box shows up when you don't have a photo selected for the profile.

The Profile Edit module is displayed, as shown in Figure 1-8. This area has a series of pages that enable you to describe your interests and background. Use the links at the top of the page to work your way through the forms, providing just the information you're willing to share with your friends or anyone else.

The Name link takes you to the place for changing your display name.

11. **If you want to add a song or a video to your profile, click the Song & Video on Profile link. Otherwise, move on to Step 12.**

The Profile Songs page opens. Figure 1-9 shows a snapshot of it.

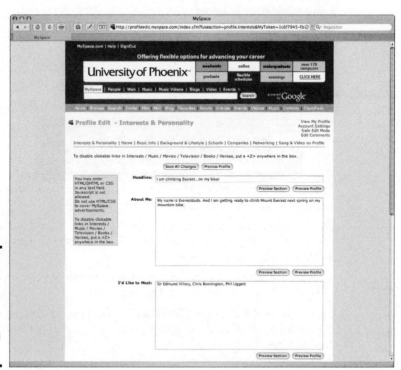

Figure 1-8:
Pouring out your heart, or at least your interests, on MySpace.

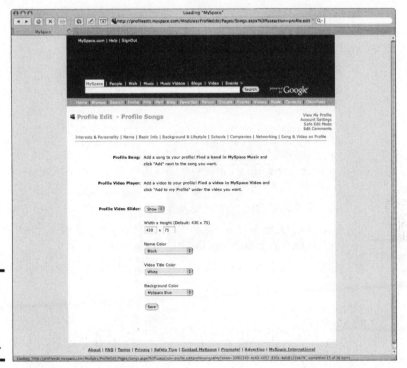

**Book II
Chapter 1**

**Creating Your Own
Space on MySpace**

Figure 1-9:
Setting up
music and
videos for
your profile.

When you add a song or video to your page, a MySpace player is embedded on your page, to allow friends or visitors to check out your favorite media.

Adding songs and videos is easy. Simply go to the band of your choice and click the Add link beside a song or the Add to My Profile link next to a video (see Figure 1-10). After you reply to a confirmation message, MySpace instantly adds it to your profile.

Before leaving the Profile Songs page, decide whether you want to display a video slider, which is a control that allows you to easily display multiple videos on your page.

Specify the height in the Width and Height boxes, along with color selections. Click Save before leaving the page.

After your profile changes have been saved, your profile page is updated to express more of your personality. Figure 1-11 shows the exciting life of Everestdude.

Figure 1-10:
Add your
favorite
videos to
your profile.

Click here to add a video to your profile.

Figure 1-11:
Run one,
run all.
Everestdude
wants to
be your
MySpace
friend.

12. **MySpace features a blog as part of your profile. If you want to post a message on your blog, click the Blog link on the top navbar.**

    The Blog Control Center is displayed (see Figure 1-12).

13. **Click the Post New Blog link.**

    The Post a New Blog Entry page is shown.

14. **Enter your blog entry in the editor.**

    Use the toolbar buttons to format your message.

    Figure 1-13 shows Everestdude's first message.

15. **Click the Preview & Post button.**

    A Confirm Blog Posting page is displayed.

16. **If you're satisfied with your post, click the Post New Blog link.**

    Figure 1-14 displays the post on your blog.

Book II
Chapter 1

Creating Your Own
Space on MySpace

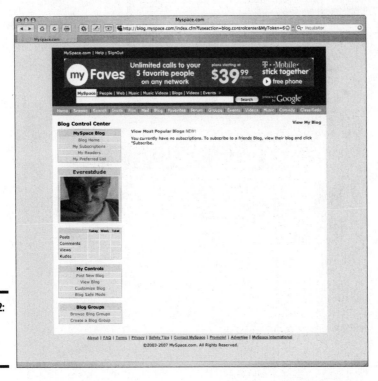

Figure 1-12:
Your
MySpace
blog.

Figure 1-13:
Typing a
blog entry.

Figure 1-14:
Viewing your
MySpace
blog.

Customizing the Look of Your MySpace Profile

Many designers look at the default MySpace profile design and groan, claiming that MySpace sets Web design back about a decade or so. If you feel the same way, you might want to give your profile a customized look.

Many Web sites provide free MySpace templates for you to use. Some look attractive, and others look garish and migraine inducing. Our best advice is to use your favorite search engine to search for **free MySpace templates** and browse through the site listings. Most sites allow you to copy the template (consisting of HTML and Cascading Style Sheets [CSS] code) to your Clipboard for pasting into MySpace later.

After you settle on a template design, follow these steps:

1. **Go to your profile page and click the Edit Profile link.**

2. **In the About Me section, paste the template code into the box, above any text you might have there. See Figure 1-15.**

3. **Click the Save All Changes button.**

Your profile (see Figure 1-16, for example) is updated to reflect the changes.

**Book II
Chapter 1**

**Creating Your Own
Space on MySpace**

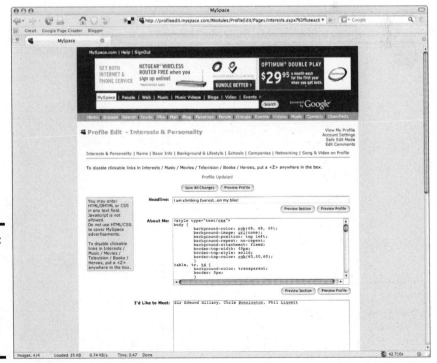

Figure 1-15: Adding a custom template in the About Me box is kludgy, but it works!

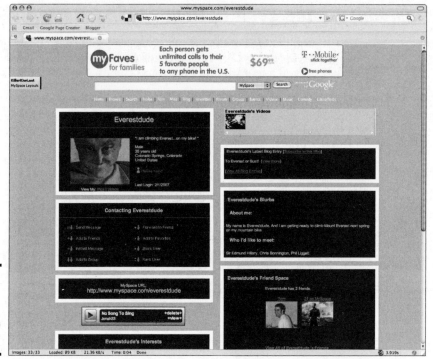

Figure 1-16:
A new and
improved
Everestdude
profile.

If you find that you don't like the new look, simply delete the HTML and CSS
code you added in the About Me box and save your changes.

Chapter 2: Creating a Basic Web Site with Google Page Creator

In This Chapter

✔ Understanding what Google Page Creator can do

✔ Signing up for Google Page Creator

✔ Creating a basic Web site

✔ Changing the look and layout of a page

✔ Working with images and text

✔ Linking your pages

✔ Publishing your site

Online Web site creators are everywhere. You can find plenty of free ones across the Web. Your Internet service provider (ISP) probably has one. Most of the big names of the Web have one, too. A few of these browser-based tools try hard to do almost everything that Adobe Dreamweaver or Microsoft Expression does on your desktop. (Trust us — they can't.) Other online builders are so limited that you can't do much of anything. However, arguably the most common attribute of these builders, other than that they work inside your browser, is that they tend to produce bland, unremarkable, or even downright ugly sites.

Google recently made public its own online Web site builder, known as Google Page Creator. Although this free tool from Google won't make the developers at Adobe or Microsoft nervous, it stands out from the crowded pack of online builders. It offers a painfree way to get a rather attractive Web site up and running in a jiffy.

In this chapter, we introduce you to Google Page Creator and walk you through the steps to build a basic Web site. Perhaps the initial site you create is a stepping stone for you — a temporary site as you begin working with Dreamweaver (see Book IV) or Expression (see Book III). Or, you may find Google Page Creator to be just the site builder you're looking for.

The Web site you create by using Google Page Creator is hosted by Google and will have the URL `your_Gmail_address.googlepages.com`. The hosting is free, but you can't specify your own domain name.

Understanding How Google Page Creator Works

REMEMBER

Here are two general principles to keep in mind as you begin to work with Google Page Creator:

✦ **You work with one page at a time.** The edits and changes you make are generally limited to the current page you're working on. Other pages in your site that you created are unaffected. A couple of examples explain the significance of this fact:

  • If you change the look of your site, you need to individually update every page on your site.

  • Your pages aren't interconnected by default. You need to manually add links before your home page will link to any other page you create.

✦ **You can edit some but not all parts of a page.** A *page* is a template with regions that you can edit, such as title, subtitle, content, and footer. Depending on the layout you select, the content region can include one, two, or three columns. You're free to add content within these regions, but you can't insert it outside of them.

Signing Up for Google Page Creator

To sign up for Google Page Creator, you must first have a Gmail account. If you have Gmail, you're all set and ready to sign up for Google Page Creator. However, if you don't have Gmail, take a quick detour and go to `gmail.google.com` first to register for an account.

After you have a Gmail account, point your Web browser to `http://pages.google.com`. As Figure 2-1 shows, you sign in using your Gmail e-mail address and password.

After you sign in, you see an introductory page, as shown in Figure 2-2. Read the Terms and Conditions section in the lower left corner of the page. Then select the check box confirming that you have read the "fine print" and click the I'm Ready to Create My Pages button.

That's it. You're ready to begin creating your Web site in Google Page Creator.

Figure 2-1:
Signing in to
Google Page
Creator for
the first time.

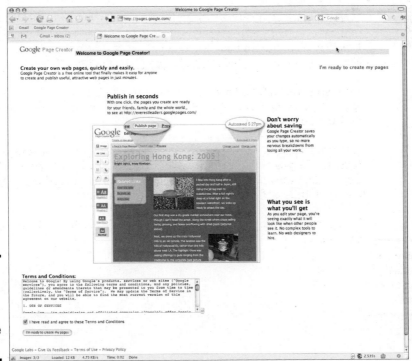

Figure 2-2:
Opening
splash
screen of
Google Page
Creator.

Creating a Basic Web Site

Google Page Creator's name helps set expectations. It isn't a "Web site builder" with tons of Web site management capabilities — it's primarily a creator of *individual* Web pages. The program allows you to create and edit a set of pages that you can group together to form a Web site.

The following steps show you how to create a basic Web site. For the site in our example, we're creating a Web site for the adventure sports company Everest Leaders. Follow these steps:

1. **Sign in to Google Page Creator.**

Follow the steps in the section "Signing Up for Google Page Creator," earlier in this chapter.

After you sign in and agree to the terms and conditions, you see a blank home page with a default design (see Figure 2-3). Don't worry about whether you want to keep the design. You can change it later.

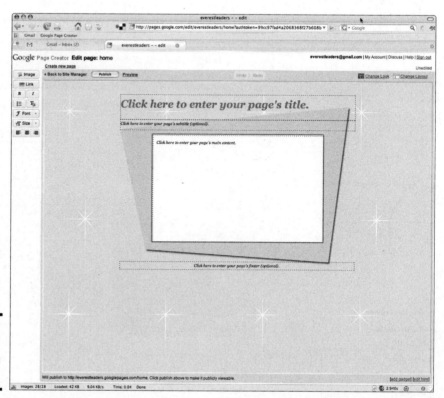

Figure 2-3: Starting out with a clean slate.

2. **Enter your home page title by clicking the text *Click here to enter your page's title* and typing some text.**

We typed `Everest Leaders`.

3. **Enter a slogan or subtitle for your page by clicking the text *Click here to enter your page's subtitle* and typing the text.**

If you don't have anything to put in this box, just leave it blank. The dummy text isn't displayed in the actual Web page.

As shown in Figure 2-4, we entered `World Leaders in Mount Everest Biking Expeditions`. (And you thought that there was no such leader!)

4. **Add text content on your home page by clicking the text *Click here to enter your page's main content* and typing some text.**

The content you enter is your visitors' introduction to your Web site. Therefore, you should provide a good introduction to who you are and the purpose of your Web site.

Book II Chapter 2

Creating a Basic Web Site with Google Page Creator

Subtitle   Title

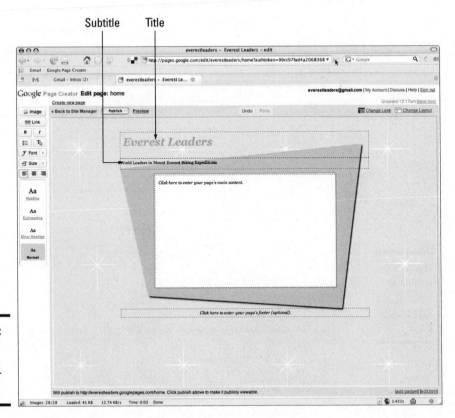

Figure 2-4:
Adding a
title and
subtitle for
the page.

We added a brief introduction to the Everest Leaders for our Web site (see Figure 2-5).

5. **Add a footer to your page by clicking the text** *Click here to enter your page's footer.*

   Type some basic copyright information and, optionally, `Contact Us` (see Figure 2-6).

   You add a mail link to the *Contact Us* text in Step 6.

6. **In the footer, select the** *Contact Us* **text with your mouse.**

7. **Click the Link button in the tools panel on the left side of Google Page Creator.**

   The Edit Link dialog box is displayed, as shown in Figure 2-7.

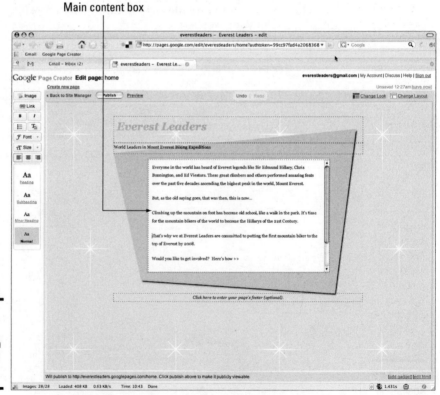

Figure 2-5: Adding an introduction to the home page.

Put footer in this box.

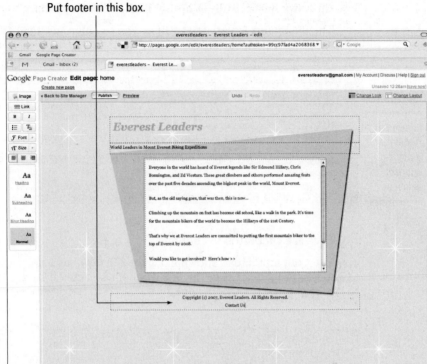

Figure 2-6:
A footer is
a great
location for
placing
copyright
information
and a way to
contact you.

Figure 2-7:
Use the Edit
Link dialog
box to
create a
hypertext
link to a URL
or another
page in
your site.

8. **Click the Email Address option in the Link To group.**

The dialog box is updated to allow you to enter an e-mail address in the space provided. See Figure 2-8.

Figure 2-8:
Adding an
e-mail
address
to link to.

Click the OK button to continue.

The Contact Us text, shown in Figure 2-9, now has a link associated with it. You see a box below the link when it's selected. Use this property box to change or remove the link.

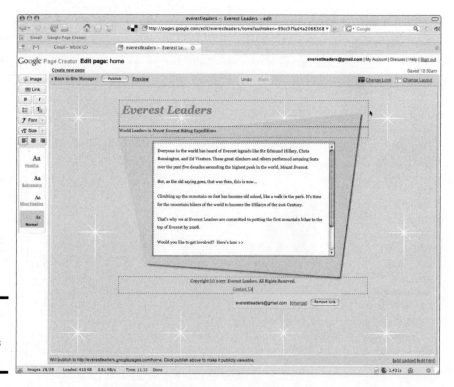

Figure 2-9:
Creating a
Contact Us
link.

You're done with the initial page for now. You'll come back and tidy up in a bit. It's time to create the rest of the pages on your site.

9. **Click the Create New Page link at the top of Google Page Creator.**

   The header displays a control for creating a new page, as shown in Figure 2-10.

10. **Enter the name of the new page, and then click the Create & Edit button.**

    We named the new page More Info.

    The new page is displayed in Google Page Creator (see Figure 2-11).

11. **Add title, subtitle, content, and footer content.**

    After you're satisfied with the results, click the Back to Site Manager link at the top of the page.

    The Site Manager is displayed, as shown in Figure 2-12.

Book II
Chapter 2

Creating a Basic Web Site with Google Page Creator

Use these controls to create a new page.

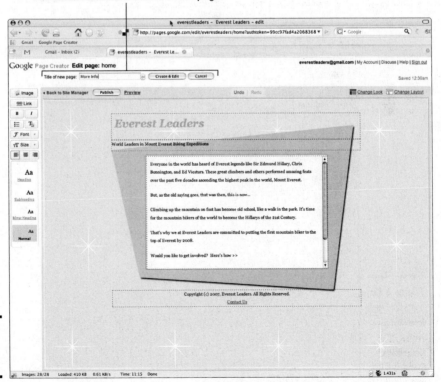

Figure 2-10:
Creating a new page.

Figure 2-11:
A new page, ready for editing.

Figure 2-12:
Google Page Creator's Site Manager is used for managing the pages of your site.

We already showed you how to create a page when you're inside the page editor. Now, we show you how to create a new page from the Site Manager window.

12. Click the Create a New Page link inside the Site Manager.

The link text is replaced with a box to add your page's title. See Figure 2-13.

13. Enter the new page name in the box, and click the Create and Edit button.

A new page is created and ready for editing.

14. Add a page title, subtitle, and footer, but don't add any content in the main content box.

One benefit of Google Page Creator is its ability to take advantage of Google's gadgets by adding them to your page. A *gadget* is a component from a third party (such as CNN, Weather.com, or ESPN) that displays a feed or some content in a rectangular box on your page. Gadgets enable you to aggregate content from other Web sites that your visitors will find useful.

Book II
Chapter 2

Creating a Basic
Web Site with
Google Page Creator

Creating a new page.

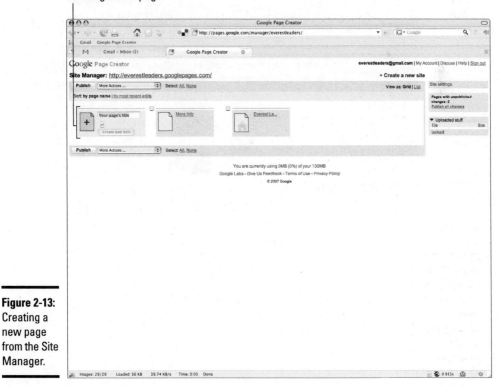

Figure 2-13:
Creating a
new page
from the Site
Manager.

15. **Click the [Add Gadget] link, in the lower right corner of Google Page Creator.**

The Add a Gadget to Your Page box is displayed (see Figure 2-14).

16. **Select a gadget from the directory to add to your page.**

Browse the categories of gadgets by using the links on the left side. The More link displays more gadgets in the same category.

In our example, we picked the Weather International gadget in the News category.

If your gadget isn't created by Google, you receive a warning message (see Figure 2-15), asking you to confirm your selection. Make sure that you trust the source before clicking OK.

Depending on your selection, a second dialog box might appear, for setting up your gadget. Fill out the dialog box and click OK.

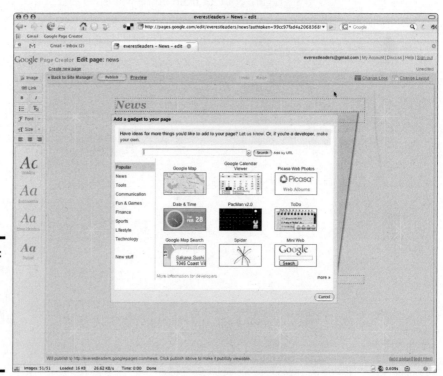

Figure 2-14: Adding a gadget to your Web page inside Google Page Creator.

Figure 2-15:
Make sure
that you trust
the source
of any third-
party
gadgets you
add to your
page.

As shown in Figure 2-16, the gadget is inserted on your page.

17. **Add gadgets or content to the page, if you want.**

Your basic Web site is now created and ready for publishing.

You might want to make changes to your site before going live. See the following two main sections to change the design or layout of your pages.

Figure 2-16:
Gadgets
provide
instant
content to
your Web
pages.

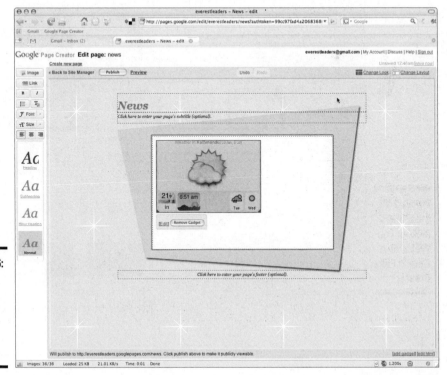

Changing the Look of Your Site

Google Page Creator has a variety of different "looks" that you can choose from as you develop your Web site. Although the Google catalog doesn't have any "high design," revolutionary-looking designs, it offers an attractive selection of more than 40 looks. The biggest downside to the designs is that most of them tend to look the same, except for their color schemes.

To change the look of your site, follow these steps:

1. **In Google Page Creator, open your home page.**

2. **Click the Change Look link, in the upper right corner of the page.**

   The Choose Look page is displayed, as shown in Figure 2-17.

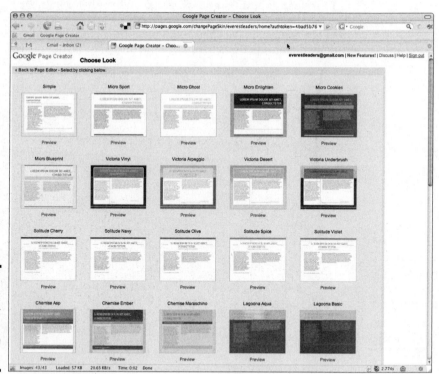

Figure 2-17: Selecting a look for your Web site in Google Page Creator.

Browse through the designs until you find the one you want to use. To preview the look on a sample site, click the Preview link below each design.

3. **Click the look you want to use for your Web site.**

   Google Page Creator updates your current page with the new look (see Figure 2-18).

4. **If you discover that you don't like the look after all, simply repeat Steps 2 and 3.**

   When Google Page Creator updates the look, it applies to only the current page you're working on. Therefore, you need to repeat Steps 2 and 3 for each page in your Web site.

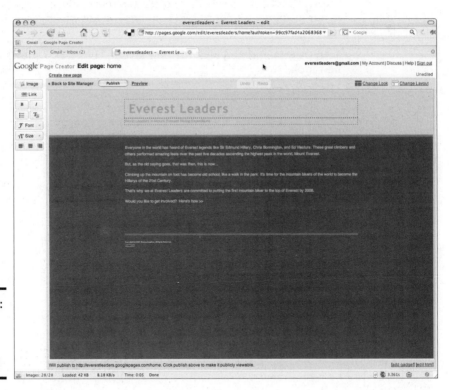

Figure 2-18:
That's the look we were looking for!

Changing the Layout of Your Page

When you create a new page in Google Page Creator, the content area is a one-column rectangular region. However, if you want to add additional columns to your page, you can do so. Follow these steps:

1. **In Google Page Creator, open the page you want to modify.**

2. **Click the Change Layout link in the upper right corner of the page.**

   The Choose Layout page is displayed, as shown in Figure 2-19. You can choose from a single column, a couple of 2-column layouts, and a 3-column layout.

3. **Click the layout you want.**

   In our example, we chose two columns (one of which is a sidebar on the left).

   Your page is updated with the new layout. Figure 2-20 shows our page's new look.

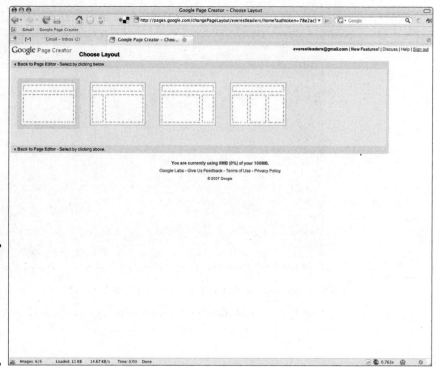

Figure 2-19:
Selecting a new layout for your page in Google Page Creator.

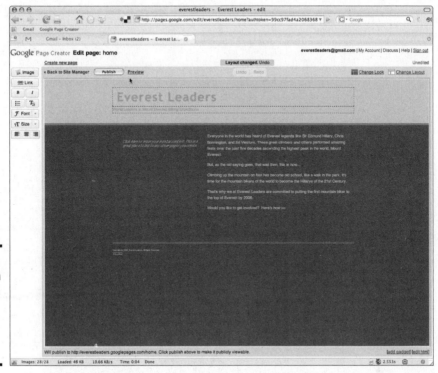

Figure 2-20:
Enough with the single-column look — it's time for a change!

Book II
Chapter 2

Creating a Basic
Web Site with
Google Page Creator

The layout changes take effect for only the current page. Therefore, you need to repeat these steps for each page you want to modify.

Adding an Image to Your Page

You can add an image to your Web page that's on either your desktop computer or a Web server. Here's how to do it:

1. **In Google Page Creator, open the page where you want to add an image.**

2. **Select the region of the page in which you want to add the image.**

3. **Click the Link button in the toolbox on the left.**

The Add an Image dialog box, shown in Figure 2-21, is displayed.

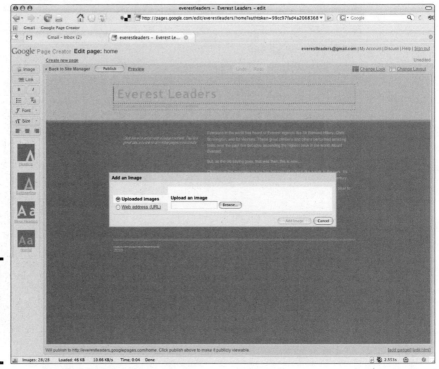

Figure 2-21:
Uploading
an image in
Google
Page
Creator.

4. If the image is on your computer, click the Browse button and select the image you want to upload and then display on your page.

If the image is already on a Web server somewhere, click the Web Address (URL) option and enter the URL.

5. Click the Add Image button.

The image is uploaded to the Google server. The Add an Image box shows the image in its listing (see Figure 2-22).

6. Select the image from the list and click the Add Image button to insert the image into your page.

Figure 2-23 shows the results.

After the image is inserted into your page, you can move it around as you want and even move it from region to region. You can also perform some basic image editing inside Google Page Creator. When you select an image, the box that's displayed below the image (refer to Figure 2-23) gives you various options for special effects resizing, cropping, and rotating.

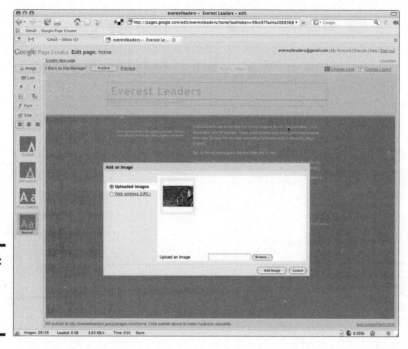

Figure 2-22:
Adding an image to your page is easy.

Image options

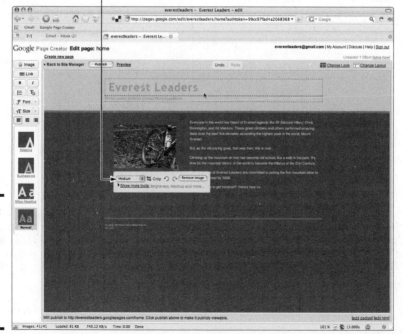

Figure 2-23:
A mountain bike picture is worth at least a couple hundred words.

Adjusting the Text on Your Web Page

Google Page Creator has several text formatting controls on the left side of the builder. These controls are shown in Figure 2-24.

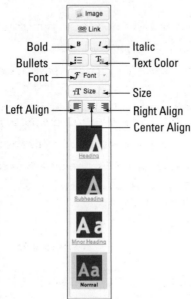

Figure 2-24:
Text formatting in Google Page Creator.

The controls are described in this list:

✦ The **Bold** button bolds the selected text.

✦ The **Italics** button italicizes the selected text.

✦ The **Bullets** button turns selected paragraphs into a bulleted list (or turns on the bullets).

✦ The **Text Color** button allows you to set the text color.

✦ The **Font** button allows you to select the current font.

✦ The **Size** button sets the font size of the current text.

✦ The three **alignment** buttons set alignment to left, center, or right.

✦ The **Heading**, **Subheading**, **Minor heading**, and **Normal** buttons are used to specify the type of paragraph.

Linking Your Pages Together

Google Page Creator doesn't come with a navigation bar (or *navbar*) control that you can drop onto your page for navigating throughout your Web site. However, you can add a set of links to perform the same function. Here's one technique:

1. **In Google Page Creator, open the home page of your site.**

2. **Click the subtitle region of your page to select it.**

   Of the regions available in a Google Page Creator page, the subtitle region is the best candidate for placing navbar style links.

3. **Enter the names of each of the pages in your Web site, and separate them with a vertical bar (|). Be sure to include the home page.**

   If you have a subtitle, press Enter first to place the links on the next line.

4. **Click the Right Align button in the toolbox on the left to align the text to the right of the region.**

   Figure 2-25 shows one author's navbar text.

Book II
Chapter 2

Creating a Basic
Web Site with
Google Page Creator

Navigation links

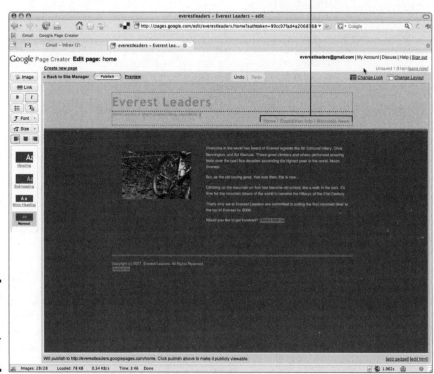

Figure 2-25:
Creating
navigation
links for your
Web site.

The text is ready to go, but you need to define the links before it's ready to roll.

5. **Define links for each of the pages of your Web site by selecting the text and clicking the Link button in the toolbox.**

   Don't put a link on the Home text, because you're already there.

   After you complete the navbar links for your home page, you will replicate the navbar on the rest of your Web site.

6. **Select the entire navbar line with your mouse.**

7. **Right-click and choose Copy from the pop-up menu.**

   The page content is copied to the Clipboard.

8. **Move to the next page in your Web site by using the Site Manager.**

9. **Click the subtitle region, and position the cursor on an empty line.**

10. **Right-click and choose Paste from the pop-up menu.**

    The navbar text is pasted into your page.

11. **Update the links as needed for the current page.**

    Select the link that's defined for the current page, and click the Remove Link button.

    Add a link to the home page by selecting its text and clicking the Link button in the toolbox.

12. **Repeat Steps 8 through 11 for each page in your Web site.**

    When you finish, you have a working navbar for your Web site.

Previewing and Publishing Your Web Site

At any time during the page creation process, you can preview the page by clicking the Preview button in the upper left corner of Google Page Creator. A new browser window appears with a preview version. A banner at the top of the page, shown in Figure 2-26, lets you know that you're in Preview mode. Close the browser window to return to the page creator window.

After you're satisfied with your Web site and are ready to go live, you can publish your pages to the live googlepages.com server.

To publish a page while in Page Creator view, click the Publish button.

To publish your entire site (or multiple pages of the site), go to Site Manager view (see Figure 2-27) by clicking the Back to Site Manager link. Select the check boxes for all the pages you want to publish (or click the All link to select them all). Then click the Publish button.

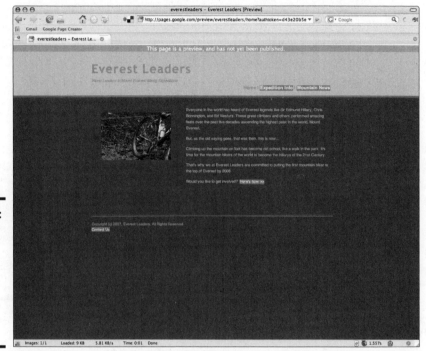

Figure 2-26:
Previewing
your page
before
publishing
helps you
catch
mistakes
and typos.

Figure 2-27:
Publish or
perish, as
they say.

After you publish, your site is available at `yourGmailAddress.googlepages.com`, where `yourGmailAddress` is your Gmail account name. Here are the results of our sample Web site, as shown in Figure 2-28.

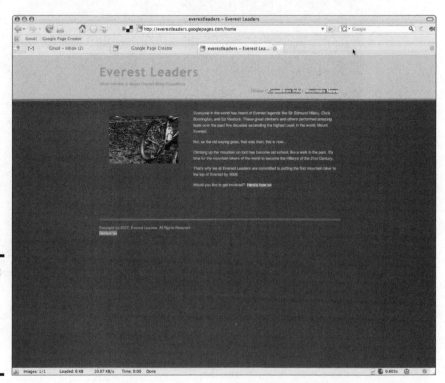

Figure 2-28: A new Google-pages Web site, ready to conquer the world.

Chapter 3: Blogging It: Creating Your Own Blog

*J*ournalists. College students. Authors. Politicians. Techies. Almost anyone. You name someone's profession or interest, and we can find a blog written by someone like that person. Blogging is taking the world by storm, and it's time for you to get on board.

In this chapter, we introduce you to the world of blogging and show you how to create your own blog in a just a matter of minutes. First, we make sure that you understand exactly what a blog is.

Understanding Blogging

A *blog,* short for W*eb log,* can be an online journal, a news-oriented site, or a place to post your vacation pictures. Blogs enable you to easily publish your thoughts, ideas, and opinions on the Web without using a traditional site.

Technically speaking, a blog is a more structured form of a traditional Web site. Standard Web sites are usually one-of-a-kind creations — each one is structured to meet the unique needs of its owner. In contrast, a blog is a Web site with these specific organizational elements:

✦ **Blog listing:** Made in the style of a journal and shown in reverse chronological order.

✦ **Home page:** Shows the latest postings, but individual entries are archived and usually organized by date.

✦ **Individual entries:** Normally appear in journal format in the blog listing (on the home page or in an archives section). However, blogging software can also assign a specific URL to a blog entry to enable it to appear on its own, individual page.

✦ **Comments:** Allow readers to express their thoughts about an entry and have them posted as part of the Web site. As you would expect, blogs that use comments can thus form an interactive community of participants.

A variety of blogs are on the Web, each with its own moniker. A *photoblog* is a photo-based blog, a *vlog* is a video-based blog, a *moblog* is a blog written using a mobile device, and a *liveblog* features real-time journaling. The collection of all blogs in the world is the *blogosphere*. A variety of free and paid blogging sites are available on the Web. In addition to Blogger (the service we focus on in this chapter), other popular free blogs include WordPress (www.wordpress.org) and LiveJournal (www.livejournal.com).

Creating a Blog with Blogger

Blogger is a free blogging service operated by Google. Using Blogger, you can get up and running with a blog in a matter of minutes. Here's a step-by-step guide to show you how.

Before you begin, make sure that you have either a Gmail account (see Chapter 2 in this minibook for details on obtaining one) or a basic Google account (see www.google.com/accounts). You need one of these accounts in order to use Blogger.

In the example in this section, we show you how to set up a blog for Everest Leaders, which is attempting a mountain bike ascent of Mount Everest. Follow these steps:

1. **Go to www.blogger.com.**

The Blogger home page, shown in Figure 3-1, provides basic information on blogging and tells you how to get started.

2. **Click the New Blogger link and sign in using your Gmail or Google account.**

3. **Enter basic name and e-mail address details in the form that appears. Click Continue.**

Be sure to select the I Accept the Terms of Service check box before continuing.

The sign-in area

Figure 3-1:
Getting
started with
Blogger.

After you click the Continue link, the Dashboard page opens (see
Figure 3-2) for managing your blogs. Consider the Dashboard your
home base inside Blogger.

You'll come back to edit your profile later, but for now, continue with
your blog.

**4. Click the Create a Blog link in the Manage Your Blogs section to begin
creating your blog.**

The Name Your Blog page is displayed, as shown in Figure 3-3.

5. Enter a title for your blog.

Some people opt for descriptive titles (Rich Wagner's Blog), and others
prefer creative ones (Tales from the Cheese Monkey Soup or Encapsulate
Obscurity).

Figure 3-2:
Dash to the
Dashboard
to manage
your blogs.

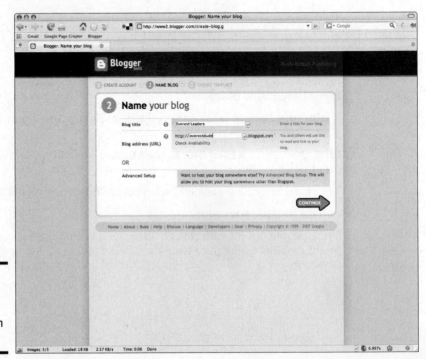

Figure 3-3:
Everything
needs a
name, even
your blog.

6. Enter the desired blog address in the space provided.

By default, Blogger hosts your blog for you, freeing you from dealing with another Web services provider. As a result, the name you enter here is the start of the Web address for your blog, followed by the `.blogspot.com` suffix.

You often want to use a portion or all of your blog title. However, because each blog address must be unique, click the Check Availability link to see whether anyone has previously taken your pick.

Because Everest Leaders started out on MySpace (refer to Chapter 1 in this minibook) as `everestdude`, I decided to choose it as the blog address.

Alternatively, if you already have a Web hosting provider, you can click the Advanced Setup link. This link takes you to a new page in which you can provide the server address and other details. The advantage to this route is that you can specify your own, unique domain name. Additionally, hosting your blog enables you to remove the Blogger navbar at the top of the page.

Click the Continue button to move on. Figure 3-4 shows the Choose a Template page that's displayed.

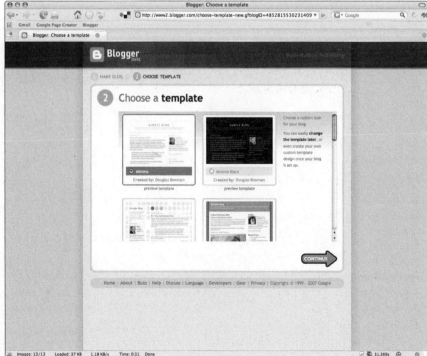

Figure 3-4:
Pick and choose the look of your blog.

7. **Select a template that matches the style you want your blog to look like.**

This initial list is only a sampling of all available templates. If you don't see any that thrill you, don't worry. Just pick one of them now and you can change the look later.

If you want to see a sample site of a template, click the Preview Template link.

After you click the Continue button, a page is displayed (see Figure 3-5) that lets you know that your blog has been created.

8. **Click the Start Posting button to continue.**

Blogger takes you to the Create Post page for typing your first entry.

Before starting to type a new post, take a moment to look around at the Web page (shown in Figure 3-6). You'll find access to all the common tasks you do as you work on your blog.

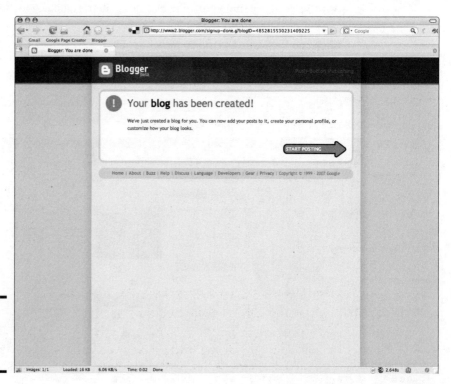

Figure 3-5:
Creating a
blog was a
breeze.

Work with your blog posts

Configure   Design   View your
your blog   your blog   live blog

Figure 3-6:
You're ready
to begin
typing a
new post.

Manage comments

Manage your previous posts

Add new blog entries

9. **Enter the title of your blog entry in the Title box.**

10. **Type your blog entry in the text box.**

The WYSIWYG editor acts as a mini-word processor, allowing you to use
the toolbar to format your text the way you want. See Figure 3-7 for
descriptions of each of the commands available as you compose an
entry.

Create link

Set text color   Left align

Italicize text   Center align

Bold text   Right align

Select a font size   Justify

Select a font   Insert image   Tweak or edit your HTML
                                code (advanced users only)

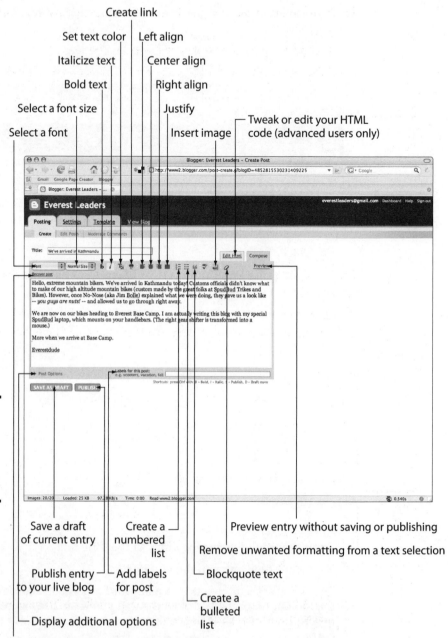

Figure 3-7:
Typing a
blog entry
by using the
WYSIWYG
editor.

Save a draft   Create a   Preview entry without saving or publishing
of current entry   numbered
                    list   Remove unwanted formatting from a text selection

Publish entry ─┐ └─ Add labels   └─ Blockquote text
to your live blog   for post
                                    └─ Create a
                                       bulleted
                                       list
└─ Display additional options

Revert to previously saved version of entry

Not all browsers support the WYSIWYG editor. If your browser doesn't
provide support, a plain-text-only version is displayed.

11. **If you want to make a link in your entry, select the text and click the Link button.**

If you don't have a link to make, skip to Step 12.

A dialog box (see Figure 3-8) appears for you to enter the URL of the link.

Figure 3-8: Entering the URL of your link.

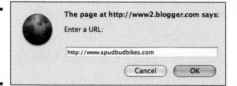

The page at http://www2.blogger.com says:

Enter a URL:

http://www.spudbudbikes.com

Cancel   OK

12. **Enter your URL in the dialog box and click OK.**

The link is added to your entry.

13. **If you want to insert an image, position your text cursor at the insertion point you want and then click the Image button.**

If you don't have an image to add now, move on to Step 14.

The Add an Image box is displayed, as shown in Figure 3-9.

Figure 3-9: Inserting an image into a blog entry.

http://www2.blogger.com – Blogger: Upload Images

Add an image from your computer   Or add an image from the web

Add another image   Add another image

/Users/rich/Public/Picture   Browse...   URL

We accept jpg, gif, bmp and png images, 8 MB maximum size   Learn more about using web images

Choose a layout.

None   Left   Center   Right

Image size:
○ Small
● Medium
○ Large

☑ Use this layout every time?

CANCEL   UPLOAD IMAGE   ☐ I accept the Terms of Service (Updated 12/13/06)

Images: 0/0   Loaded: 13 KB   5.97 KB/s   Time: 0:02   Done   2.185s

14. **To add an image from your computer, click the Browse button and locate the file on your drive.**

You can also add an image posted on Flickr or elsewhere on the Web by entering its URL on the right. (See the section "Posting to your blog from Flickr," later in this chapter.)

If you have multiple images, you can click the Add Another Image link to upload each of these images at the same time.

15. **Select the position in which you want the image to occur, relative to the text around it.**

16. **Choose the image size (small, medium, or large).**

17. **Select the I Accept the Terms of Service check box and click Upload Image.**

After the upload is complete, a confirmation box is displayed. Click the Done button in the box to return to the Blogger editor.

As Figure 3-10 shows, the image is inserted into your entry.

18. **Click the Post Options link to display additional options.**

You can specify whether you want to allow reader comments for the entry. You can also tweak the time and date that Blogger records this post.

For now, you can leave these options unchanged.

Figure 3-10:
A picture
can spiff up
an otherwise
dull entry.

19. **Enter one or more labels for this post, and separate each entry with commas.**

Labels are posted with each blog entry (usually at the bottom). Readers of your blog can then click a label to display a page that lists each blog entry which contains that label.

Labels are optional, and especially useful if you blog on a wide variety of topics.

You're ready to publish your blog.

20. **Click the Publish button.**

Blogger publishes your blog to the URL you previously defined and informs you when the process is complete. (See Figure 3-11.)

21. **Click the View Blog link.**

Blogger displays your blog in a new browser window. Figure 3-12 shows our results.

Figure 3-11:
Publishing usually takes just a few moments.

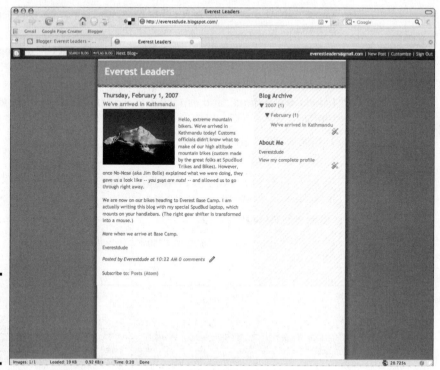

Figure 3-12:
We made it!
One of us
now has his
own blog!

Managing Your Blog Posts

Each of your blog entries is available in the Edit Posts list, as shown in
Figure 3-13. To access Edit Posts, click the Posts link in the Blogger Dashboard.
Or, if you're already working with your blog, click the Posting tab and then
click the Edit Posts link.

You can perform several tasks here:

✦ **Edit a post.** Click the Edit link beside the entry you want to edit. Blogger
displays the post in the WYSIWYG editor.

✦ **View the live version of a post.** Click the View link to see the individual
post on your blog.

✦ **View the text of a post.** You can click the arrow to view the text of the
post just below the entry.

✦ **Delete posts.** Click the Delete link to banish the post from your blog forever.

✦ **Label posts.** You can apply a new or existing label to one or more entries by selecting the entry's check box and then choosing the appropriate item from the Label Actions list.

✦ **Search for posts.** When you first start out with a new blog, you can easily locate a particular entry you want to work with. However, when your blog grows to include a large number of entries, finding it can be a challenge. Use the Search box to look up an entry.

Clicking the Moderate Comments link gives you access to a facility for reviewing comments posted on your blog by readers. However, you need to enable comment moderation in your blog settings first. (See the "Working with Comments" section, later in this chapter, for more details on managing comments on your site.)

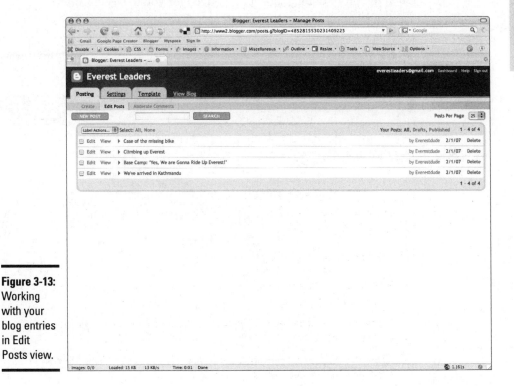

Figure 3-13:
Working
with your
blog entries
in Edit
Posts view.

Designing Your Blog Look

Blogger gives you considerable control over the template, fonts, colors, and layout of your blog. Just as important, the way in which you can modify your blog design is a breeze.

Changing the design template

Perhaps the most important decision you make in your blog design is the template you decide to use. When you initially created your blog, you had a limited set of templates from which to choose. Here's how to update the template with one you prefer:

1. **Click the Template tab.**

2. **Click the Pick New Template link.**

   A directory of templates is displayed for you to select from (see Figure 3-14).

Figure 3-14: Choose your new look.

3. **Browse through the template listings and select the template of your choice by clicking its radio button.**

   Note that many template designs have more than one variety. Click the radio button to update the mini-design preview.

4. **Click the Save Template button.**

   Your blog is updated to reflect the new look.

   Figure 3-24, later in this chapter, shows you the new look that the Everest Leaders blog took on.

You can also search around on the Web for third-party templates. If you find one, click the Template tab and then the Edit HTML button. On this page, you can upload a template file or paste the template's HTML code into the box that's provided. Here are some sites that offer free or open source templates:

✦ www.geckoandfly.com/blogspot-templates

✦ blogger-templates.blogspot.com

✦ www.blogskins.com

Modifying the page elements

When you initially create your blog, it sports a standard set of page elements, including these:

✦ Blogger-branded navbar at the top of the page

✦ Header

✦ Posts (the body of the page)

✦ Sidebar with Blog Archive and About Me sections

You can edit each of these elements by clicking the Templates tab and then clicking the Page Elements link. (You can click the Layout link from the Dashboard page as well.) Figure 3-15 shows the page.

To change the navbar style, click the Edit link and choose from four color styles.

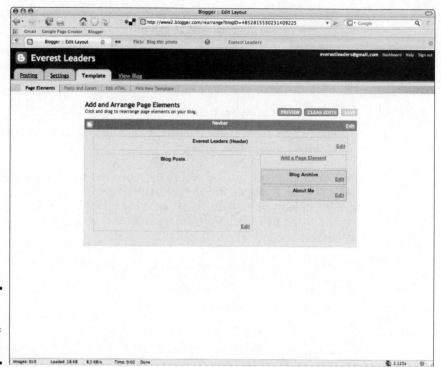

Figure 3-15:
Changing
the layout of
your page.

You cannot remove the navbar if you host your blog on Blogger. However, if you publish via FTP to another server, an option is displayed that enables you to hide it.

To modify the title or description of your blog, click the Edit link in the Header box.

To customize the layout of your post, click the Edit Posts link. Figure 3-16 shows the dialog box that's displayed. Use it to determine which parts of a post you want displayed and how them to be laid out.

Blogger also allows you add page elements to the sidebar to incorporate additional content to your blog. Click the Add a Page Element link to insert an element. The Choose a New Page Element dialog box is displayed, as shown in Figure 3-17.

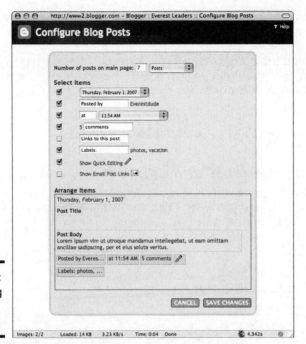

Book II
Chapter 3

Blogging It:
Creating Your
Own Blog

Figure 3-16:
Customizing
the look of
your posts.

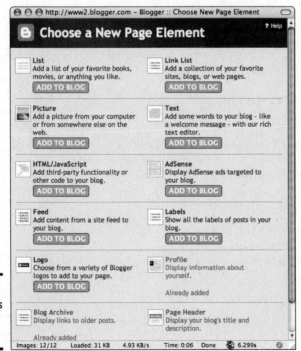

Figure 3-17:
Free goodies
to add to
your blog.

Choose from any of the selections. Click its Add to Blog button to insert. The page layout is updated to show your new element. (See Figure 3-18.)

You can change the order of the page elements in the sidebar by simply dragging them around with your mouse. However, moving elements around is limited to the sidebar only. You can't move any of the other regions of the page.

Click the Save button when you finish making changes.

Changing the fonts and colors

Although the template you choose has default fonts and colors it uses, you can customize them if you want. Click the Template tab, and then click the Fonts and Colors button. A page is displayed, as shown in Figure 3-19, with settings at the top of the page and a preview window at the bottom.

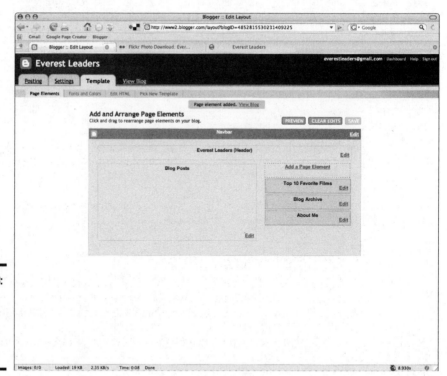

Figure 3-18: Adding a page element into your blog's sidebar.

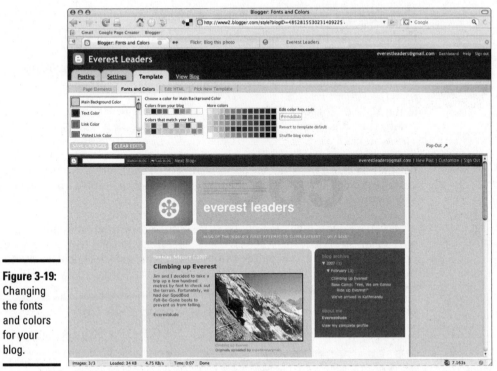

Figure 3-19:
Changing
the fonts
and colors
for your
blog.

The list box displays the default colors and fonts for your blog. As you select a font from the list, the settings area is updated automatically to display font information.

After you customize your look, click the Save Changes button.

Making Posts Outside of Blogger

Although you can make entries to your blog by using the Create Post page we discussed in the "Creating a Blog with Blogger" section, earlier in this chapter, you might find it more convenient to post using alternative means.

After these entries are posted, you can edit them just like any other blog entry inside Blogger.

Posting to your blog from e-mail

Posting to your blog can be literally as easy as sending an e-mail message. To do so, you set up a special e-mail address to send your posts to. Configure it by clicking the Settings tab and then clicking the Email link. Figure 3-20 shows the page that's displayed.

In the Mail-to-Blogger Address section, supply a name in the box that's provided. The name is used as a unique e-mail address for posting to your blog. The syntax is *yourblogname.newwordyousupply*@blogger.com. In our example, we used everestleaders.post@blogger.com, although you can choose a more secure word that people can't guess, to prevent an unwanted party from posting on your blog. Check the Publish box and click Save Settings.

After you enable e-mail posting, go to your e-mail software and compose a post as an e-mail message (see Figure 3-21). After you send the message, it's posted on your blog in a matter of moments (see Figure 3-24, a little later in this chapter).

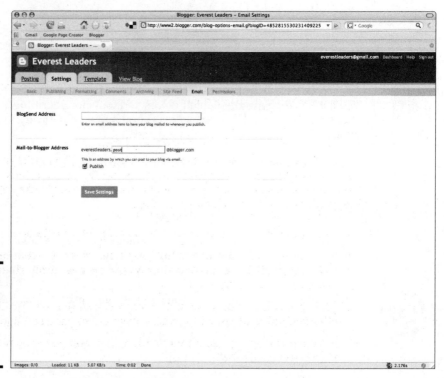

Figure 3-20: Setting up the e-mail posting option for your blog.

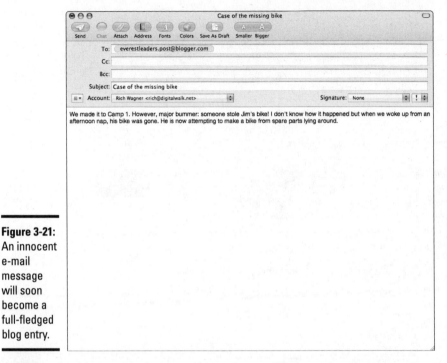

Figure 3-21:
An innocent
e-mail
message
will soon
become a
full-fledged
blog entry.

You cannot include pictures or other attachments with your e-mail. Blogger strips them out during the posting process.

Posting to your blog from Flickr

If you upload and share your photos on Flickr.com, you don't have to upload your images to Blogger again in order to post them on your blog. Flickr has a feature that enables you to post a photo directly from Flickr onto your Blogger blog. To do so, follow these steps:

1. **Click the Blog This link when viewing any of your photos.**

When you do this the first time, Flickr takes you through a setup process to link your Flickr account to your Blogger account. You're asked to confirm the setup link by e-mail.

2. **After the connection is set up, you can click the Blog This link and click the name of your blog in the drop-down list (see Figure 3-22).**

Next, a new page appears that allows you to compose a blog entry inside Flickr (see Figure 3-23).

The Blog This link

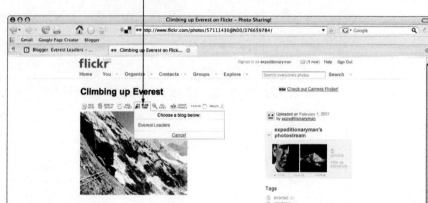

Figure 3-22:
Creating a
photoblog
has never
been easier.

3. Click Post Entry to post your new entry.

Figure 3-24 shows the blog with entries entered from the Blogger site, e-mail, and Flickr.

Figure 3-23:
Adding blog
text to
accompany
the picture.

Posted from Flickr   Posted from e-mail   Posted from Blogger

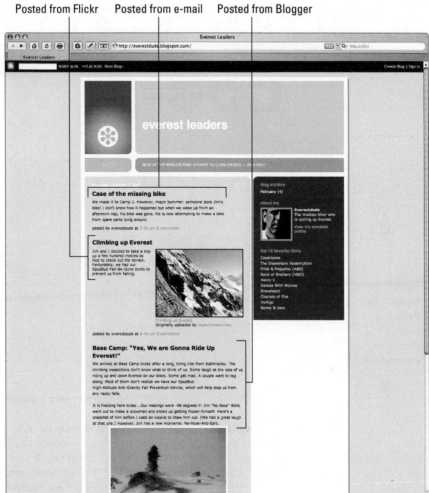

Figure 3-24:
Adding
entries from
e-mail,
Flickr, and
Blogger.

Working with Comments

Perhaps the most noteworthy setting is the Comments page (see Figure 3-25), which enables you configure how you want to deal with comments. Reader comments are a major component of many blogs because they provide

✦ Interaction between the blogger and the audience reading the blogs

✦ A sense of community for people coming to your site

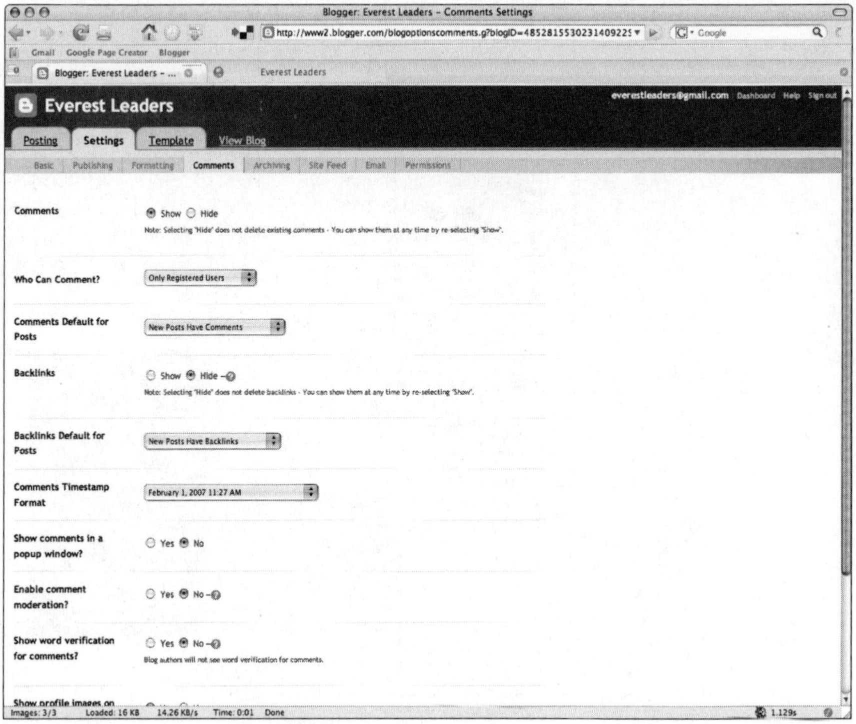

Figure 3-25:
Setting
up blog
comments.

Here some questions to consider as you configure your comment support:

✦ **Do you want to allow comments?** The biggest decision you need to make is whether you want to allow people to comment on your blog entries. By default, this feature is enabled. However, if you prefer to disable comments, click the Hide button in the Comments section to turn it off. (You can also enable or disable comments for individual blog entries, as discussed in the section "Creating a Blog with Blogger," earlier in this chapter.)

✦ **Who do you want to be able to make comments?** After you decide to allow comments, decide who can post: any ol' Joe or Jody, only registered Blogger users, or members of the blog (for Team Blogs, which is configured by clicking the Permissions link).

✦ **Do you want to review comments before they're posted?** By default, a comment is automatically posted publicly within moments after the reader saves it. However, if you're concerned about inappropriate comments being posted on your site, you can choose to review comments first.

The Moderate Comments page, accessible from the Postings tab, is the location for reviewing new comments. However, you need to enable moderated comments first by choosing the Yes option in the Enable Comment Moderation box.

✦ **Do you want to display comments in a pop-up window?** I recommend clicking the Yes button in the Show comments in a Popup Window section. If you don't, the comments page you display looks visually like Blogger.com, not like your template style. However, the popup window looks visually more neutral (see Figure 3-26), thus working well with a variety of styles.

Figure 3-26:
Displaying comments in a pop-up window.

Chapter 4: Getting Started on eBay

*e*Bay is one of the best examples of why the World Wide Web is revolutionary. It does more than just make purchasing books or DVDs more convenient: Sometimes, it makes other types of commerce *possible*.

Before the Internet became popular, buying used or hard-to-find items was an activity relegated to garage sales, flea markets, collector's shows, or out-of-date printed catalogs. Because of the geographical limitations, it would be virtually impossible for Mickey, a Seattle-based collector, to try to sell a rare movie poster to Donald, an interested buyer in Leominster, Massachusetts. Mickey wouldn't know that Donald, living 3,500 miles away, would have any interest. Donald, unless he happened to stumble into a flea market in the Pacific Northwest, would never know that a rare print of his favorite poster was even available. Enter eBay. Like a matchmaker of the commerce world, eBay eliminates the age-old geographical hurdles that have always existed.

In this chapter, you'll discover the world of eBay and get started in selling your own goods on the world's most popular online auction site.

If you want to dive deeper into the world of eBay, check out the many titles about eBay published by Wiley, including *eBay For Dummies,* 5th Edition, and *Starting an eBay Business For Dummies,* 2nd Edition, both by Marsha Collier.

Selling an Item at eBay

Before you sell an item at eBay, you first need to have an account. If you don't have one yet, go to `www.ebay.com` and click the `register` link to sign up. Follow the on-screen instructions and then you're set to roll.

In this section, we walk you through the process of listing your item at eBay.

Before beginning, make sure that you have one or more pictures of the item you want to sell. (See the "Photo tips" section, later in this chapter, for pointers on making your products looks great in pictures.)

1. **Go to www.ebay.com.**

Make sure that you're signed in before continuing.

2. **Click the Sell link on the main navigation menu.**

Before you can sell anything through eBay, you need to create a seller's account. To obtain one, you need to provide credit card and checking account information. eBay prompts you for this information, as shown in Figure 4-1.

3. **Click the Create Seller's Account button.**

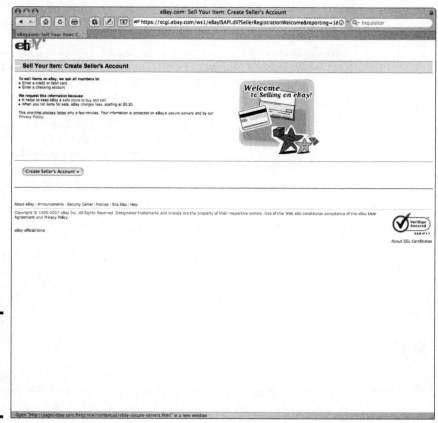

Figure 4-1:
You need to begin by creating a seller's account.

4. **Enter credit or debit card information in the spaces provided.**

When you sell something on eBay, eBay gets a percentage of the auction amount. Normally, these funds are taken from the credit card you provide. See Figure 4-2.

5. **Click Continue.**

6. **Enter checking account information on the Place Checking Account on File page.**

eBay doesn't withdraw money from your checking account unless you authorize it to. However, it requires this information as a way to confirm your identity.

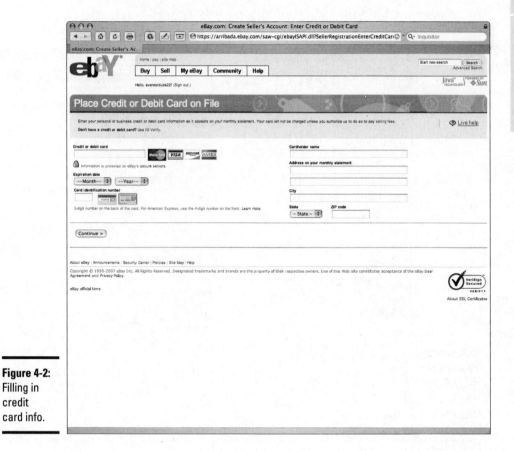

Figure 4-2:
Filling in
credit
card info.

7. Click Continue.

With those financial details out of the way, you're ready to sell, sell, sell! The initial Sell page opens, as shown in Figure 4-3.

Now that you have a seller's account, clicking Sell from the main eBay navigation menu opens this page.

You're ready to start listing your item.

8. Enter the item you're selling in the box provided and click Sell It.

eBay looks at the text you enter and makes its best guess about the category it should be listed under. It shows categories in the Sell: Select a Category page that's displayed, as shown in Figure 4-4.

Figure 4-3:
The first step in listing an item.

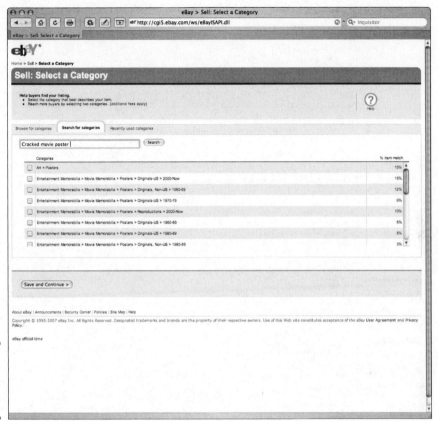

Figure 4-4:
Selecting a
category for
your item.

The text you enter is used only to determine the item's category. It isn't used as the name for your auction listing.

9. Select the check box for the *most* appropriate category for your item.

You can choose more than one category, but you have to pay extra for two categories.

10. Click the Save and Continue button.

The Sell: Create Your Listing page is displayed (see Figure 4-5).

11. Enter the title of the item in the Title box.

Describe the item as clearly and concisely as possible.

Figure 4-5: How well you describe your item makes a big impact in how much you can make.

Be sure to check out other items in the same category to see whether other sellers commonly use certain terms or phrases to describe products. If those terms are appropriate for your item, use them. In our example of selling a rare, new movie poster, potential buyers would look for the terms *mint* and *rare*.

You can optionally add a subtitle, though it costs an additional fee.

12. Click the Add Pictures button.

A text description gets people to look at your item, but doesn't sell it. Because buyers can't touch the product, they at least want to see a picture that clearly shows what they're buying and the condition it's in.

An attractive, descriptive picture is a critical factor in getting the best price possible for your item. See the section "Presenting Your Goods," later in this chapter, for some photo tips to consider.

A window is displayed for adding images (see Figure 4-6).

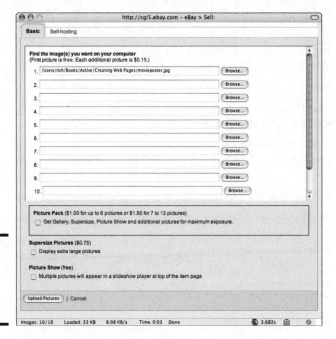

Figure 4-6:
Adding an
image to
your item
listing.

13. **Click the Browse button beside the first box and select the image you want to add.**

14. **Add additional images, if you want.**

Photos from various angles can give potential buyers a good idea of what you're selling, so you might want to upload multiple images. Keep in mind, however, that eBay charges extra if you add more than one picture.

15. **Click the Upload Pictures button.**

eBay uploads the picture (or pictures) to its server. You return to the main Sell: Create Your Listing page.

16. **Enter a full description of your item listing in the Description box.**

Provide all the details you can think of that potential buyers will want to know about the product. Also, we recommend adding shipping and payment details.

See the "Presenting Your Goods" section, a bit later in this chapter, for tips on what to write.

17. **Use the formatting bar to add text formatting to your description.**

You can also click the HTML link to add HTML markup tags to your description. (See Book VI if you want to know more about HTML.)

Use formatting to help enhance the listing, and use the design recommendations that we discuss elsewhere in this book — namely, in Books I and V. You want to convey a professional look and tone.

Figure 4-7 shows the listing for our movie poster.

18. **In the How You're Selling area, enter the starting price, number of items, and duration of the auction.**

For the starting price, we recommend starting with a low price to encourage bids and get the auction rolling. This amount shouldn't be the price you're expecting to get from the item.

For the duration, a longer timeframe can often be to your advantage.

19. **In the Payment methods you accept, check the items you want.**

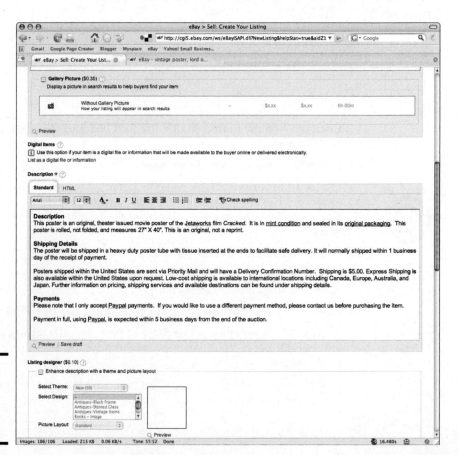

Figure 4-7:
A description fills in details for the buyer.

You should read more on the eBay page concerning the various options. Also, visit `www.paypal.com` to fully understand everything related to PayPal.

20. In the Shipping box, specify the cost of shipping.

Click the Shipping Wizard link if you need help.

21. Click Save and Continue.

A page is displayed that provides a boatload of add-ons — all designed to make your listing stand out.

When you're just getting your feet wet, we recommend sticking to the basics. Later, as you gain experience with what works and what doesn't, you might want to add one or more of these promotional tools.

22. Scroll down to the Preview Your Listing section and read through your entry.

Optionally, you can click the Preview link to display the page in a mini-preview window, as shown in Figure 4-8.

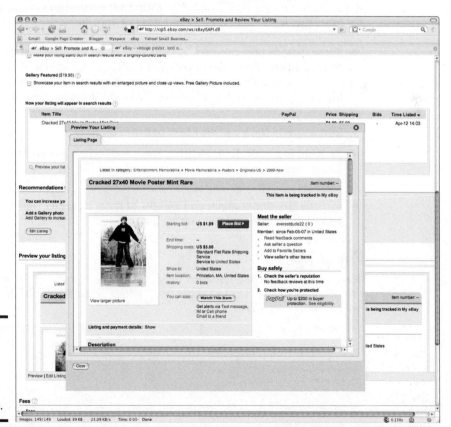

**Book II
Chapter 4**

**Getting Started
on eBay**

Figure 4-8:
Make sure
that you
carefully
preview
your listing.

23. **If you want to make a change to the listing, click the Edit Listing link.**

Make necessary changes before continuing.

24. **Click Continue.**

Your listing is now ready to go live on eBay!

You can watch the progress of your auction by clicking the My eBay link on the navigation bar.

Presenting Your Goods

Exactly how eBay sellers describe items in descriptive text and display them in photos is a major factor in separating amateurs from pros and failures from successes in online sales. As you write product descriptions and show photos in your item listings, consider the following tips.

Writing tips

Make sure that your text descriptions are well written and compelling. Here are some tips for writing up a description of your items:

✦ **Show candor and honesty in your text descriptions (and photographs) by noting any flaws that exist.** You're likely to garner a higher feedback score from satisfied customers while gaining confidence from potential bidders because more people are likely to bid on an item that's thoroughly described.

✦ **Run a spell check on your text before you post it.**

✦ **Be brief but complete.** Mention any extras, such as including the item's original box. (Having the original box can increase an item's value.)

✦ **Include the dimensions and weight of most items as well as the model and make and how long you've had it.**

Photo tips

Here are some simple guidelines for getting a good photo of the item you're trying to sell. These simple tips include some basic photo composition.

Composition

Take a few minutes to set up your shot to showcase your items to their best.

✦ **Invest in an inexpensive tripod so that the image doesn't get blurred.** Or, get a camera with a built-in image stabilizer.

✦ **Photograph your items in front of a backdrop.** For a simple backdrop, you can buy a few, large, flexible pieces of white posterboard (at an art store); a large piece of unlined white paper (also at an art store); or a plain white bed sheet. Place your object in front of this background to isolate the object and make it stand out. Ensure that the backdrop fills the entire frame of the photo.

Book II
Chapter 4

Getting Started
on eBay

Some people turn the background white by using *knockout* tools (graphics programs include various fill and select tools that can make this job a bit easier). If possible, just use a white background when you take the shots.

✦ **Avoid tilting the camera so that the object looks like it's about to slide off the table.** You can adjust tilt later in a graphics application, but it's best to get it straight off the bat.

✦ **Crop when shooting.** That is, get in close enough to eliminate unnecessary space around the item being photographed. However, you can always crop in an image editor later before uploading.

✦ **Mix it up.** Vary the exposure, the distance between the camera and your item, and the angle from which you shoot.

✦ **Get close to the object, to fill the frame.**

✦ **Take close-up shots.** Use the camera's macro button if you're closer than a few feet from the object. For example, get close to the details and take shots of a fine, hand-painted porcelain design, but also note any flaws, cracks, chips, or whatever makes your item less than perfect.

✦ **Provide scale.** Put a familiar object in the shot, such as a penny, a little ruler, or a pencil. This object helps viewers understand the size of the item.

✦ **Take lots of photos and then choose the best shots.**

Lighting

To also help create the best possible product photos, here are a few tips for getting the lighting right in your photos:

+ **Use adequate lighting.** Remember to keep the auto contrast and other auto features in your camera turned on.

+ **Watch out for shadows.**

+ **Try a few shots with the camera's flash.** Keep in mind that outdoor light from the sun is nearly always best.

For more tips on digital photography, check out *Digital Photography For Dummies,* 5th Edition, by Julie Adair King (Wiley).

Opening a Store in eBay Stores

After you get your feet wet with individual eBay auctions, you might see the opportunity to dive further into online commerce. eBay allows you to move closer to your own, custom online e-commerce site by opening an eBay Stores store for a relatively small monthly fee.

Opening an eBay store (`stores.ebay.com`) is an easy and quick way to set up an online commercial presence without a lot of hassle. You get to customize your "storefront" page, track sales and visits, and get a unique Web address. eBay Stores also has an in-store search feature.

Directing traffic and trust

When you use eBay Stores, you get the added benefit of the exposure on eBay itself with various ways to direct eBay visitors to your store. If someone visits your eBay auction, he's already providing evidence of a targeted interest in your kind of products. When you link to your eBay Store from your auction, the customer can then browse all your product listings.

In addition to an obvious interest in your product, potential buyers are also likely to feel comfortable within the eBay universe and feeling a general sense of trust in the eBay umbrella. In other words, when you open a store within the eBay universe, you're not asking buyers to trust some independent, unknown Web site. Instead, you're asking them to trust eBay itself.

Opening a store in eBay Stores is easier than setting up a full shopping cart solution on your own Web site. It includes

✦ **Order tracking:** You don't have to construct a complex order-tracking and customer-servicing system because they're built in.

✦ **Payments:** As with normal eBay auctions, PayPal (`www.paypal.com`) is available as a payment method.

✦ **Operating cost:** The cost to sell items within an eBay Stores store is far less than selling on an eBay auction. It costs only two cents per listing per month for each item you want to sell.

If you want to maintain a normal Web site for your normal business but provide an eBay store as an option for people to shop with you online, simply provide links between each site. When you do this, make sure that your eBay store has a page design that's consistent with your main Web site.

To see how some of the best eBay stores look, visit this page to view some prizewinners: `pages.ebay.com/storefronts/bestinstores.html`.

Book III

Microsoft Expression Web

The 5th Wave   By Rich Tennant

MOUSE PAD HELP CENTER

It sounds like you may still have your pad in the packaging, sir...

No ma'am, the pad goes on the desktop, not the floor.

Try turning the pad over...

Anyone have any experience with a round pad?!

Contents at a Glance

Chapter 1: Getting to Know Microsoft Expression Web

In This Chapter

✔ Introducing the Expression Web workspace

✔ Exploring the editing window

✔ Discovering the task panes

✔ Customizing the workspace

*E*xpression Web is the premier Web site design tool from Microsoft. If you've used Microsoft Office applications, such as Word, you'll find Expression Web fairly easy to pick up. Better yet, if you've used FrontPage, you'll discover many similarities between the two software products. In truth, Expression Web comes from the same software lineage as the older FrontPage.

Expression Web is the flagship product in the new Microsoft Expression Studio. Others products in the software suite include Expression Design (for illustrations and graphic design), Expression Blend (for user interface design), and Expression Media (for organizing your digital assets). In this book, we focus on Expression Web.

This chapter introduces you to Expression Web and walks you through the major features of its working environment. In the remaining chapters of this book, you'll roll up your sleeves and create pages with it.

Exploring the Expression Web Workspace

When you launch Expression Web, the main workspace (as shown in Figure 1-1) is displayed in full glory.

An untitled HTML document is created for you automatically. You can immediately begin working with it.

You compose and design your Web pages in the editing window. Each toolbar and task pane that surrounds the editor help you construct or manage your Web site.

Tag properties   Toolbox

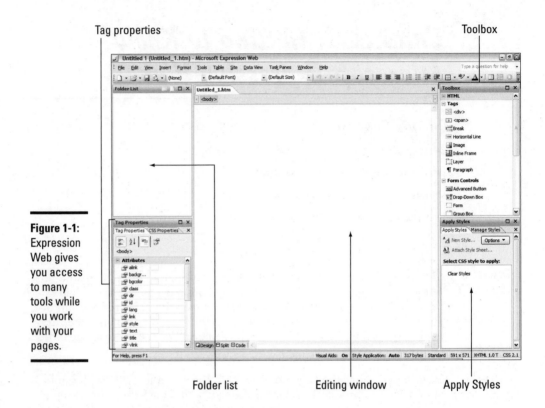

Figure 1-1:
Expression
Web gives
you access
to many
tools while
you work
with your
pages.

Folder list   Editing window   Apply Styles

Exploring the Editing Window

The Editing window is the spot inside Expression Web where you'll spend much of your time. Figure 1-2 points out the major features that you can work with.

Pay special attention to the Design, Split, and Code buttons at the bottom of the Editing window. By default, Expression Web displays the document in *Design view* (see Figure 1-2), which features a visual look at the Web page that approximates what it will look like in a browser.

Click the Code button to display the document in *Code view,* which reveals the HTML (Hypertext Markup Language) code of the page (see Figure 1-3). If HTML looks like Greek to you, be sure to check out Book VI.

File tabs   Quick Tag Selector bar   Close button

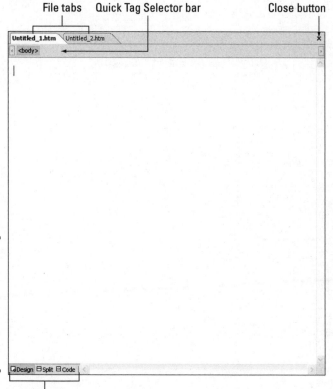

Untitled_1.htm   Untitled_2.htm   x

‹ ‹body›

Design Split Code

Figure 1-2:
Quick
access
productivity
tools
surround
the Editing
window.

Design/Split/Code view buttons

**Book III
Chapter 1**

**Getting to Know
Microsoft
Expression Web**

Finally, you can split the difference by viewing the document in Split mode (see Figure 1-4). *Split mode* provides a split screen to display the code on the top and the design view on the bottom.

In addition to the buttons on the bottom of the editing window, you can also choose the Design, Split, and Code items from the View⇨Page submenu.

Figure 1-3:
Code view displays a document's HTML source code.

Figure 1-4:
Split view enables you to see both Design and Code views.

Discovering the Tag Selector

A Web page is written in HTML. Expression Web doesn't force you to hand-code your pages, of course. However, the more you know about the HTML for your document, the greater control you can have over it.

When you work in Design view, Expression Web always gives you quick access to the tags you are working within its Tag Selector, shown just below the file tabs in the Editing window.

When you click your mouse anywhere on the document, the Tag Selector displays a nested order view of the HTML for that insertion point. For example, Figure 1-5 shows the Tag Selector when the mouse is inside a paragraph of text. The paragraph is contained by several div elements and then the body element.

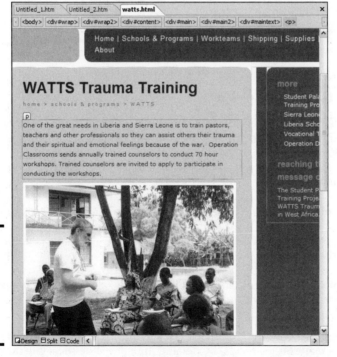

Figure 1-5: Select various HTML tags, using the Tag Selector.

Book III
Chapter 1

Getting to Know
Microsoft
Expression Web

Each tag is a button that, when clicked, selects the element inside the Editing window. Or, you can click the down arrow on the right side of the button to display a drop-down list of options (Select Tag, Select Tag Contents, Edit Tag, Remove Tag, Insert HTML, Wrap Tag, Positioning, and Tag Properties), as shown in Figure 1-6.

Figure 1-6:
You can
access
several
features
from the Tag
Selector.

Working with Task Panes

Surrounding the Editing window is a set of task panes that provide additional functionality to help you with your Web site design and management. These task panes are normally displayed on the sides of the Expression Web window, although each can be detached from the side and displayed as a floating window.

Each of the task panes can be accessed from the Task Panes menu.

Here are some of the task panes that will come in handy as you use Expression Web:

✦ **Toolbox:** The Toolbox (see Figure 1-7) is used to add common HTML elements to your page. (You can also add ASP.NET controls from the Toolbox, although we don't cover that in this book.)

✦ **Apply Styles and Manage Styles panes:** The Apply Styles and the Manage Styles panes, by default, appear inside the same task pane window. Use the Apply Styles task pane to quickly apply CSS (Cascading Style Sheet) styles to your document. The Manage Styles pane, on the other hand, is used for managing your style rules and external style sheets. Figure 1-8 displays the Apply Styles pane.

Figure 1-7:
The Toolbox
lets you
drag and
drop HTML
elements
into your
Web page.

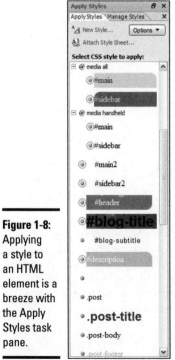

Figure 1-8:
Applying
a style to
an HTML
element is a
breeze with
the Apply
Styles task
pane.

✦ **Folder List pane:** The Folder List task pane, shown in Figure 1-9, is used to view and manage the files of your Expression Web site. You can create, open, rename, or delete pages and folders from inside of the task pane. This pane is empty if you're working on a standalone page outside a site.

✦ **Tag Properties and CSS Properties panes:** By default, the Tag Properties (see Figure 1-10) and CSS Properties (see Figure 1-11) task panes are bundled inside the same task pane. The Tag Properties pane allows you to view and edit all the available attributes of the current HTML element in your document. The CSS Properties pane displays the CSS rules and properties for the selected element.

Figure 1-9:
The Folder List pane is a mini Windows Explorer packed inside Expression Web.

Figure 1-10: Get the inside scoop on any element with the Tag Properties pane.

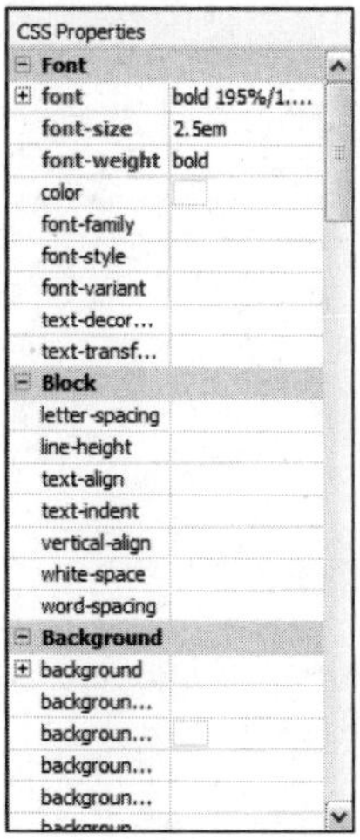

Figure 1-11: The CSS Properties task pane allows you to see the current rules applied and available rule settings.

Viewing Your Web Site

When you open a Web site in Expression Web, a Web Site tab is displayed on the far left of the document tabs. Inside this window is a listing of the site's assets, including local folders, remote Web sites, reports, and hyperlinks. These different assets can be viewed through the view buttons on the bottom of the window. Figure 1-12 shows the Web Site view.

Web Site tab

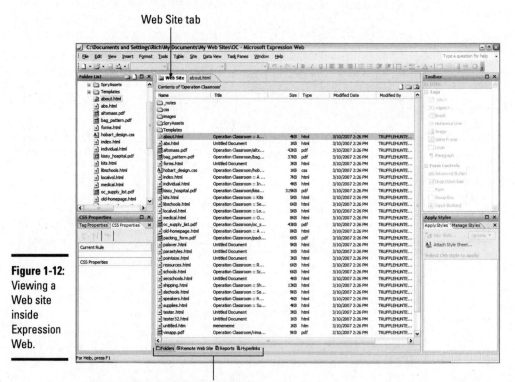

Figure 1-12: Viewing a Web site inside Expression Web.

Folders/Remote Web Site/Reports/Hyperlinks buttons

Customizing Your Working Environment

Expression Web enables you to customize your working environment, enabling you to tailor it just the way you want to.

Customizing the task panes

Here are several display options that you can perform with the task panes:

✦ **Showing and hiding a task pane:** All the task panes can be accessed from the Task Pane menu. You can show or hide a task pane by choosing its menu item from list. You can also hide an open task pane by clicking its Close button.

✦ **Maximizing the task pane:** You can click the Maximize button on the task pane to expand the size of the pane (and shrink any other panes adjacent to it). Click the Restore button to return to the normal size.

✦ **Undocking and docking a task pane:** You can undock any of the task panes and create a floating window. To do so, drag the caption bar of the task pane and drag onto the Editing window. The task pane undocks and floats on top of the workspace. You can also right-click and choose Float from the pop-up menu.

To dock a floating task pane, drag the task pane to the side of the application window that you wish to dock. Expression Web docks the pane for you. Or, you can right-click the caption bar and choose Dock.

Customizing the Page Editor

The Expression Web page editor comes with an impressive assortment of options that you can customize by choosing Tools⇨Page Editor Options (as shown in Figure 1-13).

Figure 1-13: The Page Editor can be customized so much it will look like an aardvark.

Chapter 2: Express Yourself: Creating Your First Site with Expression Web

In This Chapter

✔ Creating a new Expression Web site

✔ Adding content to the home page

✔ Previewing your pages in a browser

✔ Publishing your site to the Web

It's time to express yourself with Expression Web. As you work your way through this minibook, you'll dive deeper into how to lay out pages and work with content. To get things started, we walk you step-by-step through creating a Web site with Expression Web.

At the end of the chapter, we show you how to publish the Web site you just created to a remote server. As a result, you need to have an established account with a Web hosting provider. If you don't, skip the section on publishing.

Creating a New Site

Before you can use Expression Web to work with pages, graphics, and other files as you develop a site, you first need to create the site itself. To create a new site, follow these steps:

1. **Choose File➪New➪Web Site.**

The New dialog box appears with the Web Site tab selected, as shown in Figure 2-1.

2. **Select the General or the Templates category.**

- *General:* Select this to begin with a blank site or to import an existing site into Expression Web.

- *Templates:* Use this to choose from a list of design templates to get you started.

3. **Select the desired site selection from the type list.**

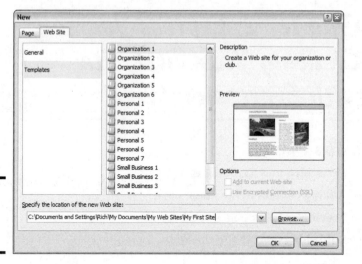

Figure 2-1:
Creating a
site starts
here.

For our purposes, we're choosing the Personal 4 template.

4. Click OK.

Expression Web creates the site and displays the Web Site window, as shown in Figure 2-2.

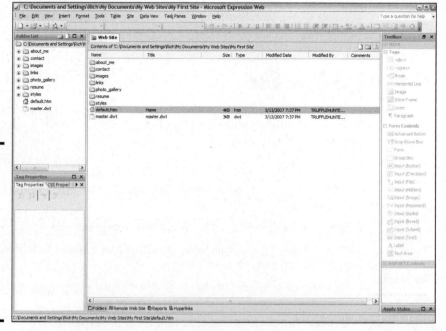

Figure 2-2:
The
template
used by
Expression
Web
creates
several
folders and
pages at
the start.

Working with the Home Page

Unless you select an empty site during the site creation process, Expression Web automatically creates a home page and names it `default.htm`.

If you select a template, it contains canned content. See the example in Figure 2-3. Or, if you choose the blank page, you have a vanilla-looking document.

To add content to the home page:

1. **Double-click the `default.htm` page in the Web Site window.**

2. **Click your cursor at the desired location in the page and begin editing the content.**

3. **(Optional) Add a link.**

   a. *Select text that you wish to link.*

   b. *Click the Insert Hyperlink button from the toolbar.*

   c. *Navigate to the link in the dialog box (or type a URL in the Address box) and click OK.*

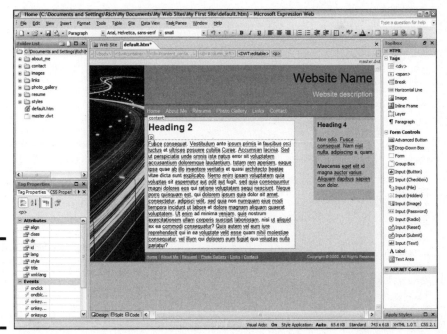

Figure 2-3: Canned content ready to be edited.

4. (Optional) Add an image.

   a. *Position your cursor at the location in which you'd like the image to appear.*

   b. *Click the Insert Picture from File button on the toolbar and then select the image you would like to insert from the dialog box that appears.*

   c. *Click OK.*

5. Add a title to your page.

   Right-click the page in the Editing window and choose Page Properties from the pop-up menu. In the Page Properties dialog box (see Figure 2-4) that appears, enter a descriptive title in the Title field and then click OK.

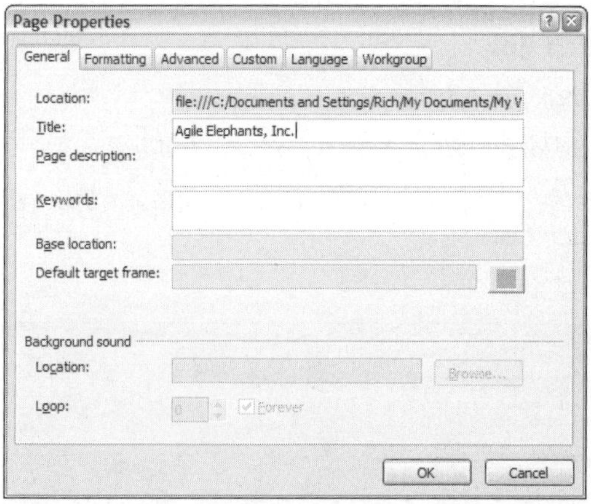

Figure 2-4:
Modifying
the title and
other page
properties.

6. Choose File⇨Save.

   It's not rocket science, but like with other documents you work with, save your Web page before it can be of much use.

7. Repeat Steps 1 through 6 for each of the pages in your Web site.

   If you use one of the templates, you might have several pages that you wish to modify.

Here, we bypassed the many features of Expression Web for working with text, links, and images. We save that discussion for Chapter 4 of this minibook.

Previewing Your Page in a Browser

Although Expression Web features a WYSIWYG (What You See Is What You Get) visual editor, some disparities always exist between what you see in Design view and what you see in the browser. Therefore, before you finish with a page, be sure to preview your page to see how it looks.

To preview a document:

1. **Click the Preview in Browser button on the toolbar.**

In the drop-down list, a list of browsers that are installed on your computer is displayed, shown at various window sizes (see Figure 2-5).

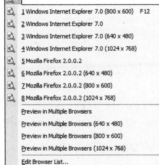

Figure 2-5:
Choose the browser and window size to preview your page.

Or, if you prefer the main menu, you can also choose an option from the File⇨Preview in Browser submenu instead.

You can modify the browser list by choosing the Edit Browser List item from the drop-down list. Additionally, you can specify whether you'd like Expression Web to automatically save the current state of the document before previewing.

2. **Choose the desired browser and window size from the list.**

Expression Web opens your page in the browser for you to preview (see Figure 2-6).

Publishing Your Site

After you preview your site and have everything ready to go, you're ready to publish it to your remote server.

**Book III
Chapter 2**

Creating Your First
Site with
Expression Web

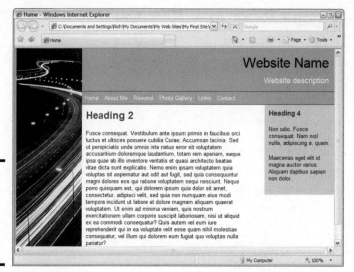

Figure 2-6:
Previewing
your
document
inside of a
browser.

Here's how to publish your newly created site:

1. **Click the Web Site button in the Editing window tab pane.**

2. **Click the Remote Web Site button at the bottom of the window.**

   Because you've not yet set anything up, an empty window is displayed (see Figure 2-7).

3. **Click the Remote Web Site Properties button.**

   The Remote Web Site Properties dialog box appears, as shown in Figure 2-8.

4. **From the Remote Web server type option group, specify the kind of Web server that you're connecting to.**

   If you have a typical Web hosting provider, you use FTP (File Transfer Protocol) to connect to the server. (If you are using another option, fill out the settings and then skip to Step 7.)

5. **In the Remote Web Site Location field, enter the FTP server information for your hosting provider.**

6. **If you have a special directory to place the site files in, add that to the FTP Directory field.**

7. **Click the Publishing tab to display publishing options.**

8. **Make any desired changes to the publishing settings.**

9. **Click OK.**

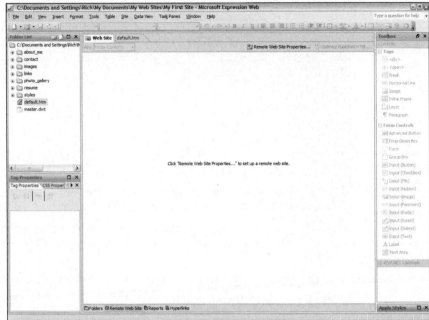

Figure 2-7:
You're ready
to connect
to the World
Wide Web
and publish
a site.

**Book III
Chapter 2**

**Creating Your First
Site with
Expression Web**

Figure 2-8:
Configuring
a Web
site for
publishing.

Expression Web attempts to connect to the server, using the information that you provide.

You are prompted for your user name and password (see Figure 2-9).

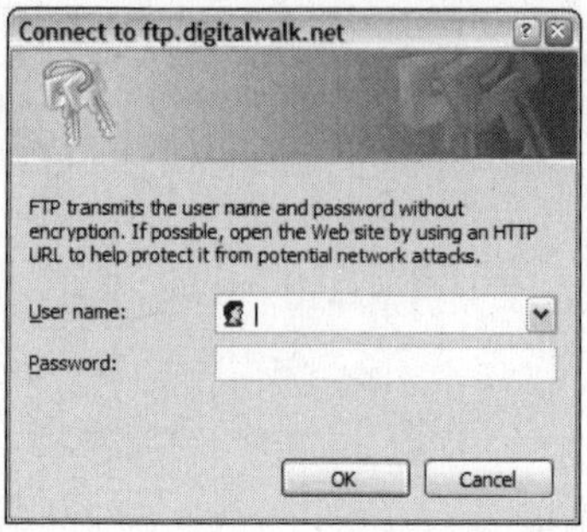

Figure 2-9:
Not so fast,
Buster!
User
name and
password
are required
for
publishing!

10. **If the directory doesn't exist on the remote server, you're asked to confirm whether you'd like to create the folder.**

After it's successfully connected, Expression Web then configures the server. The status is shown in the Remote Web Site view of the Web Site window.

11. **In the Publish All Changed Pages section, select Local to Remote.**

12. **Click the Publish Web Site button.**

Expression Web connects to the server and begins transferring files to the remote server (see Figure 2-10).

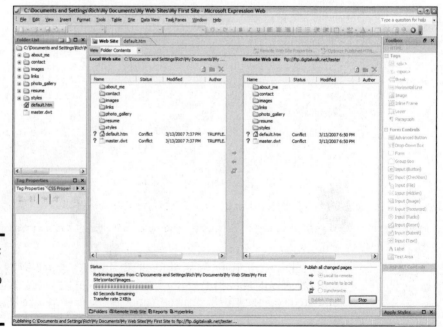

Figure 2-10:
Uploading
local files to
the live
server.

Expression Web displays the results of the transfer in the Status pane. If the upload was successful, congratulations! You published your first site using Microsoft Expression Web.

Importing a Site into Expression Web

Perhaps you have an existing site that you'd like to import into Expression Web and begin using. To import a Web site, follow these steps:

1. **Choose File⇨Import⇨Import Site Wizard.**

The Import Web Site Wizard dialog box is displayed, as shown in Figure 2-11.

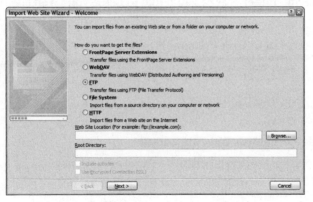

Figure 2-11: You can get a head start by importing work you've already done with another Web tool.

2. **Decide the transmission method in which you would like to retrieve the files.**

- *FTP:* If you're importing an old site of yours that you have on a Web server, select FTP (if you have your user name and password information).

- *HTTP:* For everything else, select HTTP.

3. **Specify the address in the Web Site Location field.**

4. **If you're using FTP, specify the Root Directory. Otherwise, go to Step 5.**

5. **Click Next to begin.**

Expression Web connects to the remote server (requesting user name and password if needed). If it's able to, the next page in the wizard is shown (see Figure 2-12).

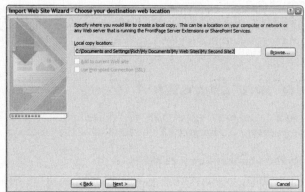

Figure 2-12:
Enter the
local folder
in which you
want to
store the
imported
files.

6. **Enter the folder where you'd like to place your Web site files.**

   A final dialog box is displayed.

7. **Click Finish to start the import process.**

   Expression Web opens the Remote Web Site view in the Web Site
   window.

8. **Select the Remote to Local radio button in the Publish All Changed
   Pages group.**

9. **Click the Publish Web Site button.**

   Expression Web connects to the Web server and begins the transfer
   process. Status is shown as the files are retrieved from the remote
   server.

10. **When the transfer process is complete, click the Folders View button
    at the bottom of the Web Site window.**

    The local files to the Web site are displayed. Site files are now ready for
    editing.

Chapter 3: Working with Text, Graphics, and Links

In This Chapter

✔ **Inserting and formatting text**

✔ **Working with images**

✔ **Adding links**

*I*t's all about the content. A Web site should be attractive and easy to navigate. If your site visitors are going to come back again and again, you need to have the content.

Much of the content that you'll be working with on your Web site consists of three basic types: text, graphics, and links. You arrange and style these pieces of content in a variety of ways by using HTML (Hypertext Markup Language) and CSS (Cascading Style Sheets), but having a solid grasp on the basics is important. You explore how to work with text, pictures, and links in this chapter.

Adding and Editing Text in Your Pages

If you've used Microsoft Word before, you already have a pretty good idea of how you'll work with text inside Expression Web. Although the underlying technologies are different, many of the ways how you format and edit your text are consistent from Word to Expression Web. This synergy makes your transition to the Web all that much easier.

Adding text

To add text to your page, just click the position in the Editing window in which you wish to type, and away you go. If you're not in any other element (beside the body), Expression Web automatically adds a paragraph element for you around your text.

Expression Web performs much like Microsoft Word when you enter text. For example, the text wraps when you reach the end of a line. Pressing Enter closes the paragraph and creates a new one. Or, to begin a new line but keep it within the same paragraph, press Shift+Enter. A line break (br) element is added.

TIP

You can also add a line break by double-clicking the Break tag in the Toolbox.

Formatting text

After you enter your text, there are two main ways in which you can format it: directly, and with styles.

Direct formatting

You can format your text in Expression Web by directly formatting it from the Common toolbar, as shown in Figure 3-1. You do this exactly as you've likely always done in Microsoft Word.

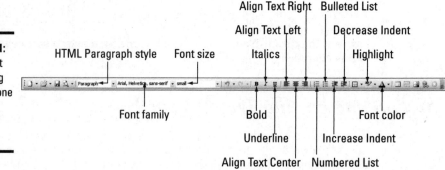

Figure 3-1:
Basic text formatting can be done from the Common toolbar.

The HTML paragraph style is a setting for the entire paragraph (by positioning the text cursor anywhere inside the paragraph), but the remaining formatting options are applied to the text selection (by selecting text with your mouse).

Here are some of the more commonly used formatting options:

✦ **Style:** The Style drop-down list displays the traditional HTML paragraph styles of text:

 • *Paragraph* (the default)

 • *Heading 1* (largest header) *through Heading 6* (smallest header)

- *Preformatted* (monospaced)

- *A series of list and definition styles*

  The list styles can also be applied using the Bulleted and Numbered list buttons.

✦ **Font:** The Font drop-down list shows the fonts that you can apply to your text. Web fonts are usually applied as a *family* (a prioritized list of font faces, separated by commas). The most common font families are shown at the top of the list.

✦ **Size:** The Size drop-down list displays a list of possible font sizes. You can use various sizing measurements:

  - *xx-small* to *xx-large*

  - *Smaller* (one size smaller than previously defined) and *Larger* (one size larger than previously defined)

✦ **Basic word processing styles:** The Common toolbar also has formatting buttons that perform just as Microsoft Word does, including Bold, Italic, Alignment, Bulleted List, Numbered List, Decrease Indent, and Increase Indent.

✦ **Highlight:** The Highlight button is a carryover from the word processor world in which you wish to highlight text, like using a colored highlighter.

✦ **Font Color:** The Font Color box allows you to select a text color from the drop-down box that is displayed.

The Format menu also has access to several dialog boxes for direct formatting of text, particularly the Format➪Font and Format➪Paragraph commands. Once again, you'll find these dialog boxes basically the same as in Microsoft Word.

Formatting with styles

Expression Web also allows you to format your text by using CSS styles. The way in which you work with styles in Expression Web is loosely based on the ways in which you apply and manage styles in Microsoft Word. If you've worked with Word styles before, you will find yourself with a head start. However, CSS styles are far more powerful (and complex) than Word styles are.

See Book V for all of the ins and outs of CSS.

Applying CSS styles to your text

To format your text using styles, display the Apply Styles task pane (see Figure 3-2). If it's not visible already, choose Task Pane⇨Apply Styles.

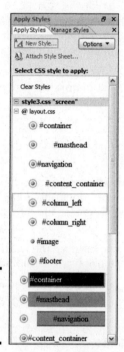

Figure 3-2:
Apply CSS styles to your text.

The Apply Styles task pane displays all the styles that are accessible from the opened document. The styles are defined in the document itself or from external style sheets linked into the document with a `link` tag. Each is displayed visually to emulate the look of the style. Here's how the style list is organized by default:

✦ **Class-based and `id`-based styles** are listed according to their source document (current or external `.css` file).

✦ **Element-based styles** are listed in the Contextual Selectors section.

✦ **Inline styles** are listed in the Inline Style section.

The Options button at the top of the task pane enables you to modify the sorting and the styles that are displayed.

To apply a style, position the cursor or select the text in which you wish to apply the style and then click the style from the Apply Styles task pane.

Managing CSS styles

You can manage your CSS styles both from the Manage Styles and Apply Styles task panes, although Manage Styles (see Figure 3-3) is generally preferred.

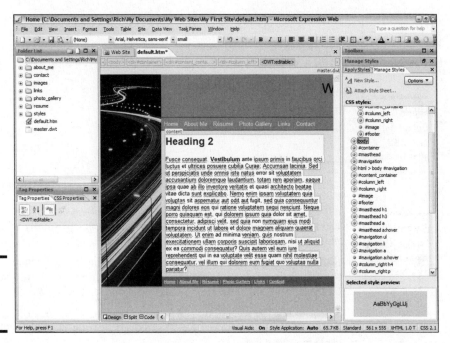

Figure 3-3:
Manage
CSS styles
from here.

**Book III
Chapter 3**

**Working with Text,
Graphics, and Links**

Here are some of the typical tasks that you will want to perform with CSS styles:

✦ **Define a new style.** Click the New Style link to define a new style. The New Style dialog box is displayed, as shown in Figure 3-4. In the Selector field, enter the pound sign (#) and a unique identifier for an id selector, a period (.) and a class name for a class selector, or select an element name from the list. Next, define the location in which the class should be defined in the Define In field. After that, format the style based on the dialog box settings. Click OK to save.

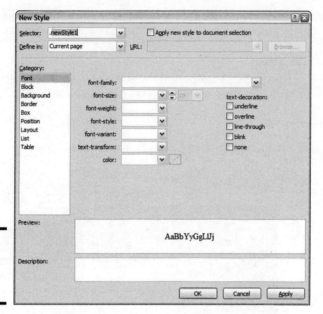

Figure 3-4:
Defining a
new CSS
style.

✦ **Attach a style sheet.** Click the Attach Style Sheet link to attach an external .css file to the current document (or optionally to all HTML pages in the site).

✦ **Edit an existing style.** You can edit an existing style by selecting it from the CSS Styles list, right-clicking, and then choosing Modify Style from its contextual menu. The Modify Style dialog box is displayed.

✦ **Jump to a style's CSS code.** If you are comfortable with CSS code, you can jump directly to a style's CSS definition code by double-clicking the style from the list.

Working with Pictures

Pictures are the second staple of any Web site. Here's how to work with them inside Expression Web.

Adding a picture to your page

To insert an image, perform the following steps:

1. **In the Editing window, position your cursor at the desired location in which you'd like to insert an image.**

2. Click the Insert Picture from File button from the Common toolbar.

You can also choose Insert⇨Picture⇨From File from the menu, if you prefer.

The Picture dialog box (as shown in Figure 3-5) is displayed.

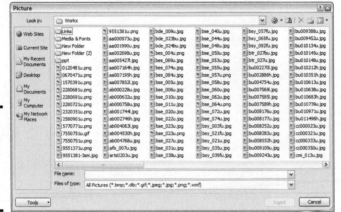

Figure 3-5:
Select
an image
to place
into your
document.

3. Select the desired image.

4. Click OK.

The Accessibility Properties dialog box is displayed (see Figure 3-6). Providing alternate text for your images ensures visually impaired persons will be better able to understand your Web site.

**Book III
Chapter 3**

Working with Text,
Graphics, and Links

Figure 3-6:
Providing
alternate
text for your
images.

5. Enter a description of the image in the Alternate Text field.

Alternate text is vital for visually impaired visitors of your site.

6. Click OK.

The image is now available on your Web page, as shown in Figure 3-7.

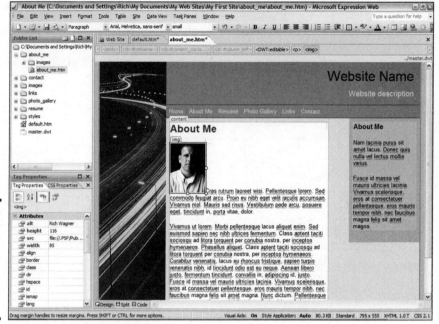

Figure 3-7:
Inserting a picture of some hayseed onto a Web page.

If the image isn't already located inside the folder of the current site, Expression Web displays a Save Embedded Files dialog box (see Figure 3-8) when you save the document. Use this dialog box to add the picture to your images folder of your site.

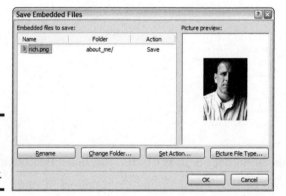

Figure 3-8:
Saving the picture into a site folder.

Modifying a picture

You can modify the properties of an image by double-clicking the image in the Editor window, pulling up the Picture Properties dialog box. The Picture Properties dialog box has two tabs: the General tab (see Figure 3-9) and the Appearance tab (see Figure 3-10).

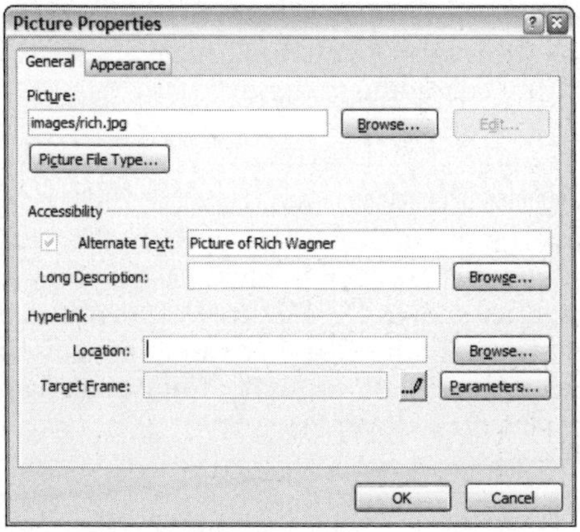

Figure 3-9:
Edit image
attributes
here.

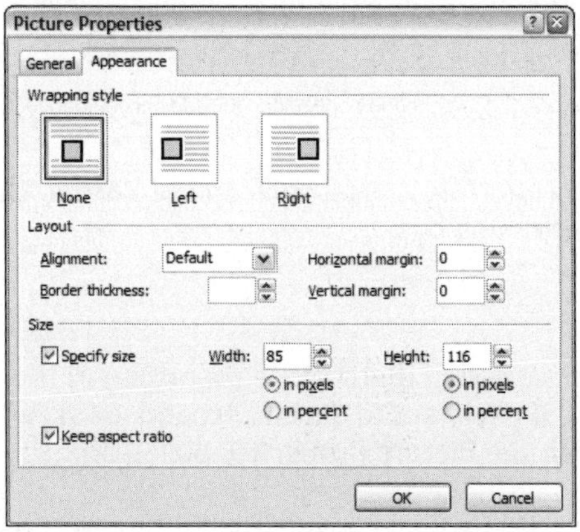

Figure 3-10:
Change the
appearance
of a picture.

In the following sections, we walk you through some of the changes you might want to make to an image's properties.

Changing the image file type

Expression Web enables you to convert your existing image into another format type through the Picture File Type button on the General tab. Use it to convert between GIF, JPEG, PNG-8, and PNG-24. See Book VII for full details on the pros and cons of these different formats.

If you have an image editor, such as Photoshop, you probably want to do most image conversion there because you'll have greater control over the quality of the conversion. However, if you don't have access to other software, this conversion utility can come in handy.

Aligning and wrapping the picture

By default, when you insert a picture into a paragraph, the image is added directly in the paragraph itself. However, in most cases, you want to wrap the text around the image instead. In the Picture Properties dialog box, use the Wrapping Style options on the Appearance tab to specify the type of wrapping you'd like to use: None, Left, or Right. You can also specify the position from the Alignment drop-down list.

Padding the image

In the Picture Properties dialog box, the Horizontal Margin and Vertical Margin fields allow you to specify the padding (in pixels) that you'd like to add around the image. (Five pixels is often a good rule.)

Adding a border

You can add a border by entering a pixel value in the Border Thickness field in the Picture Properties dialog box.

Sizing the image

Expression Web places the actual dimensions (in pixels) of the image in the Width and Height fields. If you want to shrink, expand, or skew the image, enter new values there in the Picture Properties dialog box.

You can also directly resize the image inside the Editing window with your mouse by clicking the image and dragging one of the border boxes. When you do this action, a Picture Action drop-down list is displayed when the picture is selected. You can specify whether you want to only modify the HTML size attributes or whether you'd like Expression Web to resize the image, using those specified dimensions.

Editing the image

Much like in Microsoft Word, the Pictures toolbar (as shown in Figure 3-11) provides image editing functionality directly within the editor itself. To access the toolbar, choose View⇨Toolbars⇨Pictures. The toolbar has a series of commands that you can access for editing the image.

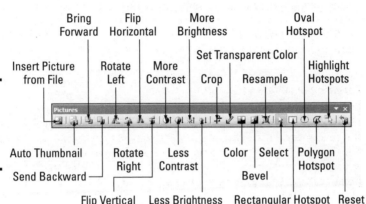

Figure 3-11:
Edit your image with the Pictures toolbar.

Labels (top): Bring Forward · Flip Horizontal · More Brightness · Oval Hotspot · Set Transparent Color · Highlight Hotspots · Insert Picture from File · Rotate Left · More Contrast · Crop · Resample

Labels (bottom): Auto Thumbnail · Rotate Right · Less Contrast · Color · Select · Polygon Hotspot · Send Backward · Bevel · Flip Vertical · Less Brightness · Rectangular Hotspot · Reset

Some commonly used features include

✦ **Auto Thumbnail:** Clicking this button creates a small thumbnail version of the selected picture. The thumbnail image is then linked to the larger image. When you save the page, Expression Web asks you to save the new thumbnail image.

✦ **Brightness and contrast:** Click the brightness and contrast buttons to tweak these image settings.

✦ **Crop:** Click the Crop button to trim the size of the image directly on your page. These changes are made to the image file itself.

✦ **Resample:** Click the Resample button to save the image based on current dimensions.

✦ **Reset:** Click the Reset button to restore the original image dimensions of the picture.

Working with Hyperlinks

Hyperlinks, quite literally, make the Web what it is today. Not surprisingly, one of the most common practices you will find yourself doing is adding links here, adding links there, adding links everywhere.

Creating a hyperlink

To insert a link:

1. **Select the text or picture you wish to serve as the link.**

2. **Click the Insert Hyperlink button on the Common toolbar.**

   You can also choose Insert⇨Hyperlink.

   The Insert Hyperlink dialog box is displayed (see Figure 3-12).

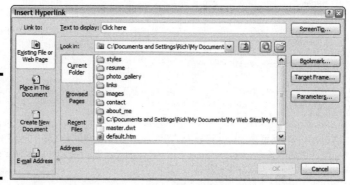

Figure 3-12: Creating a link using the Insert Hyperlink dialog box.

3. **If needed, edit the link text in the Text to Display field.**

4. **Select the desired option from the Link To list.**

   The options are as follows:

   • *Existing File or Web Page* links to a file in your site or to a URL on the Internet.

   • *Place in This Document* links to a bookmark previously defined within the current document.

   • *Create New Document* links to a new document that you subsequently create.

   • *E-mail Address* links to an email address.

   The dialog box updates based on the selection you make.

5. **If you're linking to an existing file or Web page, navigate to the selected file or type the URL in the Address field.**

6. **(Optional) To specify the target window for the linked document, click the Target Frame button.**

The Target Frame dialog box that opens can be used to specify the window or frame in which the linked page should be displayed. You can choose the following options:

- *Page Default (none)* makes no changes.

- *Same Frame (_self)* displays the document in the same window that sent the link.

- *Whole Page (_top)* opens the returning document in the top level window (replacing any frames).

- *New Window (_blank)* opens the returning document in a new window.

- *Parent Frame (_parent)* displays the document in the parent window of the current one.

7. Click OK to create the link.

Removing a hyperlink

You can delete a link that you previously created by selecting the text or the image that the link is assigned to. Right-click and choose Hyperlink Properties from the contextual menu. In the Edit Hyperlink dialog box, click the Remove Link button.

You can also simply remove the URL value from the `href` property in the Tag Properties task pane.

Creating an image map and hotspots

To link different portions of an image to different URLs, use the Hotspot buttons on the Pictures toolbar (refer to Figure 3-11) to create an image map.

You can create hyperlinks to images just like text so that when the image is clicked, the user is taken to a new URL. However, you can also define regions inside of an image *(hotspots)* and assign each a specific URL to go to when clicked. An image that contains hotspots is an *image map*.

To create an image map:

1. Select the image to which you'd like to add hotspots.

2. From the Pictures toolbar, select the desired hotspot tool based on the shape you'd like to create.

For most uses, the Rectangular Hotspot tool works just dandy.

3. **Drag your mouse over the image to set the hotspot in the dimensions you desire. Release the mouse when you're satisfied with the size.**

   Expression Web displays the Insert Hyperlink dialog box.

4. **Enter the URL you wish to associate with the clickable region in the Address field. Or, navigate to the file of your choice via the dialog box.**

5. **Click OK to add the link.**

6. **Repeat Steps 2–5 for each hotspot you wish to add.**

If you wish to resize, reposition, or remove a hotspot after it's added, click it with your mouse inside of the Editing window and manipulate it according to the desired action.

Chapter 4: Laying Out Your Page with Expression Web

> Senator, I served with Jack Kennedy. I knew Jack Kennedy. Jack Kennedy was a friend of mine. Senator, you are no Jack Kennedy.
>
> —Senator Lloyd Bentsen

*N*o matter which side of the political spectrum you're on, it's hard to deny that this line from a U.S. vice presidential debate in the 1980s has become one of the more popular political quotes of the 20th century.

That quote came to mind when we began recalling the constant comparisons that we've been making between Microsoft Word and Expression Web throughout this minibook. After all, for many normal tasks, they could just as well be the same product. However, the pages that emerge from the two products should not look the same. If you're going to create a well-designed Web site, you want to do more than populate it with online versions of word processing documents. Instead, use the tools available in Expression Web to create sophisticated, standards-based page layouts.

And, in the end, you'll want to be able to look at the Microsoft Word icon and tell it, "I worked with Expression Web to create my Web site. Expression Web was a friend of mine. Word, you are no Expression Web." (However, if you do this, we recommend not speaking directly out loud while others are present, or you could find yourself winding up on YouTube.)

In this chapter, we show you how to work with the most important page layout tools inside Expression Web, including `div` elements and layout tables.

Working with div Elements

The div element is the most important component in HTML for laying out Web pages. The div element, by itself, isn't visible by default and does little more than serve as a rectangular container for blocks of content. However, when combined with Cascading Style Sheets (CSS), you can position them exactly as you wish on your page to create a visual masterpiece of splendorific satisfaction. Okay, maybe we're getting carried away, but you can find well-designed sites around the Web making effective use of div blocks.

Before starting out this section, we recommend having at least a basic knowledge of what CSS positioning is. See Book V for more on positioning div elements using CSS.

Adding a div element

You can add a div element onto a page by double-clicking the <div> tag in the Toolbox task pane. (Or you can choose Insert⇨HTML⇨<div>.) The div element, displayed as a dotted rectangular box, is added at the current cursor position. See Figure 4-1. Note that Expression Web doesn't let you insert a div element inside a paragraph.

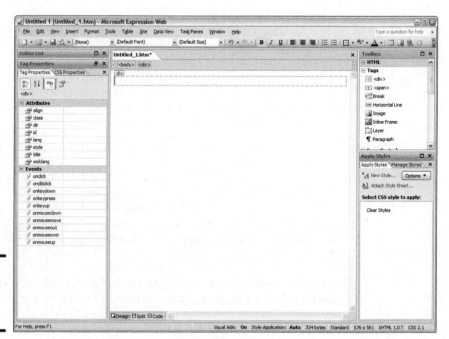

Figure 4-1:
Add a div element to a page.

You can add content to the `div` element or position it. To add content, simply begin typing just as you would the document body.

Sizing and positioning a div element

You can resize the `div` directly by selecting it and then using the handles on the border to change its dimensions. However, the kind of positioning that you can perform using your mouse is limited because you're working within a flow-based environment in which everything normally is positioned in a left-to-right, top-down manner.

Therefore, to position your `div`, you want to use CSS. If you already have a style defined in a style sheet for your `div`, you can use the Apply Styles task pane to apply the style to the `div` that you just created. However, if you don't have a style already created, you can perform the following:

1. **Choose Format⇨Position.**

   The Position dialog box is displayed (see Figure 4-2).

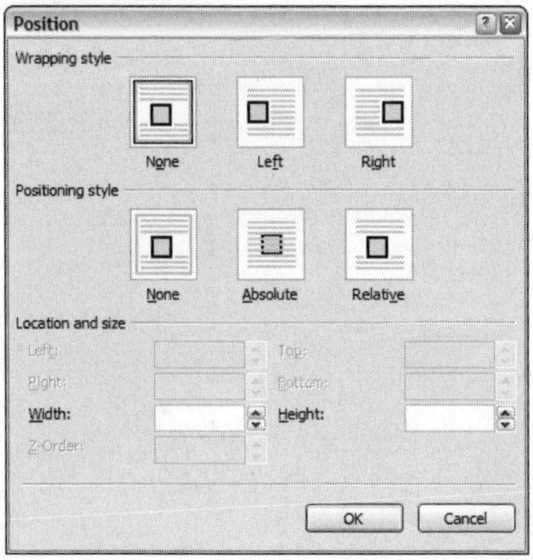

**Book III
Chapter 4**

Laying Out Your
Page with
Expression Web

Figure 4-2:
Set the
position
and size of
a `div`
element.

2. **In the Wrapping Style section, specify the type of wrapping you would like the `div` to have, relative to the normal document text.**

   The Left and Right settings add a float CSS property to the `div`.

3. **In the Positioning Style section, indicate whether the `div` should be positioned in an absolute, fixed position or relative to other elements around it. Or, if you don't want to specify, click None.**

If you choose Absolute, the `div` element is not wrapped around other elements. Therefore, the `div` element might be overlain above or beneath other content.

In most cases, you want to position the `div` relative to other elements on the page to ensure that they don't overlap.

4. **If you choose Absolute in Step 3, indicate the Left, Right, Top, and Bottom values in the spaces provided.**

   These values are not used when the `div` is relatively positioned.

5. **Indicate the desired dimensions of the block in the Width and Height fields.**

6. **Click OK.**

   The div is repositioned and resized based on your settings. Figure 4-3 shows a right-wrapped block sized to 150 x 300 pixels.

In addition, as Figure 4-3 shows, the CSS Properties task pane displays the properties you set. You can use the task pane to tweak these positioning values, if desired.

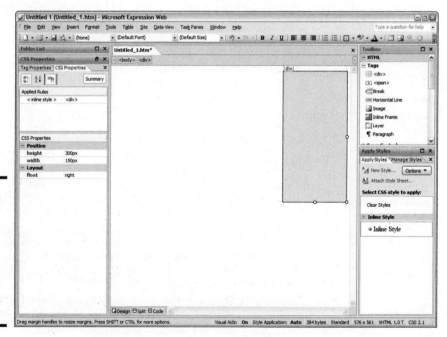

Figure 4-3:
A floating `div` element makes a useful sidebar for the rest of the page.

The Positioning toolbar, as shown in Figure 4-4, is useful for tweaking various aspects of the position and size settings. You can access this by choosing View⇨Toolbars⇨Positioning.

Figure 4-4: Tweak the position, size, and order of elements.

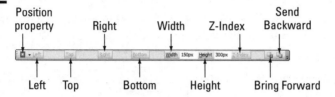

Position property   Right   Width   Z-Index   Send Backward

Left   Top   Bottom   Height   Bring Forward

Formatting a div element

Because a `div` element is a blocked container of content, it has no "appearance" to it other than the content that is packaged inside of it. However, you can use CSS to apply formatting to it — giving it a background, border, margins, and padding.

As you get more and more comfortable with creating CSS style sheets (see Book V), you will likely find yourself creating class-based styles for your `div` elements so that they look uniform across your Web site.

However, you can also apply formatting directly to `div` elements. Here's how:

1. **Select the `div` element in the Editing window.**

Figure 4-5 shows the `div` element that we'll modify.

2. **Activate the CSS Properties task pane.**

If the task pane is not visible, choose Format⇨CSS Properties.

Be sure that the Summary view isn't enabled, or else you can't see all the formatting properties. If the list shows only a handful of properties, click the Summary button to see the full list. See Figure 4-6.

3. **Click the Show Categorized List button on the CSS Properties task pane.**

4. **In the Background category, set a background color by choosing a color from the drop-down list.**

Alternatively, you could specify a background image instead.

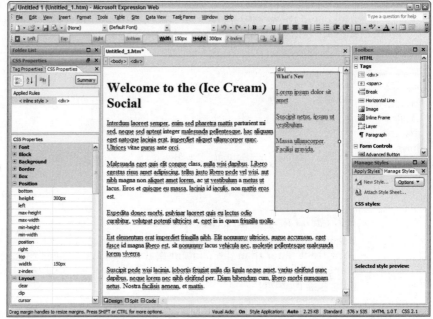

Figure 4-5:
A `div`
element
needs
formatting
to stand out
from a
page's
content.

5. **In the Border category, expand the border property and define its three subproperties.**

This example sets `border-width` to `thin`, `border-color` to black (`#000000`), and `border-style` to `solid`.

6. **In the Box category, specify the margin properties to offset the `div` element from other elements on the page.**

To move the `div` down from the top of the page, use the margin-top property. For this example, we specified `50px`.

To offset the `div` from the rest of the page content, we defined the left and bottom margin to be `10px`.

We didn't specify the margin-right property because we'd like it to be aligned to the side of the page.

7. **In the Box category, specify the padding properties to offset the content of the `div` with its border.**

Typing **5px** in the padding property defines the same value for all four sides.

Figure 4-7 shows a newly formatted `div` element.

Show categorized list   Show set properties on top

Show alphabetized list   Show all set properties

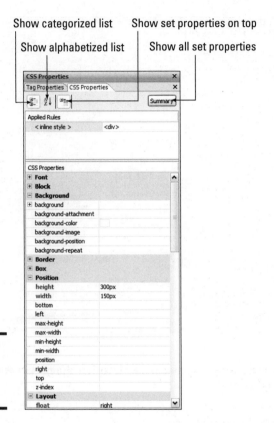

Figure 4-6:
The CSS
Properties
task pane.

The CSS Properties task pane provides a full list of formatting properties. Glance through the list for a better understanding of the `div`-formatting capabilities of CSS.

Working with Layout Tables

In the earlier days of the Web before `div` elements, tables were the main ingredient used for any page design recipe. And although `div` elements are now strongly preferred by Web designers as a way to lay out pages, Expression Web does provide layout tables as an alternative for page design.

A *layout table* is a just like a normal HTML table you define. However, it has special formatting capabilities inside Expression Web that aren't available with normal tables.

Figure 4-7:
A `div`
element
can be
formatted
from
the CSS
Properties
task pane.

A layout table is designed to be a fixed width rather than relative to the size of the browser.

Inserting a layout table

To add a layout table to your Web page, choose Table⇨Layout Tables. The Layout Tables task pane is displayed, as shown in Figure 4-8.

The Layout Tables task pane allows you to draw your table and cells manually through the Insert Layout Table link and drawing tools in the New Tables and Cells section. When you add a cell in the desired location, the layout tool automatically adds the appropriate rows and columns to position your cell.

If you prefer, you can use a predefined layout template from the Table Layout list. For most purposes, you can find a layout that suits your needs from the Table Layout list. When you select a layout option, its surrounding border becomes lighter. After you decide on one, click it to insert into the current page, as shown in Figure 4-9.

Figure 4-8:
The Layout
Tables
task pane.

The layout table is inserted and displayed with the Layout Tool turned on. When the table is selected in the Tag Selector, the dimensions of the various cells are shown in labels surrounding the cells.

Use the Show Layout Tool button on the Layout Tables task pane to toggle between normal Table view and enhanced Layout view.

Use the Layout Tables task pane to specify basic table properties, including width, height, and alignment. Selecting the Auto-Scale Cells with Table check box causes the cells to expand and collapse based on the table size.

Editing layout cells

You can perform several different tasks when in Layout mode:

✦ **Resize cells.** You can also resize the various table cells to the desired size by dragging the borders with your mouse and moving them into a new position.

Resizing your layout table directly with your mouse is arguably the single handiest aspect of the Layout Tables feature.

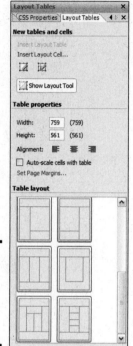

Figure 4-9:
A layout
table is
added to
the current
document.

✦ **Adjust row and column properties.** With the entire table selected or a single cell, the row/column sizes are shown in label boxes. Click the down arrow on a box to set specify various column and row options.

✦ **Insert a layout cell.** Click the Insert Layout Cell link to add a new cell to the layout table. You can specify the size and location of the new cell in the Insert Layout Cell dialog box. You can also add a layout cell by clicking the Draw Layout Cell button and using your mouse to draw the cell.

✦ **Delete a layout cell.** To remove a cell from the layout table, select the cell and then right-click. From the popup menu, choose Delete⇨Delete Cells.

Chapter 5: "Been There, Formatted That" with Dynamic Web Templates

In This Chapter

✔ Understanding Dynamic Web Templates

✔ Creating a new Dynamic Web Template

✔ Marking editable regions

✔ Attaching and detaching Dynamic Web Templates

*W*e humans just don't like to repeat something we've already done. "Been there, done that" is the familiar saying. That's why Microsoft Word, for example, has its ubiquitous `Normal.dot` template that allows you to specify the default formatting of new documents you create. Or, if you're really adventurous, you can create your own customized templates for more specialized needs.

Not to be outdone, Expression Web has its own version of "been there, formatted that." In this chapter, you'll discover how to work with Dynamic Web Templates to help you maintain a consistent page design across your site.

Understanding Dynamic Web Templates

A *Dynamic Web Template* in Expression Web is an HTML document that contains a page layout, formatting, and page elements. After it's defined, the Dynamic Web Template can be attached to new pages. The new documents take on these settings and layout. Later, when you wish to make changes, edit the template; all the created documents are updated.

Keep the following in mind when working with Dynamic Web Templates:

✦ You can create your own customized Dynamic Web Template or use a premade one when you create a new site from a template.

✦ A Dynamic Web Template file has a `.dwt` extension and is normally stored in a site's root folder.

✦ A Dynamic Web Template is divided between editable and non-editable regions. You can specify which regions in your template can be edited or have content added to them. Other parts of the page are locked.

If you look at the source code of the template, editable regions are enclosed with `<!-- #BeginEditable -->` and `<!-- #EndEditable -->` comments.

✦ The document head has a section that can be modified by going into Code view.

✦ You can go into Code view and modify non-editable regions. However, when you return to Design view, Expression Web notifies you what you did and asks you whether to discard these changes the next time the document is updated from the template.

Creating a Dynamic Web Template

Because a Dynamic Web Template is a special kind of HTML document, creating one is quite similar to creating an ordinary Web page. Here's how to create one:

1. **Choose File⇨New⇨Page.**

The New dialog box is displayed, as shown in Figure 5-1.

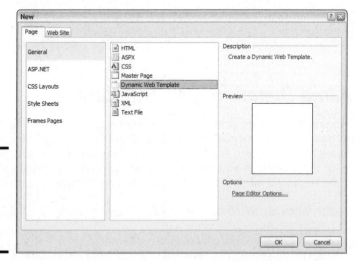

Figure 5-1:
Create
a new
Dynamic
Web
Template.

2. **From the General group, choose the Dynamic Web Template item from the list.**

3. **Click OK.**

   The `Untitled_1.dwt` document is displayed in the Editing window (see Figure 5-2).

   Expression Web adds a `div` element to the document body and marks it as an editable region.

   If you find it helpful, use it. Otherwise, feel free to delete it and mark editable regions later.

4. **Edit the design and layout of your Dynamic Web Template.**

   With `div` elements or layout tables, organize your template into non-editable and editable zones.

5. **Add content and features that you'd like to appear on every page created from the Dynamic Web Template.**

6. **Add placeholder text in a region that you will mark as editable.**

7. **Select the editable region (`div`, table cell, text selection, paragraph, and so on) with your mouse.**

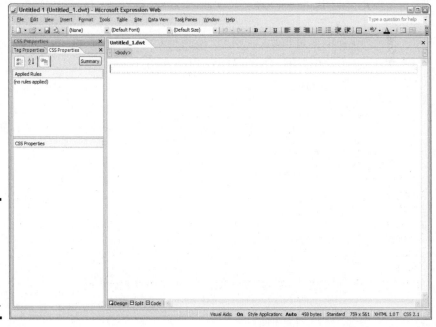

Figure 5-2:
A new template document is now ready for customizing.

8. **Right-click and choose Manage Editable Regions from the contextual menu.**

   The Editable Regions dialog box is displayed, as shown in Figure 5-3.

Figure 5-3:
Add a new
editable
region.

9. **Enter the name of the editable region in the Region Name field.**

10. **Click Add.**

    Expression Web marks the selection as an editable region. If the region has no content, the region's name is added in parentheses as canned text.

11. **Repeat Steps 6–10 for each editable region on your page.**

    Your basic Dynamic Web Template is ready to go.

12. **Choose File⇨Save.**

    The Save As dialog box is displayed.

13. **Navigate to the desired site folder you wish to add the template to.**

14. **Enter a name in the File Name field.**

15. **Click Save.**

    Expression Web saves the Dynamic Web Template, adding a .dwt extension.

You can also transform an HTML document you have already created into a Dynamic Web Template. To create a template from an existing page:

1. **Open an existing page into the editing window.**

2. **Remove any content that you do not wish to be part of the Dynamic Web Template.**

3. **Select the content region that you want to be editable.**

4. **Right-click and choose Manage Editable Regions from the contextual menu.**

   The Editable Regions dialog box is displayed.

5. **Enter the name of the editable region in the Region Name field.**

6. **Click Add.**

   Expression Web marks the selection as an editable region. If the region has no content, the region's name is added in parentheses as canned text.

7. **Repeat Steps 3–6 for each editable region you would like to define.**

   Your basic Dynamic Web Template is ready to go.

8. **Choose File⇨Save As.**

   The Save As dialog box is displayed.

9. **From the Save as Type drop-down list, choose Dynamic Web Template (*.dwt).**

10. **Navigate to the desired folder in the Folder box.**

11. **Add a name in the File Name field.**

12. **Click Save.**

   Expression Web save the document as a template and adds a `.dwt` extension to it.

Using a Dynamic Web Template to Create a New Page

After you build your template, you're ready to create new pages based on it. To do so, follow these steps:

1. **Choose File⇨New Page.**

   The New dialog box is displayed.

2. **From the General category, click the Create from Dynamic Web Template item.**

   Figure 5-4 shows the dialog box.

3. **Click OK.**

   The Attach Dynamic Web Template dialog box is shown.

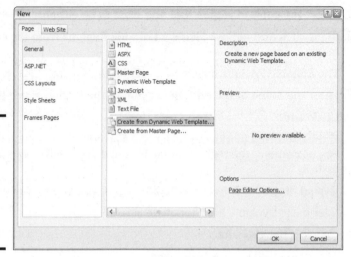

Figure 5-4:
Create
a new
document
from a
Dynamic
Web
Template.

4. **Locate the desired `.dwt` file in the Folder box.**

5. **Click Open.**

   A new document based on the Dynamic Web Template is displayed in the Editing window.

6. **Modify the content inside of the editable regions of the page.**

   You can't modify the content of non-editable regions.

7. **Choose File⇨Save.**

   Save your document as you would a normal Web page.

Making Changes to Your Dynamic Web Template

The "dynamic" in the Dynamic Web Template is the linkage that is maintained between a template and the documents that were created from it. As a result, when you modify a template and then save it, Expression Web asks you whether you wish to update all related documents as well.

To modify a template and then update all documents attached to that template

1. **Choose File⇨Open to open the Dynamic Web Template `.dwt` file in the Editing window.**

   Alternatively, you can open the template by using one of two other options:

- *If you have the site opened that contains your template:* Click the Web Site button on the Editing window tabbed pane and then double-click the template in the folder list.

- *If you have a Web page opened in the Editing window that is already attached to the template*: Choose Format⇨Dynamic Web Templates⇨ Open Attached Dynamic Web Template.

The Dynamic Web Template is opened in the Editing window.

2. **Edit the document.**

3. **Choose File⇨Save.**

A message box, such as the one shown in Figure 5-5, is displayed. It asks whether you would like to update attached documents at this time.

Figure 5-5:
Decide
whether to
update the
attached
documents.

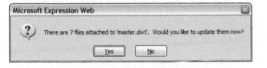

4. **Click Yes to confirm the update action.**

Or, if you don't want to for whatever reason, click No.

If you click Yes, Expression Web goes through each attached document files and updates them as needed. Changes are reflected the next time you open them.

Be sure to upload the changed files to the Web server.

Attaching and Detaching a Dynamic Web Template

As you can see in the earlier "Using a Dynamic Web Template to Create a New Page" section, when you create a new document based on a Dynamic Web Template, you attach the template to the page. However, Expression Web allows you to attach a template to an existing page.

To attach a template to an opened document:

1. **Choose Format⇨Dynamic Web Template⇨Attach Dynamic Web Template.**

The Attach Template dialog box is displayed.

2. **Choose the desired template.**

3. **Click Open.**

Expression Web evaluates the editable regions of the current document with the Dynamic Web Template and seeks to map between the two. When the two don't match, the Match Editable Regions dialog box is shown; see Figure 5-6.

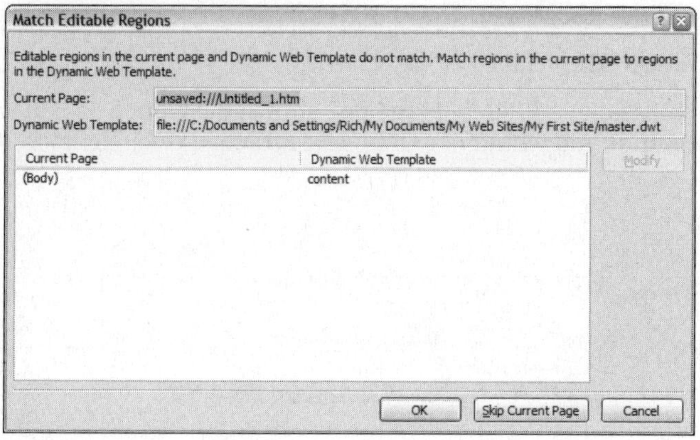

Figure 5-6:
"Match-
maker,
match-
maker,
make me a
match...."

4. **Match the regions as best as possible to retain the existing content.**

5. **Click OK.**

Expression Web attaches the Dynamic Web Template and makes the appropriate changes.

If you need to detach a document from a Dynamic Web Template, choose Dynamic Web Template⇒Detach Dynamic Web Template from the menu. Expression Web breaks the link and removes all trace of the former Dynamic Web Template.

Book IV

Dreamweaver

The 5th Wave — By Rich Tennant

"Are you using that 'clone' tool again?!"

Contents at a Glance

Chapter 1: Getting to Know Dreamweaver

In This Chapter

✔ **Working with the Dreamweaver workspace**

✔ **Exploring the Document window**

✔ **Using toolbars, inspectors, and panels**

✔ **Customizing the workspace**

*A*dobe Dreamweaver CS3 (formerly Macromedia Dreamweaver) is the *de facto* standard Web site design tool for both Microsoft Windows and Mac OS X. Web professionals use Dreamweaver because of its power, features, and extensibility. If you're a beginner with the product, don't feel shell shocked. You can quickly become productive in the Dreamweaver visual environment, all while gradually discovering the many capabilities it has to offer.

This chapter introduces you to Dreamweaver CS3 and gives you a guided tour around the major features of its workspace. We don't talk yet about how to use Dreamweaver to create Web pages. First, we want you to "kick the tires" of Dreamweaver and get comfortable with its working environment.

Introducing the Dreamweaver Workspace

When you launch Dreamweaver, a welcome screen is displayed, as shown in Figure 1-1. From this screen, you can start creating a new page or opening an existing file.

By default, the welcome screen appears every time you start Dreamweaver. To bypass this window, select the Don't Show Again check box before proceeding.

Windows and Mac versions: Any difference?

The Windows and Mac versions of Dreamweaver are nearly identical in functionality. In fact, the only noticeable difference between the two is arguably that the Windows version (refer to Figure 1-2) keeps the panels, the toolbars, and the Document window inside the main Dreamweaver application window. However, following Mac interface conventions, the Mac version has no main application window. The Insert bar, Document window, and panels all float around the desktop, as shown in the figure.

Click the HTML button under the Create New section or any other option you want to select. The new file is created inside the Dreamweaver workspace (see Figure 1-2).

You compose and design your Web pages in the Document window. Each of the bars, inspectors, and panel windows that surround the document help you construct or manage your document or site.

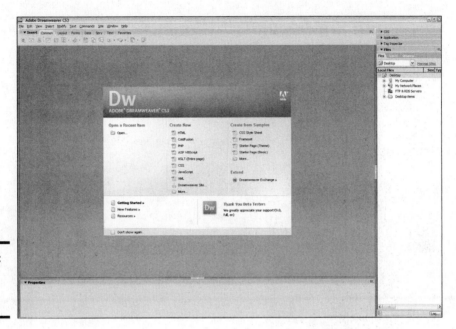

Figure 1-1:
Welcome
to Dream-
weaver.

Document window's page tab

Insert bar

Menu bar

Document window's
Code/Split/Design buttons

Document window

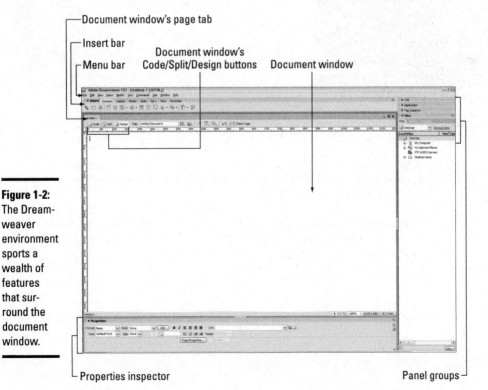

Figure 1-2:
The Dream-
weaver
environment
sports a
wealth of
features
that sur-
round the
document
window.

Properties inspector

Panel groups

Exploring the Document Window

The Document window is where you spend almost your time as you work in Dreamweaver. As you get started, familiarize yourself with several parts of the document environment. Figure 1-3 highlights the major features.

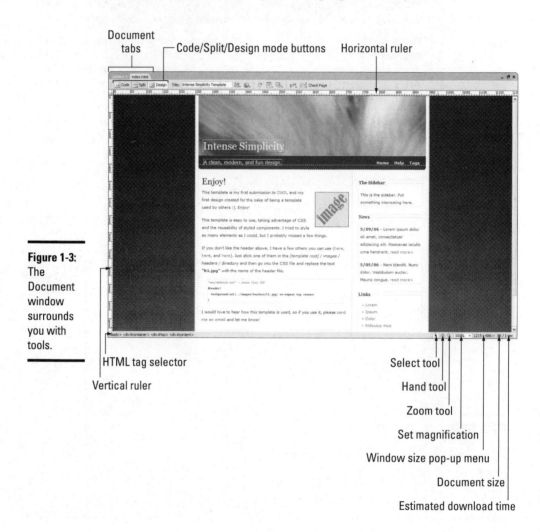

Figure 1-3: The Document window surrounds you with tools.

Document tabs

Code/Split/Design mode buttons

Horizontal ruler

HTML tag selector

Vertical ruler

Select tool

Hand tool

Zoom tool

Set magnification

Window size pop-up menu

Document size

Estimated download time

Perhaps the most important feature to notice as you begin to work with Dreamweaver is the use of Code, Split, and Design buttons on the top Document bar. You use these buttons to select which mode to work in:

✦ **Design mode:** By default, Dreamweaver displays the document in Design mode, a visually oriented look at the page, which is similar to (but not exactly) how it will appear in the browser. Figure 1-3 shows this view.

✦ **Code mode:** The document can also be viewed in Code mode, which reveals the HTML code of the page (see Figure 1-4). Don't worry if this code looks intimidating. You can avoid this mode for now, if you like. After you read Book VI, you will probably spend more time working in Code view.

✦ **Split mode:** You can also display Split mode (see Figure 1-5), which displays both Design and Code views.

You can also access these views by choosing View➪Code, View➪Design, or View➪Code and Design.

Figure 1-4: Diving into the nitty gritty HTML code of a document.

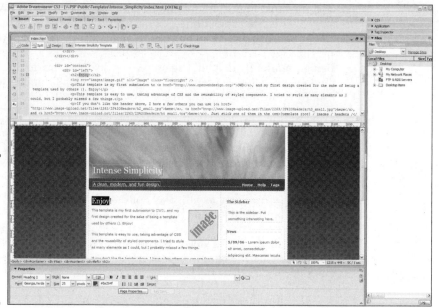

Figure 1-5:
The split-screen document view offers the best of both worlds: design and code.

Working with Toolbars

When you first start using Dreamweaver, you may be overwhelmed by the sheer number of menus, bars, inspectors, panels, and other controls that can surround the Document window. You make sense of them all as you work through this chapter, but for now, we start with toolbars.

The Insert bar

You use the Insert bar (shown in Figure 1-6) to add various elements to your page. It's visually separate from the Document window, although it always acts on the active document.

Figure 1-6:
Use the Insert bar to add elements to your page.

The Insert bar has seven sections, grouped (by default) on separate tabs:

✦ **Common:** These elements are the most common elements you drop on most pages, including links, images, and tables.

✦ **Layout:** These elements are related to the layout of a page, including `div` and table elements. (Check out Chapter 4 in this minibook for full details on working with the layout controls.)

✦ **Forms:** All elements that you can place and work with in forms are located in this section. (Chapter 5 in this minibook covers how to work with forms in Dreamweaver.)

✦ **Data:** These elements relate to displaying server-side data inside a Web page. (Most of the functionality in this section of the Insert bar is beyond the scope of this book.)

✦ **Spry:** *Spry* is a framework for the Ajax technology, which allows designers to incorporate XML data into their pages without refreshing the entire page. The elements in this section all place Spry widgets in your page. (Again, because of the complexities of working with Ajax, we don't cover it in this book. If you want more information on Ajax, check out *Ajax For Dummies,* by Steve Holzner, PhD [Wiley]).

✦ **Text:** These elements are for formatting text inside your page. You find bold, italic, headings, and all the usual text suspects here. (Check out Chapter 3 in this minibook for more on working with text.)

✦ **Favorites:** The Favorites section is a handy depository for you to place all the elements you use most.

To add or remove elements, right-click (or Ctrl+click on the Mac) the Favorites tab and choose Customize Favorites from the pop-up menu. The Customize Favorite Objects dialog box is displayed (see Figure 1-7). Use the controls in the dialog box to set the elements, and then click OK.

Figure 1-7:
Configuring your favorites for speedy access to frequently used elements and objects.

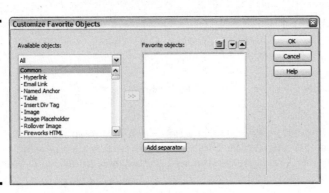

If you have a childhood fear of tabs or simply don't have the stomach for them, you can also organize these element groups on a drop-down menu instead. To change this view, right-click the top of the Insert bar (or click the menu button in the toolbar's upper right corner) and choose Show As Menu. The tabs are replaced with a drop-down menu, as shown in Figure 1-8.

Figure 1-8:
You can view the Insert bar as a menu.

To return to the tabbed view, choose Show As Tabs from the Insert bar's drop-down menu.

Document toolbars

The Document window has three toolbars that are displayed as part of the window:

✦ **Document toolbar:** The Document toolbar (see Figure 1-9) is used to control basic document-level functionality. (Chapter 2 in this minibook shows you how to work with several of these commands.)

Figure 1-9:
The Document bar provides basic functionality as you work with your page.

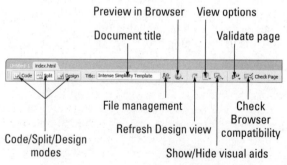

Preview in Browser   View options

Document title   Validate page

Code/Split/Design modes

File management

Refresh Design view

Show/Hide visual aids

Check Browser compatibility

✦ **Standard toolbar:** The Standard toolbar, shown in Figure 1-10, is like the basic toolbar in Microsoft Word. You can create a new file, save the existing one, and perform standard editing operations (such as cut, copy, paste, and undo).

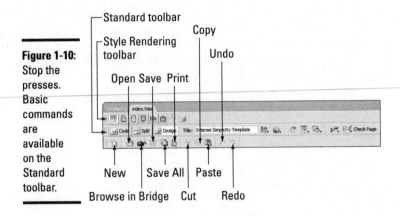

Figure 1-10: Stop the presses. Basic commands are available on the Standard toolbar.

Standard toolbar
Style Rendering toolbar
Copy
Undo
Open Save Print
New
Save All
Paste
Browse in Bridge
Cut
Redo

✦ **Style Rendering toolbar:** You can use the Style Rendering toolbar (refer to Figure 1-10) to specify different CSS style sheets if you're outputting your Web page to multiple mediums (standard Web, handheld, printer, or TV).

By default, the Standard and Style Rendering toolbars are hidden, so you need to make them visible to use them. You can show or hide any of the toolbars by choosing View➪Toolbars and then selecting or deselecting a toolbar from the list. Alternatively, if a toolbar is displayed, you can right-click it to display the Toolbar pop-up menu and then toggle the toolbar of your choice.

Checking Out the Properties Inspector

You use the Properties inspector for viewing and setting the most common properties (or attributes) of the selected element inside the active document. Because every page element you work with has different attributes, the Properties inspector is updated each time you select a different element.

The Properties inspector has two modes: Basic and Expanded. Figures 1-11 and 1-12 show Basic and Expanded modes, respectively, for an image element. Basic mode shows the core set of properties, and Expanded mode displays an additional set of lesser used properties. You can toggle between these modes by clicking the expander arrow in the lower right corner of the Properties inspector.

Book IV Chapter 1

Getting to Know Dreamweaver

Figure 1-11:
Basic
properties
in the
Properties
inspector.

Expander arrow

Figure 1-12:
Expanded
properties
in the
Properties
inspector.

You can toggle the visibility of the Properties inspector by choosing
Window⊏>Properties. Windows users can also press Ctrl+F3, and Mac
users press ⌘+F3.

Working with Panels

Dreamweaver sports several panels that provide additional functionality to
help you in your Web site design and management. You can display these
panels in their own, floating window or grouped into panel groups. When a
panel is docked with a group, it appears as a tab inside the panel group
window.

Here are some panels that are particularly useful as you get started with
Dreamweaver:

+ **CSS Styles (see Figure 1-13):** View and edit the CSS rules and properties
  of an element or page. (See Chapter 5 in this minibook for more on working with CSS style sheets in Dreamweaver.)

Figure 1-13:
The CSS
Styles panel
provides a
visual way
to work with
style sheets.

+ **Files (see Figure 1-14):** Use the Files panel to view and manage the files of your Dreamweaver site. When working on individual Web pages, you can work with the Files panel much like you work with a standard file system dialog box. However, when you work with sites in Dreamweaver (see Chapter 8 in this minibook), you can use the Files panel to work with both local and remote site files.

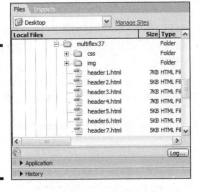

Figure 1-14:
The Files
panel
provides
quick
access to
your site
files.

✦ **Tag Inspector (see Figure 1-15):** View and edit attributes of the current HTML element in your document. You can think of the Tag inspector as something like the Properties inspector "on steroids" because it lists every attribute in a categorized (or, optionally, alphabetical) list.

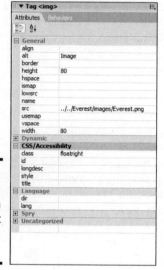

Figure 1-15:
Get the full lowdown on any element with the Tag inspector.

When you're starting out, you'll probably find the Properties inspector easier to work with. However, the Tag inspector is a helpful place to look for hard-to-remember properties.

✦ **Results:** The Results panel (see Figure 1-16) displays the results of searches and other reporting tools, such as the Browser Compatibility Check, Link Checker, and FTP Log. By default, the Results panel is displayed in the bottom of the window, under the Properties inspector.

Figure 1-16:
The Results panel displays results of searches.

✦ **Reference (see Figure 1-17):** The Reference panel is your home base for online reference documentation for HTML, CSS, JavaScript, and other Web technologies.

Figure 1-17:
Become a
Web expert
inside the
Reference
panel.

Reference tab

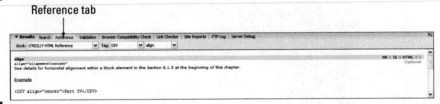

By default, the Reference panel is part of the Results panel, but you can move it elsewhere by grouping it with another panel group or by itself in a new group.

✦ **History (see Figure 1-18):** Think of the History panel as a beefed-up Undo/Redo list. You can use it to retrace your steps to undo changes you made to the document. If you want to get fancy, you can retrace your steps or even copy a series of steps and use them again.

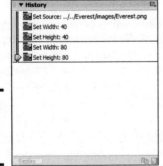

Figure 1-18:
History will
teach you
something.

**Book IV
Chapter 1**

✦ **Code Inspector (see Figure 1-19):** The Code inspector pops up a mini window that displays the HTML code of the document. The active element that you're working with is selected for you in the window.

**Getting to Know
Dreamweaver**

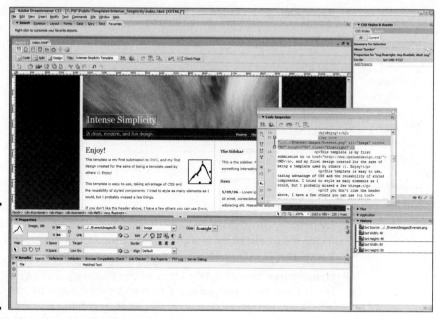

Figure 1-19:
Get a peek
behind the
scenes with
the Code
inspector.

Customizing Your Workspace

Perhaps the biggest attraction of Dreamweaver is the wealth of features at your disposal as you're creating your Web site. However, because you can display so many elements in panel groups and toolbars, you can quickly clutter your work area with a set of features you never use. Fortunately, in Dreamweaver you can tweak your working environment just the way you like it and then save your workspace for future use.

Showing and hiding a panel

You can access all panels from the Window menu. You can show or hide a panel by selecting its menu item from list. You can also hide a panel that's open by right-clicking its tab and choosing the Close *PanelName group* command from the pop-up menu.

Press F4 to toggle the visibility of all panels and inspectors. This keyboard shortcut is useful for temporarily eliminating distractions as you work on your Web page.

Undocking and docking a panel group

In the Windows version of Dreamweaver, panel groups are normally docked at one side of the application window. To undock and create a floating panel group, click the dotted bar in the upper left area of the panel group title bar and drag it onto the Document window. The panel group undocks and floats on top of the workspace.

To redock, drag the panel group to the side of the application window that you want to dock. Dreamweaver recognizes your intention and redocks the window.

Note that in the Mac version, panel groups always float.

Removing a panel from a group

To move a panel from a panel group, right-click the Panel tab and choose the Group *PanelName* With menu item. The submenu displays other panel groups. Choose one of them or choose the New Panel Group item if you want it to go off on its own. For an even easier method, drag the panel tab and drop it to a new location.

Saving a workspace layout

After you arrange the panels, toolbars, and inspectors the way you want them, choose Window⇨Workspace Layout item⇨Save Current. In the Save Workspace Layout dialog box, give your new, customized workspace a name and click OK. The new layout is added to the Workspace Layout list. Dreamweaver uses this new layout each time it starts until you change it. You can display these panels in their own floating windows or grouped into panel groups. When a panel is docked with a group, it appears as a tab inside the panel group window.

You can customize your workspace layout to make effective use of the available screen space. If you have a small monitor, you can eliminate all the extras and focus on the bare essentials for creating a Web site. However, if you have a larger screen, you can take advantage of the extra space to create the ultimate Web site design environment, such as the one shown in Figure 1-20.

**Book IV
Chapter 1**

**Getting to Know
Dreamweaver**

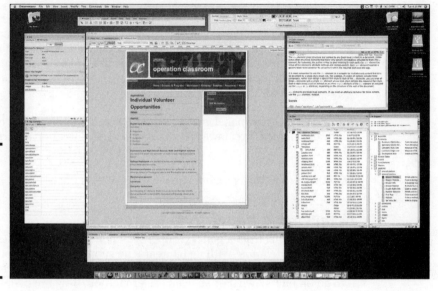

Figure 1-20:
If we only
had a little
more space
to display
the rest
of the
panels. . . .

Chapter 2: Nuts and Bolts: Creating Your First Dreamweaver Web Site

C hapter 1 in this minibook gives you the showroom tour of Dreamweaver, giving you a chance to kick its tires. In this chapter, you take a test drive to see how this baby runs in the real world. We walk you through the basic steps of creating and publishing a simple one-page Web site. You can use the rest of the chapters in this minibook to begin to develop more complex pages and sites.

Because you publish your Web site to a remote server at the end of this chapter, we assume that you already have an established account with a Web hosting provider. If you don't, skip the "Publishing Your Site" section.

Launch Dreamweaver and let's rock and roll.

Creating a New Site

You can create individual Web pages inside Dreamweaver, but the tool is really suited for working with sites. When you create Web pages inside a site, you can take advantage of many site-related features, such as a site map and a link checker.

hen you create a new site in Dreamweaver, you're asked to pick a particu-
r folder on your computer to store all the pages and assets of the site. An
set is any file that's used by a Web page, such as an image, Flash file, style
eet, or JavaScript file.

To create a new site, follow these steps:

1. **Choose Site⇨New Site.**

The Site Definition dialog box appears. The Advanced tab is displayed
by default. Click the Basic tab. Figure 2-1 shows you the dialog box that's
displayed.

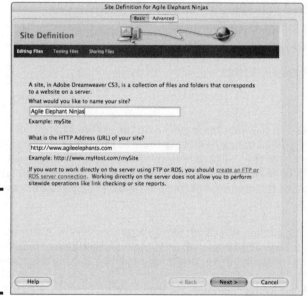

Figure 2-1:
Creating
a basic
Dream-
weaver site
in a snap.

2. **Enter a descriptive name for your site in the space provided.**

Dreamweaver uses this name to label the folder and uses the name
inside the application itself. The name isn't used when you publish your
site on a real Web server.

3. **Enter the URL of your Web site.**

4. **Click Next.**

The Editing Files, Part 2 page appears.

5. **Select the No, I Do Not Want to Use a Server Technology option.**

A message asks whether you want to work with server-side technologies. (We know, we know: Server-side technologies, such as ColdFusion and ASP.NET, sound intriguing — perhaps even alluring. But, for this exercise, no matter how much you're tempted, just say No!)

6. **Click Next.**

The Editing Files, Part 3 screen appears (see Figure 2-2).

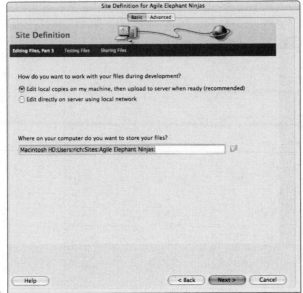

Figure 2-2:
You can easily make setup decisions because you're guided by Dream-weaver each step of the way.

7. **Select the option labeled Edit Local Copies on My Machine, Then Upload to Server When Ready (Recommended).**

This method is the typical way in which most Web designers work — create and test locally, and then upload to a server when you're ready to go live.

8. **Specify the location in which you want to store your site files.**

You can use the Browse button to navigate to a specific folder.

9. **Click Next.**

The Sharing Files page is displayed.

10. **Select from the drop-down list the way in which you connect to the remote Web server.**

If you have a typical Web hosting provider, you use FTP to connect to the server. (If you're using another option, fill out the settings and then skip to Step 12.)

The dialog box is updated to display specific options depending on the method chosen. Figure 2-3 shows the FTP options.

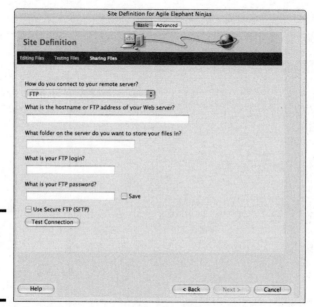

Figure 2-3: Specifying remote server options.

11. **Enter in the text boxes the FTP server information for your hosting provider.**

If you're like use, you probably scribbled down this information on a sticky note months ago and can't find it now. (We'll wait while you go look for it.)

After you enter the information, click the Test Connection button to ensure that the information is correct.

12. **Click Next.**

The Sharing Files, Part 2 screen appears.

13. **Select the No, Do Not Enable Check In and Check Out option.**

Selecting Yes allows you to check out files from the server and prevent other users from modifying them. However, for now we keep it simple and don't deal with that advanced functionality.

14. **Click Next.**

A summary page give you the basic details of what you just configured in the series of dialog boxes.

If you see any problems, click the Back button and fix the error. When you're satisfied, continue.

15. **Click Done.**

Dreamweaver creates the site for you and displays it as the active site in the Files panel, as shown in Figure 2-4.

You can specify more site details and options by choosing Site⇨Manage Sites. In the Manage Sites dialog box, select the new site and click Edit. The Site Definition dialog box is displayed. Check out Chapter 8 in this minibook for complete details on managing your site.

Figure 2-4:
The Files panel is the first point of access for your site assets.

Creating a New Document

After your site is created, you're ready to add a Web page to the site. To create a Web page, follow these steps:

1. **Choose File⇨New from the menu.**

The New Document dialog box is displayed, as shown in Figure 2-5.

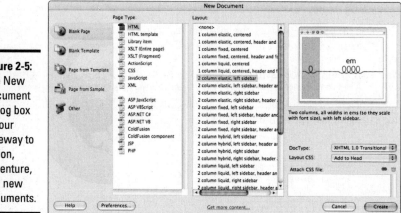

Figure 2-5: The New Document dialog box is your gateway to action, adventure, and new documents.

2. **Select HTML from the Page Type list.**

You can create other document types later, but for now, stick with good ol' HTML.

3. **Select a layout from the Layout list.**

The Layout list provides a large set of Web page layouts you can choose from. Or, if you would rather start with a blank page, click <None>.

We picked the 2 Column Elastic, Left Sidebar option for this example.

4. **Select XHTML 1.0 Transition from the DocType drop-down list.**

See Book VI for more on the different document types and versions of HTML.

5. **Select Add to Head from the Layout CSS drop-down list.**

In Chapter 6 of this minibook, we talk more about using separate style sheets, but for now, stick with the default option.

6. **Click the Create button.**

A new document, named Untitled-1, is created for you and appears in the Document window.

Figure 2-6 shows the document that's created by using the 2 Column Elastic, Left Sidebar layout.

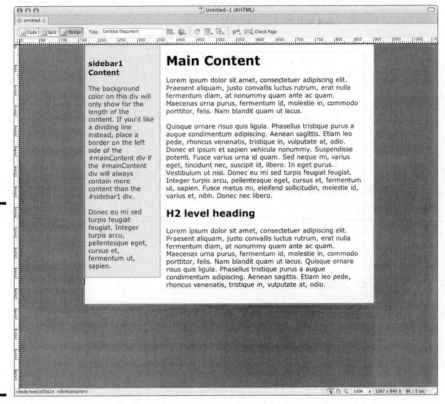

Figure 2-6: When you select a layout in the New Document dialog box, you get a head start on your page design.

Adding Content to Your Page

Much of your time in Dreamweaver is spent sitting in front of the Document window and either tweaking the page layout or adding content. Chapters 3 through 7 of this minibook focus on these tasks, so for now, we keep the discussion straightforward.

To add content, follow these steps:

1. **Click the cursor at the location you want in the document and type away.**

   If you used one of the default layouts, you have to remove some canned text — unless you have a particular fondness for greeked text.

2. **Add a link (optional).**

   Select text that you want to link, and then enter the URL you want to link to in the Link box of the Properties inspector.

3. **Add an image (optional).**

   Position the cursor at the location in which you want the image to appear. Click the Images button on the Common Insert bar and select the image you want to insert in the dialog box that appears. Click OK.

4. **Add a title to your page.**

   In the Title box of the Document toolbar, add a descriptive title for your page.

We don't provide much instruction here for working with text, links, and images. We save that discussion for Chapter 3 in this minibook.

Saving a Page

Just like with any other document you work with on your computer, you need to save your Web page in Dreamweaver before it can be of much use. To save your document, follow these steps:

1. **Choose File⇨Save.**

   The Save As dialog box appears. The default location is your site folder.

2. **Enter a name for the file.**

   If you're creating your home page, name the file **index.html**.

3. **Click Save.**

Previewing Your Page in a Browser

Although Dreamweaver's Design mode is visual, it isn't identical to how the page will appear inside a browser. As a result, before publishing the Web server, you should always preview your page *and* your entire site in a browser to see how they look and test how they perform.

To preview a document, follow these steps:

1. **Click the Preview in Browser button on the Document toolbar.**

A list of browsers installed on your computer is displayed. See Figure 2-7.

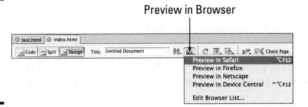

Figure 2-7:
Previewing
your
document
inside a
browser.

Preview in Browser

Or, if you prefer the top menu, you can also choose File➪Preview in Browser instead.

2. **Select a browser from the list.**

Dreamweaver opens your page in the browser for you to preview.

You can edit the browser list by choosing Edit Browser List from the drop-down list to display the Preferences dialog box. From there, you can add and remove browsers and assign keyboard shortcuts to them.

Publishing Your Site

After you preview your site and everything is ready to go, you're ready to publish your document to the Web hosting server. After you do this, the world can view your Web page.

Here's how to publish your page:

1. **Click the File Management button on the Document toolbar.**

A drop-down list of options is displayed, as shown in Figure 2-8.

2. **Select Put.**

Dreamweaver uploads the document and all dependent files to the server.

Book IV
Chapter 2

Nuts and Bolts

File management

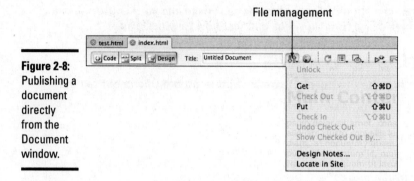

Figure 2-8:
Publishing a
document
directly
from the
Document
window.

From the Document window, you publish only the active document (and any dependent files). However, thumb over to Chapter 8 in this minibook to see you how you can publish the entire site from the Files panel.

Chapter 3: Formatting and Layout Basics

In This Chapter

✔ **Inserting and formatting text**

✔ **Inserting images**

✔ **Adding links**

✔ **Inserting tables**

✔ **Creating `div` elements**

Much of the time you work with Dreamweaver is spent inside the Document window. You create a layout. Add content to fill it in. Format the content to look good *and* be easy to read. In this chapter, you explore the basic aspects of formatting and laying out your Web page. We start by focusing on the big three: text, images, and links. After that, we explore how to work with key layout elements, including tables and `div` elements.

Working with Text

Images and multimedia may get all the acclaim, but text is the meat and potatoes of every Web page. Dreamweaver allows you to work with text inside your document in much the same way you would work with Microsoft Word or another word processor.

Inserting text

To insert text, click the location in the Document window in which you want to type. Just like in a word processor, text automatically wraps to the next line when you reach the edge of the line.

When you press the Return (or Enter) key, Dreamweaver begins a new paragraph (the p element). Or, to begin a new line but not create a new paragraph, you can add a line break (the br element). To do so, you can either press Shift+Return (or Shift+Enter) or add a br element by clicking the Line Break button on the Text Insert bar.

Changing the text formatting

Entering text is the easy, no-brainer part of working with text. Much of the work you do with text involves formatting it. You can modify either a text selection (by selecting text with your mouse) or an entire paragraph (by positioning the text cursor anywhere inside the paragraph). When you do, the text properties are displayed in the Properties inspector, as shown in Figure 3-1.

Figure 3-1:
Modify text formatting in the Properties inspector.

 Although the Format and Style settings in the Properties inspector work on the entire paragraph, the other property settings work on a text selection. Therefore, if you set the font size when no text is selected, the font size is turned on at the insertion point but has no effect on the current paragraph.

HTML versus CSS: Shootout at the Style Corral

Anytime you format text in Dreamweaver, you have to make a fundamental choice: *To CSS or not to CSS.* In other words, do you use old-school HTML formatting or CSS styles? Or, do you use some combination of the two?

With traditional HTML formatting, you format your text directly by using the Properties inspector. With CSS, you define styles in the CSS Styles panel (or in the style sheet itself) and then apply a style to your text by using the Properties inspector.

 Dreamweaver allows you to specify the type of code it creates behind the scenes when you work with the Properties inspector. In the Preferences dialog box, look for the Use CSS Instead of HTML Tags check box in the General category.

 ✦ If you prefer to work with HTML, deselect the check box.

 ✦ If you prefer CSS, select that option. Dreamweaver creates a document-specific style for you (named Style1, Style2, and so on) when you work with the non-CSS controls (except for bold and italics) in the Properties inspector.

Formatting text with HTML styling

To format by using HTML styling, use these features from the Properties inspector:

✦ **Format:** The Format drop-down list displays the traditional HTML paragraph "styles" of text:

- Paragraph (the default)
- Heading 1 (largest header) through Heading 6 (smallest header)
- Preformatted (monospaced)

Figure 3-2 shows the formatting styles.

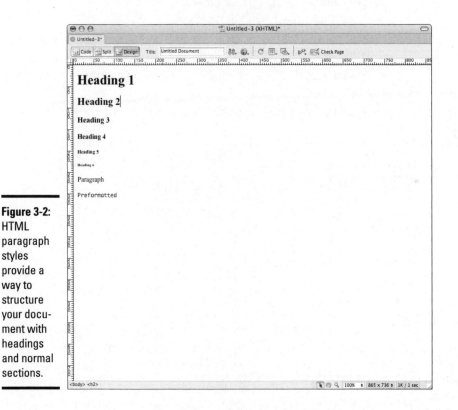

Figure 3-2:
HTML
paragraph
styles
provide a
way to
structure
your docu-
ment with
headings
and normal
sections.

TIP

Here's a plug for CSS: CSS enables you to customize the formatting of each of these HTML styles. As a result, you can use the built-in heading hierarchy that these paragraph styles give you but still use CSS. (See Book V for more on CSS.)

✦ **Font:** The Font drop-down list displays the font faces you want to assign to your selection. Fonts are usually arranged in families (a list of font faces separated by commas). The first font is used if it's available on the user's machine. If not, the next font is chosen, and so on.

Select Default Font when you don't want to specifically apply any font formatting. When you do so, the browser uses the default font setting defined elsewhere when it renders the document.

✦ **Size:** The Size drop-down list displays a list of possible font sizes. You can use various sizing measurements:

- *Sizes ranging from 9 to 36:* Specify the numeric size of the font. Use the drop-down box beside it to specify the measurement unit (typically points, pixels, or picas).

- *xx-small to xx-large:* A collection of constants (xx-small, x-small, small, medium, large, x-large, xx-large) to define as an absolute sized font.

- *Smaller, Larger:* One size smaller or larger, respectively, than previously defined.

Figure 3-3 displays various font size options.

Figure 3-3:
You can size your font by using relative and absolute measurements.

✦ **Color:** Use the color box to select a text color from the palette that appears. You can also specify an HTML color code in the box that's provided.

✦ **Basic word processing styles:** The Properties inspector also has several buttons that format text just like a standard word processor does: Bold, Italic, Alignment, Bulleted List, Numbered List, Indent, and Outdent (see Figure 3-4).

Figure 3-4:
Word
processing
formats.

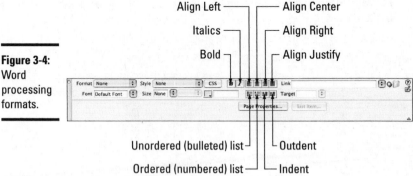

If you're familiar with HTML code, the Text Insert bar is a handy way to quickly insert HTML tags. The labeling of the buttons, however, assumes that you have basic knowledge of HTML.

Formatting text with CSS

If you define your text styles with CSS, the Styles drop-down box is your primary control to work with in the Properties inspector. After you define your styles and link your CSS style sheet to the current document (see Chapter 5 in this minibook), you can simply select a style from the list.

If you need to modify a style, the CSS button in the inspector is a quick way to display the CSS Styles panel.

Working with Images

If text is the meat and potatoes of any Web page, images are the appetizers, desserts, and fancy drinks all rolled up into one. In other words, they usually give a Web page pizzazz and character.

Inserting an image

To insert an image, follow these steps:

1. In the Document window, position the cursor at the location in which you want to insert an image.

2. Click the Image button on the Common Insert bar.

Or, choose Insert⇨Image.

In either case, the Select Image Source dialog box is displayed, as shown in Figure 3-5.

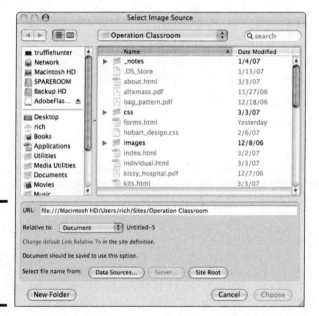

Figure 3-5: Selecting an image to place in your document.

3. Navigate to the image in the Select Image Source dialog box.

4. Click OK (Windows) or Choose (Mac).

If the image isn't already located inside the folder of the current site, Dreamweaver asks whether you want to copy the image into the site's root folder (see Figure 3-6). Click Yes to have Dreamweaver perform this process. In the Copy File As dialog box, you can specify a new filename for the image, if you want.

Figure 3-6:
Images
should be
inside your
site folder,
to ensure
that they're
accessible
during
publishing.

This file is outside of the root folder of site 'Agile
Elephant Ninjas',
and may not be accessible when you publish the site.

Your root folder is:
Macintosh HD:Users:rich:Sites:Agile Elephant Ninjas:

Would you like to copy the file there now?

Cancel   No   Yes

The Image Tag Accessibility Attributes dialog box is displayed (see
Figure 3-7) after this step has been completed.

Figure 3-7:
Be sure to
provide
alternative
text for your
images.

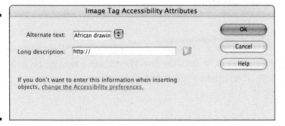

Image Tag Accessibility Attributes

Alternate text: African drawin

Long description: http://

OK

Cancel

Help

If you don't want to enter this information when inserting
objects, change the Accessibility preferences.

REMEMBER

5. Enter a description of the image in the Alternate text box.

Alternative text is important for users who are visually impaired and use
a screen reader for browsing your site. It's also useful for people who
have disabled images in their browsers.

6. Click OK.

If the image isn't already located inside the folder of the current site,
Dreamweaver copies the image into the site's image folder.

The image is now available on your Web page.

Modifying an image

You can modify the properties of images by selecting the image in the
Document window and then working with the Properties inspector
(see Figure 3-8).

Figure 3-8:
Modify
image
attributes by
using the
Properties
inspector.

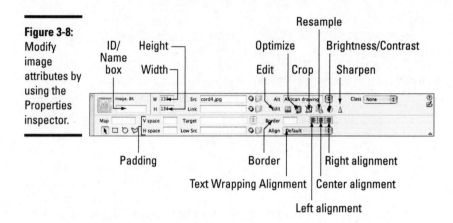

You can perform a variety of tasks from the Properties inspector. We cover
them in the following sections.

Adding an `id` attribute

Enter a text value in the box beside the thumbnail image to assign a unique
name to the image. Dreamweaver adds this text as both `name` and `id` attributes to the image.

Sizing the image

Dreamweaver places the width and height (in pixels) in the W and H boxes.
If you want to shrink, expand, or skew the image, enter new values.

For an even easier method, you can directly resize the image inside the
Document window with your mouse by clicking the image and dragging one
of the border boxes. The W and H values are automatically updated.

If you want to change the dimensions of your image, use an image editing
program. Don't rely on the W and H values to do the resizing for you.

Adding a border

You can add a border by entering a width value (in pixels) in the Border box.

Even better, you can modify this setting by using CSS instead, which is
discussed in Book V.

Padding the image

Use the V Space and H Space boxes to specify the padding (in pixels) that you want to add around the image.

You can modify this setting by using the CSS `padding` property, if you prefer. The `padding` property, discussed in Book V, provides much greater precision than the built-in HTML attributes.

Aligning the image

When you insert an image into a paragraph of text, the image is added directly in the paragraph itself, right alongside of the text. The line spacing is automatically expanded to account for the size of the image. However, in most cases, you wrap the text around the image instead. Use the Align drop-down box to set a text wrapping option.

Alternatively, if you prefer to align the image to the page (no text wrapping), click the Left Align, Center Align, or Right Align button.

Editing the image

The Edit portion of the Properties inspector has a series of commands that you can access for editing the image:

✦ **Edit:** Click the Edit button to work with the image by using an external image-editing program. You can specify in the File Types/Editors preferences which editor you want to use.

✦ **Optimize:** Click the Optimize button to display the Image Preview dialog box (see Figure 3-9). Rather than use Photoshop or another editor, you can tweak the size or image quality of the image right inside Dreamweaver.

✦ **Crop:** Click the Crop button to trim the size of the image directly on your page. These changes are made to the image file itself.

✦ **Resample:** Click the Resample button to enhance the image quality.

✦ **Brightness and Contrast:** Click the Brightness and Contrast button to change these image settings.

✦ **Sharpen:** Click the Sharpen button to improve the quality of blurry images.

✦ **Reset Size:** If you make a change to the image, a Reset Size button is displayed. Click the Reset Size button to restore the original width and height settings of the image.

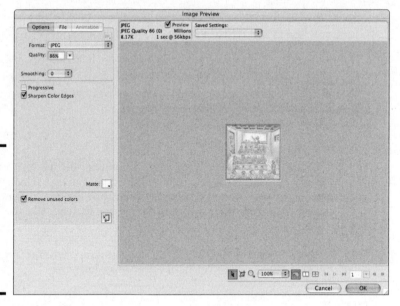

Figure 3-9:
Optimize
your image
right inside
Dream-
weaver.
Nothing
could be
easier.

Connecting the Dots: Adding Links

You often want to link text, images, and other elements to other pages on the Web. To insert a link, select the text or image and then look for the Link box in the Properties inspector (see Figure 3-10).

Figure 3-10:
Creating a
link.

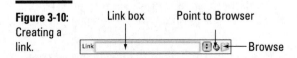

Creating and deleting a link

You have three ways to specify the link:

✦ **Manually:** Enter the URL in the box provided.

✦ **Browse:** If the file you're linking to is in your site, click the Browse button to specify the document in the Select File dialog box.

✦ **Point & Click:** If the Files panel is opened, the easiest (and coolest) way to create a link is to click the Point to File button and then drag the mouse to the file in the Files panel in which you want to link. Dreamweaver displays an arrow as you perform this process (see Figure 3-11). Release the mouse button over the file you want, and Dreamweaver creates the link.

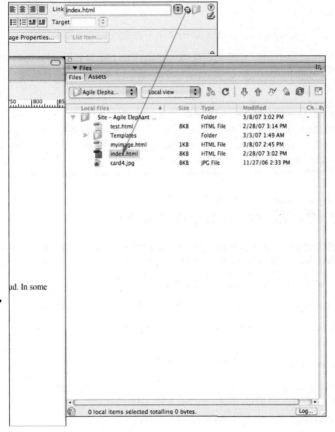

Figure 3-11:
Point to File is the coolest way to create a link in Dream-weaver.

You can delete a link that you created by selecting the text or the image that the link is assigned to. In the Properties inspector, remove the text in the Link box.

Specifying the target window

You can use the Target drop-down list in the Properties inspector to specify the window or frame in which the linked page should be displayed. You can select from these options:

✦ `_blank` opens the returning document in a new window.

✦ `_parent` displays the document in the parent window of the current window.

✦ `_self` displays the document in the same window that sent the form.

✦ `_top` opens the returning document in the top-level window (replacing any frames).

Using named anchors

To create a link to another spot on the current page (or a particular location on another page), you need to create a named anchor. A *named anchor* is a bookmark to a specific location on the page.

Creating a named anchor

To create a named anchor, follow these steps:

1. **In the Document window, position the cursor at the location in which you want to insert the named anchor.**

2. **Choose Insert⇨Named Anchor.**

3. **Specify a name for the anchor in the Named Anchor dialog box.**

This name isn't displayed in the text, but is used for behind-the-scenes purposes.

4. **Click OK.**

The anchor is added at the current cursor position. An anchor icon is displayed in your document, to represent the invisible bookmark.

Linking to a named anchor

To link to a named anchor, select the text or image you want to link from and then display the Properties inspector.

To link to an anchor on the same page, in the Link box, enter a pound sign (#) and then the exact name of the named anchor. Alternatively, you can use the Point to File button and drag the mouse to the named anchor in your document.

To link to an anchor on another page, follow the instructions in the "Creating and deleting a link" section, earlier in this chapter, but add a # and the name of the named anchor at the end of the URL. For example, to link to the `section2` named anchor at `www.digitalwalk.net/intro`, you enter **www.digitalwalk.net/intro#section2**.

Creating an image map and hotspots

If you want to link different portions of an image to different URLs, you can use the Hotspot tools in the Image Properties inspector (see Figure 3-12) to create an image map.

Figure 3-12:
Create a hotspot for your image.

Image map name = Map   Label

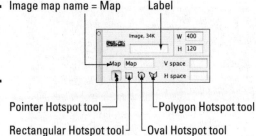

Pointer Hotspot tool ———   └─Polygon Hotspot tool

Rectangular Hotspot tool ┘   └─Oval Hotspot tool

A *hotspot* is a clickable region of an image that is assigned a URL. An *image map* is an image that contains hotspots.

To create an image map with hotspots, follow these steps:

1. **Select the image to which you want to add hotspots.**

   The Image Properties inspector is displayed. (If not, choose Window⇨ Properties.)

2. **Assign a unique name to the image map in the Map box.**

3. **From the Properties inspector, select a hotspot tool based on the shape you want to create.**

   Normally, you use the Rectangular Hotspot tool.

4. **Drag your mouse over the image to set the hotspot in the dimensions you want. Release the mouse button when you're satisfied with the size.**

Dreamweaver prompts you to specify alternative text for the hotspot from the Hotspot Properties inspector.

5. **Specify alternative text in the Alt box.**

6. **Enter the URL you want to associate with the clickable region in the Link box.**

7. **Repeat Steps 4 through 6 for each hotspot you want to add to the image map.**

Figure 3-13 shows an image map with four hotspots.

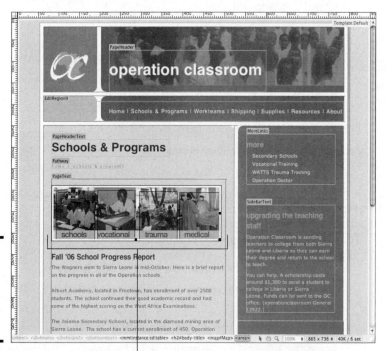

Figure 3-13:
An image map is shown inside a document.

This image has four hotspots.

You can resize and reposition hotspots by directly manipulating them with your mouse inside the Document window.

Working with Tables

A decade ago, tables were the underpinning of almost every well-designed Web page. To position elements in exact positions on the page, designers were forced to assemble a complex arrangement of tables to achieve the look they were striving for. Fortunately, `div` elements have been introduced over the past few years, which largely eliminate the need to use HTML tables as layout tools. As a result, tables can go back to their original purpose — as a way to display tabular data.

Choose Insert⇨Table to add a table. You can also click the Table button on the Common Insert bar. The Table dialog box is displayed, as shown in Figure 3-14.

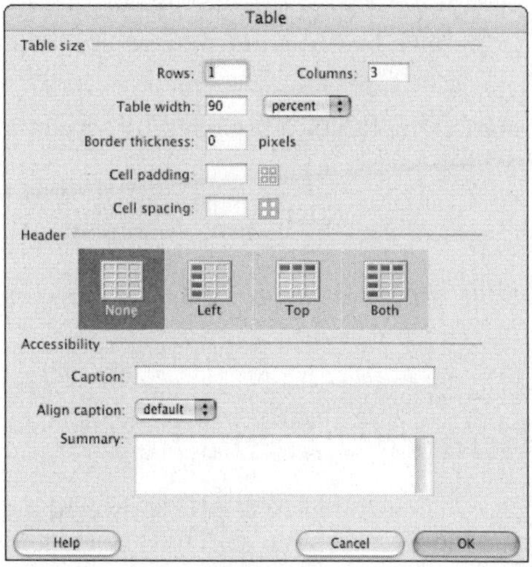

Figure 3-14:
Adding a
table.

Fill out these options in the dialog box:

✦ **Rows and Columns**: Enter numbers for the basic dimensions of the table.

✦ **Table Width:** Enter a value that specifies the total width of the table. The value can be either fixed (in pixels) or relative (as a percent of the total browser width).

✦ **Border Thickness:** Specify the pixel size of the surrounding table border. If you choose 0, no border is displayed.

If no value is entered, most browsers default to a 1 value.

✦ **Cell Padding and Cell Spacing:** Enter values (in pixels) to determine the padding and spacing of the table cells. *Padding* is the space between the edge of a cell and its contents. *Spacing* is the space between cells.

If no values are specified, browsers typically display the cell padding as 1 and the cell spacing as 2.

✦ **Header:** If you want to add a heading, click to select a style (left, top, or both).

Headers are especially helpful for visually impaired people who use screen readers.

✦ **Caption:** Enter text if you want a caption displayed next to the table. Use the Align Caption drop-down box to determine where the caption should be placed.

✦ **Summary:** To summarize the table (often used by screen readers), enter text in the Summary box.

When you click OK, the table is inserted in your document.

If you need to delete a table, click the border of the table to select it. Press Delete (or Backspace).

Divide and Conquer: Using div Elements

The div element is a relative newcomer to the HTML world but has proven to be an important part of modern Web pages. The div element is used in combination with CSS to create blocks of content that can be precisely positioned on a page.

Be sure that you have a well-rounded understanding of CSS before working with div elements. See Book V for full details on how to work with div elements that can be positioned with CSS.

Adding a div element

You can add a div element by clicking the Insert Div Tag button on the Layout Insert bar. The Insert Div Tag dialog box is displayed, as shown in Figure 3-15.

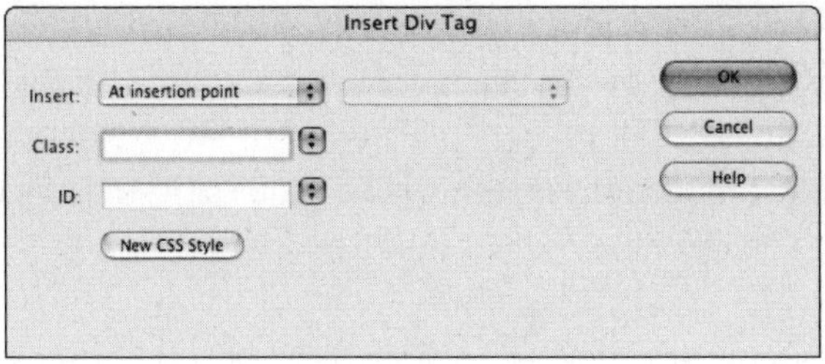

Insert Div Tag

Insert: [At insertion point ▼] [▼]

Class: [_____] [▼]

ID: [_____] [▼]

[New CSS Style]

OK

Cancel

Help

Figure 3-15:
Adding
a `div`
element.

You see these options in the dialog box:

✦ **Insert:** You can decide whether you want to insert the `div` element at the insertion point or before or after a specific element in your document.

✦ **Class:** Select the CSS class that you want to attach to the `div`.

✦ **ID:** Choose from `div` IDs defined in an attached style sheet, or else add a new ID.

Clicking OK adds the `div` at the specified location, with placeholder text added to it.

Adding an AP div

Dreamweaver also enables you to "draw" an absolutely positioned (AP) `div` element to your page. An *AP* `div` is a `div` element that has a fixed position assigned to it.

Unlike other `div` elements, which normally wrap around other elements, an AP `div` is a different beast. It's placed in specific screen coordinates and is displayed either above or below regular page content (depending on its z-index property in the Properties inspector).

To add an AP `div`, follow these steps:

1. **Click the Draw AP Div button on the Layout Insert bar.**

2. **In the Document window, position the mouse cursor in the upper left corner in which you want to add the AP `div`.**

Notice how the cursor changes to a crosshair pointer.

3. **Click the mouse button and hold it down while you drag the mouse cursor to the lower right corner of the `div` element.**

A blue box is created as you move your mouse.

4. **Release the mouse button when you're satisfied with the dimensions of the div.**

   Your result should look something like what's shown in Figure 3-16.

Blue box

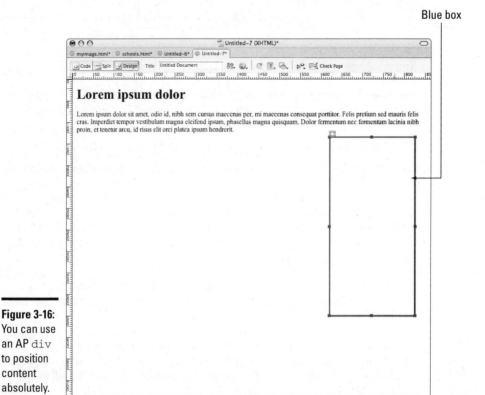

Figure 3-16:
You can use an AP div to position content absolutely.

5. **Add content inside the div element.**

If you want to move the AP div, you can select the element and then grab the blue box handle in its upper left corner. Drag the element to a new location.

Chapter 4: Enhanced Page Elements: Flash Controls and Spry Widgets

In This Chapter

- Enriching the user experience with Flash media and interface controls
- Enhancing page functionality with Spry widgets

Dreamweaver provides built-in support for making sophisticated user interfaces. You can add not only Adobe Flash media to your Web page but also Flash-powered controls and Spry widgets to create highly interactive pages — without writing a single line of JavaScript code.

In this chapter, we show you how to work with Flash media and controls. Then we set our sights on how to add the three most useful Spry widgets to your Web site.

Working with Flash Controls

You can add a Flash media file to your Web page, to provide a richer user experience for your site visitors. However, in addition to Flash media that you create yourself (see Book IX) or obtain from another source, you can work with special Flash page elements that come with Dreamweaver.

Inserting Flash content

You can add normal Flash content to your Web page much like you would add an image. Here are the steps:

1. **In the Document window, position the cursor at the location in which you want to insert the Flash media.**

2. **Click the Media button on the Common Insert bar, and select the Flash item from its pop-up menu.**

   Or, choose Insert⇨Media⇨Flash.

In either case, the Select File dialog box is displayed.

3. **Navigate to the Flash media file in the Select File dialog box.**

4. **Click OK (Windows) or Choose (Mac).**

If the Flash file isn't already located inside the folder of the current site, Dreamweaver asks whether you want to copy the file into the site's root folder. Click Yes to have Dreamweaver perform this process. In the Copy File As dialog box, you can specify a new filename for the Flash file, if you want.

The Object Tag Accessibility Attributes dialog box is displayed (see Figure 4-1) after this step has been completed.

Figure 4-1:
Even Flash
media
should use
accessibility
settings for
the visually
impaired.

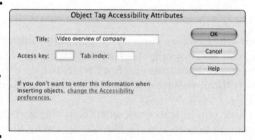

5. **Enter a description of the media in the Title box.**

6. **Optionally, add tab index and access key options.**

7. **Click OK.**

The Flash media file is now available on your Web page.

You can set various Flash-related options by selecting the Flash file from the Properties inspector, as shown in Figure 4-2.

Figure 4-2:
Working
with the
Flash media
file inside
Dream-
weaver.

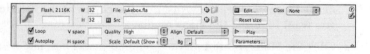

Adding Flash buttons

In Dreamweaver, you can create Flash buttons, which use the Adobe Flash technology to provide a richer user experience than ordinary HTML buttons or links do. Flash buttons have rollover or animated effects built into them, so you don't need to worry about adding scripts yourself.

Think of a Flash button as more of a link replacement than a push button replacement. For example, you can't use a Flash button in place of a Submit or Reset button in a form. Instead, you can assign only a single action when the button is linked — to jump to a URL.

Keep in mind, however, that if a user's computer doesn't have Flash installed, your button isn't displayed and the link doesn't work.

Here's how to add a Flash button to your page:

1. **In the Document window, position the cursor at the location in which you want to insert the Flash button.**

2. **Click the Media button on the Common Insert bar, and then choose Media⇨Flash Button from the pop-up menu.**

   Or, choose Insert⇨Media⇨Flash Button.

   The Insert Flash Button dialog box is displayed, as shown in Figure 4-3.

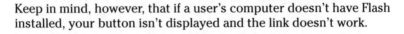

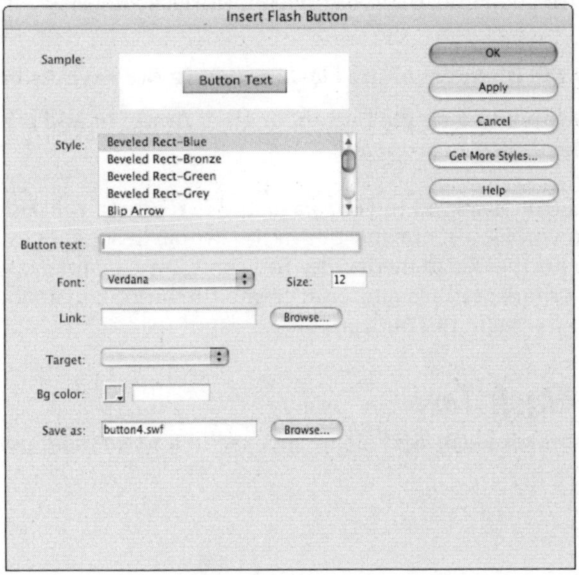

Figure 4-3: The Dreamweaver do-it-yourself Flash button creator.

3. **Scroll the button styles in the Style list and select the style of your choice.**

   The list includes generic buttons, ecommerce-related buttons, and tabs.

4. **Type some text for the button in the Button text box.**

5. **Select a font typeface and size in the Font and Size boxes, respectively.**

6. **Enter a URL in the Link box.**

   This page is displayed when the button is clicked.

7. **If you want to specify a target for the link, select one from the Target drop-down list.**

   The available options are described in this list:

   - `_blank` opens the returning document in a new window.
   - `_parent` displays the document in the parent window of the current one.
   - `_self` displays the document in the same window that sent the form.
   - `_top` opens the returning document in the top-level window (replacing any frames).

8. **In the Bg Color box, select the background color of the page on which you're inserting the Flash button.**

   This setting ensures that your button works seamlessly with your page design.

9. **Specify the filename of the Flash button in the Save As box.**

10. **Click OK to add a single button, or click Apply to add a button but leave the dialog box open.**

The Flash button is added to your page and is ready to roll. However, you notice when you view its properties in the Properties inspector that it's now treated as a normal Flash media file. You can't, for example, change the button text or link settings after you create the button. Instead, you need to go back and re-create the button.

Adding Flash Text

The Dreamweaver Flash Text element is useful for two main purposes:

✦ **Create text-based links that allow you to do the following:**

- Specify a rollover effect when the mouse hovers over the text.
- Use any font available on your system (rather than a Web-friendly font for normal text).
- Get anti-aliased letters (for a smoother look).

✦ **Use purely as a vehicle to display anti-aliased text content on your page.** Suppose that you want to display an introductory paragraph in a fancy scripted font that site visitors aren't likely to have on their systems. Using Flash Text, you can ensure that the text is displayed exactly as you expect.

Follow these steps to add a Flash Text element to your document:

1. **In the Document window, position the cursor at the location in which you want to insert the Flash Text.**

2. **Click the Media button on the Common Insert bar and then choose Flash Text from the pop-up menu.**

Or, choose Insert⇨Media⇨Flash Text.

The Insert Flash Text dialog box is displayed (see Figure 4-4).

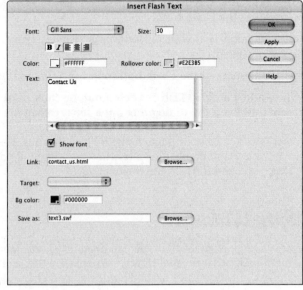

Figure 4-4:
Create text-based rollover links with any font of your choice.

3. **Select the font typeface and size in the Font and Size boxes.**

   If the Show Font check box is selected, your selected font is displayed in the Text box. However, your font size isn't reflected in the box.

4. **Format the text the way you want, by using the Bold, Italic, and Alignment buttons to specify additional formatting options.**

5. **Use the Color and Rollover Color boxes to assign coloring for the text.**

6. **Enter the text for the Flash control in the Text box.**

7. **Enter a URL in the Link box.**

   This page is displayed when the text is clicked.

8. **If you want to specify a target for the link, select from the Target drop-down list.**

   The available options are described in this list:

   - _blank opens the returning document in a new window.
   - _parent displays the document in the parent window of the current one.
   - _self displays the document in the same window.
   - _top opens the returning document in the top-level window (replacing any frames).

9. **In the Bg Color box, select the background color of the page on which you're inserting the Flash text.**

   This setting ensures that your button works seamlessly with your overall page design.

10. **Specify the filename of the Flash button in the Save As box.**

11. **Click OK to add a single Flash Text element, or click Apply to insert an element and keep the dialog box open for creating more.**

Your Flash text is added to your page. As with Flash buttons, Flash text elements are normal Flash media files after they're created. If you want to modify the text, you need to re-create the control.

Working with Spry Widgets

A *Spry widget* is a page element that you can drop into your page to provide enhanced functionality that normal HTML elements, by themselves, cannot provide. Examples of widgets are tabbed controls, menu bars, collapsible panels, and self-validating form elements. To perform their magic, Spry widgets combine a variety of Web technologies (HTML, CSS, JavaScript, and XML).

In the past, to achieve some of these effects, you had to either hand-code the source yourself or do a lot of copying and pasting of HTML and JavaScript code from a third party. However, Dreamweaver enables you to work with Spry widgets visually, directly inside the Document window, and set their properties by using the Properties inspector.

Be careful when you're using Spry widgets: You can break them if you aren't careful. Consider, for example, Flash media files. You can insert, delete, or modify a Flash file's properties — nothing more. In contrast, Spry widgets aren't standalone, "black box" objects. You still work with HTML in your page — with CSS and JavaScript simply "hooked up" to it. As a result, you can accidentally break something about the widget when you're working in the Document window, particularly in Source view. Here's a good rule of thumb: If the widget code gets corrupted, delete and then reinsert it from scratch. Therefore, be sure to back up your Web pages regularly, to ensure that you don't lose your Spry widget settings.

Unfortunately, to customize the look of the Spry widgets, you need to roll up your sleeves and work with the underlying CSS style sheets. Dreamweaver doesn't have access to the formatting properties from the Properties inspector. To locate the rule you want to modify, click the Customize This Widget link in the Properties inspector.

To access Spry widgets, choose Insert⇨Spry or use the Layout, Forms, and Spry sections of the Insert bar. Start with the widgets on the Layout Insert bar, as shown on Figure 4-5.

Spry menu bar   Spry accordion

Figure 4-5:
Spry Insert
bar.

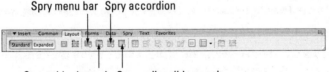

Spry tabbed panel   Spry collapsible panel

Some Spry widgets are for more advanced purposes, such as working with XML data. Three layout widgets, however, are particularly useful for everyday use: the Spry Menu Bar, Spry Tabbed Panels, and Spry Collapsible Panel. The Spry Accordion is also available, although it's a control that's less common on the Web.

Adding a Spry Menu Bar

A menu bar is one of the most common elements of any Web site, yet because it combines HTML, CSS, and JavaScript, it can be a pain to create from scratch. That's the beauty of the Spry Menu Bar: You can create a basic menu bar by simply dropping a widget onto the page and adding links from the Properties inspector.

To add a Spry Menu Bar, follow these steps:

1. **In the Document window, position the cursor at the location in which you want to insert the menu bar.**

2. **Click the Spry Menu Bar button on the Layout Insert bar.**

Or, choose Insert⇨Spry⇨Spry Menu Bar.

The Spry Menu Bar dialog box is displayed (see Figure 4-6).

Figure 4-6:
You can create a horizontal or vertical menu bar.

3. **Click to select an orientation (horizontal or vertical) for the menu bar.**

4. **Click OK.**

The menu bar is added to your page, as shown in Figure 4-7.

5. **Select the menu bar with your mouse to display its properties.**

Figure 4-8 displays the Spry Menu Bar Properties inspector.

6. **Create a multi-level menu structure by using the controls provided in the Properties inspector.**

The second and third levels are always under the selected item in the level above them.

Click the plus sign (+) button to create a new item on the associated level. Or, click the minus sign (–) button to remove the current selection.

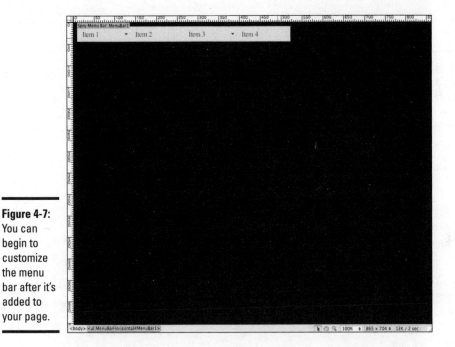

Figure 4-7:
You can begin to customize the menu bar after it's added to your page.

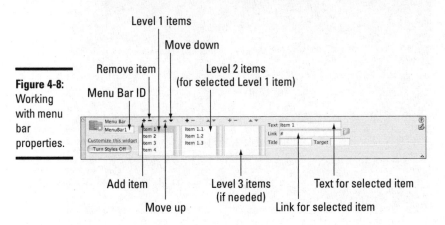

Figure 4-8:
Working with menu bar properties.

Level 1 items

Move down

Remove item

Level 2 items
(for selected Level 1 item)

Menu Bar ID

Add item

Move up

Level 3 items
(if needed)

Text for selected item

Link for selected item

Enter the text label and link URL in the Text and Link boxes, respectively. The Title box is used for accessibility purposes.

Figure 4-9 shows the Properties inspector with a menu bar defined.

Figure 4-9:
Creating a
multi-level
menu bar.

Figure 4-10 shows the finished menu bar in a browser.

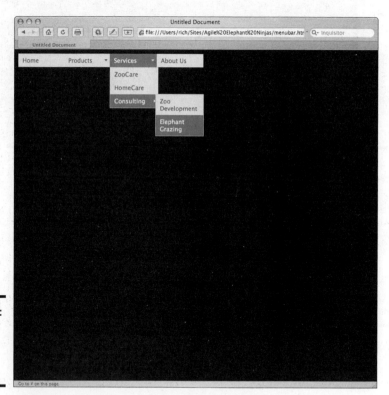

Figure 4-10:
The Spry
Menu Bar
inside a
browser.

Adding a Spry Tabbed Panel

The Spry Tabbed Panels widget provides a way to display multiple overlapping panels of content, each associated with a tab.

The tabbed panel isn't intended to be used as a tabbed menu bar. Instead, it's meant to be used inside a single Web page.

To add a Spry Tabbed Panel, follow these steps:

1. **In the Document window, position the cursor at the location in which you want to insert the tabbed panel.**

2. **Click the Spry Tabbed Panel button on the Layout Insert bar.**

Or, choose Insert⇨Spry⇨Spry Tabbed Panel.

The tabbed panel is added to your page, as shown in Figure 4-11.

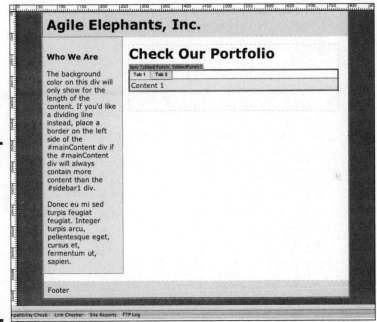

Figure 4-11: The tabbed panel is a useful way to display content while minimizing the use of screen real estate.

3. **Select the tabbed panel with the mouse to display its properties.**

Figure 4-12 displays the Spry Tabbed Control Properties inspector.

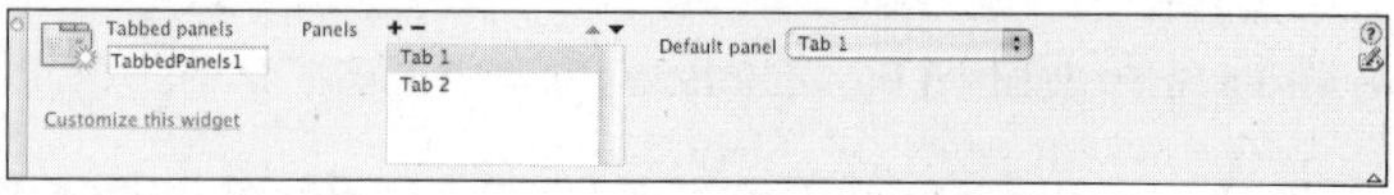

Figure 4-12:
Setting
up the
properties
of a tabbed
control.

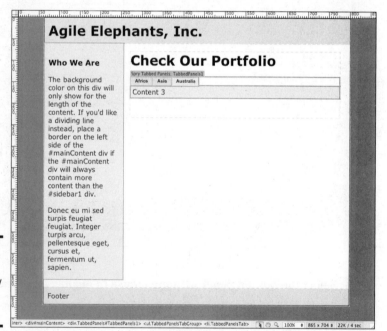

4. Use the + and – buttons to add the number of tabs you want.

Unlike with the menu bar, you don't label the tabs in the Properties inspector. You do that directly in the document.

5. In the Document window, click the left side of the tab you want and then enter the new name.

Figure 4-13 shows the renamed tabs.

Figure 4-13:
Label the
tabs directly
on the Web
page.

6. **Select a tab to view its content by hovering the mouse over the right side of the tab.**

   As Figure 4-14 shows, an eye icon is displayed on the tab.

7. **Add content to the selected tab panel.**

   Figure 4-15 displays the finished tabbed panel inside a browser.

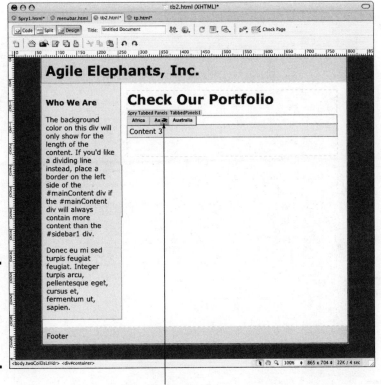

Figure 4-14: Beware! Your tab might be watching you.

Eye icon

Adding a Spry Collapsible Panel

The Spry Collapsible Panel is a handy way to display content that you want a user to be able to expand or collapse as needed. To add a collapsible panel, follow these steps:

1. **In the Document window, position the cursor at the location in which you want to insert the collapsible panel.**

2. **Click the Spry Collapsible Panel button on the Layout Insert bar.**

Or, choose Insert⇨Spry⇨Spry Collapsible Panel.

The collapsible panel is added to your page, as shown in Figure 4-16.

Figure 4-15: The Spry Tabbed Control inside a browser.

3. **Select the collapsible panel with the mouse to display the panel's properties.**

Figure 4-17 displays the Spry Collapsible Panel Properties inspector.

4. **In the Display drop-down box, specify the state of the panel in Design view.**

5. **In the Default State drop-down box, indicate whether the panel should be opened or closed by default.**

6. If you want to animate the collapse-and-expand process, select the Enable Animation check box.

We recommend it. It's cool!

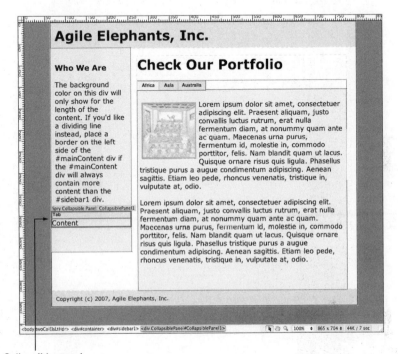

Figure 4-16:
Adding a collapsible panel to a sidebar on a page.

Collapsible panel

Figure 4-17:
Setting up the properties of a collapsible panel.

7. Add content to the collapsible panel by selecting the panel and typing away.

If the panel is collapsed, press the eye icon to the right of the header.

Figures 4-18 and 4-19 show the collapsible panel in both states.

Figure 4-18:
A collapsible panel in its collapsed state.

Figure 4-19:
The collapsible panel was expanded when the user clicked the header.

Chapter 5: Forms Follow Function

In This Chapter

✔ Working with HTML forms in Dreamweaver

✔ Making accessible forms

✔ Adding text fields, check boxes, lists, and other controls

✔ Adding a jump menu

*F*orms are the primary vehicle in HTML to enable site visitors to interact with your Web site. It doesn't matter whether they're typing in a search box or entering all their personal details on an order form, an HTML form is used to collect data and send it to a remote server.

In this chapter, we show you how to set up forms in Dreamweaver. However, a form isn't a standalone module. It always works with a CGI (Common Gateway Interface) program running on the server to process the input. Therefore, make sure that you have the URL and assorted details to connect your form to the server program.

If you want a primer on HTML forms, thumb through Book VI.

Adding a Form

Although the form element in HTML doesn't show up on the Web page itself, it contains the other form elements that users interact with, such as text boxes and buttons. The form element also contains the information necessary to connect with the CGI program on the server.

To add a form, follow these steps:

1. **Click the Forms tab on the Insert bar (shown in Figure 5-1), and then click the Form button.**

You can also choose Insert➪Form➪Form.

An empty form container is added to your document. As Figure 5-2 shows, the container is displayed as a rectangular box with a red dotted outline.

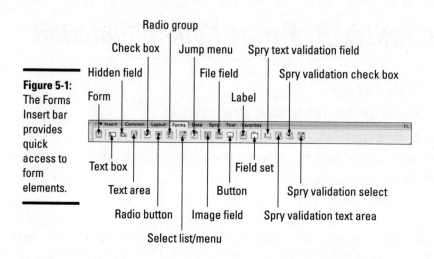

Figure 5-1: The Forms Insert bar provides quick access to form elements.

Radio group

Check box | Jump menu | Spry text validation field

Hidden field | File field | Spry validation check box

Form | Label

Text box | Field set

Text area | Button | Spry validation select

Radio button | Image field | Spry validation text area

Select list/menu

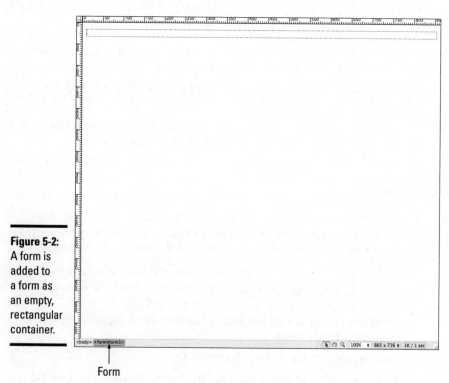

Figure 5-2: A form is added to a form as an empty, rectangular container.

Form

2. Click the form to display its properties in the Properties inspector, shown in Figure 5-3.

Figure 5-3:
Selecting
a form
displays its
properties.

	Form name	Action		Target	Class None
	form1	Method POST		Enctype	

3. Enter a unique name in the Form Name box.

Use normal alphabetical and numeric characters, not spaces or special characters.

4. In the Action box, enter the URL for the CGI program that resides on the server.

Many times, these programs are in a `cgi-bin` subdirectory on your Web server; for example, `http://www.myserver.com/cgi-bin/fprocess.pl`.

5. Select a transmit method (Default, GET, POST) in the Method drop-down list.

`GET` appends the form data to the request URL. As a result, users can see this information in the browser's address box.

`POST` embeds the form data in the HTTP request, which is hidden from the user when the form is sent.

`Default` uses the default setting in the browser, which is usually the `GET` method.

Check the details of the CGI program you're using to see which transmit method it's expecting.

6. (Optional) To specify the window to display the data returned by the CGI form processor, select a value from the Target drop-down box. Or, leave this box blank (which is more typical).

`_blank` opens the returning document in a new window.

`_parent` displays the document in the parent window of the current window.

_self displays the document in the same window that sent the form.

_top opens the returning document in the top-level window (replacing any frames).

7. **Select a MIME encoding type from the Enctype drop-down list if your CGI program requires it.**

   The application/x-www-form-urlencode value is usually used with the POST method.

   If you're uploading a file as part of the form submittal, use multipart/form-data value.

   Otherwise, you can leave this box blank.

The basic shell of your form is ready to go. You're ready to add elements to it.

Making Your Form Elements Accessible

Accessibility is a key issue to consider as you create your forms, in order to ensure that they can be used by all visitors to your site, even those who use nontraditional browsers. By default, Dreamweaver provides support for these accessibility features.

When you add a form element to your document by using the Forms Insert bar, the Input Tag Accessibility Attributes dialog box is displayed, as shown in Figure 5-4.

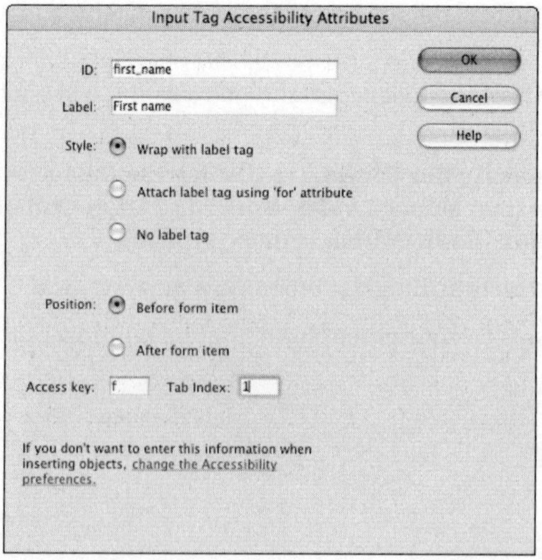

Figure 5-4:
Accessibility matters! Make your forms work for everyone.

Here's how to fill out the dialog box to make the element accessible:

1. **Add a unique ID value in the ID box.**

Add a name that effectively describes the data you're capturing, such as first_name for a First Name text box.

2. **Enter a descriptive label in the Label box.**

Dreamweaver uses this text as the label for your field.

Skip this step if you don't want to use a label.

3. **In the Style option group, choose the way in which you want to associate the label with the field.**

Here are your options:

- *Wrap with Label Tag:* Wraps an HTML label element around the text field. Normally, this option is the easiest to work with.

- *Attach with Label Tag Using "for" Attribute:* Associates a label element with the text field by using the label tag's for attribute.

- *No label tag:* Omits a label element. You have to add your own text or label element later if you want to identify the field for users.

4. **In the Position option group, decide whether the label should be placed before or after the field.**

If you choose the No Label Tag option in Step 3, you can skip this step.

5. **Enter a single letter in the Access Key text box if you want to add a hot key for keyboard access to the text field.**

Windows users press Alt+letter, and Mac users use Control+letter to select the text field.

If you add an access key, be sure to explicitly let users know about this shortcut. Otherwise, it's never used.

6. **Enter in the Tab Index text box a number value that indicates the order in which you want this field to be selected when a user presses the Tab key.**

7. **Click OK.**

If you prefer not to have the Input Tag Accessibility Attributes dialog box displayed when you add a form element, click the Change the Accessibility Preferences link in the dialog box to display the Preferences dialog box. In the Accessibility category, deselect the Form Elements check box and click OK.

Adding Form Elements

HTML provides several different types of elements for capturing data from a user and sending it to the remote server for processing. Table 5-1 lists the common HTML elements according to the type of data they capture.

Table 5-1	Common HTML Elements by Type
Type of Information	*HTML Elements*
Text	Text field (single line), Textarea (multi-line), Password field (masked input)
Yes/No	Check box
Multiple choice	Select list, Radio group
Hidden	Hidden field
File upload	File field
Action buttons	Submit button, Reset button, Push button

Capturing text

The most common type of data you capture is plain-text input. HTML provides three types of text elements:

✦ **Text field** captures single lines of text.

✦ **Textarea** provides space for multiple lines of text.

✦ **Password field** allows a masked control for entering sensitive passwords. An asterisk or dot appears in the control for each character the user enters.

To add a text field, follow these steps:

1. **In the document window, position the text cursor at the spot in which you want to place the new field inside your form.**

Don't worry if you haven't created a form yet. Dreamweaver asks whether you want to create one when it adds the text field.

2. **Click the Text Field button on the Forms Insert bar.**

By default, the Input Tag Accessibility Options dialog box is displayed.

3. **Enter accessibility options based on instructions in the section "Making Your Form Elements Accessible," earlier in this chapter.**

When you close out the Input Tag Accessibility Options dialog box, the text box is added to the form.

4. **Select the text box with your mouse to display the TextField properties on the Properties inspector.**

Figure 5-5 shows the Properties inspector.

Figure 5-5:
Capture text
in a text
field.

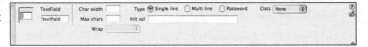

5. **Specify the type of text field in the Type option group: single line, multi-line, or password.**

6. **Enter a value in the TextField box if this box is blank.**

   If you entered an ID value in the Input Tag Accessibility Options dialog box, this value is already displayed.

7. **If you want to adjust the default visible width of the text box, enter a value in the Char Width box.**

   The width is approximately the number of characters that can be displayed in the box.

8. **Optionally enter a value in either the Max Chars (Single Line, Password) or Num Lines (Multi Line) box.**

   If you selected Single line or Password in the Type group, you can optionally enter a value in the Max Chars box. If this field is blank, users can enter as many characters as they want. If you enter a value, users are limited to the number of characters you specify. For example, for a U.S. state field, you can limit the size to two characters.

   Or, if you selected Multi Line in the Type group, you can specify the number of lines that should be displayed in the box.

9. **If you selected Multi Line in the Type group, you can specify how to wrap text in the Wrap drop-down list. Otherwise, skip to Step 10.**

   Off and Default prevent users from wrapping text to the next line.

   Virtual shows word wrap in the text element but sends the data to the server as a single string.

   Physical wraps text in the text element and sends the data to the server in the same format.

10. **If you want to specify an initial value inside the element, enter it in the Init Value box.**

Creating a drop-down list box

A *drop-down list box* (or *drop-down menu*) gives you a way to get multiple-choice values from users without taking up much real estate on your form. Here's how to add one of these elements to your form:

1. **In the Document window, position your text cursor at the spot in which you want to place the new drop-down list box inside your form.**

   Dreamweaver asks whether you want to create a list box when it adds the text field.

2. **Click the List/Menu button on the Forms Insert bar.**

   By default, the Input Tag Accessibility Options dialog box is displayed.

3. **Enter accessibility options based on instructions in the section "Making Your Form Elements Accessible," earlier in this chapter.**

   When you close out the Input Tag Accessibility Options dialog box, the drop-down list box is added to the form.

4. **Select the list with your mouse to display the List/Menu properties on the Properties bar.**

5. **Click the List Values button to display the List Values dialog box.**

   Figure 5-6 shows the List Values dialog box.

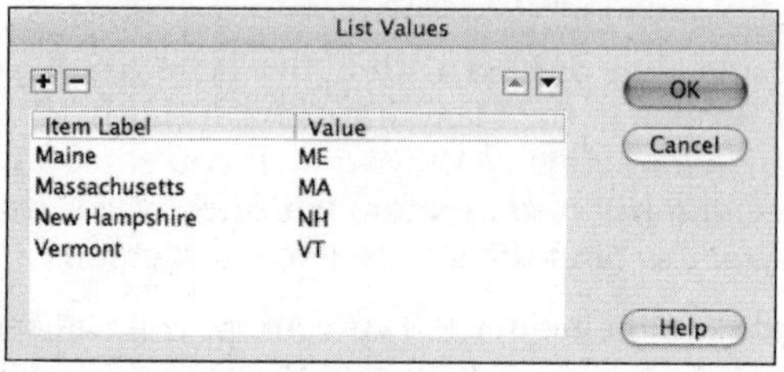

Figure 5-6:
Entering list box values.

6. **Click the + button to add a new list item in the List Values dialog box.**

7. **Enter in the Item Label column the text that you want to be displayed in the list box.**

8. **Press Tab to move the cursor to the Value column.**

9. **Enter in the Value column a value that you want to send to the server program when this item is selected.**

10. **Repeat Steps 6 through 9 for each item in your list.**

11. **Click OK when your list is ready to go.**

12. **By default, Menu is selected in the Type group for a drop-down list box. However, if you want to display a full list, choose List.**

Although the List type isn't often used, it allows a user to select multiple items inside the list box when the Allow Multiple check box is selected.

13. **If you want to select a default value, select an item from the Initially Selected list.**

Adding a check box

A *check box* is the simplest HTML control because it's used for capturing yes/no (Boolean) values. If the check box is selected, a checked value is sent to the server.

To add a check box, follow these steps:

1. **In the Document window, position the text cursor at the spot in which you want to place the new check box inside your form.**

2. **Click the Check Box button on the Forms Insert bar.**

By default, the Input Tag Accessibility Options dialog box is displayed.

3. **Enter accessibility options based on instructions in the section "Making Your Form Elements Accessible," earlier in this chapter.**

When you close out the Input Tag Accessibility Options dialog box, the drop-down list box is added to the form.

4. **Select the check box with your mouse to display the Checkbox properties on the Properties bar.**

5. **Enter in the Checked Value box the value that you want to be sent to the server.**

6. **Indicate the default value of the check box in the Initial State group.**

Adding a radio group

A drop-down list box (see the section "Creating a drop-down list box," earlier in this chapter) is perhaps the most popular way to display a multiple choice list of items in a form. However, you can also display a set of mutually exclusive items, by using a radio group.

To add a radio group, follow these steps:

1. **Position the text cursor at the spot in which you want to place the new radio group.**

2. **Click the Radio Group button on the Forms Insert bar.**

The Radio Group dialog box is displayed, as shown in Figure 5-7.

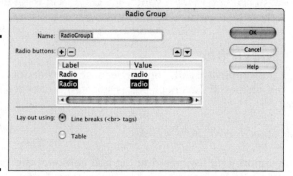

Figure 5-7:
Say what
you will —
radio
buttons are
an exclusive
set to be
around.

3. **Click the first default item in the Label column. Enter text that you want to be displayed beside the button.**

4. **Press Tab to move the cursor to the Value column.**

5. **Enter in the Value column a value that you want to send to the remote server when this radio option is selected.**

6. **Repeat Steps 3 through 5 for the second default item.**

7. **Click the + button to add more items, if needed.**

8. **Repeat Steps 3 through 7 for each item in your list.**

9. **Choose the layout of the radio group from the Lay Out Using group:**

To separate each entry on a separate line: Select the Link Breaks
(
 Tags) option.

To separate each entry by placing each in its own cell in a table: Choose
Table.

10. **Click OK.**

The radio group is added to your form.

You can work with each individual radio button (such as its initial state) by selecting it with your mouse and modifying its properties by using the Properties inspector. However, after you create the group, you cannot view the properties of the radio group as a whole by using the Properties inspector.

Powering up with buttons

The form element links the form to the remote program, and the input controls, such as text field or drop-down list box, capture the data. The final pieces of the puzzle are button controls, which are used to give the form power — by telling the form element to send the data to the server.

You can use one of three buttons:

+ The **Submit** button tells the form to submit the form data to the server.

+ The **Reset** button clears all data entered on the form.

+ The **Push** button does nothing with the server, but can be programmed by using JavaScript to perform an action. (See Book VIII for more on JavaScript.)

To add a button, follow these steps:

1. **In the Document window, position the text cursor at the spot in which you want to place the new button inside your form.**

If the cursor isn't inside a form, Dreamweaver asks whether you want to create one when it adds the button.

2. **Click the Button button on the Forms Insert bar.**

By default, the Input Tag Accessibility Options dialog box is displayed.

3. **Enter accessibility options based on instructions in the section "Making Your Form Elements Accessible," earlier in this chapter.**

When you close out the Input Tag Accessibility Options dialog box, the drop-down list box is added to the form.

A Submit button is created by default.

4. **Select the button with your mouse to display the Button properties on the Properties bar.**

Book IV
Chapter 5

Forms Follow
Function

Validating form values

You can use JavaScript to validate the values that users enter on your form. Using JavaScript form validation, you can check for required fields as well as for the correctness or validity of the data being sent *before* transmitting the data. See Book VIII for details on how to add validity-checking scripts to forms.

You can also consider using the new Spry validation widgets, found on the Forms Insert bar: Spry Validation Text Field, Textarea, Checkbox, and Select.

5. **Select a button type based on the value of the Action group.**

   Use Submit Form for submit buttons. Use Reset Form for reset buttons. Use None for plain push buttons.

6. **If you want to change the button text, enter a value in the Value box.**

Creating a Jump Menu

Although a jump menu isn't an element you would see on a normal data-entry form, it's one of the most practical uses of a drop-down list box. A *jump menu* is a list of links in which a user goes to a URL based on the selection in the list box. You can create a jump menu the hard way, by using JavaScript and a normal drop-down list box. However, Dreamweaver simplifies this process with its Jump Menu control. Here's how to use it to add a jump menu to your page:

1. **In the document window, position the text cursor at the spot in which you want to place the new jump menu inside your page.**

2. **Click the List/Menu button on the Forms Insert bar.**

   The Insert Jump Menu dialog box is displayed, as shown in Figure 5-8.

3. **Enter the display text of your first link in the Text box.**

   You may want to add a (Jump to) or (Choose one) prompt as the first item in the list.

4. **Enter the URL of the first link in the When Selected, Go to URL box.**

5. **Click the + button to add a new jump entry.**

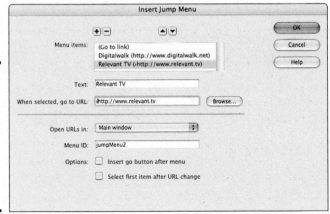

Figure 5-8:
Dream-
weaver
makes it
easy to
create a
handy-
dandy jump
menu.

6. **Repeat Steps 3 through 5 as needed until your list of jumps is completed.**

7. **If you want a Go button to appear alongside the jump menu, select the Insert Go Button after Menu check box.**

8. **If your first item is a prompt, such as** Jump to, **select the Select First Item after URL Change check box.**

9. **Click OK.**

Dreamweaver adds the drop-down jump menu and JavaScript code auto-matically to your Web page.

After the jump menu has been inserted, Dreamweaver treats the element just like a traditional drop-down list box.

Chapter 6: Working with CSS

In This Chapter

✔ Working with the CSS Styles panel

✔ Creating CSS rules visually rather than in plain code

✔ Creating an external CSS style sheet

✔ Linking your document to an external style sheet

*C*ascading Style Sheets (CSS) is a companion technology to HTML that provides a far more powerful way to control the formatting and layout of your Web page than using HTML alone.

In this chapter, we show you how to work with CSS inside the Dreamweaver environment. In particular, you explore how the use of the Dreamweaver enhanced CSS features is much easier and more productive than working with the CSS source code alone.

Because this chapter focuses on using CSS in Dreamweaver, it doesn't attempt to explain what CSS is. Therefore, before you read this chapter, we recommend thumbing through Book V so that you know general information about CSS rules, the workings of the `style` element, and the basics of linking external style sheets (`.css` files) into a document.

Managing Styles with the CSS Styles Panel

Although CSS enables you to create visually appealing Web pages, CSS is, on its own, somewhat technical to work with. Therefore, unless you prefer to get your hands dirty with CSS style sheet code, you will find the CSS Styles panel to be your styling guru inside Dreamweaver. You can use the CSS Style panel to keep track of the CSS rules associated with either the selected (or current) element or the entire document. To view the CSS Styles panel, choose Window➪CSS Styles.

Working with styles of the selected element

When you click the Current button at the top of the CSS Styles panel, you toggle the display to Current mode, as shown in Figure 6-1.

Toggle between Current and All modes

Summary for Selection pane

Rules pane

Properties pane

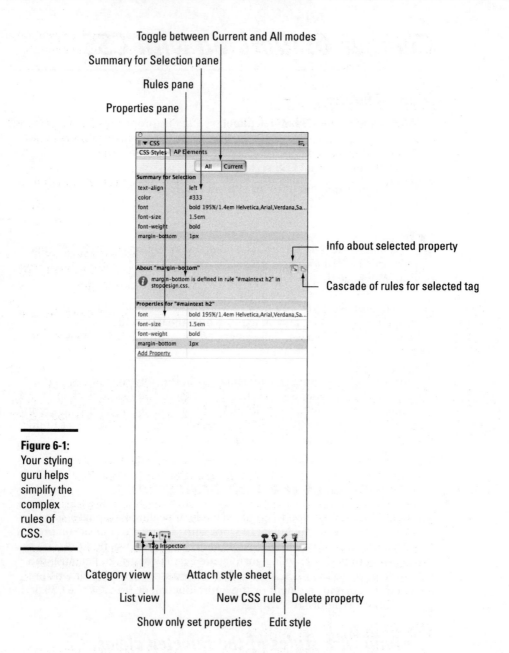

Info about selected property

Cascade of rules for selected tag

Figure 6-1:
Your styling
guru helps
simplify the
complex
rules of
CSS.

Category view

List view

Show only set properties

Attach style sheet

New CSS rule

Edit style

Delete property

The Current mode panel is divided into three panes: Summary for Selection pane, Rules pane, and Properties pane. We describe each of these panes in the following sections.

Summary for Selection pane

The Summary for Selection pane displays the CSS properties for the selected element in a rule-value list. The summary pane is read-only, although you can double-click it to display a dialog box for editing the rule.

When you select a property, the Rules and Properties panes are updated to display property information associated with its rule.

Rules pane

The Rules pane either tells you where the selected property is defined in your source code or lists the cascade of rules for the selected element. The buttons to the right of the pane toggle between these two modes.

Given the cascading nature of CSS, the Rules pane can be extremely helpful in tracking down a style rule.

Properties pane

The Properties pane provides a way to edit the style properties of the selected rule. By default, the properties shown in the list are explicitly set in your CSS code. You can then tweak a property by selecting a new value from its drop-down list or typing your own.

The Properties pane has two other modes, each of which you can access from the button set on the left side of the status bar (refer to Figure 6-1).

Category view shows all possible properties arranged in categories. Set properties are placed at the top of each category and shown in blue text.

List view lists possible properties in alphabetical order. Set properties are displayed in blue text at the top of the list. List view, although complete, can make quite a long list to have to scroll down and navigate to a specific property.

Working with all styles

The CSS Styles panel can also toggle to All mode, to work with rules in the whole document. As shown in Figure 6-2, the panel is divided into an All Rules pane and a Properties pane.

Book IV
Chapter 6

Working with CSS

Toggle between Current and All modes

All Rules pane

Properties pane

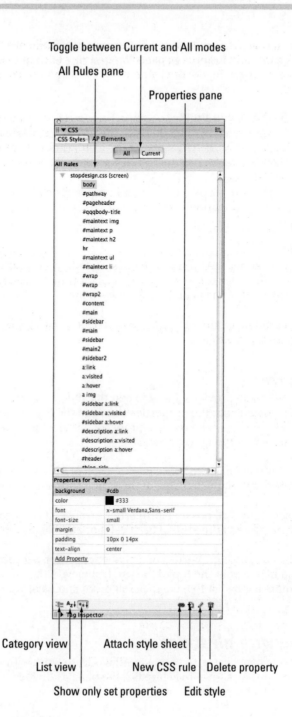

Figure 6-2:
Viewing
style
information
for the
whole
document.

Category view

List view

Show only set properties

Attach style sheet

New CSS rule

Edit style

Delete property

The All Rules pane displays in a tree-like structure all CSS rules associated with the document. Rules are organized by their containers — either a `style` element inside the document or an external style sheet attached to the HTML file.

The Properties pane acts the same way as it does in Current mode. (See the section "Working with styles of the selected element," earlier in this chapter.) The pane provides a way to edit the properties of the CSS rule selected in the All Rules pane. You can also view the Properties pane in Category and List views.

Creating a New CSS Rule

Rather than your having to go to the document source and create a new CSS rule, Dreamweaver provides a visual way to do that, from within the CSS Styles panel. Follow these instructions to add a CSS rule to your document or style sheet:

1. **Click the New CSS Rule icon (see Figure 6-3), in the lower-right corner of the CSS Styles panel.**

Figure 6-3:
Adding a
new rule
from the
CSS Styles
panel.

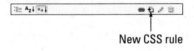

New CSS rule

The New CSS Rule dialog box is displayed, as shown in Figure 6-4.

Figure 6-4:
Rules, rules,
rules. Even
style sheets
need some
structure.

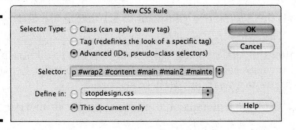

2. Choose the type of selector from the Selector Type options.

Your options are described in this list:

- *Class:* Use Class when you want to apply the style rule by using the `class` attribute of the elements.

- *Tag:* Use Tag when you want to add to or redefine an existing HTML tag's properties.

- *Advanced:* Use Advanced when you need to apply the rule to a particular `id` value or to a pseudo-class (such as `a:active`, `a:link`, and `a:visited` links).

3. Enter the appropriate value in the text box based on your selection from Step 2.

If you choose Class, enter a period followed by the class name in the box. Remember that a valid class selector begins with a period.

If you choose Tag, select an HTML tag from the drop-down list.

If you choose Advanced, enter the selector value. This value is an `id` for `id`-specific rules or the name of a pseudo-class (from the drop-down list).

4. Choose the location in which you want to add this new rule.

Here are your options:

- *Existing style sheet:* If you choose this option, select a style sheet file that you already created.

- *New style sheet:* Select the (New Style Sheet file) item from the Define In drop-down list.

- *Current document:* Select the This Document Only option if you want to embed the style rule inside a `style` element of the current document.

5. Click OK.

The CSS Rule Definition dialog box is displayed, as shown in Figure 6-5.

6. Modify all the properties you want to set inside the dialog box.

One of the greatest benefits to using Dreamweaver for creating style rules is that this dialog box gives you full access to all possible properties at your disposal. Therefore, feel free to go to town. Leave no stone unturned. Leave no CSS property overlooked.

See Book V for more details on the these specific properties.

7. Click OK.

Your style rule is created in the location you specified.

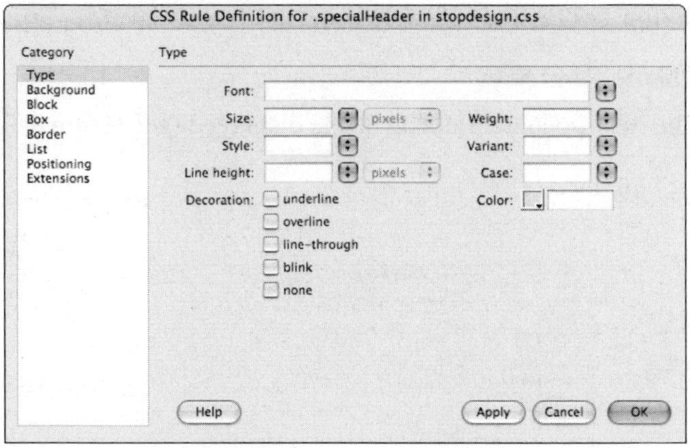

Figure 6-5:
Define your
style rule in
the comfort
of your own
CSS Rule
Definition
dialog box.

Editing Style Properties and Rules

You can edit both style properties and complete rules in the CSS Styles panel. To edit a property of the selected rule, simply use the Property pane in the CSS Styles panel.

To edit a rule:

✦ **If you're in Current mode:** Double-click a property in the Summary for Section pane to display the rule in which the property is defined. Or, click the Edit Style icon on the bottom of the panel.

✦ **If you're in All mode:** Double-click a rule in the All Rules pane (or select the rule and click the Edit Style icon).

The CSS Rule Definition dialog box is displayed (refer to Figure 6-5). Make the changes you want and click OK.

Creating an External Style Sheet in Dreamweaver

Because a CSS style sheet is a code-oriented document, you work with a style sheet in the Document window only in Code view. These types of documents have no Design view. If you're comfortable with CSS code, you will feel at home writing style rules by hand. However, if you prefer not to stare at a source code file with strange-looking CSS syntax, you can use the CSS Styles panel as a visual interface to the style sheet definition.

Here's how to create a CSS style sheet in Dreamweaver:

1. **Choose File⇨New.**

The New Document dialog box is displayed (see Figure 6-6).

Figure 6-6:
Choosing to
create a
CSS style
sheet from
the New
Document
dialog box.
You get no
frills in the
Layout or
Preview
boxes
because a
style sheet
is all text
based.

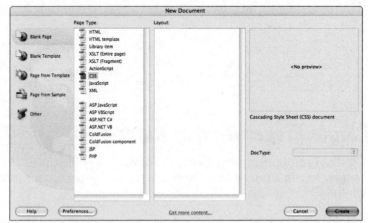

2. **Select CSS from the Page Type list.**

3. **Click Create.**

An untitled style sheet is created and displayed in the Document window (see Figure 6-7).

4. **Add CSS style rules to the style sheet.**

You can use the CSS Styles panel with a style sheet, freeing you from dealing directly with the source code. See the "Creating a New CSS Rule" section, earlier in this chapter, for more details on using the CSS Styles panel to create new rules.

5. **Choose File⇨Save.**

Save the style sheet in the location that you want in your site.

```
1  @charset "UTF-8";
2  /* CSS Document */
3
4
```

```
1K / 1 sec
```

Figure 6-7:
An eager
young style
sheet, ready
to set the
world on
fire.

Applying and Removing a Style in Your Document

After styles are defined in your style sheets, you're ready to apply them to elements in your Web pages. If you're comfortable working with HTML, you can apply a style by making source code changes. But, if you prefer to work with Dreamweaver visual editor, here's how to apply a style in Design view:

1. **Select the text or element that you want to apply a style to.**

2. **Click the Style drop-down list in the Properties inspector.**

   Alternatively, you can choose Text⇨CSS Styles to perform the same task.

   Figure 6-8 shows the list of styles available in my document.

3. **Select the style you want to use.**

   Your selection is then updated to reflect the new style properties.

If you want to remove a style, select the text or element and choose the None option from the Style drop-down list in the Properties inspector.

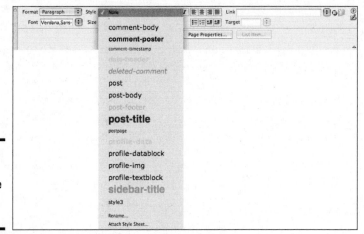

Figure 6-8:
Listing
styles in the
Properties
inspector.

Linking to an External Style Sheet

You can link to an external style sheet by following these steps:

1. **Choose Text⇨CSS Styles⇨Attach Style Sheet.**

The Attach External Style Sheet dialog box is displayed, as shown in
Figure 6-9.

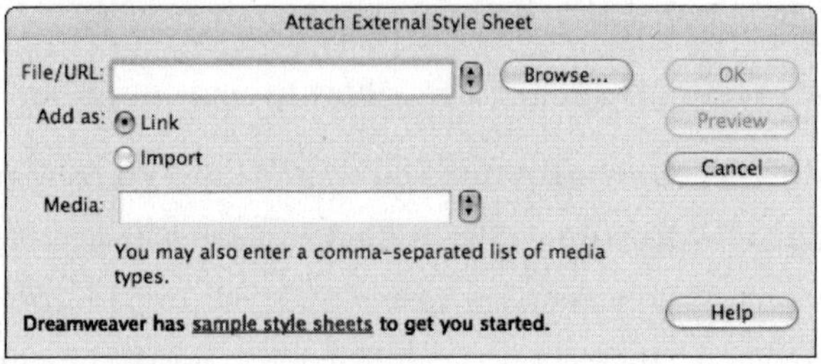

Figure 6-9:
Hear the
wedding
bells ring —
wedding a
style sheet
to an HTML
document.

2. **Enter the style sheet you want to attach in the File/URL box.**

3. **Click the Link button to attach the style sheet in the typical way.**

Alternatively, if you want to nest style sheets, use the Import option.

You can use the advanced technique known as *nesting* to reference a .css style sheet from another style sheet using an @import url ("stylesheet.css") command in the CSS code.

4. Select the screen item from the Media drop-down list.

Or, if the style sheet you're attaching is for a specific media (such as a handheld device or printer), select the appropriate alternative.

5. Click OK.

Getting a Kick-Start with Sample Styles

Dreamweaver has several sample style sheets that you can access by clicking the Sample Style Sheets link in the Attach External Style Sheet dialog box (refer to Figure 6-9). The Sample Style Sheets dialog box is shown (see Figure 6-10). None of the styles in these samples will set the world on fire with its innovation or high design flair. However, they're all good tools that can give you a kick-start as you work with styles in Dreamweaver.

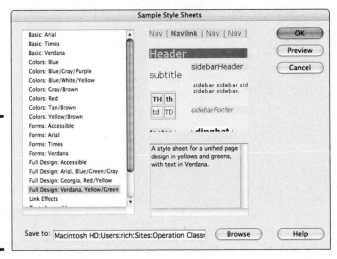

Figure 6-10:
Dream-
weaver
gives you a
start with
some kinda
ugly style
sheets.

**Book IV
Chapter 6**

Working with CSS

Chapter 7: When DWT Calls: Using Templates for a Consistent Look

In This Chapter

↙ Grasping the key concepts of templates

↙ Creating a template from scratch

↙ Transforming an existing document into a template

↙ Creating a new document based on a template

*A*fter you develop a killer page design and your text and layout formatting are exactly the way you want them, you should reproduce this common look throughout your Web site. The old-fashioned way was to create a master HTML file and then use it as the basis for starting each new document you created. Although that method can still work, its shortcomings become clear when you want to make a change to the master file. To do so, you have to open each of your documents and make the change.

Templates solve this problem. They provide an easy way for you to create a master document, but at the same time maintain a link with the created documents. Therefore, any time you want to tweak the template, all the created documents can be updated as well.

In this chapter, you discover how to use templates to simplify managing your Web pages and help maintain a consistent look across your site.

Understanding Dreamweaver Templates

A *template* in Dreamweaver is a special file that serves as a master document for site pages. Here are the key concepts to understand when working with Dreamweaver templates:

✦ **A Dreamweaver template is a Web document with Dreamweaver-specific instructions inside it.** A template file for an HTML document has a `.dwt` extension and is used only inside Dreamweaver, not on your live Web site.

✦ **A template page is divided between editable (unlocked) and non-editable (locked) regions.** A non-editable region helps you ensure that content or layout code is consistent and unaltered across all template-based pages. The editable regions give you a way to provide custom content for a page.

✦ **When editing a template, you edit both editable and non-editable regions.** When working with a document created from the template, however, you can make changes only in the editable regions.

✦ **Inside the document body of a template-based page, only editable regions can be edited.** Inside the document head, Dreamweaver automatically creates an editable section for you for adding scripts and style instructions, for example.

✦ **A template is always enclosed inside a Dreamweaver site, and its file is stored in a special Templates subfolder, under the site's root folder.**

If you don't want to create a template yourself, you can find many pre-made templates available on the Web, although most of them are commercial products. You can check out `www.dreamweaver-templates.org` for reviews of both free and commercial templates.

Creating a Template

The process of creating a template is much like creating a normal Web page, except that you define editable and non-editable regions for the document. We show you two ways.

From scratch

Here's how to create a template from scratch:

1. **Choose File⇨New.**

The New Document dialog box is displayed.

2. **Click the Blank Template button on the left.**

Figure 7-1 shows the template selections.

3. **Select HTML Template from the Template Type list.**

Or, if you feel a hankering for Web programming, you can select one of the other template types.

4. **Select a layout from the Layout list.**

The layouts are identical to the ones you can choose from when creating an ordinary HTML document. Select <None> if you prefer to start from a blank page.

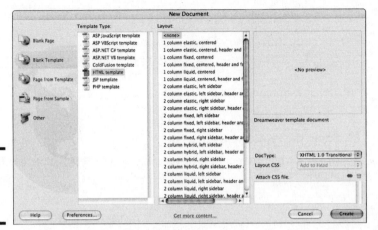

Figure 7-1:
Create
a new
template.

5. **Select a document type in the DocType drop-down list.**

6. **Select from the Layout CSS drop-down list the location where you want to place CSS style information.**

7. **Click the Create button.**

   The template you created is shown in the Document window.

8. **Edit the design and layout of your template.**

   Using `div` elements or tables, organize your template into non-editable and editable zones.

9. **Add content and features that you want to appear on every template-created page.**

   Company logos, navigation bars, and footers are typical examples of "global" content that is locked in non-editable regions.

10. **Add placeholder text in the regions that you will mark as editable.**

11. **Select the placeholder content with your mouse.**

   You can make almost anything an editable region: a single word, phrase, paragraph, image, `div` element, table, or individual table cell.

12. **Choose Insert➪Template Objects➪Editable Region from the menu.**

   Or, you can click the Templates drop-down button on Common tab of the Insert bar and then choose the Editable Region menu item.

   The New Editable Region dialog box is shown (see Figure 7-2).

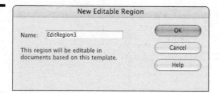

Figure 7-2:
Add an
editable
region to a
template.

13. **Name the region and click OK.**

Dreamweaver marks the selection as an editable region, as shown in
Figure 7-3.

Editable region

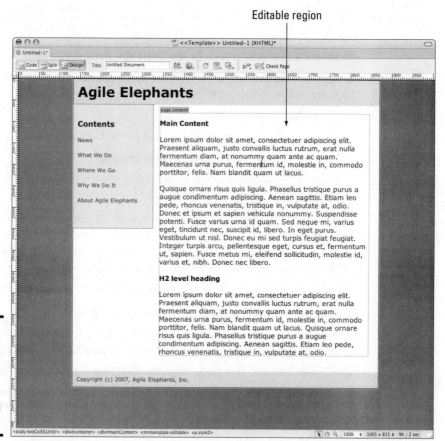

Figure 7-3:
Editable
regions are
indicated
with a
surrounding
blue box.

Your basic template is ready to go.

14. Choose File⇨Save.

The Save As Template dialog box (shown in Figure 7-4) is displayed.

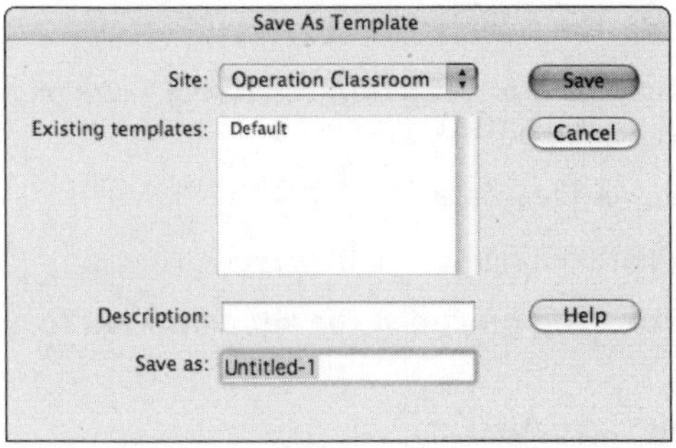

```
                    Save As Template
         Site:  [ Operation Classroom ▲▼ ]    ( Save )
Existing templates:  Default                    ( Cancel )



    Description:  [_____]           ( Help )
      Save as:  [ Untitled-1        ]
```

Figure 7-4:
Saving a
template for
later use.

15. Select from the Site drop-down list the site you want to add the template to.

16. Add a name in the Save As box.

17. Click Save.

Dreamweaver saves the template in the Templates folder of the selected site and adds a .dwt extension.

Defining document-relative links in your template can be tricky. Dreamweaver expects the document-relative link to be based on the path *from* the Templates subfolder *to* the linked document. It's *not* the path from the template-based document to the linked page. You can help make sure that the correct path is stored by using the folder icon or the Point to File icon in the Properties inspector as you create the link.

From an existing page

In addition to allowing you to create a template from scratch, Dreamweaver enables you to transform an existing Web page into a template. Here's how:

1. Open an existing page in the Document window.

After you save the document as a template, none of the existing content or layout is editable. Therefore, you need to define editable regions.

2. **Select the content that you want to be editable.**

3. **Choose Insert⇨Template Objects⇨Editable Region.**

   The New Editable Region dialog box is shown (refer to Figure 7-2).

4. **Name the region and click OK.**

   Dreamweaver marks the selection as an editable region.

5. **Repeat Steps 2 through 4 for any other areas of your page that you want to be unlocked for editing.**

6. **Choose File⇨Save As Template.**

   The Save As Template dialog box is displayed.

7. **Select from the Site drop-down list the site you want to add the template to.**

8. **Add a name in the Save As box.**

9. **Click Save.**

   Dreamweaver saves the template in the template folder of the selected site and adds a .dwt extension.

Using a Template to Create a New Page

After your template is built, you're ready to create new pages based on it. To do so, follow these steps:

1. **Choose File⇨New.**

   The New Document dialog box is displayed.

2. **Click the Page from Template button.**

   The page is updated to display a lists of sites, as shown in Figure 7-5.

3. **Select the site that contains the template you want to use.**

4. **Select a template from the template list box.**

   The preview box displays a thumbnail version of the template.

5. **Select the Update Page When Template Changes check box to maintain a link with the template.**

   If you select the check box, any changes you make in the template are updated in the new document.

   If you deselect the box, the link between the template and the document isn't preserved.

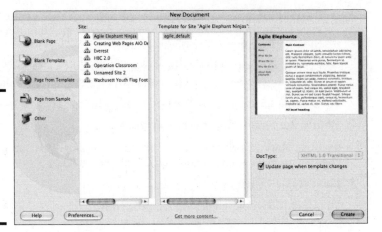

Figure 7-5:
The New Document dialog box gives you access to all your templates.

6. Click Create.

A new page based on the template is displayed in the Document window.

7. Edit the editable regions of the page.

Notice that the locked regions can't be edited or deleted, in either Design or Source view.

8. Choose File⇨Save.

Save your document as you would save a normal Web page.

The Ripple Effect: Making a Change to Your Template

Templates provide a quick way to create a new document based on a pre-built page layout. However, the real power of templates comes into play when you need to tweak the original template. Because the template maintains a connection with the documents created from it, you can automatically apply changes to all the pages by simply changing the master file. (You can also decide not to update the pages, if you want.)

To change a template and update all documents based on that template, follow these instructions:

1. Open the template file.

You have three options:

- If you're traditional, choose File⇨Open from the menu to display the Open dialog box. Navigate to the template file you want to modify and click Open.

- If you're already working with the site that contains your template, save some time and head to the Files panel, and then double-click the template in the Templates folder.

- Even better, if you have a document open that's attached to the template, choose Modify⇨Templates⇨Open Attached Template.

The template is opened in the Document window.

2. **Modify the template the way you want.**

Because you're working with the original template, you can make changes to both editable and non-editable regions.

3. **Choose File⇨Save.**

The Update Template Files dialog box, shown in Figure 7-6, is displayed. It lists all files that are attached to the template.

Figure 7-6:
Template
changes
can auto-
matically
update
created
documents.

4. **Click the Update button to update all the documents list.**

Or, if you don't want to, click the Don't Update button.

Dreamweaver works through each of the files in the list and makes the appropriate changes.

Attaching and Detaching a Template

When you create a document based on a template, you automatically attach the template to the new page. However, you can also attach a template to an existing page. When the page is attached, Dreamweaver applies the content of the template to the existing content.

To attach a template to an opened document, follow these steps:

1. **Choose Modify⇨Templates⇨Apply Template to Page.**

The Select Template dialog box is displayed.

2. **Select a template.**

3. **Click Select.**

Bringing the template structure into an existing document can cause unexpected results to the existing formatting, so we recommend creating a new file from the template and then copying and pasting the text from the original document.

Alternatively, you can detach a file from its template. When you do so, Dreamweaver unlocks all the non-editable regions, enabling you to make any changes you so desire. To detach a template from an open document, choose Modify⇨Templates⇨Detach from Template.

Chapter 8: Think Outside the Page: Managing Your Web Site

In This Chapter

✔ Creating a site

✔ Configuring site settings

✔ Working with the Files panel

✔ Transferring local and remote files

✔ Using the site map

✔ Checking site links

The first seven chapters in this minibook focus on how to work with the Adobe software package to create well-designed, attractive Web pages. However, it's time to think "outside of the page" and focus on the Web site as a whole. Besides sporting a top-notch document editor, Dreamweaver serves as an ideal tool for managing your Web site. In this chapter, we show you how to use Dreamweaver to simplify the process of managing and working with local and remote files.

Creating and Configuring a Site

In Chapter 2 of this minibook, we walk you through a step-by-step example of creating a basic site in Dreamweaver. In this example, we show you how to do a more advanced setup and configuration.

To create a site, follow these steps:

1. **Choose Site⇨New Site.**

   The Site Definition dialog box is displayed. If you created a basic site in Chapter 2, the Basic tab is active. Otherwise, the Advanced tab is visible.

2. **If necessary, click the Advanced tab to make it active.**

   Figure 8-1 shows the Advanced tab with the Local Info page selected.

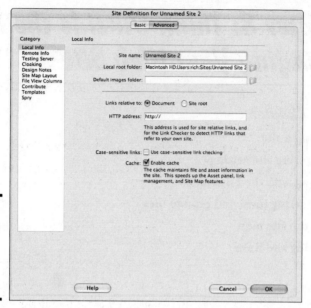

Figure 8-1:
Setting up a
new Web
site in
Dream-
weaver.

3. **Enter a descriptive name for your site in the Site Name box.**

4. **In the Local Root Folder box, specify the location on your hard drive for storing site files.**

   Your local root folder is the working directory for your site.

5. **In the Default Images Folder box, give the default location in which you want to place site images.**

   It's often an images subfolder under your root.

6. **Specify how you want Dreamweaver to handle relative links in the Links Relative To option group.**

   If you select Document (the default), Dreamweaver creates document-relative links to another file on your site. If you select Site Root, Dreamweaver prefixes the full site root URL before each link.

7. **Enter the URL for your Web site in the HTTP Address box.**

   This setting is used primarily when you specify Site Root in Step 6, but it comes in handy when verifying absolute URLs in the Dreamweaver link checker.

8. **Select the Case-Sensitive Links check box if you want the link checker to check for case.**

   If your Web host uses a Unix server, be sure to select this option.

9. **Select the Cache check box (the default) to enable Dreamweaver to store a site-based cache.**

   A cache helps improve the performance of site management tasks and to enable the Assets panel.

   The local settings of your site are ready. It's time to move to the remote server settings.

10. **Click the Remote Info item in the Category box.**

11. **Select an access method from the Access drop-down box.**

   FTP is the typical method if your site is hosted by an ISP or on a server you access over the Web.

   Here are the other, advanced options:

   • **Local/Network:** Use Local/Network if your Web server is on the same machine or local-area network that you use.

   • **RDS:** Use RDS if you're connecting to a ColdFusion server.

   • **WebDav:** Use WebDav if you connect to a server using Web-based Distributed Authoring and Versioning (WebDav) protocol.

   Figure 8-2 shows the Remote Info page for FTP access.

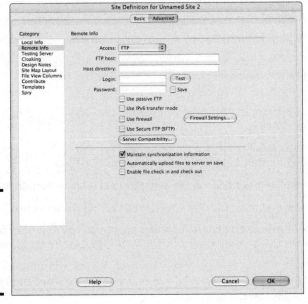

Figure 8-2:
Most users configure their sites for FTP access.

12. Enter remote server details for the access method you selected in Step 11.

13. Select the Maintain Synchronization Information check box if you want to keep the local and remote files in sync.

The synchronization process is performed on the Files panel.

14. Select the Automatically Upload Files to Server on Save check box if you want Dreamweaver to publish your local files each time you save them.

15. Select the Enable File Check In and Check Out check box if you plan to use Dreamweaver's multi-user file management capabilities.

Your remote server settings are all gathered.

You can specify several other, advanced-level categories of settings, including

- **Testing Server:** Useful only if you're using Dreamweaver to create dynamic pages with a server-based technology, such as ColdFusion, ASP, PHP, or JSP.

- **Cloaking:** Useful if you want to mask certain folders or file types from normal site operations.

- **Design Notes:** Enables the ability to add extra comments to your site. This option is normally used in environments in which multiple designers or contributors are working together on the same site.

- **Site Map Layout:** Allows you to customize the look of your site map. (See the "Viewing the Site Map" section, later in this chapter.)

- **File View Columns:** Lets you customize the Files panel. (See the "Working with the Files Panel" section, later in this chapter.)

- **Contribute:** Used only if you plan to use your site with Adobe Contribute.

- **Templates:** Provides a single setting for use with site templates. (See Chapter 7 in this minibook for more details.)

- **Spry:** Useful only if you're using the Spry Ajax components.

16. Click OK.

Your Web site is created. Dreamweaver opens the new site in the Files panel.

Editing Site Settings

All the site settings are made within the Site Definition dialog box. You can access the Site Definition dialog box for a site by performing these steps:

1. **Choose Site⇨Manage Sites.**

The Manage Sites dialog box (shown in Figure 8-3) is displayed.

Figure 8-3: Choose from any of your sites to edit.

2. **Select your site from the list.**

3. **Click the Edit button.**

The Site Definition dialog box is displayed.

However, as a shortcut, you can quickly display the Site Definition dialog box of your active site by double-clicking the site name in the Site drop-down list, located on the Files panel toolbar. Much easier!

Working with the Files Panel

The Files panel is your command-and-control center for your Dreamweaver site. You perform most site management tasks there. Figure 8-4 shows the Files panel in its normal mode.

Managing local files

Use the Files panel hierarchical directory to manage your site files. You can use the window much like a Windows Explorer or Mac Finder window to open, move, rename, and delete files.

Put files

List of sites View Get files Check out

Figure 8-4:
The Files
panel is
used for site
manage-
ment tasks.

Click to show File Activity window Check in Expand to show
local/remote sites

Refresh view

Connect to remote server Synchronize

Managing remote files

Although the default display of the Files panel shows the local files, Dreamweaver enables you to connect to the remote server to display a live view of the server files as well. You can view the remote server files in one of two ways:

✦ **Select Remote view from the View list on the Files panel toolbar.** The local view is replaced with a live view of the server.

✦ **Better yet, click the Expand/Contract button on the Files panel tool-bar, and then click the Connect to Remote Host button.** The expanded view displays a side-by-side view of the local and remote directories, as shown in Figure 8-5.

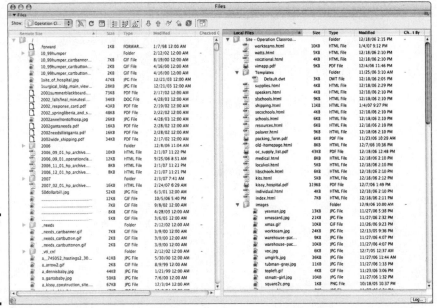

Figure 8-5:
Viewing
remote and
local files
side by side.

When you're done working with the remote files, you can click the Disconnect from Remote Host button on the Files panel toolbar.

Customizing Files Panel view

If you want to customize the columns that appear in the Files panel, follow these steps:

1. **Choose Site⇨Manage Sites.**

2. **Select your site from the list.**

3. **Click the Edit button.**

 The Site Definition dialog box is displayed.

4. **Click the File View Columns item in the Category list.**

5. **Modify the columns the way you want on the File View Columns page.**

6. **Click OK.**

Working with the Assets Panel

An *asset* is any resource that your Web site uses, such as images, Flash files, script files, and even links. Dreamweaver provides a centralized location for managing these various types of assets in the Assets panel.

To access the panel, choose Window⇨Assets or press F11 (or Alt+F11 on a Mac). Or, if your Files panel is visible, you normally find the Assets panel as a tab in the same panel group. The Assets panel is shown in Figure 8-6.

Asset type   Preview pane

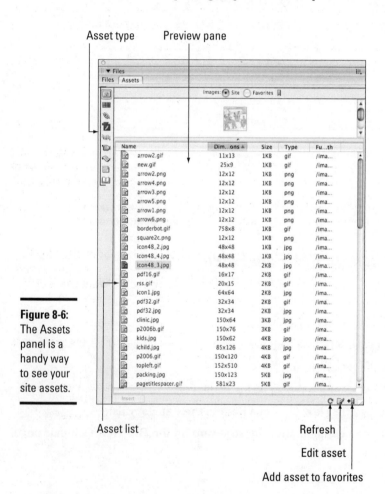

Figure 8-6: The Assets panel is a handy way to see your site assets.

Asset list

Refresh

Edit asset

Add asset to favorites

Here are the most useful tasks you can perform in the Assets panel:

✦ **Drag and drop assets to your pages.** You can drag and drop a file-based asset, such as an image of a Flash file, from the Assets panel to your document.

✦ **Create a library of favorite assets.** Most Web designers use certain assets repeatedly — perhaps a bullet image, color scheme, or script file. You can click the Add to Favorites button in the Assets panel or right-click and choose Add to Favorites from the pop-up menu. You then have the asset readily available, no matter which site you open.

✦ **Copy an asset to another site.** You can also copy an asset from your current site to another site by right-clicking it and choosing a site from the Copy to Site submenu.

Managing Local and Remote Files

Because the typical Web site in the Dreamweaver environment involves both local files (for designing and testing) and remote files (on a live server), most of your site management responsibilities normally focus on making sure that these two versions are working together properly with each other.

Transferring files

The most common action you perform when working with your site files is to upload (or put) a local file on the remote server. If you want to put on the remote server a document you're working on, click the File Management button on the Document toolbar (see Figure 8-7) and then select Put from the drop-down list of options.

Alternatively, you can upload a local file by selecting it in the Files panel and then clicking the Put button on the toolbar.

If you want to copy your entire set of local files to the remote server, select the root site folder in the Files panel and then click the Put button. Dreamweaver uploads all the site's pages and other assets to the server.

You can also retrieve a file that's on your remote server and copy it back to your local computer. To do so, open the Files panel in Remote view (see the "Managing remote files" section, earlier in this chapter). Select the file or files you want to download, and then click the Get button on the Files panel toolbar.

File management

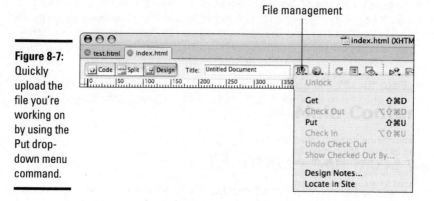

Figure 8-7:
Quickly upload the file you're working on by using the Put drop-down menu command.

Automatically uploading files to the server

You usually manually upload your local files to the Web server after you thoroughly test and proof them. However, Dreamweaver allows you to upload your local files automatically, every time you save them.

To do so, follow these steps:

1. **Choose Site⇨Manage Sites.**

2. **Select your site from the list.**

3. **Click the Edit button.**

The Site Definition dialog box (shown in Figure 8-8) is displayed.

4. **Click the Remote Info item in the Category list.**

5. **Select the Automatically Upload Files to Server on Save check box.**

6. **Click OK.**

The option to automatically upload files to the server helps ensure that your local and remote files are always in synch. However, you run the risk of "putting up" a file that is a work in progress and not ready for live viewing yet.

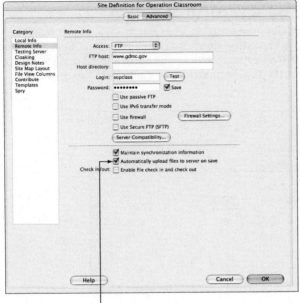

Figure 8-8:
When you save, this option takes you live with your latest changes.

You can choose to automatically upload files.

Viewing the Site Map

The Files panel displays your Web site in a traditional file-system-oriented hierarchy, just as you find in Windows Explorer or the Mac Finder. Although that view is helpful when you're working with files, it isn't reflective of the linked relationships that exist among the pages of your site.

That's where the site map comes in handy. The Dreamweaver *site map* is a visual look at your Web site that shows the site structure. However, the site map limits the view to two levels. The home page is shown at the top level, with other site pages that are linked in the home page displayed at the second level. Pages are arranged in the map based on the order in which links appear in the document source.

The site map shows interrelationships between a site's pages. You can also use the site map to add, edit, or delete links.

The site map gives you a visual look at your local files. It doesn't work with files located on your remote server.

Displaying a vertical site map

To view the site map from the Files panel, choose the Map View item from the toolbar's View drop-down list. The file-based contents of the panel are replaced with a vertical site map, as shown in Figure 8-9. The home page is displayed at the top, with arrows to each of its linked pages.

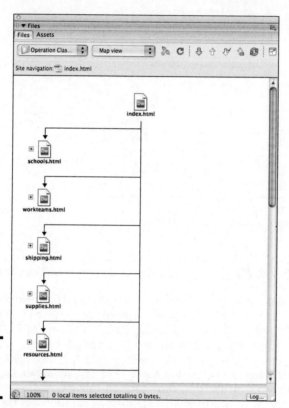

Figure 8-9: Viewing the site map.

Displaying a horizontal site map

You can also display a wider site map when the Files panel is in expanded mode. To expand the Files panel, click the Expand/Collapse button on the toolbar.

After you're in Expanded mode, click the Site Map button displayed on the toolbar. A drop-down menu is displayed. Choose Map Only to view just the site map. Choose Map and Files to view the site map on the left panel and the normal Local Files view on the right. Figure 8-10 shows the site map with the Map Only option.

Site Map button

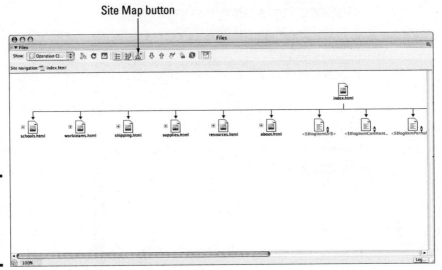

Figure 8-10:
Viewing the
site map in
horizontal
mode.

Working with the site map

You can perform various tasks inside the site map:

✦ **Display dependent files for level-two pages.** You can click the +
button next to a page icon to display a list of all dependent files
(see Figure 8-11).

✦ **Change the root page.** You can optionally treat a secondary page as the
root for the site map. To do so, click the Page icon and choose View As
Root from the pop-up menu.

✦ **Manage links.** You can add, remove, and modify links by selecting a
page icon and right-clicking to display a pop-up menu. Choose the
appropriate item.

The problem with managing links in the site map is that you're working
with a page's links outside of their context on the page. We're sure that
you'll see, for nearly all purposes, that working with links is far better
when you're working inside the Document window.

**Book IV
Chapter 8**

**Think Outside the
Page: Managing
Your Web Site**

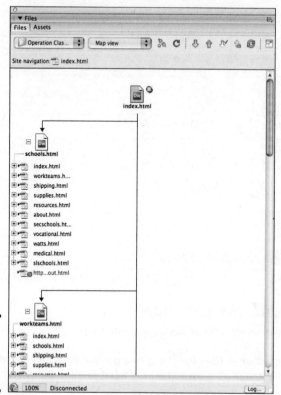

Figure 8-11:
Listing the
dependents
of a file.

Customizing the site map

If you want to customize the display options of the site map, follow these
steps:

1. **Choose Site⇨Manage Sites.**

2. **Select your site from the list.**

3. **Click the Edit button.**

   The Site Definition dialog box is displayed.

4. **Click the Site Map Layout item in the Category list.**

5. **Modify the display options the way you want.**

   The most common change is to click the Page Titles option, under Icon
   Labels, to display the page title with the icon.

6. **Click OK.**

Managing Links

Dreamweaver manages site links for you so that you can verify and make global changes.

To check the links in your site, choose Site⇨Check Links Sitewide. Dreamweaver begins checking the links throughout your site's pages and displays the results in the Link Checker panel.

Suppose that you linked to a page throughout your site but you need to change its filename or location. Rather than manually work through each page and change the link, you can make the global change by using the Change Link Sitewide command.

To change a link sitewide, follow these steps:

1. **Choose Site⇨Change Link Sitewide.**

The Change Link Sitewide dialog box is displayed, as shown in Figure 8-12.

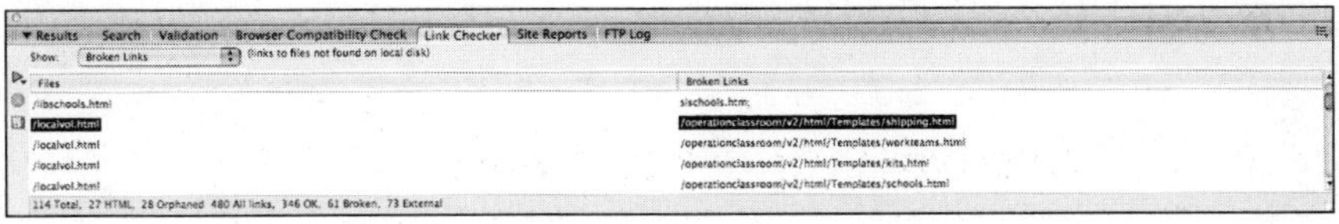

Figure 8-12:
The Change
Link
Sitewide
saves you
time
searching
through
your Web
site for link
changes.

2. **In the Change All Links To box, enter the URL you want to modify.**

Use the Browse button if you want to locate it in your site.

3. **Enter the new URL in the Into Links To box.**

4. **Click OK.**

**Book IV
Chapter 8**

**Think Outside the
Page: Managing
Your Web Site**

Book V

Cascading Style Sheets

The 5th Wave   By Rich Tennant

SUPER FRUITCAKE
RESEARCH PROJECT
"Deep Fruit"
20 tFlops x
NUT CLUSTER
MASSIVE DR
PARALLEL

"Hold on people. It seems the Japanese have a 40 teraflop fruitcake in development, and plan to release it -get this -one week before Christmas! Okay, we've got our work cut out for us."

Contents at a Glance

Chapter 1: Styling Your Web Pages with CSS

In This Chapter

✓ **Understanding what Cascading Style Sheets can do for you**

✓ **Introducing the basics of CSS**

✓ **Dissecting a CSS rule**

✓ **Applying a style**

✓ **Understanding inheritance and cascading**

*W*hen the Web was introduced in the early 1990s, Web page creators had to rely on the HTML markup language to display the content and assign all the formatting to it. The problem was, however, that HTML was designed to display content, not format it. Not surprisingly, Web designers were forced to go through hoops to get an HTML document to look the way they wanted.

Although that method worked in the "wild west" days of the Web, the powers that be (a standards body known as the W3C) soon realized that a better solution was needed. The result was *Cascading Style Sheets (CSS),* a technology introduced back in 1996. The initial version of CSS showed promise in taking the formatting responsibilities from HTML, but it was plagued by inconsistent implementations by the major browsers. Therefore, CSS in those days was, to be frank, pretty lame because you couldn't count on the browser to format the page the way you designed it.

That was then; this is now. Fortunately, with more than a decade under our collective belts, things have significantly changed for the better. In fact, neither of us can possibly imagine creating a Web site without using CSS as a basic tool in our Web site toolbox.

In this chapter, we introduce you to CSS and help you feel comfortable with some of the terminology and basic principles. Then, in the remaining chapters of this minibook, we show you how to use CSS to add style to your Web site.

Expression Web (see Book III) and Dreamweaver (see Book IV) offer built-in support for CSS. Or, if you aren't using these Web site design tools, you can always work with CSS using a plain text editor, such as Notepad.

Why Use CSS?

CSS is a styling language that you can use to make your Web site look good and be easier to manage. We get into the particulars of how CSS works in the sections that follow, but here are three basic reasons that CSS is helpful:

✦ **CSS gives you greater control over your page design.** CSS has many formatting settings that HTML, by itself, does not provide. As a result, you can have much greater control over the look of your Web page by using CSS than just using normal HTML.

✦ **CSS allows you to separate your site content from the formatting instructions.** The HTML document, therefore, becomes the place where you work with content, and the CSS style sheet serves as your place to set up your styles.

✦ **CSS enables you to manage styles across your site in one central location.** Although you can define CSS styles inside a single Web page, its real power becomes evident when you use a separate CSS style sheet that every page in your Web site can access. When you set up your site like this, you can easily give your entire site a consistent look and feel. You can also make global changes from a single location.

In the end, CSS enables you to create a more attractive, well-designed Web site and make it much easier to manage and organize.

Suppose that you're working in a multiuser environment in which you design the page while someone else programs the HTML or scripting code. With CSS, a designer can work primarily with a separate style sheet rather than wade through the programmer's HTML files.

Introducing CSS

You use CSS to define style definitions that look something like CSS:

```
body {
  font-family: 'Lucida Grande', Arial, Tahoma, sans;
  background-color: #000000;
}
```

When you create CSS styles, you typically write instructions in a `style` element inside an HTML document or in an external style sheet. A *style sheet* is just a plain text file that's linked into a Web page. The browser applies the styling rules to the HTML document when it displays the page. A CSS style sheet has a `.css` extension. See the section "Applying CSS Styles to a Web Page," later in this chapter, for more on attaching a style to an HTML element.

Make the rules — don't break 'em

Although an element is the basic ingredient of an HTML document, a rule is the primary building block of CSS. A *rule* selects the elements in which you want to apply formatting to and then indicates what should be done to them. In other words, a rule is a code statement that says "Hey, you — do this!" It consists of two parts: the *selector* (the "Hey, you" part) and the *declaration* ("do this"):

+ The **selector** identifies one or more HTML elements that you want to work with. You commonly select an element by its type, `id` attribute, `class` attribute, or position in the document hierarchy. We cover selectors in detail in Chapter 2 of this minibook.

+ The **declaration** consists of a property and a value (known as a *property-value pair*) that specifies how to format the elements identified by the selector.

A CSS rule looks like this:

```
selector { property: value }
```

CSS is flexible with spacing, so you can put a rule all on one line or else spread it out over multiple lines, like this:

```
selector {
  property: value
}
```

A rule can have one or more property-value pairs defined inside curly brackets. If you have multiple properties specified, you need to separate each one with a semicolon. For example, each of the following is a valid rule:

```
h1 { font-size: 18px; font-weight: bold; }
h2 {
  font-size: 16px;
  font-weight: bold;
}
```

Caged formatting match: CSS versus HTML

If CSS and HTML ever get into a cage formatting match, put your money on CSS. With CSS, you can do many things that are either difficult or impossible when using ordinary HTML. For example, you can

✔ Customize text indention

✔ Gain considerable control over formatting, such as adding borders and padding around blocks of text

✔ Precisely position or tile background graphics

✔ Manage margins effectively

✔ Manipulate character and word spacing with great precision, in addition to using *kerning* (adjusting the spacing between lines of text) and justification

✔ Provide unique navigation tools for the user

✔ Specify the *Z-axis* (what is on top, as though you fanned a deck of cards and some cards were on top, overlapping others) for text and graphics

When you apply these rules to a Web page, all h1 elements are formatted as 18 pixels, bold, and h2 elements are formatted as 16 pixels, bold; for example:

```
<html>
    <body>
        <h1>This h1 heading is 18 pixels and bold.</h1>
        <h2>This h2 heading is 16 pixels and bold.</h2>
        <p>This is normal text.</p>
    </body>
</html>
```

Being (kinda sorta) insensitive about case

CSS is case insensitive, except for the parts that reference specific parts of an HTML document (such as an element name, id attribute, or class attribute). However, the standard convention is to use lowercase for CSS code, which keeps it consistent with XHTML documents (see Book VI). We highly recommend following the lowercase convention.

Applying CSS Styles to a Web Page

You have three different ways that you can apply CSS styles to an element in your document:

✦ Define it in the head of the document.

✦ Define it in an external style sheet.

✦ Define it inside the element tag itself.

We discuss each way in this section.

Using embedded styles

The style element is used to contain CSS code that you want to work with inside a given Web page. CSS styles contained inside the page itself are often called *embedded styles*.

Suppose that you want to use 10-point Arial as the default font for all paragraph text in a Web page. You can add the following style element inside the <head> section of your document:

```
<style type="text/css">

p {
  font-family: Arial;
  font-size: 10pt;
}

</style>
```

All the paragraph text in your document is displayed in 10-point Arial type when you display the text.

Now suppose that you want to redesign your site and use 12-point Georgia instead. To adjust the paragraph style for all p elements inside your page, you only need to tweak the CSS rule:

```
<style type="text/css">

p {
  font-family: Georgia;
  font-size: 12pt;
}

</style>
```

When the document is displayed, all paragraphs are displayed in the new font settings.

You can control whether a CSS style applies to a single paragraph, certain paragraphs, a whole page, or the entire site. We explore this topic fully in Chapter 2 of this minibook.

Using an external style sheet

A style sheet is an ordinary text file (with a `.css` extension) that you can use to define your styles across multiple pages on your Web site. You need to link only to the style sheet into your HTML document to then apply the styles.

Suppose that you create a file named `global.css` that contains the following code:

```
p {
   font-family: Georgia;
   font-size: 12pt;
}
```

We want to apply that default style across our Web site. Therefore, for each page, we need to connect to the `global.css` file. The standard way in which you can link the style sheet is with the `link` element, which is added inside the document head:

```
<link rel="stylesheet" rev="stylesheet" href="global.css"
   type="text/css" media="screen" charset="utf-8" />
```

Note that, in this example, the `global.css` is located in the same folder as the HTML file.

Using inline styles

Every visible HTML element has a `style` attribute that you can use to directly add CSS properties. Because you selected the element in which you want to apply the style to by yourself, you don't add the selector portion of a CSS rule for inline styles. You define only the CSS properties. For example, if you want to set the font for a paragraph by using an inline style, your code would look something like this:

```
<p style="font-family:Georgia; font-size:12pt">Welcome to the
   ice cream social.</p>
```

Note that multiple properties need to be separated by semicolons.

Use inline styles sparingly. They can be handy by freeing you from defining your style elsewhere; the style definition is good for only that element and cannot be reused.

Inheriting Properties

An HTML document is made up of a set of elements that form a *containment hierarchy*. The html element is "king of the hill" because it contains every other element in the page. The head and body elements are the other two major containers and typically contain many more elements. For example, consider the following document:

```
<html>
<head>
</head>
<body>
<div>
<p>this is a <span>paragraph</span></p>
</div>
</body>
</html>
```

The span element is contained by the p, div, body, and html elements. We could write the hierarchy to look something like this:

```
html > body > div > p > span
```

The containment hierarchy is important to understand as you begin to work with CSS. When you apply CSS rules to your HTML document, the CSS properties can occasionally have a ripple effect throughout the document. The reason is that *some* properties are inherited by an element (a *child*) that's contained inside another element (the *parent*).

The font and most other text-related settings, for example, are inherited properties. Therefore, if you set the font-family property in the body element, all elements inside the document body take on this property:

```
body {
   font-family: Arial, Tahoma, sans;
}
```

Therefore, if you have another element that you don't want to have this property, you need to explicitly write a rule that changes the font-family to something else.

Other properties aren't inherited, including the margin, border, padding, and background properties.

Therefore, consider the following code snippet:

```
<div style="font-family:Arial; border:1px solid black">
<p>My paragraph</p>
</div>
```

The paragraph inherits the font-family property, but not the border property, from the parent div element. However, suppose that you want the paragraph to inherit the border. For these occasions, CSS has an inherited property value that you can use to explicitly force a property to be passed from parent to child. Therefore, by adding border:inherited as a paragraph style, both the div and the p elements have a border around them:

```
<div style="font-family: Arial; border: 1px solid black">
<p style="border:inherited"> My paragraph</p>
</div>
```

Cascading Styles

Because cascading is the initial word in the technology, you probably won't be surprised to know that cascading is an important concept to understand when working with CSS. *Cascading* refers to the prioritizing that takes place when more than one property declaration applies to the same element in your HTML document. In other words, which style declaration wins out? The winner is based on the following levels of priority, starting with the highest:

✦ **Style weight (use of !important)**

You can add !important to the end of a property declaration. When you do so, the defined property always wins; for example:

```
body {
    background-image: url(../images/bgd.gif);
    background-repeat: repeat-y !important;
}
```

◆ **Style origin (author versus user)**

Not only can you as a Web page designer (the *author*) define CSS styles, but users can also specify their own style sheets in most modern browsers. The author style wins over the user style of the same weight. A user style overrides the author's style only when `!important` is used by the user and not specified by the author. The author and user style both win over default browser settings.

The origin ranking goes like this:

- Author styles
- User style sheet
- Default browser settings

REMEMBER

Because any `!important` declarations you make in your style sheet always win, be sure to use them wisely. A user may have a good reason for making a style change (such as the need for a larger-than-normal font size to account for poor eyesight).

◆ **Selector type**

The more specific selector wins over the more general one. Therefore, the general order is

- ID selector
- Class selector
- Descendent selector
- Type selector

See Chapter 2 of this minibook for a full description of these different kinds of selectors.

◆ **Style proximity**

When two rules carry the same weight, the one defined "closer" to the element wins out. Here's the order:

- Inline style (an element's `style` attribute)
- Embedded style (a `style` element)
- External style sheet (`.css` file) attached via a `link` element
- External style sheet (`.css` file) attached via an `@import` statement

Chapter 2: Selectively Speaking: Working with Selectors

In This Chapter

✔ **Understanding how selectors work**

✔ **Selecting regular HTML tags**

✔ **Selecting specific elements through class and id selectors**

✔ **Working with multiple elements in the same rule**

✔ **Selecting all elements in a document**

✔ **Performing some advanced selection techniques**

✔ **Exploring pseudo-classes and pseudo-elements**

CSS packs a warehouse full of styling properties and options that you can use to format your HTML documents. But it also sports something else that's as important but often overlooked: a powerful way to select the exact elements you want to format.

Fishermen know that different hooks are needed to catch different species of fish. Some fish go for a good old-fashioned hook and worm, whereas others are suckers for those mail-order specialty lures. In the same way, CSS provides several different types of selectors that you can use to specify the elements in your Web site that you want to apply formatting to. In this chapter, you explore how selectors work and put them to use in your style sheets.

Type Selectors: Selecting an Element by Its Type

A *type selector* allows you to select an element by its type by using the name of the element as the selector for the CSS rule. A type selector selects the element regardless of where it is inside the hierarchy of a document. Consider the following HTML document:

```
<html>
<head>
</head>
<body>
<h1>The Martians</h1>
<p>The Martians seem to have calculated their descent with
    amazing subtlety--<span>their mathematical learning is
    evidently far in excess of ours</span>--and to have
    carried out their preparations with a well-nigh perfect
    unanimity.</p>
<div>
<p>Had our instruments permitted it, we might have seen the
    <span>gathering trouble</span> far back in the nineteenth
    century.</p>
</div>
</body>
</html>
```

Suppose that you to color the span elements blue. To do so, use span as the
selector and then assign the color property a value of blue:

```
span { color: blue }
```

When this style is applied to the HTML document, the span text is displayed
in blue.

Class Selectors: Selecting an Element by Class

Using a *class selector*, you can also select HTML elements based on the value
of its class attribute, no matter its position in the document hierarchy. The
selector is defined as the name of the class prefixed by a dot.

Consider the following HTML document:

```
<html>
<head>
</head>
<body>
<h1 class="attn">The Martians</h1>
<p>The Martians seem to have calculated their descent with
    amazing subtlety--<span>their mathematical learning is
    evidently far in excess of ours</span>--and to have
    carried out their preparations with a <span
    class="attn">well-nigh</span> perfect unanimity.</p>
```

```
<div>
<p>Had our instruments permitted it, we might have seen the
   <span class="attn">gathering trouble</span> far back in
   the nineteenth century.</p>
</div>
</body>
</html>
```

Suppose that you want to color red the elements that have a `class` attribute set to `attn`. You can define a class selector for this operation this way:

```
.attn { color: red }
```

This rule colorizes both the h1 and the two span elements.

Combining type and class selectors

You can combine type and class selectors to narrow a particular selection. Suppose that you define the following rules:

```
/* Only applies to H1 with a class of attn */
h1.attn { color: red }

/* Only applies to span with a class of attn */
span.attn { color: blue}
```

The h1 is displayed in red, whereas the two span elements are colored blue.

Combining classes

CSS also enables you to combine classes for an element. Suppose that you have the following two style rules:

```
.attn { font-weight: bold }
.supersize { font-size: 160% }
```

TIP

Comments welcome

CSS supports comments, which enables you to add descriptive information inside your style sheet. Comments are identified by a `/*` at the start and `*/` at the end:

```
/* Add comment here */
```

If you're familiar with JavaScript, these comment symbols should be familiar to you.

If you have an element that you want to apply both rules to, you can place both of them in the same `class` attribute:

```
<span class="attn supersize">Hello, I am Michael, please
    notice me!</span>
```

ID Selectors: Selecting an Element by id

If you use `id` attributes to uniquely identify individual elements, you can use the attributes as a way to select specific elements from your HTML document. The key difference between an `id` selector and a `class` selector is that an `id` is used once per page, whereas a `class` can be applied to many elements on a given page.

An *id selector* is defined in your CSS rule by typing the `id` value, prefixed with a pound sign (#); for example:

```
#top {
    position: relative;
    width: 900px;
    margin: 0 auto;
}
```

This rule could then be applied to a `div` element with `top` as its `id`:

```
<div id="top"><img src="banner.jpg"/></div>
```

As with class selectors, you can combine type and `id` selectors. For example, the `#top` rule could also be defined as

```
div#top {
    position: relative;
    width: 900px;
    margin: 0 auto;
}
```

Universal Selectors: Selecting All Elements

Using a *universal selector*, you can select all elements inside a document by using the wildcard character (*). For example, to set a 0 margin for every element, you would use

```
* { margin: 0 }
```

Use care when declaring universal selectors because they can have unexpected side effects from working with inheritance (discussed in Chapter 1 of this minibook).

Multiple Selectors: Selecting More than One Element

You can select multiple elements for a rule by listing each element name in a comma-separated list. Suppose that you want all headings to have the Georgia typeface. Rather than define a rule for each heading separately, you can combine them into a single rule, such as

```
h1, h2, h3, h4, h5, h6 { font-family: Georgia }
```

You can also do this for class and id selectors. For example, to apply the same formatting to the blogitem and comments classes, you can define the following code:

```
.blogitem, .comments {
    display: block;
    padding: 2px 10px 15px 2px;
}
```

Descendant, Child, and Adjacent Sibling Selectors: Selecting an Element Based on Hierarchy

You can select elements based on their position in the overall document hierarchy in one of three ways: descendant, child, or adjacent sibling selectors.

Child and adjacent sibling selectors aren't supported in Microsoft Internet Explorer 6.0 or earlier, so use caution if using them in your style sheets.

Descendant selectors

A *descendant selector* selects elements based on their position in the document hierarchy. Consider the following sample document:

```
<html>
<head>
</head>
<body>
```

```
<h1>The Martians</h1>
<p>The Martians seem to have calculated their descent with
    amazing subtlety.</p>
<div>
<p>Had our instruments permitted it, we might have seen the
    gathering trouble far back in the nineteenth century.</p>
</div>
<div>
<p>"The chances against anything manlike on Mars are a
    million to one," he said.</p>
</div>
</body>
</html>
```

A type selector enables you to select all the paragraph elements, but if you want to select only the paragraphs inside the div elements, you can use a descendant selector:

```
div p { font-size: 9pt }
```

Note that the p doesn't have to be a child element of the div element, directly inside it. It just has to be a descendant somewhere in the hierarchy.

Child selectors

If you want to select an element that's a direct child of another element, you can use a child selector. A *child selector* separates the parent and child elements with a > arrow:

```
div > p { font-size: 9pt }
```

When you use this syntax, the right-side element must be a direct child of the element on the left.

Adjacent sibling selectors

This selector is used much less often, but it's worth a mention here. You select an element in an HTML document based on the element that's adjacent to it in a document. If two elements are separated with the + operator, the second element is selected only if it immediately follows the first element. For example, if an h1 is immediately followed by an h2 element, the following rule applies:

```
h1 + h2 { margin-top: -5px }
```

Attribute Selector: Selecting an Element by Attribute

Although you never display attributes with CSS, you can select elements based on their attributes. You can use these *attribute selectors* in three common ways:

✦ **Presence of an attribute:** To test an element to see whether it contains an attribute, place the attribute name in square brackets after the element name. For example, to select all `img` elements that have an `alt` attribute defined:

```
img[alt] { padding-right: 5px }
```

✦ **Exact value of an attribute:** To select an element based on the value of an attribute, you add the information to the selector. For example, the following line selects all `img` elements that have a particular `src` value:

```
img[src="banner.jpg"] { margin-top:1px }
```

✦ **Partial value of an attribute:** You can also select an element based on the partial value of an attribute by using a `~=` operator rather than an equal sign (=) and then writing a space-separated list of words. For example, to select all `img` elements with `alt` text that contains `"newswire"`:

```
img[alt~="newswire"] { margin: 5px }
```

Microsoft Internet Explorer versions 6.0 and earlier don't support selecting elements by attributes.

Understanding Pseudo-Classes and Pseudo-Elements

Pseudo-classes are a special type of selector that aren't based on the HTML code, but rather on conditions applied by the browser. The pseudo-class is defined by using this syntax:

elementname:pseudoclassname

Pseudo-classes are most commonly used with links. You can create a unique style for each of the different states of a link: unvisited, visited, active, and hover. For example, the following code defines pseudo-classes for an `a` link:

```
a:link     { color: black; text-decoration: none; }
a:active   { color: blue; text-decoration: none; }
a:visited  { color: gray; text-decoration: none; }
a:hover    { color: blue; text-decoration: underline; }
```

Pseudo-elements, on the other hand, are parts of an element. You can use pseudo-elements to specify formatting for the first letter and first line of a block level element, such as a paragraph or heading; for example:

```
p:first-line: { font-size: 110%; }
p:first-letter: { font-size: 300%; float: left; font-variant:
    small-caps; }
```

Chapter 3: Formatting Text

In This Chapter

✔ Assigning a typeface to your text

✔ Setting basic font properties

✔ Adding style to your text

✔ Colorizing your text

✔ Working with paragraph settings

*H*ey, you — *do this.* That's the essence of a CSS rule. The selector picks the elements to work with, and the properties assign formatting styles to them. In Chapter 2 of this minibook, we explain the *Hey, you* part, by focusing on the ins and outs of selecting different parts of your document. In this chapter, we follow up with the *do this* part for your text. We begin by showing you how to format various character properties before moving into paragraph properties.

At Face Value: Assigning a Font Face

One of the most important design decisions you make in your Web site is your font selection. Your font style either complements your overall design or clashes with it.

Whatever your ultimate selection, you need to be sure that the fonts you select are widely available on the computers of the people coming to your Web site. If the font you pick isn't available for the browser, the browser substitutes another, similar style font.

The most common fonts fall into two categories — *serif* and *sans serif.* A serif typeface has short cross lines, or curves, at the ends of its character strokes. Some common serif typefaces are Times Roman, Times, Garamond, and Palatino. Sans serif fonts are typefaces that don't have serifs. Helvetica, Arial, Verdana, and Lucida Grande are common serif typefaces.

Which font should you use?

As you consider the fonts to standardize for your Web site, consider these tips:

✔ You may want to select different fonts for your normal text and headings. However, don't choose more than one serif and one sans serif per page.

✔ Back in the early days of the Web, serif fonts, such as Times New Roman, were usually the default fonts for a Web page because studies have shown them to be more readable. Sans serif fonts were usually reserved for headlines. However, many Web designers are now choosing sans serif fonts as the standard font for body text.

✔ Georgia and Verdana are slightly larger at a given point size than other fonts in their family. The reason is that these two typefaces were created to be easy to read on a computer display.

Use the `font-family` property to define a set of fonts, organized by order of priority. This property can be composed of specific font names, generic font families (see Table 3-1), or (more commonly) both. Consider, for example, the declaration `font-family: Helvetica, Arial, Verdana, sans-serif;`. The browser would first look for Helvetica font. If that typeface isn't found, it tries to use Arial and then Verdana. Finally, if none of these is found, it reverts to any sans serif font it can find.

Table 3-1	Generic Font Family Names
Name	*Font example*
serif	Times New Roman
sans-serif	Arial, Lucida Grande
monospace	Courier New
cursive	Zapf-Chancery
fantasy	Andy, Critter

To define Arial to all p elements, you would write

```
p { font-family: Arial }
```

However, you often want to use a list of fonts rather than a single one. When you use a series of fonts, the browser tries your preferred font choice first (the first in the list). If this font isn't available, the browser continues down the list. Adding the appropriate generic font family name as a final item ensures that the general style of the typeface is used. Suppose that you want to use the sans serif style Lucida Grande font as the default font for your site, but you want to have a set of acceptable alternatives. You can define the rule in the body selector and have it look something like this:

```
body { font-family: "Lucida Grande", Arial, Verdana,
    sans-serif }
```

Notice that if the font name is composed of multiple words, you need to enclose the name in quotation marks.

In a second example, you want to assign the default paragraph font to be a serif font, headings to be sans serif, and a special `url` class to be in monospace. The CSS rules look like the following:

```
p { font-family: "Palatino Linotype", "Times New Roman",
    serif; }

h1,h2,h3 {font-family: "Lucida Grande", Arial, Verdana,
    sans-serif; }

p.url { font-family: "Courier New", Courier, monospace; }
```

If you're unsure how closely two typefaces match, look closely at the upper-case *Q* and the ampersand (&). These characters are among the most distinctive in the typeface alphabet.

Sizing Up Your Text

You can set the font size that uses CSS by using the `font-size` property. You have several different ways to specify an absolute or relative sized font:

✚ **Points:** Points are probably the most popular way in which we think of sizing a font because applications like Microsoft Word use points. A *point* is ½2 of an inch. The downside to points is that different screen resolutions can size points differently, so they may vary slightly from computer to computer. To specify a point size, use a numeric value along with `pt` following it. For example, to specify 10 point for a paragraph, use

```
p { font-size: 12pt; }
```

Em & ems: Melt in your mouth, not on the page

In the publishing world, the em is traditionally the width of the letter *m*. You may have heard the term *m dash* or *em dash*. It's a horizontal line — like these — that's equivalent to the width of the typeface's *m* (although it isn't strictly a precise equivalent in many typefaces).

Em units are different for each typeface and type size. As a result, using em allows you to specify what happens *relative* to the given font used in a browser. The result is in proportion to the other qualities of the typeface and surrounding text.

✦ **Pixels:** Pixels offer greater ability to precisely size your font, regardless of which screen resolution the page is displayed on. However, the downside is that if a user wants to have the fonts enlarged for visibility, pixel sizing doesn't adjust well to them. To specify a specific pixel size of a font, use a numeric value along with px following it:

```
p { font-size: 12px; }
```

✦ **Ems:** The *em* unit is one of the lesser known of the font sizing units, but it's a great choice to use. (See the sidebar named "Em & ems: Melt in your mouth, not on the page.") An *em* is the same as the font height, making it relative to the default browser font. One em is equal to the default browser font, which is commonly set to medium-size text by users. To specify a font size in ems, use a numeric value along with em after it. In this example, we're setting the paragraph font to be 90 percent of the size of the default font set by the user:

```
p { font-size: 0.9em; }
```

Because the *em* unit is relative to the user's browser settings, your page layout can potentially be adversely affected if the user chooses a default font size significantly larger than your design accounts for.

✦ **Absolute size keyword:** If unit sizes aren't your cup of tea, you can set the size based on the following keywords: xx-small, x-small, small, medium, large, x-large, and xx-large. For most browsers, medium is 10 point or 12 point with the other keywords proportional to that size. For example, the following line defines the h1 as extra-large:

```
h1 { font-size: x-large; }
```

✦ **Percentage:** To set a font size based on the relative percentage of the font size of the parent, you can specify a percentage value; Consider this example:

```
body { font-size: 10pt; }
p { font-size: 95%; }
h1 { font-size: 120%; }
```

In this example, the body element sets the main font to be 10pt. The default paragraph font is 95 percent of the body's font value (because the body will contain every paragraph), whereas h1 is 120 percent of the body's font setting.

✦ **Relative size keywords:** You also can set the size of a font relative to the parent element's font size by using the larger and smaller keywords. For example, to make the size of the span text smaller in proportion to its parent, you use

```
span { font-size: smaller; }
```

✦ **Other units of measurement:** Although points, pixels, and ems are the most commonly used units of measurement, others are available, including

- **Picas (pc):** Picas are a subset of points. One *pica* equals 12 points.

- **Millimeters (mm)**

- **Centimeters (cm)**

- **Inches (in)**

- **x-height (ex):** x-height is the distance between the tops of the lower-case letters (excluding ascenders, like the top of the *d* or *b*) and the imaginary line on which all the letters appear to rest (the *baseline*).

Giving Your Font a Makeover: Adding Style

Before CSS, your ability to add character styles to your text was limited to HTML's <b> (bold) and <i> (italics) tags. However, CSS provides many more properties and variations that you can use, including font-style, font-weight, font-variant, font-stretch, and text-decoration. We show you each of these in this section.

Adding italics with font-style

The `font-style` property is used to define italicized text. There are three values: `italic`, `normal`, or `oblique` (a fancy word for *slanted*); for example:

```
p { font-style: normal; }
span { font-style: italic; }
```

We recommend avoiding `oblique`. It merely tilts the normal typeface and looks inferior to normal italics.

Like two peas in a pod, bold and italics go hand in hand. If we want to highlight text, we tend to either bold or italicize or do a combination of the two. Even in Web design products such as Dreamweaver and Expression Web, the Bold and Italics controls are side by side. However, CSS separates them into individual properties. You don't set a bold property with `font-style`. Instead, bolding is done by using the `font-weight` property (see the next section).

Bolding your text with font-weight

The `font-weight` property is used to bold text. For common uses, the `normal` or `bold` keywords can be used; for example:

```
p .bodytext { font-weight: normal; }
p .intro { font-weight: bold; }
```

You can also specify a numeric value from 100 to 900 to specify the weight of text. A 100 value is the lightest, and 900 is the darkest. The `normal` keyword is equivalent to 400; `bold` is the same as 700.

Finally, you can use the keywords `lighter` and `bolder` to lighten or darken the text based on the relative value of the parent element.

Underline and decorate with text-decoration

The `text-decoration` property can be used to underline your text or apply other special formatting. The possible values are `underline`, `overline`, `line-through`, and `blink`. For example, to underline an `a:hover` pseudo-class, use the following rule:

```
a:hover { text-decoration: underline; }
```

Overlining (`overline`), which is used far less frequently, can be used for a visual effect or as a way of separating zones of text.

Bold or italic?

When should you use italic, bold, and under-lining? Most typefaces have several variants, with boldface and italic the most common. Boldface is most often used in headlines — big and thick — but it's used less often in body text because it can be distracting.

If you want to emphasize something in body text, you should normally use *italics* rather than **bold** or ALL CAPS.

However, nothing is set in stone. You may want to use bold formatting in your page text to give readers a way to quickly scan for important items. The classic example of this technique is a gossip column where the names of the celebrities are in bold. You use this technique in situations where you aren't using subhead-ings but you want to give readers an efficient way to skim through the text and locate topics of interest.

The `line-through` value is commonly known in other applications (such as Microsoft Word) as *strikethrough*.

The `blink` value generally isn't recommended because blinking text can be a first-class annoyance to readers.

Capping it with text-transform and font-variant

You can use the `text-transform` property to change the case of your text. The keyword values for this property are shown in Table 3-2.

Table 3-2	`text-transform` **Keyword Values**
Value	*What It Does*
capitalize	Changes the first character of each word to uppercase
uppercase	Changes all characters in the text to uppercase
lowercase	Changes all characters in the text to lowercase
none	Cancels the inherited value

For example, to change the text of an h2 element to uppercase, use this rule:

```
left h2 { text-transform: uppercase; }
```

The `font-variant` property can be used to set turn off and on small caps formatting. The two values are `normal` and `small-caps`. For example, if you want to apply small caps to the h1 element, you can use the following:

```
h1 { font-size: 1.2em; font-variant: small-caps; }
```

Spacing out your text

The `letter-spacing` and `word-spacing` properties can be used to increase or decrease the spacing between letters or words. The value is a specific length value (typically in em or pixel units) or the `normal` keyword. Suppose that you want to make a `#pathway` selector's `letter-spacing` value to be 15 percent of the normal spacing. You use the following rule:

```
#pathway { letter-spacing   : .15em; }
```

Reducing the space between some of the characters with `letter-spacing` often improves the look and readability of headings.

Flexing your text with font-stretch

The `font-stretch` property allows you to set condensed, extended, or normal typeface from a font family. There are several absolute keywords (ranging from most compressed to most expanded):

✦ `ultra-condensed`

✦ `extra-condensed`

✦ `condensed`

✦ `semi-condensed`

✦ `normal`

✦ `semi-expanded`

✦ `expanded`

✦ `extra-expanded`

✦ `ultra-expanded`

CSS also allows you to use the relative keywords `wider` and `narrower` to stretch or compress at the next value.

For example, to expand a `span` element to the maximum possible, use the following rule:

```
span { font-stretch: ultra-expanded; }
```

The `font-stretch` isn't widely supported in browsers and should be used with the expectation that many users may not see this font variation.

All-Inclusive: Putting It All Together with the font Property

In the earlier sections of this chapter, we show you how to apply font styles one at a time. But CSS provides the `font` "shorthand" property, which can be used to set the most common font-related settings in a single property. The properties you can set include `font-style`, `font-variant`, `font-weight`, `font-size`, `line-height`, and `font-family`. The syntax is

```
selector {
  font: font-style font-variant font-weight font-size/
    line-height font-family;
}
```

Each property is separated with a space (no semicolons or commas).

Note that the line height can be specified in the font property when you separate the font size and line height with a `/`.

The first three values in your list (`font-style`, `font-variant`, and `font-weight`) are optional and can be listed in any order. For example, you can reverse the order in the preceding with no ill effects:

```
p { font: italic bold 12px "Times New Roman", serif; }
```

However, the `font-size` and `font-family` properties are required (although `line-height` is optional) and must be in the correct order.

The following sample rules are defined by using the `font` property:

```
p { font: 12px "Trebuchet MS", Arial, Helvetica, sans-serif;
    }
td { font: 75%/1em Arial, Helvetica, sans-serif }
div { font: 10pt/11pt "Times New Roman", Times, serif }
span { font: 60% sans-serif }
p { font: italic bold 1.5em/2 Arial, Helvetica, sans-serif }
div #sidebar h1 { font: bold small-caps 130%/130% Arial,
    sans-serif }
```

Color Me Beautiful: Setting the Text Color

The color of text can be adjusted by using the `color` property. (No, there's no `text-color` property.) The value of the `color` property can be a reserved color keyword or an RGB color value:

✦ **Color keywords:** The 16 common keyword color names are aqua, black, blue, fuchsia, gray, green, lime, maroon, navy, olive, purple, red, silver, teal, white, and yellow. For example:

```
h1 { color: green; }
```

✦ **RGB hex number:** RGB (Red-Green-Blue) is the standard color encoding scheme that defines the color spectrum through separate numeric values (0–255) for red, green, and blue colors. The format of a RGB color value in hexadecimal notation is a pound (#) symbol followed by hexadecimal value representing the color. For example, to define black text, you use

```
body {color: #000000; }
```

✦ **RGB value:** You can also define a color by using the rgb(r, g, b) function in which r, g, and b are numbers (0 through 255) or percentages (0 to 100 percent); for example:

```
div { color: rgb(255, 0, 0); }
```

Formatting Paragraph Properties

CSS also has several paragraph-oriented properties that you can specify, including alignment, indentation, and line height.

Aligning text

Block style elements take up the full width of the page or container they are inside. The following sample elements are block level by default: p, div, headings (h1. . .h6), lists and list items (ul, ol, li), table, and form. You can set the text alignment of block level elements with the text-align property. The possible values are left, right, center, and justify. For example, to center align the h2 element, use the following rule:

```
h2 { text-align: center; }
```

Suppose that you want to center all content inside the browser and left-align the text. You can use text-align to perform both these alignment settings. A div (<div id=main></div>), which is the master container, centers all content. Two div elements (rightcolumn and leftcolumn) then set the text alignment to left:

```
#main { text-align: center; }
#rightcolumn, #leftcolumn { text-align: left; }
```

Indenting your text

The `text-indent` property sets the indention of text of the first line of the block level element. You can either use a positive or negative length (usually in em or pixel units) or a percentage relative to the parent. For example, if you want to slightly indent the first line of p, you add this rule:

```
p { text-indent: 2%; }
```

Adjusting the line height

The `line-height` property adjusts the height between lines in your block level element's text.

Line heights are often adjusted for two primary reasons: Headlines often look better with less white space between the lines, and normal body text is more readable with slightly *more* white space between its lines.

You can use a number, length (usually in em or pixel units), or percentage value. When a number is used, the line height is set by multiplying the number you provided with the font size. For example, to set a paragraph line height to be slightly more normal, you can specify

```
p { line-height: 1.35em; }
```

Here's a second example, using pixel units:

```
p#summary { font-size: 11px; line-height: 15px; }
```

Finally, to double-space a paragraph with a 12px font size, you can use any of the following:

```
p { line-height: 2; }
p { line-height: 2.0em; }
p { line-height: 200%; }
p { line-height: 24px; }
```

Chapter 4: The Gang of Four: Formatting Box Properties

In This Chapter

✓ Exploring block and inline elements

✓ Framing elements with padding and borders

✓ Adding space with margins

✓ Working with backgrounds

✓ Customizing the mouse cursor with CSS

*F*rom a CSS perspective, an HTML document is much like a UPS truck at Christmas time — boxes, boxes everywhere. A page is composed of a nested set of boxes that represent the various elements on the page. Every visible element has a rectangular region surrounding it. Although this rectangular box is normally invisible, you can define styles that format various parts of the box.

In this chapter, you explore how to format these four box-related properties: the *margin* around the element, a colored or shaded *border,* the *padding* between the border and content, and the background.

Understanding Blocks and Inline Elements

Each element, no matter whether it's a p, div, or span, is displayed on the page as a rectangle. This box can flow in the document as either a block or inline:

✦ A *block-level element* occupies the full width of the container it's inside. A block element begins on a new line, and the next block element begins on the next line of the document. The elements that are block level by default include p, div, h1...h6, ul, ol, li, table, and form. You can also define a block-level element with the display:block property.

✦ An *inline element* is added to the normal flow of the document. It occupies only the width that's required, not the whole line, and does not force a new line after it. A span is a notable example of an inline element. You can also define an inline element with the display:inline property.

The display property becomes especially important when you begin to position elements by using CSS. (See Chapter 5 for more on positioning.) However, it's also helpful to understand as you begin to format different parts of the element.

Discovering the "Box" Properties Surrounding an Element

You can think of an element on your page much like a painting on display in an art gallery. The painting itself is displayed on a canvas. It usually has a mat around it that adds space between the painting and the outer frame. The frame is either solid or decorated and helps give focus to the painting inside it. Finally, every framed painting has a certain amount of spacing between it and other paintings around it.

In much the same way, surrounding the content area of an element are optional padding (like the mat), border (like the picture frame), and margin (like the spacing from other art) properties, as shown in Figure 4-1.

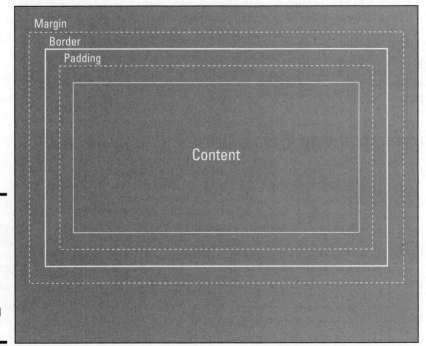

Figure 4-1:
An element's box is composed of its content, padding, border, and margins.

Understanding box dimensions

To determine the *width* of an element's box, add the content width to any left and right margins, borders, or padding. Likewise, the *height* of an element's box is the sum of the content height plus any top and bottom margins, borders, and padding.

For each of these elements, you can define all four sides by using its short-cut property (`padding`, `border`, and `margin`). When you do so, you define each side by starting at the top and going clockwise around the box in the following order: top, right, bottom, and left. For example, the following rule defines a 5 pixel space on the top, no right or left margin, and a 10-pixel bottom margin:

```
div #top { margin: 5px 0 10px 0; }
```

Alternatively, you can define individual sides through `-left`, `-right`, `-top`, and `-bottom` subproperties. We explain how in the sections that follow.

See Chapter 3 for more information on the units of measurement (such as ems or pixels) that you can work with in defining these properties.

Padding the Elements

The *padding* of an element is the amount of space between an element's content and its border. You can set this property by using the `padding` property. Acceptable values are lengths (usually in `em` or `px` units) or percentage values. For example, to add a slight padding to all four sides of a `div` element, you can use the following rule:

```
div { padding: .5em; }
```

You can also use `padding-top`, `padding-right`, `padding-bottom`, or `padding-left` to specify the padding on one of the box sides. The following rule uses these subproperties to define left and right padding:

```
img .leftside { padding-left: 10px; padding-right: 0px; }
img .rightside {  padding-left: 0px; padding-right: 10px; }
```

Making a Run for the Border

A *border* surrounds the content of an element, by surrounding any padding that you specified for an element. Margins, on the other hand, lie outside the border frame and separate the element from elements around it. Whereas the `padding` and the `margin` properties of an element deal only with size, a border has more properties to think about, including border style, width, and color.

border-style

The `border-style` property is required for setting the border. Because the property defaults to `none`, you need to explicitly define it, or else the other border properties (`border-width` and `border-color`) are simply ignored. There are nine border styles, as shown in Table 4-1.

Table 4-1	`border-style` **Values**
Value	*Border Appearance*
none	No border, causing the `border-width` and `border-color` values to be disregarded (default)
solid	Solid line
dotted	Dotted line
dashed	Dashed line
double	Double line (two single lines and the space between equals the `border-width` value)
groove	3D groove (based on color value)
ridge	3D ridge (based on color value)
inset	3D inset (based on color value)
outset	3D outset (based on color value)

You can also define the style for one of the box borders by using `border-top-style`, `border-right-style`, `border-bottom-style`, or `border-left-style`.

Figure 4-2 shows the various border styles (using a very wide 8-pixel border) when rendered by Internet Explorer. Other browsers may display the border styles slightly differently. For example, Firefox renders dotted lines as small dashed lines. Firefox also employs black, rather than gray, for the shadows in the bottom four, frame-like, borders.

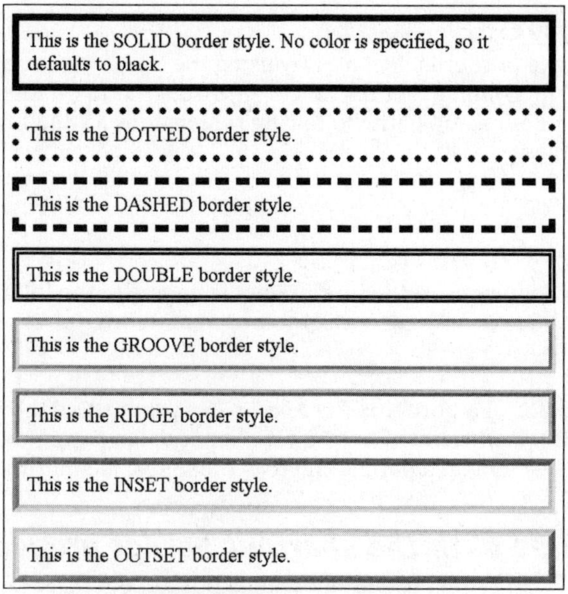

This is the SOLID border style. No color is specified, so it defaults to black.

This is the DOTTED border style.

This is the DASHED border style.

This is the DOUBLE border style.

This is the GROOVE border style.

This is the RIDGE border style.

This is the INSET border style.

This is the OUTSET border style.

Figure 4-2:
The border
styles you
can specify.

border-width

You can assign a width to the entire box by using the `border-width` property. Possible values are the width keywords (`thin`, `medium`, or `thick`) or a relative length value (usually in `em` units). The default width is `medium`, which is the equivalent of 2 or 3 pixels.

You can specify the size of one of the border sides by using the `border-top-width`, `border-right-width`, `border-bottom-width`, or `border-left-width` property.

Suppose that you want to add a medium solid border to a particular `div` element and a thin groove border to the second `div` element. Here's the style code:

```
#div_one { border-width: medium; border-style: solid; }
#div_two { border-width: thin; border-style: groove; }
```

Use the width keywords to ensure consistent border widths across your Web site. Because the width keywords are absolutely sized, thin, medium, and thick are identically sized regardless of the font size of a given element. However, if you use a relative units (such as ems), the border size varies on the size of the element's font.

border-color

The color of the border is declared by using the `border-color` property and accepts the common set of CSS colors discussed in Chapter 3 concerning text color. For example, the following rule defines a solid blue thin border for a link element:

```
a { border-style: solid; border-width: thin; border-color:
   blue; }
```

You can also define one of the borders by using one of the following: `border-top-color`, `border-right-color`, `border-bottom-color`, or `border-left-color`.

The default color of a border is the text `color` property of the element (usually black). If an element has no text (an `img`, for example), the `color` property of the element's parent (such as the `body`) is inherited.

Saving time with the shortcut border property

You can use `border` (along with individual border sides `border-top`, `border-right`, `border-bottom`, and `border-left`) as a shortcut property to define the border width, style, and color in a single statement. The general syntax is

```
selector { border: border-width border-style border-color; }
```

Using the shorthand property, you can condense the earlier link property definition into a single statement:

```
a { border: thin solid blue; }
```

We recommend that you stay conservative and subtle in your use of borders. In almost every case, a relatively thin, solid border looks far more attractive than some specialty borders. For example, Rich uses the following style for his images on his Web site:

```
img { border: 6px #fff solid; margin: 0px 0px 5px 0px; }
```

Figures 4-3 and 4-4 show how Rich uses this style fin two portions of his home page.

My Favorite Films of All Time

1. Casablanca
2. The Shawshank Redemption
3. It's A Wonderful Life
4. Babette's Feast
5. Field of Dreams
6. Pride & Prejudice (A&E Version)
7. The Band of Brothers (HBO)
8. Chariots of Fire
9. Amélie (Le Fabuleux destin d'Amélie Poulain)
10. Groundhog Day
11. Braveheart
12. Princess Bride
13. Les Miserables (1998 version)
14. Signs
15. The Lord of the Rings trilogy
16. Benny & Joon
17. Vertigo
18. Sense & Sensibility
19. The Count of Monte Cristo
20. A Little Princess
21. Double Indemnity
22. Forrest Gump
23. The Incredibles
24. The African Queen
25. Henry V (1989 version)
26. The Truman Show

Figure 4-3:
A solid
border can
be used to
make an
image blend
well into the
overall
design.

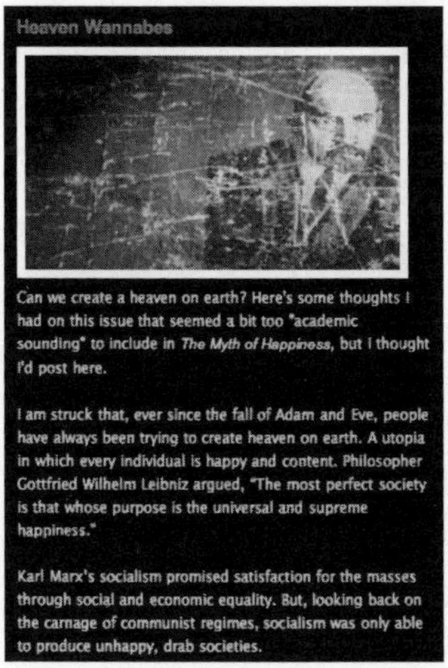

Heaven Wannabes

Can we create a heaven on earth? Here's some thoughts I
had on this issue that seemed a bit too "academic
sounding" to include in *The Myth of Happiness*, but I thought
I'd post here.

I am struck that, ever since the fall of Adam and Eve, people
have always been trying to create heaven on earth. A utopia
in which every individual is happy and content. Philosopher
Gottfried Wilhelm Leibniz argued, "The most perfect society
is that whose purpose is the universal and supreme
happiness."

Karl Marx's socialism promised satisfaction for the masses
through social and economic equality. But, looking back on
the carnage of communist regimes, socialism was only able
to produce unhappy, drab societies.

Figure 4-4:
Padding is
eliminated
to create an
interesting
effect with
the image
and border.

Mixing and matching borders

You don't need to surround an element with all four sides of a frame. You can define only the borders that make sense in your Web site design. For example, if you want to define a thin border on the right and bottom sides of your images, you can use this declaration:

```
img { border-style: none solid solid none; border-width:
   thin; }
```

Or, consider a gaudier example. Suppose that you want to style the borders of images so that the top and right are dotted and the left is dashed. As you can see from the following code snippet, we used the none style to remove the bottom border:

```
img { border-style: dotted dotted none dashed; }
```

This code results in the odd, mixed-border look shown in Figure 4-5.

Figure 4-5:
Mix and
match
borders, if
you want.

A final example shows you how to use the inset command with colors to create a beveled look. Here's the CSS and HTML code:

```
<html>
<head>
<style type="text/css">
```

```
img {
  border-top: silver inset;
  border-right: silver inset;
  border-bottom: silver inset;
  border-left: silver inset;
  border-width: 12px;
}
</style>
</head>
<body>
<img src="ghouse.jpg" alt="ghouse.jpg" width="320px"
    height="264px" alt="My House"/>
</body>
</html>
```

Figure 4-6 shows the result.

Figure 4-6:
Use the
`inset`
command to
create a
border like
this.

Give Me Some Space: Adding Margins around An Element

The `margin` property is used to set the amount of space between the element box and other elements. You can define the property in unit lengths (often using ems or pixels), percentage value, or the keyword `auto`.

You can also specify the margin for one side of the element by using `margin-top`, `margin-left`, `margin-right`, and `margin-bottom`.

Suppose that you want to add a small amount of space after each h1 heading. To do so, add a bottom margin with this code:

```
h1 { margin-bottom: .75em }
```

The margin is always transparent, enabling the parent element's background to show through.

The auto constant is used to center an element either horizontally or vertically. Because margin: auto deals with positioning, we show you how to work with it in Chapter 5.

Zeroing out default margin and padding settings

Many browsers add a default margin and padding around block level elements. Although this can be handy for normal page composition, it can be problematic when you're trying to achieve a more precise design effect. You can ensure that you're starting from a level margin and padding the playing field by adding the following to the body element:

```
body { margin: 0; padding: 0; }
```

Using automatic margins with auto

When specifying the size of content or a margin, you can use specific measurements, such as 1em or 15px. Alternatively, you can use the auto keyword to let the browser calculate the correct measurement. Suppose that you want to maintain a fixed margin of 15px on the right of a paragraph but want the browser to automatically set the left margin so that the 15px right margin is always maintained. The code looks like this:

```
p { margin-right: 15px; margin-left: auto; }
```

The result of this style is that the paragraph is frozen at a specific horizontal location within the browser window (15 pixels from the right), even if the user stretches or shrinks the browser window.

As shown in this example, if you specify left and right margins but don't specify the width of an element, the element stretches its width to accommodate and maintain the requested margins.

However, if you set all three properties dealing with horizontal space — width, margin-left, and margin-right — to an absolute size (such as 250px), you can easily create a rule that the browser can't logically apply. As a result, one of these three width measurements must give way to the others. The margin-right property is the only setting ignored by the browser and its value is, in effect, treated as being auto.

Adding a Background

Every element has a background property that's transparent by default but can be assigned with the `background` properties. The background of an element lies behind its content and padding but does not include the border or margin. The background is applied to the element box regardless of whether it is block level or inline.

You can assign a color or image as the background of an element by using either the `background-color` or `background-image` properties:

✦ The `background-color` property can take any color value or the keyword `transparent`. For example, to set the `body` background to black, use the following line:

```
body { background-color: #000000; }
```

✦ The `background-image` property displays the specified image as the background and accepts either a URL (by using the `url()` function) or the `none` keyword. For example, to set an image as the background for the document body, use this:

```
body { background-image: url( "/images/bg.gif" ); }
```

The value of the `url` function can be inside quotes or not. Therefore, the following code also works:

```
body { background-image: url( /images/bg.gif ); }
```

You can use the `background-repeat` property to specify how the image should be repeated if space permits in the element's box region. Possible values are shown in Table 4-2.

Table 4-2	`background-repeat` **Values**
Value	*Image Is Displayed As*
`repeat`	Repeated both horizontally and vertically
`repeat-x`	Repeated horizontally
`repeat-y`	Repeated vertically
`no-repeat`	Not repeated

For example, to repeat a background image vertically for the entire body, you can use the following:

```
body {
  background-image: url( "../images/bg.gif" );
  background-repeat: repeat-y;
}
```

Getting Mousy with the Cursor

We want to mention one more CSS property in this chapter. Although it's less useful than the other box properties we discuss in this chapter, it can be helpful under certain situations.

CSS enables you to modify the shape of the cursor when it moves over an element with the `cursor` property. The list of common cursor values is shown in Table 4-3.

Table 4-3	Common `cursor` Keywords
Keyword	*What It Displays*
`auto, default`	Normal mouse cursor
`wait`	Hourglass cursor
`crosshair`	Gun-style crosshair cursor
`text`	I-beam text selection cursor
`pointer`	Hand cursor
`help`	Question mark cursor

For example, to change the mouse cursor to the question mark shape when the mouse hovers a link, you use

```
a { cursor: help; }
```

Chapter 5: Positioning with CSS

In This Chapter

✔ Centering elements on the page

✔ Floating elements on a page

✔ Adjusting the flow of floating elements

✔ Creating a div-based layout

✔ Aligning text vertically

✔ Styling horizontal lines

C SS does more than just style your Web page. You can also use it to position your elements. In this chapter, we begin by showing you how to center your elements on the page. Next, you explore how to create floating elements to create powerful, easy-to-use layouts. Finally, we wrap up with a discussion on how to align your text vertically inside an element.

Also, if you want to explore the absolute positioning of div elements by using CSS inside Dreamweaver, check out Book IV.

Centering Elements on the Page

You can center an element horizontally by setting the left and right margins to auto. Suppose that you have a fixed width div element (with an id="main") that serves as the container of all content in your page. By default, the div aligns itself to the left side of the browser. However, by setting the left and right margins to auto, it centers the element in the middle of the browser. After you add a zero margin at the top, here's the code:

```
#main {
  width: 796px;
  margin-left: auto;
  margin-right: auto;
  margin-top: 0;
}
```

However, here's a shortcut way to compact the three properties into a single declaration:

```
#main {
  width: 796px;
  margin: 0 auto;
}
```

Although this technique is the preferred way to horizontally center with CSS, you need to add additional rules to account for a bug in earlier versions of Internet Explorer that didn't work right with this CSS rule. Specifically, you need to center everything in the body with `text-align: center` and then reset the `text-align` property in child elements by using `text-align: left`. Here's how the centering code now looks:

```
body {
  text-align: center;        /* IE workaround */
}

#main {
  width: 796px;
  margin: 0 auto;
  text-align: left;          /* IE workaround */
}
```

Breaking Normal Flow with Floating Elements

As we discuss in Chapter 4 of this minibook, most of the page elements you format — such as paragraphs and `divs` — are block elements. When you add them to your page, they're added to the normal top-to-bottom "flow" of the document. The block level element takes up the full width of the container it's inside of and separates itself from other block elements with a line before and after it.

However, you can use the `float` property to break out of the normal body text flow. When you assign the float property to an element, it becomes a "floating" block and you can specify whether it should moved to the left or right of the current line. The possible values are `left`, `right`, and `none`.

When you float an element, the browser moves the element as far to the left or right as possible at the current line in which the element is defined. Therefore, block level elements defined in the HTML code above the floating element aren't affected. However, block level elements below it wrap around the floating element and flow its content down the side (the right side of a left float and the left side of a right float).

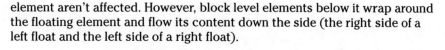

To float an element, you must explicitly define its width. Otherwise, results can be unpredictable when rendered by the browser.

To demonstrate, we begin with a mini-example to show you how it works and then move on to a full example. Here's a mini HTML document:

```
<html>
<head>
</head>
<body>

<div id="sidebar">
<h2>Sidebar</h2>
<p>Sidebar text.</p>
</div>

<h1>Main Content</h1>
<p>Regular document text.</p>

</body>
</html>
```

In this example, we want float the `div` on the right side of the page to function like a sidebar. To do so, we define the following CSS style:

```
#sidebar {
  float: right;
  width: 150px;
  margin: 0px 20px 5px 10px;
}
```

The rule sets the float to the right, sets the width of the block element to 150px, and then assigns a margin to add some spacing between the floating element and the rest of the page.

Listing 5-1 shows the same logic in a full HTML document (complete with dummy text).

Listing 5-1   Floating_element.html

```
<!DOCTYPE html PUBLIC "-//W3C//DTD XHTML 1.0 Transitional//EN"
    "http://www.w3.org/TR/xhtml1/DTD/xhtml1-transitional.dtd">
<html xmlns="http://www.w3.org/1999/xhtml">
<head>
<meta http-equiv="Content-Type" content="text/html; charset=UTF-8" />
<title>Floating Me</title>
<style type="text/css">

body {
    color: #FFFFFF;
    background-color: #000000;
    font-family: 'Lucida Grande', Arial, Helvetica, Tahoma, sans;
    font-size: 11px;
}

#sidebar {
  float: right;
  width: 150px;
  margin: 0px 20px 5px 10px;
}

</style></head>

<body>
<div id="sidebar">
<h2>Sidebar</h2>
<p>Lobortis aenean. Tincidunt lacinia, phasellus turpis, fringilla rhoncus. In
    tortor magna, vitae litora ipsum, quis vitae. Cras nunc, sit integer, turpis
    nulla. Amet vitae vehicula, congue ante.
  Felis nullam mauris. Turpis vitae. Pretium cum ipsum, cursus duis. Enim ut a,
    at ut sodales, gravida lacus. At nullam.
  Non donec in, metus sed sed. Phasellus mi dui, amet possimus dui. Libero eget,
    dolor urna ipsum. Sed nullam, nunc mauris. Vitae ullamcorper vestibulum, dis
    est, iaculis nullam.
  Ipsum fringilla, quisque amet sapien. Omnis suspendisse praesent, vel justo
    justo, phasellus ullamcorper. Quam montes. Odio nibh. Mauris hac. Nulla
    eget.
  Mauris felis, suspendisse odio. Amet dui. Amet pellentesque. Viverra justo
    alias, metus tristique ut. Quam inceptos, sodales egestas, erat ullamcorper
    fringilla.</p>
</div>
<h1>Main Content</h1>
<p>Lorem ipsum dolor sit amet, id ante imperdiet tortor dignissim laoreet,
    vehicula in etiam et, donec lectus gravida ultrices in sed duis, vestibulum
    eiusmod purus adipiscing dictumst vivamus. Varius rhoncus, dignissim
    dignissim. Ac sollicitudin, aliquam pede fames, pretium ridiculus gravida
    accumsan massa. Amet odio aliquet facilis suspendisse elementum convallis,
    mauris dictum malesuada mattis aenean, scelerisque dui elit, eu facilisi
    sodales tortor viverra augue elit, neque amet suscipit magna neque ac. Massa
    tortor vestibulum phasellus neque nec, nec orci quam, mauris elit pretium
    fermentum sociosqu nihil massa, suscipit suspendisse. Dolor praesent.
    Suspendisse ac felis egestas reprehenderit sem morbi, ut enim semper lacus,
    lorem sit. Nunc tempor ultricies nunc. Et suscipit metus velit, morbi orci
    ultrices pellentesque dui suspendisse curabitur, ultricies ultrices lacinia
    ut varius nunc, elit mi. Ut tempor curabitur facilisis velit magna maecenas,
    lectus vel et mattis, laoreet dolor ornare, ipsum vitae sagittis tristique,
    ornare libero.</p>
```

```
<p>  Ultricies libero, mauris parturient, dolor rhoncus, suscipit nunc nemo
     blandit risus malesuada, quisque varius aliquam et. Nunc in posuere auctor.
     Habitasse sed lorem, elit sociis. Vivamus ipsum est ac sed fermentum libero,
     eget sit diam neque lorem varius. Mauris senectus dolor, habitasse sodales.
     Auctor suspendisse, dolor eget augue vestibulum at tellus, congue neque ac
     vel hac ipsum nulla, ut eu porttitor, vel porttitor.</p>
<p>  Sem pharetra elit penatibus. Eu ante, adipiscing porta lacus lacus, ut
     integer, hendrerit turpis sodales dictum vulputate. Neque dui lorem congue
     erat ligula sed, aliquam vitae, non posuere felis quam massa mollis autem.
     Vel curabitur turpis cum, sed vitae tempor, libero interdum quam nonummy,
     non arcu tempor dignissim feugiat. Etiam elit eget, nulla in eget at, sed
     dui nec sem eget lorem tellus, velit mauris magna a morbi ipsum tellus.
     Suspendisse maecenas convallis, mi libero rutrum, nec dapibus rutrum. Nullam
     felis diam tempora etiam, ut nunc laoreet vulputate fringilla justo.</p>
<p>  Amet amet diam, sollicitudin nullam felis odio sit in, vivamus suspendisse
     aliquam eget, amet neque libero ipsum magni aliquam dictum, vitae wisi.
     Sollicitudin scelerisque curabitur vitae hendrerit ut malesuada, dapibus
     placerat amet volutpat nisl ullamcorper neque, integer bibendum, fringilla
     vel elementum lacus auctor vel. Nulla sed interdum sociosqu ac. Et urna, ac
     wisi non lorem at sociis commodo, purus aliquam posuere. Risus quam sed amet
     metus ac. A nam duis. Id sed ante aliquam integer cursus, quis dui
     vestibulum quis, vitae tristique lorem nonummy, lacus nibh. </p>
<p>Lorem ipsum dolor sit amet, suspendisse odio. Turpis litora. Vivamus feugiat.
     Dui quis nulla. Nisl ultricies orci, dis id et, nunc vel sit.</p>

</body>
</html>
```

Figure 5-1 shows the results displayed in a browser.

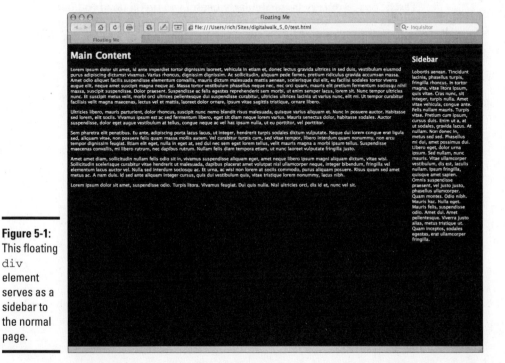

Figure 5-1:
This floating
`div`
element
serves as a
sidebar to
the normal
page.

When you're determining the overall width that your element will occupy on a page, be sure to account for the padding, border, margin, and content width.

Tweaking a Float with clear

When you use the float property, you may occasionally want to add further control over the flow of the document around the floating element. You can use the clear property to prevent an element from appearing in the same horizontal space as the floating panel. The possible values include: left, right, both, and none.

When an element has a left, right, or both value assigned to the clear property, it's pushed down below the floating element and rendered on the next available line.

Suppose that you want to ensure that a heading is displayed below a floating image:

```
<img src="monkey_sighting.gif" height="230" width="40"
    style="float: right">
<h1 style="clear: right">Monkey Sighted at HBC</h1>
```

The clear property is particularly useful when you need to float multiple images or divs on top of each other rather than side by side. Suppose that you want to display three images on the right side of a page. You assign them with a class of floatMonth:

```
<html>
<head>
</head>
<body>
<img src="nov.png" class="floatMonth">
<img src="dec.png" class="floatMonth">
<img src="jan.png" class="floatMonth">
<p>These images show the results of the last three months of
    the sales performance for...</p>
</body>
</head>
```

You could then define a CSS class that uses clear and float:

```
img.floatMonth {
  float: right;
  clear: right;
  margin: 5px;
}
```

The `clear` property forces each the images to be displayed top down, with the normal paragraph text flowing alongside on the left.

Creating a Layout Using float and clear

After you get comfortable working with the `float` and `clear` properties, you can begin to grasp the power that these CSS styles can give you when designing a page. Suppose that you want to create a three-column page layout with a header and footer. Using `div` elements for these block sections, here's the basic HTML:

```
<html>
<head>
<title>Three Column Liquid Layout</title>
</head>
<body>
<div id="header">Header</div>
<div id="leftcolumn">Left column</div>
<div id="rightcolumn">Right column</div>
<div id="bodytext">Main page text goes here.</div>
<div id="footer">Footer</div>
</body>
</html>
```

Without CSS, these block level elements would be displayed sequentially, from top to bottom on the page. However, by using the `float` and `clear` properties, you can transform this basic structure into the sophisticated page layout you're after.

To begin, zero all default `margin` and `padding` settings with the following rule:

```
body {  margin: 0px; padding: 0px; }
```

Next, the `header` and `footer` `div` elements need to span the entire width of the page (100 percent width). However, because the `footer` `div` is last, you also need to explicitly use clear: both to ensure that it's always positioned beneath the leftcolumn, rightcolumn, and bodytext div elements. Here are the rules to style these two elements:

```
#header {
    width: 100%;
    background-color: #CCCCCC;
}

#footer {
    width: 100%;
    clear: both;
    background-color: #CCCCCC;
}
```

The middle div elements contain the page content. You define the widths of these three blocks to be percentage-based: The bodytext column gets 60 percent of the width, and leftcolumn and rightcolumn each get 20 percent. leftcolumn floats left, and rightcolumn floats right, but you also set the bodytext float to the left so that it fits well into this structure. Here's the code:

```
#leftcolumn {
    float: left;
    width: 20%;
    height: 600px;
    background-color: #999999;
}

#rightcolumn {
    float: right;
    width: 20%;
    height: 600px;
    background-color: #999999;
}

#bodytext {
  float: left;
  background: #fff;
  width: 60%;
  height: 600px;
}
```

Because this page layout expands or contracts based on the size of the browser window, it's often called a *liquid* layout. If you want to fix the size of the columns, you can change the width percentage values to an absolute unit value (such as pixels or ems). This *fixed* layout isn't resized based on the size of the browser window.

Listing 5-2 shows the full code for this example.

Listing 5-2   Three-Column Liquid Layout

```
<html>
<head>
<title>Three Column Liquid Layout</title>
<style type="text/css">
body {   margin: 0px; padding: 0px; }

#header {
    width: 100%;
    background-color: #CCCCCC;
}

#footer {
    width: 100%;
    clear: both;
    background-color: #CCCCCC;
}

#leftcolumn {
    float: left;
    width: 20%;
    height: 600px;
    background-color: #999999;
}

#rightcolumn {
    float: right;
    width: 20%;
    height: 600px;
    background-color: #999999;
}

#bodytext {
  float: left;
  background: #fff;
  width: 59%;
  height: 600px;
}
</style>
</head>
<body>
<div id="header">Header</div>
<div id="leftcolumn">Left column</div>
<div id="rightcolumn">Right column</div>
<div id="bodytext">Main page text goes here.</div>
<div id="footer">Footer</div>
</body>
</html>
```

Figure 5-2 shows the results of this page layout in a browser.

Figure 5-2:
A liquid
layout takes
advantage
of floating
`div`
elements.

Aligning Text Vertically

The `vertical-align` property specifies how text aligns vertically in relation to another element, such as other text (superscripting, for example) or to an image (captioning, for example).

You can give the `vertical-align` property any of the following eight descriptive values: `bottom`, `baseline`, `middle`, `sub`, `super`, `text-top`, `text-bottom`, and `top`. Or, you can supply a specific measurement (such as 4px) or a percentage.

The alignment is made relative to any `line-height` property used with the text. Most values that can be used with `vertical-align` are self describing, but `text-bottom` means that the baseline is ignored and that the imaginary line is drawn at the bottom of the typeface's descenders (such as a line at the bottom of the letters *p* and *y,* which both have descenders).

The *baseline* is an imaginary line drawn between characters that have no descenders. The baseline is the default to which everything aligns unless you specify otherwise with the `vertical-align` property.

Superscripting

You can achieve superscripting (such as adding a degree symbol to a temperature) by modifying the vertical alignment. Superscripted (and subscripted) characters are often printed in a smaller typeface than the surrounding text (think of footnote numbers, for example). However, if you superscript (or subscript) a character by using the `vertical-align` property, the character's text size isn't automatically reduced. If you want that effect, you can add a font size specification to your style. To get the effect you want — both superscription and text size reduction — you should combine the `super` value with a percentage downsizing of the `font-size` property. Here's an example:

```
<html>
<head>
<style type="text/css">
  span.super { vertical-align:
    super; font-size: 70%; }
</style>
</head>
<body>
<p>Hello, I am here to
    stay<span
    class="super">SUPER-
    SCRIPT</span>.
</p>
</body>
</html>
```

Book VI

HTML/XHTML

The 5th Wave   By Rich Tennant

Contents at a Glance

Chapter 1: Exploring HTML and XHTML Documents

In This Chapter

✓ Understanding HTML tags and formatting

✓ Knowing why XHTML is important to use

✓ Finding out about DOCTYPE declarations

✓ Exploring the structure of a Web page

*1*f I were to sit down with Peter Jackson and watch any of *The Lord of the Rings* epics, the film I would view would be quite different from the one he would see. Through "movie magic," I would be transported to Middle-earth alongside Frodo, Sam, Aragorn, and the rest of the Fellowship as I rooted for them to succeed in their quest to destroy the Ring. In contrast, Peter surely would not look at what was on-screen as much as he would replay what was going behind the scenes. He would likely remember the exact special effect that was used in a particular shot, the last-minute script edit that was made, or the specific camera angle someone suggested.

In the same way, you can view Web pages differently, depending on your point of view. You can look at the page as it's presented to you in the browser. Or, if you have an understanding of HTML and XHTML, you can consider what's going on "under the hood." In this chapter, you discover the basic tasks that go on behind the scenes of any Web page. What's more, after you get a solid understanding of this concept, perhaps you will want to join the Fellowship of the HTML.

Before starting on your journey, open your favorite text editor and browser so that you can try out the examples in this chapter.

Under the Hood: Understanding HTML

A Web page is written in *Hypertext Markup Language (HTML),* a tag-based programming language used for presenting information. It consists of two types of data:

✦ **Content:** Text and graphics that you want to display on the page.

✦ **Instructions:** A defined set of formatting elements, or *tags,* that determine how text and graphics are displayed and arranged on a page. These instructions are invisible when the page is displayed in a browser.

Most of the elements you normally work with format content: They specify the font or style of a paragraph of text, the exact placement of a JPG photo, or the number of rows in a table, for example. However, a few other elements apply more generally to the entire HTML document: They specify the title of the page or the structure of the document, for example.

When a browser opens a Web page, the browser presents the content based on the instructions contained in the page.

Opening and closing tags

HTML elements usually consist of a pair of tags that are denoted by angle brackets that enclose a piece of content:

```
<element>Content</element>
```

The *opening tag* (`<element>`) declares the start of an instruction to be performed. The *closing tag* (`</element>`) specifies the end of the instruction. Everything inside the opening and closing tags is considered the element's *content.* As you can see from this example, the opening and closing tags are nearly the same, except that the closing tag has a forward slash (/) just before the element name.

Suppose that you want to format a sentence in a Web page so that it looks like this:

> **Phil:** There is no way this winter is *ever* going to end as long as that groundhog keeps seeing his shadow.

The HTML code you write looks like this:

```
<p><strong>Phil:</strong>There is no way this winter is
    <em>ever</em>going to end as long as that groundhog keeps
    seeing his shadow.</p>
```

Because the p element is used to define a paragraph, everything inside the start and end p tags is considered to be in it. The strong element declares bold text, so text inside it is bolded. The em element is for italicized words, so all the text inside the em element is formatted in italic.

As you can see in the previous example, you often need to nest or enclose elements inside other elements. When you do so, you apply multiple elements to some or all of the same content. The p element contains all the text of the paragraph as well as the nested `strong` and `em` elements, both of which apply to only a single word of the paragraph.

Now suppose that you want to make a piece of text both bold and italic. You surround the text with both elements:

```
<strong><em>Mind over matter.</em></strong>
```

In well-written HTML, the element that appears first in the code must close last. As you develop Web pages, follow this rule: In first, last out; last in, first out. Older-style HTML was somewhat flexible in being able to close elements in varying orders.

Case doesn't matter — sort of

In traditional HTML, tags are case insensitive. Therefore, all the following lines of HTML code are treated identically by a browser:

```
<strong>Phil:</strong>
<STRONG>Phil:</STRONG>
<Strong>Phil:</Strong>
<sTRONG>Phil:</StRoNg>
```

In years past, personal preference usually determined the case of tags. SOME PEOPLE LIKED UPPERCASE. others preferred lowercase. A Few Oddballs Liked Mixed Case.

In XHTML, all elements must be in lowercase. Although case doesn't matter to HTML, it makes a *big* difference with XHTML, HTML's successor (which is discussed later in this chapter). We strongly recommend using lowercase for your HTML coding, to avoid problems later.

The devil is in the attributes

If the expression "The devil is in the details" is true, watch out for attributes. Most elements also include additional information inside the opening tag. These *attributes* further define the behavior of the HTML element. An attribute is expressed as a *name-value pair*, with the attribute name on the left side of the equal sign and the value on the right side:

```
<element attributename="attributevalue">Content</element>
```

The attribute value is normally enclosed in quotes. And, although traditional HTML considers quotation marks optional, we recommend getting used to using them because XHTML requires them.

Consider the a element as an example. It declares a hyperlink:

```
<a>Visit my home page.</a>
```

You can see that the a opening and closing tags used by themselves are insufficient. I specified which text should be hyperlinked but didn't tell the browser where to go when the text is clicked. The href attribute provides that vital piece of information:

```
<a href="http://www.digitalwalk.net">Visit my home page.</a>
```

Although many attributes are optional, some elements (such as the a element example) have required attributes.

Blanks are blanked

HTML doesn't do much with blank spaces, tabs, and empty lines when formatting text on a page. In fact, it ignores them! As a result, both of the following paragraphs are presented the same way in a browser:

```
<p><strong>XHTML</strong> is the next big thing.</p>
```

is equivalent to

```
<p>             <strong>XHTML</strong>   is      the       next
big
thing.</p>
```

Both lines are displayed this way:

```
XHTML is the next big thing.
```

HTML's way of dealing with spaces lets you be flexible in writing your HTML documents, but you can't resort to good old-fashioned tabs and spaces for manual formatting and text alignment. Instead, you need to use HTML-specific instructions for that sort of thing.

XHTML: An Extreme HTML Makeover

The HTML markup language spawned the Web revolution, back in the 1990s. However, as the popularity of the Web grew, the shortcomings of the markup language became increasingly apparent to Web designers. The biggest problem with HTML is its *laissez-faire* flexibility: inconsistent rules and sloppy shortcuts, for example. The laxness of HTML is reminiscent of a grandfatherly teacher not in control of his classroom: He sees his students turning in papers late and only partially answering questions. However, rather than discipline them, he simply shrugs his shoulders and says, "I'm sure they mean well."

The problem is that HTML's flexibility leads to ambiguity and other problems in trying to process more complex pages in more complex platforms and environments, such as cellphones and handheld devices.

Enter XHTML. Built on the Extensible Markup Language (XML) technology, XHTML is a better organized and structured version of HTML.

Because all future Web development will focus on XHTML, I strongly recommend using XHTML to develop your Web pages.

Fortunately, the exact differences between HTML and XHTML are fairly straightforward and distinguishing between them shouldn't be traumatic for even an old-fogy HTML coder:

✦ **XHTML elements and attributes must be lowercase.** As I say earlier in this chapter, HTML is case insensitive: `<table>`, `<TABLE>`, and `<tAbLe>` are considered identical. However, in XHTML, all elements and attribute names must be in lowercase letters.

✦ **XHTML elements must always be closed.** In HTML, several tags were often used with just the opening tag, such as `<p>` (paragraph), `<br>` (line break), and `<hr>` (horizontal line). But, in XHTML, every start tag needs to have a matching end tag. A starting `<p>` tag, for example, needs a `</p>` to close it.

✦ **Empty XHTML elements can be written using shorthand notation — a single tag closed with `/>`.** Although every element must be properly closed, an element with no content between the opening and closing tags can close by itself. For example, the `hr` element adds a horizontal line to the page. But, because it never would have any text or other content inside it, it would always have to be expressed as

```
<hr></hr>
```

However, by using the shortcut notation, you can reduce this example:

```
<hr/>
```

Typically, the XHTML elements that you self-close include `br`, `hr`, `img`, `input`, `link`, and `meta`.

✦ **XHTML documents must have one root element that encloses all the others.** Although most HTML pages always enclosed the code inside an `html` element, you technically can get by without one. However, an XHTML document must always enclose all XHTML elements inside the `html` root element.

✦ **Images must have an alternative text attribute.** In HTML, `img` elements (used to display images) had an *optional* `alt` attribute for supplying an alternative text description for a graphical image. In XHTML, this attribute is required.

✦ **XHTML documents must have a valid DOCTYPE.** Although later versions of HTML encouraged the use of a `DOCTYPE` element (see "The DOCTYPE element," later in this chapter), XHTML requires it.

Table 1-1 shows several examples of HTML code and the same code after it's cleaned up in XHTML.

Table 1-1	Converting Old HTML into XHTML
HTML	*XHTML*
`<p>Go to the hill,` `ye sluggard.`	`<p>Go to the hill,` `ye sluggard.</p>`
` `	` `
`<img src="photo1.jpg">`	`<img src="photo1.jpg"` `alt="Portrait" />`
`<Table></TABLE>`	`<table></table>`

Throughout this book, I often use *HTML* in a generic sense to refer to the markup code of a Web page. However, even as I do so, I always follow the XHTML conventions.

Surveying the Document Structure of a Page

An HTML document uses special elements to define and describe the structure of a page. You can generally break any document into two parts: the head and the body. The *head* contains important document-level information about the page, and the *body* contains the content and the formatting elements. A skeleton HTML page looks something like this:

```
<!DOCTYPE html PUBLIC "-//W3C//DTD XHTML 1.0
    Transitional//EN" "http://www.w3.org/TR/xhtml1/DTD/
    xhtml1-transitional.dtd">
<html xmlns="http://www.w3.org/1999/xhtml">
<head>
<meta http-equiv="Content-Type" content="text/html;
    charset=ISO-8859-1" />
<title>Untitled Document</title>
</head>
<body>
Content goes here.
</body>
</html>
```

Each of these elements is described in the following sections.

The DOCTYPE element

The first element you encounter in any Web page is perhaps the most con-fusing to look at. The DOCTYPE declaration looks something like this:

```
<!DOCTYPE html PUBLIC "-//W3C//DTD XHTML 1.0 Transitional//
    EN" "http://www.w3.org/TR/xhtml1/DTD/xhtml1-transitional.
    dtd">
```

Okay, I admit, the DOCTYPE element just looks weird. Everyone was just get-ting comfortable with the conventions of HTML and XHTML elements, and then DOCTYPE comes along and seems to break all the rules. A DOCTYPE begins with an exclamation point. The name is all in uppercase. Its attributes don't follow the name-value pair rules that I describe earlier in this chapter. To top it off, it has no closing tag.

The DOCTYPE element doesn't follow the normal markup rules because, technically speaking, it isn't an HTML or XHTML element. Instead, it's a *document type declaration*. The DOCTYPE element declares the type of docu-ment that the file contains and the version of HTML or XHTML that's used. A browser looks at this information to determine how to render the page as accurately and efficiently as possible. A document type declaration appears only at the top of an HTML or XHTML document — before the html element.

Whether you're working with HTML or XHTML, you find three basic DOCTYPE varieties:

✦ **Strict:** The most restrictive type; requires you to code presentation instructions in Cascading Style Sheets (CSS), not in HTML or XHTML. (Refer to Book V for more on CSS.) See the nearby sidebar "That's a no-no in a strict DOCTYPE" for a listing of features not allowed with a Strict DOCTYPE.

That's a no-no in a strict DOCTYPE

The Web may be an ideal platform to express yourself, but if you're using a Strict DOCTYPE, you have to mind your p's and q's — or at least your elements and attributes. The following list outlines the general restrictions of the Strict DOCTYPE:

🖍 **Elements not allowed with a Strict DOC-TYPE**: center, font, iframe, strike, and u.

🖍 **Attributes not allowed with a Strict DOCTYPE**: align (except with certain table elements, such as td, th, and tr), alink, background, bgcolor, border (except on the table element),

height (except for img and object), hspace, language, link, name, noshade, nowrap, target, text, vlink, vspace, and width (except for the col, colgroup, img, object, and table elements).

A few differences also exist in the placement of certain elements inside other elements. Text and images aren't allowed immediately inside the body element and must be contained in a p, div, or other block-level element. Text placed inside blockquote elements must be enclosed in a p or other block-level element. Finally, an input element must not be directly placed inside a form element.

✦ **Transitional:** Provides more flexibility, allowing you to retain some older-style HTML presentation elements and attributes. However, the term Transitional specifies that it's a temporary solution for transferring old, legacy HTML code into the newer markup standards. The W3C expects this DOCTYPE to be phased out eventually.

✦ **Frameset:** Used when you want to place frames inside your document.

Use the Strict DOCTYPE unless you have a compelling reason to use one of the other alternatives. Using Strict now helps ensure that your Web page doesn't, from a coding standpoint, become outdated. It also helps ensure that the browsers processing the document will use the strictest rendering available (which ensures that the designer gets the greatest level of control over how the page is displayed to users).

Table 1-2 lists the typical DOCTYPE declarations for XHTML and HTML. As you can see in the example, the !DOCTYPE element declaration is somewhat technical. Fortunately, most Web site applications, such as Dreamweaver and Expression, automatically add this declaration for you when you create a new HTML page.

Table 1-2	DOCTYPE Declarations
DTD	*Declaration*
XHTML 1.0 Strict	`<!DOCTYPE html PUBLIC "-//W3C//DTD XHTML 1.0 Strict//EN" "http://www.w3.org/TR/xhtml1/DTD/xhtml1-strict.dtd">`
XHTML 1.0 Transitional	`<!DOCTYPE html PUBLIC "-//W3C//DTD XHTML 1.0 Transitional//EN" "http://www.w3.org/TR/xhtml1/DTD/xhtml1-transitional.dtd">`
XHTML 1.0 Frameset	`<!DOCTYPE html PUBLIC "-//W3C//DTD XHTML 1.0 Frameset//EN" "http://www.w3.org/TR/xhtml1/DTD/xhtml1-frameset.dtd">`
HTML 4.01 Strict	`<!DOCTYPE HTML PUBLIC "-//W3C//DTD HTML 4.01//EN" "http://www.w3.org/TR/html4/strict.dtd">`
HTML 4.01 Transitional	`<!DOCTYPE HTML PUBLIC "-//W3C//DTD HTML 4.01 Transitional//EN" "http://www.w3.org/TR/html4/loose.dtd">`
HTML 4.01 Frameset	`<!DOCTYPE HTML PUBLIC "-//W3C//DTD HTML 4.01 Frameset//EN" "http://www.w3.org/TR/html4/frameset.dtd">`

The html element

The `html` element is much like an envelope: It exists only to neatly bundle up all the content inside it. In an HTML or XHTML document, only the `DOCTYPE` declaration appears outside of it. In traditional HTML, the `html` element had no parameters. However, with XHTML, the XML namespace declaration should be declared as an attribute:

```
<html xmlns="http://www.w3.org/1999/xhtml">
</html>
```

If the term *XML namespace* makes your head spin, don't worry about what it means. It's just more technical jargon that the browser uses to understand which kind of document it's working with.

The head element

The `head` element serves as a place to store information related to the document, although it doesn't appear as content inside the browser itself. The `head` section contains the document title, links to external style or script files, and other meta information, such as the character set or document author.

The title element

The `title` element is located inside the `head` element. The text that appears inside the element provides a descriptive title for the document. The browser typically displays the title text in the browser window or tab:

```
<title>Digitalwalk :: About Digitalwalk</title>
```

The title is also one of the most important pieces of content on your Web page for search engines. Google and other search engines factor in the document title heavily when they evaluate the Web page. In addition, the title is used as the main entry in search result listings.

Therefore, although you should limit your title to fewer than 80 characters, make sure that it's expressive and descriptive enough to adequately describe your page. Moreover, savvy Web designers creatively incorporate specific keywords that they want associated with their pages in search results.

The meta element

The `meta` element is a general-purpose element to specify meta-related information about the document, such as author, date, keywords, description, and character set (often referred to as *meta tags*). Here are two general rules of thumb for using the `meta` element:

+ It must be placed inside the `head` element.

+ It never contains any content and is always self-closed (ends with `/>`).

The following sections describe the most commonly used meta tags.

Content type declaration

This type of meta tag is often used to declare the content of the document to the browser:

```
<meta http-equiv="Content-Type" content="text/html;
    charset=ISO-8859-1" />
```

Most Web site builders automatically add this information when you create a new document.

Meta description

A meta description tag is often used by search engines for the summary text that's displayed for the page in the search engine listings. Here's an example:

```
<meta name="description" content="Wimbly Tech Online solves
    all of your technology needs in 5 seconds or less."/>
```

However, the content in your meta description tag matters only for search engines that support it. Google, for example, ignores this tag. Instead, Google generates the summary text automatically based on the content of your document.

If you use the meta description tag, use as your descriptor the text from the first couple of sentences in your HTML page's content.

Meta keywords

**Book VI
Chapter 1**

Exploring HTML and
XHTML Documents

The meta keywords tag is a popular way to provide search engines with specific keywords to index as they process your Web page. However, because of misuse by Web site designers over the years, this tag is much less important now. In fact, most major search engines ignore it! However, if you want to supply it to search engines that still use the tag, the code looks like this:

```
<meta name="keywords" content="Waterslides,Hoses,Water fun,
    HydroDance" />
```

Here are a few tips for using meta keywords:

+ Limit the number of keywords to fewer than 20.

+ Avoid repeating words, even if a word appears in more than one term.

+ Use only keywords that are relevant to the content of your document.

The body element

The body element encloses the content of the Web page — and is where most of your real work takes place. Any text that's placed between the opening and closing body tags is displayed in the browser. For example, consider this HTML document:

```
<!DOCTYPE html PUBLIC "-//W3C//DTD XHTML 1.0 Transitional//
    EN" "http://www.w3.org/TR/xhtml1/DTD/xhtml1-transitional.
    dtd">
<html xmlns="http://www.w3.org/1999/xhtml">
<head>
<meta http-equiv="Content-Type" content="text/html;
    charset=ISO-8859-1" />
<title>Creating Web Pages</title>
</head>
<body>
```

```
All of the text I place inside the document body is shown in
   the browser.
</body>
</html>
```

When this page is viewed in a Web browser (see Figure 1-1), the text inside the browser is displayed and everything else remains hidden from the user's view. Notice that the content of the `title` element is displayed on the browser window's title bar.

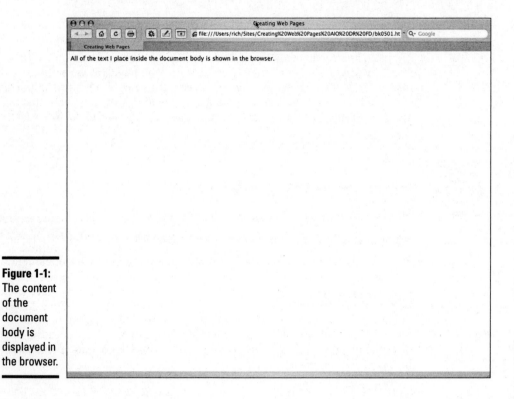

Figure 1-1:
The content of the document body is displayed in the browser.

Chapter 2: Working with Text and Links

In This Chapter

✓ Working with paragraphs and other document elements

✓ Adding bold and italic text

✓ Specifying font properties for your pages

✓ Creating links to Web pages and e-mail addresses

In this chapter, we show you how to work with the most common HTML elements that help you format text on your Web pages. We also show you how to create links to other Web pages.

Giving Your Document Structure

Any document you compose and edit contains at least a basic structure and formatting. Without these basic formatting techniques, text is extremely difficult to read. You already divide a page of text into distinct paragraphs, often grouping related paragraphs with a single heading. For special words or phrases, you emphasize the text by changing its text style. In fact, this sort of practice is probably second nature, to the point that you don't even think about doing it when you're writing e-mail messages or creating Word documents.

However, when you work with the source of an HTML document, you need to think about giving the document some structure because you can't format it like you would with an old typewriter by pressing Enter and Tab.

Making a paragraph

The p element is used to contain a paragraph of text. The opening tag (<p>) is placed at the beginning of the paragraph, and the closing tag (</p>) serves as the caboose. For example, the following HTML code shows two paragraphs of text:

```
<p>"Not much of a blowing up, I am sure," Mrs. Ellison said;
    "and as likely as not, a shilling at the end of it."</p>
<p>"Well, Mary, I must own," the squire said pleasantly,
    "that a shilling did find its way out of my pocket into
    his."</p>
```

Each paragraph appears as a block of text with an extra blank line at the end to divide it from the next paragraph. Figure 2-1 shows this code in a browser window.

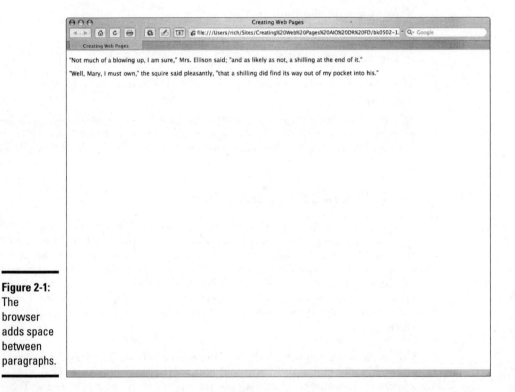

Figure 2-1:
The browser adds space between paragraphs.

When you use traditional HTML, be sure to add the closing tag (</p>) to the end of a paragraph — even though you don't have to. Traditional HTML allows you not to add the closing tag; however, as we discuss in Chapter 1, this practice isn't compatible with XHTML.

Adding a line break

The br element serves as a way to end a line manually or create an empty line of text. It's the equivalent of pressing Enter in your e-mail message or word processing document and starting a new line.

The br element forces a new line when it's used and does not add space around other paragraphs. Unlike the p element, br never contains any content by itself and, in fact, is often located inside a p element, as shown in this example:

```
<p>"Not much of a blowing up, I am sure,"<br/>
Mrs. Ellison said.<br/>
"And as likely as not, a shilling at the end of it."</p>
```

The two br elements force new lines to be added, as shown in Figure 2-2.

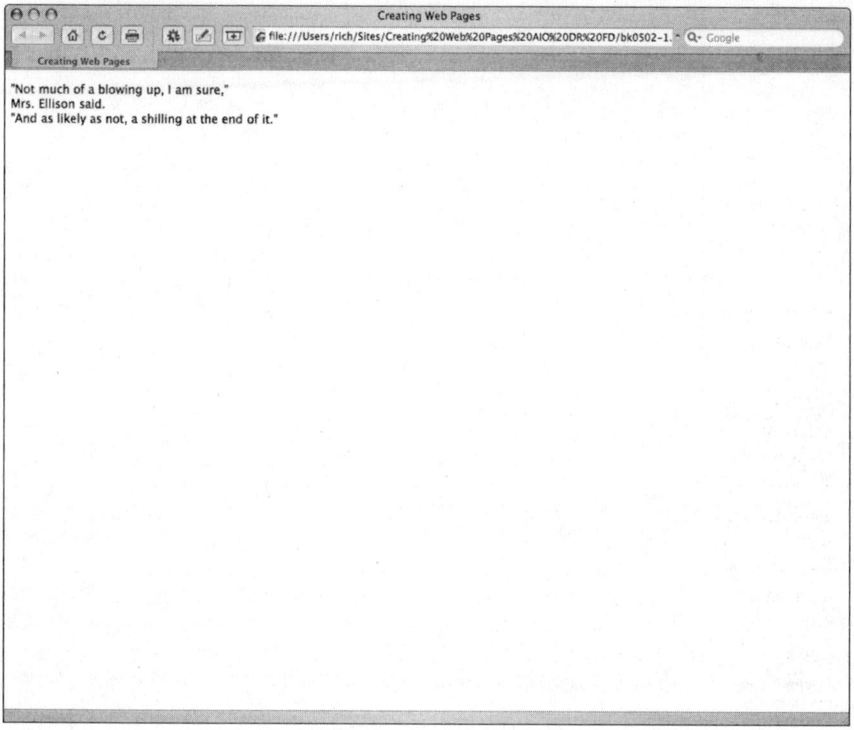

Figure 2-2:
Using the
br element
to force
new lines.

Making a heading

Most Web pages have a paragraph or groups of paragraphs offset by headings. HTML supports six levels of headings with the h1, h2, h3, h4, h5, and h6 elements. The h1 element is the topmost and largest; the h6 element is the smallest heading. Here are some examples:

```
<h1>This is heading 1</h1>
<h2>This is heading 2</h2>
<h3>This is heading 3</h3>
<h4>This is heading 4</h4>
<h5>This is heading 5</h5>
<h6>This is heading 6</h6>
```

The HTML is displayed in the browser, as shown in Figure 2-3.

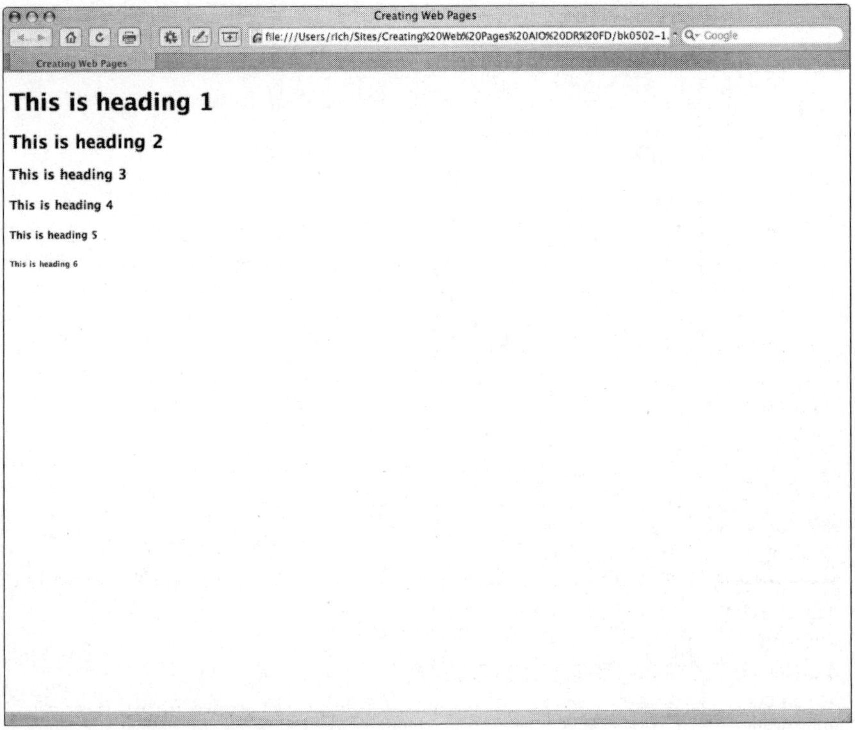

Figure 2-3: HTML headings give a hierarchical structure to your Web page.

Adding a horizontal line

You may want to visually offset one block of text from another. One way to do this is to use an hr element, which adds a horizontal line (or rule) to your document. For example, the following hr tag separates two sections of a page:

```
<p>The next day Mrs. Whitney and Reuben moved, with all their
   belongings, to Lewes.</p>
<hr/>
<h1>Chapter 3: The Burglary At The Squire's.</h1>
<p>"What is that woman Whitney going to do with her boy?" the
   squire asked the schoolmaster, when he happened to meet
   him in the village about a month after she had left. "Have
   you heard?"</p>
```

Figure 2-4 shows the horizontal line in the browser.

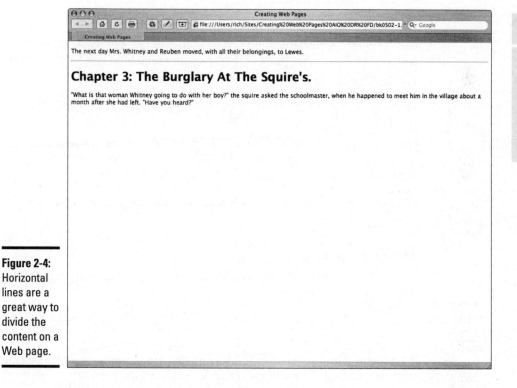

Figure 2-4:
Horizontal
lines are a
great way to
divide the
content on a
Web page.

Grouping inline text

Within a paragraph, you may have a reason to group part of the text so
that you can add styling to it rather than to the entire paragraph. The span
element is used to perform this sort of behind-the-scenes grouping, as
shown in this example:

```
<p>One morning in the spring, <span>the squire looked</span>
   in at Mrs. Whitney's shop.</p>
```

Without any attributes, the `span` element does nothing to the text. Instead, you typically use it with the `style` attribute, as shown a little later in this chapter, in the section "Fontastic! Specifying the Typeface, Size, and Color."

Emphasizing Your Text with Bold and Italics

Whether the Web site you're creating is megahuge or teeny-weeny, your most common formatting task is emphasizing text with bold and italics. This section describes the two elements you use for adding these two popular text effects.

Bolding text

Use the `strong` element when you want to **strongly emphasize** a portion of text. Strong text is displayed in the browser with a bold typeface, as shown in this example:

```
<p>I told the daring skater to <strong>stop</strong> ice
    dancing with scissors.</p>
```

Use the `strong` element to ensure compatibility with future browsers. Traditional HTML had a `b` tag for bolded text, but this element is being phased out in newer versions of HTML and XHTML.

Heading elements (`h1` to `h6`) automatically bold the text, so you don't need to add `strong` tags.

Italicizing text

The `em` element is used when you want to emphasize text with italics, as shown in this example:

```
<p>A <em>tilde</em> is popularly known as a "squiggly
    mark".</p>
```

Traditional HTML sported an `i` tag for italics. However, because this element is being phased out, use the `em` element instead.

Fontastic! Specifying the Typeface, Size, and Color

Until now in this chapter, all the HTML formatting you looked at uses HTML elements to change the look of the text. However, after you begin to work with font properties — such as typeface, size, and color — you need to begin working with Cascading Style Sheets (CSS) styling. (Refer to Book V for full details on CSS.) In years gone by, HTML designers used a `font` tag to set character formatting. However, the font tag is obsolete in newer versions of HTML and XHTML, so we strongly recommend that you avoid using it.

In this section, we show you the basics of using CSS to format text with the style attribute of the p and span elements. You can use the style attribute to set a style rule for all the content within a single element. The generic code looks like this:

```
<element style="css-property:value;another-css-property:
    value">Content</element>
```

CSS properties are declared as name-value pairs, separated by colons. Semicolons are used to separate more than one CSS property.

In addition to applying inline styles, you can apply style rules globally with the style element or by using an external stylesheet. (For the full scoop on these items, be sure to flip to Book V.)

Setting the typeface

The typeface or font face of a block of text can be set by using the CSS property font-family. The font-family property is a comma-separated list of fonts you want to use. The browser uses the first font in the list that's available on the user's system. Here's an example that specifies three typefaces:

```
<span style="font-family:Arial, Helvetica, sans-serif">"Is
    this the road to Lewes?" Reuben asked.</span>
```

In this example, the browser looks for the Arial typeface first and then for Helvetica if Arial isn't located. If neither is available, the browser uses any sans serif (smooth-looking) font.

Multiple-word font names must be placed within quotation marks. Therefore, when using inline styles with the style attribute, be sure to use single quotation marks. For example, if you specify Times New Roman as the font, here's what the style declaration looks like:

```
<p style="font-family:'Times New Roman', Times, serif">"Is
    this the road to Lewes?" Reuben asked.</p>
<p style="font-family:Arial, Helvetica, sans-serif">"Lewes?
    Noa, this baint the road to Lewes. I don't know nothing
    about the road to Lewes. This bee the road to Hastings, if
    you goes further. So they tell me; I ain't never been
    there."</p>
```

Figure 2-5 shows the two paragraphs as displayed in the browser.

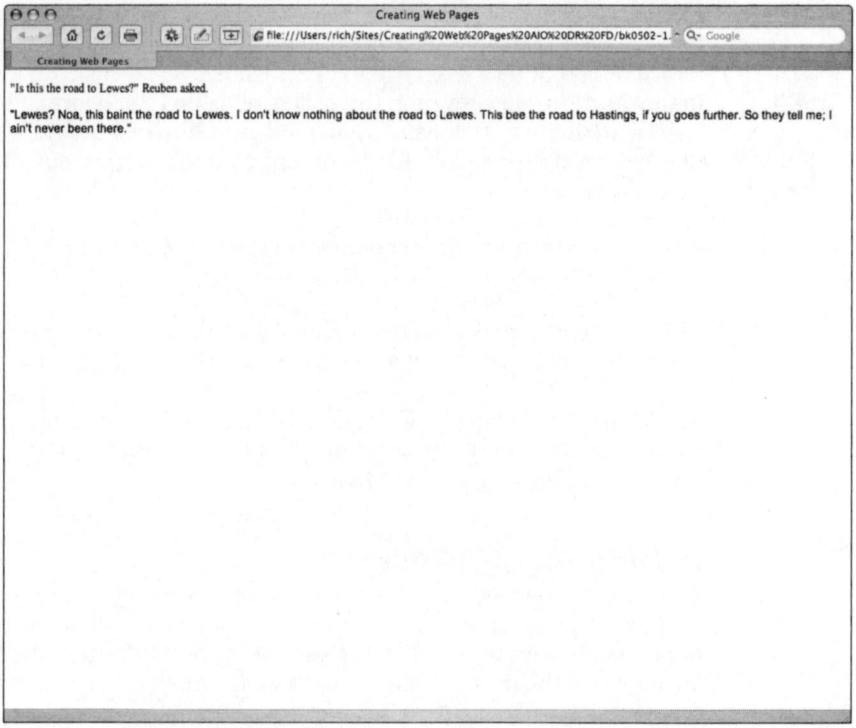

Figure 2-5:
Setting
the font
typeface in
a Web page.

Sizing the text

The size of the text is set using the CSS property `font-size`. You can set an *absolute* font size or have the size be *relative* to the browser's default font size.

Absolute sizes

To set the absolute font size, you can use a collection of constants: `xx-small`, `x-small`, `small`, `medium` (default), `large`, `x-large`, and `xx-large`. The following bit of code sets the sentence font to extra small, which is roughly three sizes smaller than the normal, default size:

```
<span style="font-size:x-small">Reuben told the story of his
    adventures from the time of leaving.</span>
```

You can also set the font size by using point or pixel size:

```
<p style="font-size:12pt">Reuben told the story of his
    adventures from the time of leaving.</p>
<p style="font-size:12px">Reuben told the story of his
    adventures from the time of leaving.</p>
```

Although point size is the unit of measurement that people are most comfortable with, point size is less precise than the collection of size constants. Different computers render point sizes differently, giving you less control of the text appearance.

Here's a code listing of several absolute size paragraphs:

```
<p style="font-size:xx-small">xx-small</p>
<p style="font-size:x-small">x-small</p>
<p style="font-size:small">small</p>
<p style="font-size:medium">medium</p>
<p style="font-size:large">large</p>
<p style="font-size:x-large">x-large</p>
<p style="font-size:xx-large">xx-large</p>
<p style="font-size:8pt">8 point</p>
<p style="font-size:10pt">10 point</p>
<p style="font-size:12pt">12 point</p>
<p style="font-size:14pt">14 point</p>
<p style="font-size:8px">8 pixels</p>
<p style="font-size:10px">10 pixels</p>
<p style="font-size:12px">12 pixels</p>
<p style="font-size:14px">14 pixels</p>
```

Figure 2-6 shows this HTML code as displayed in the browser.

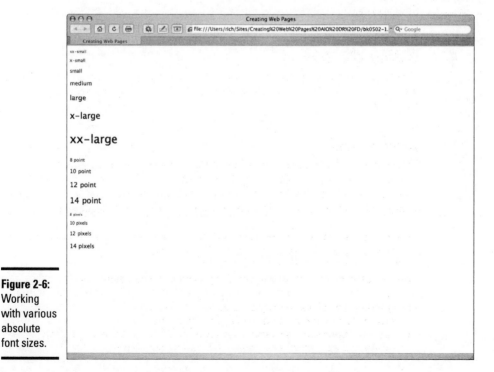

Figure 2-6:
Working with various absolute font sizes.

Relative sizes

To set the size of the text relative to the base font size, you can use the constants `smaller` and `larger`. In addition, you can specify a percentage of the base font size. This bit of code shows several relative size options:

```
<p style="font-size:smaller">Smaller</p>
<p style="font-size:90%">90% of Normal</p>
<p>Default font size - the standard bearer</p>
<p style="font-size:larger">Larger</p>
<p style="font-size:300%">300% of Normal</p>
```

The browser displays the code snippet, as shown in Figure 2-7.

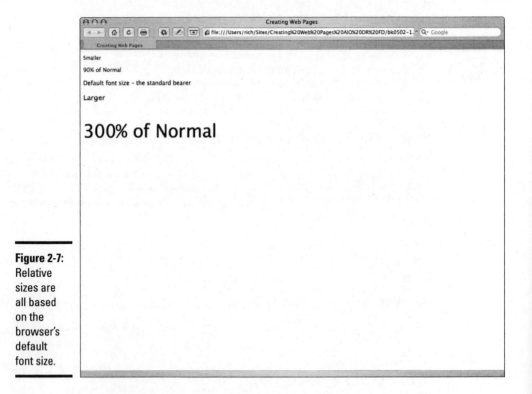

Figure 2-7:
Relative sizes are all based on the browser's default font size.

Giving your text some color

You can specify the color of your text by using the CSS property `color`. You can assign a color by using a predefined color keyword or a hexadecimal (hex) value.

HTML and CSS define 17 color constants for standard colors: `aqua`, `black`, `blue`, `fuchsia`, `gray`, `green`, `lime`, `maroon`, `navy`, `olive`, `orange`, `purple`, `red`, `silver`, `teal`, `white`, and `yellow`, as shown in this example:

```
<p style="color:navy">Can I see my mother?" Reuben asked
   next.</p>
```

However, because you can use millions of colors, you often want to use a hexadecimal color value, which is a technical-looking hex number prefixed with a hash character (#). It can be either three or six digits long, as shown in this example:

```
<p class="color:#ffffff">White</p>
<p class="color:#000000">Black</p>
<p class="color: #66FFCC">Spindrift</p>
```

Book VI
Chapter 2

Working with Text and Links

Fortunately, most of the software applications you use in Web design and development allow you to easily copy these hex values from color selector dialog boxes and paste them directly into your code.

Creating Links

Links, links, links — it's all about links. In a very real way, links make the Web go 'round. Links drive everything people do on the Web. You read a Web page and then click a hyperlink to jump to another page on the site for more details. Or, you search for a term on Google.com and then click the top result to jump to the associated site.

As you construct your Web site, carefully think about how you want to use links to help increase its usefulness to your visitors. Ask yourself these types of questions:

✦ What other information on your site is relevant to your current page?

✦ What other sites can you link to that provide more details about a particular topic?

Dissecting a URL

After you have any link-related decisions worked out, you're almost ready to create links in your document. However, before we jump into the HTML instructions, we give you an overview of URLs. A Uniform Resource Locator (URL) is the technical term for a Web address. A *URL* (pronounced either "you-are-ell" or "earl") is the unique identifier that's used to access any Web page, graphical element, or other resource.

Here's an example:

```
http://www.digitalwalk.net/more/about.html
```

URLs are composed of these three main parts:

✦ *Protocol:* Most Web links use the `http://` protocol, which simply tells the Web server that a document or other Web resource is being requested by the browser. Other protocols you might encounter include `mailto` (for creating a new e-mail message to the specified e-mail address), `ftp` (for a file on an FTP server), and `https` (for a Secure Sockets Layer transaction).

✦ *Domain name:* The domain name, such as `www.digitalwalk.net`, identifies the Web site containing the document. The domain name points to a particular Web server that hosts the site itself.

✦ *Path:* The path points to the exact location of the page on the Web server. This part (such as `/more/about.html`) often looks similar to a folder-and-filename combination that you work with on your local computer. The path can also include an anchor (prefixed with the # character), which indicates a link to a specific bookmark on a page. (See the later section "Linking to a location inside a page").

Although you don't need to worry about case when working with the protocol and domain name, the path portion of a URL is often case sensitive on many Web servers.

Distinguishing between absolute and relative URLs

Two types of URLs exist: absolute and relative. Here's a description of both types:

✦ *Absolute URL:* Provides the full address (including protocol, domain name, and path) of the page or other resource you're pointing to. Here's an example:

```
http://www.wiley.com/resources/extras.html
```

✦ *Relative URL:* Also an address to a Web page, but described in relationship to the current page. For example, if the `extras.html` page is linking to another page (`more.html`) that sits in the same domain and directory (`www.wiley.com/resources/`), the relative URL is simply

```
more.html
```

Or, if you want to point to a file that's in the directory above the current file location, you can use this relative URL:

```
../index.html
```

 You might find it helpful to think of an absolute URL much like a full mailing address that you give to someone who lives far away from you: "We live at 122 Reed Lane, Fremont, MS 34531". A relative URL, on the other hand, is much like an informal address that you give to someone who lives in your neighborhood: "We live on the corner of Reed and Lamotte."

When you add a link to your Web page, use absolute URLs for all resources you point to that aren't part of your site. For links to other pages on your domain, you can use either absolute or relative paths, although relative URLs are often easier to work with.

Making a link

The HTML anchor element (a) is used to define a link in your page to another document. To use the anchor, you enclose text inside the <a> and </a> tags and then specify the URL by using the href attribute. Follow these steps to make a link:

1. Inside the HTML page's body, locate or enter the text that you want to serve as the link on your page.

Here's an example:

```
<p>
Go to Digitalwalk for more information.
</p>
```

2. Enclose the link text with the a element.

In the following example, you use only part of the text:

```
<p>
<a>Go to Digitalwalk</a> for more information.
</p>
```

3. Specify the URL you want to link to inside the href attribute:

```
<p>
<a href="http://www.digitalwalk.net">Go to
    Digitalwalk</a> for more information.
</p>
```

This code jumps to the `www.digitalwalk.net` URL when the `Go to Digitalwalk` text is clicked in the Web page.

If the page you're linking to is on your site, you can use a relative URL instead, as shown in this example:

```
<p>
<a href="index.html">Home</a>
</p>
```

To make a link from an image, see Chapter 4 in this minibook.

To customize the visual look of your links by using CSS, refer to Book V.

Linking to a location inside a page

Although most links you create link to other pages on the Web, you might occasionally want to link to a specific section on the same page. Typical examples are a Return to Top link at the bottom of a page or a table of contents that links to each section of the document.

To link to a specific location on a page, you first define a *named anchor,* an invisible HTML element that serves as the placeholder bookmark. Don't be confused: The named anchor uses the same a element as normal links. However, rather than use the `href` attribute, a named anchor uses the `name` attribute. After the named anchor is defined, you can link to the named anchor by using the a element.

When you link to a named anchor, you specify the named anchor as the value of the `href` attribute, prefixed with a pound sign (#). For example, to link to the named anchor `topofpage`, you use the following code:

```
<a href="#topofpage">Return to top</a>
```

Here's how to set up a link to a named anchor:

1. **Create a named anchor at the destination you want to jump to by using the link with the a element. Enter a value in the name attribute that effectively describes the location:**

   ```
   <a name="section1"></a>
   ```

   Note that you don't need to place text inside the named anchor.

2. **Create a link to the named anchor, by specifying its name (prefixed with a # sign) in the `href` attribute:**

   ```
   <a href="#section1">Section 1: Understanding Political
       Reform</a>
   ```

Linking to an e-mail address

You can link to an e-mail address from your Web page, to provide an easy and direct way for site visitors to send e-mail to you. To do this, use the `mailto` protocol (rather than the familiar `http://`) inside the `href` attribute, as shown in this example:

```
<a href="mailto:info@digitalwalk.net">info@digitalwalk.net</a>
```

If you want to add a subject line, you can specify it inside the `href` value after the e-mail address. To do so, add `?subject=` followed by the subject text. Here's an example:

```
<a href="mailto:info@digitalwalk.net?subject=Question for
    You">info@digitalwalk.net</a>
```

Book VI
Chapter 2

Note that `mailto:` links are good only when users use e-mail clients on their computers. They don't work with browser-based e-mail.

Linking to a picture, PDF document, or file

You can link to resources other than HTML pages on the Web. You can use the a element to jump to JPG pictures, Adobe Acrobat documents (PDF files), Microsoft Word or Excel documents, ZIP files, and more. To link to one of these file types, you simply point to the URL of the file:

```
<a href="manuals/netspud_102.pdf">Read user manual</a>
```

Depending on the type of document you're pointing to, the file is either downloaded on the user's computer or displayed like another Web page inside the browser itself. For example, a picture or PDF document is usually opened in the browser.

Opening the link in a new browser window

When you click a link on a Web page, the normal action is to replace the existing page with the destination page inside the browser window. However, you may occasionally want to define a link that opens in a new browser window and leaves the existing page unchanged. This technique is especially helpful when you're linking to an external site. To do this, add a `target` attribute to your link code, as shown in this example:

```
<a href="http://www.digitalwalk.net" target="_blank">Go to
    Digitalwalk</a> for more information.
```

Chapter 3: Presenting Information with Lists and Tables

In This Chapter

✔ **Creating bulleted and numbered lists**

✔ **Using images for bullets**

✔ **Working with nested lists**

✔ **Creating tables to organize tabular data**

✔ **Formatting tables**

The typical Web page contains large amounts of text. But there's more to organizing text on a page than just positioning sentences and paragraphs. A Web page filled with lines of text may contain good content, but the eyes of a visitor quickly glaze over if you don't break the text into readable chunks. Lists and tables are therefore excellent organizational tools that help make your Web pages easier and quicker to read. In this chapter, you discover how to create lists and tables.

Creating a Bulleted List

A bulleted list is one of the most common ways to organize a series of items, whether it's a single word, phrase, sentence, or occasionally even an entire paragraph. Each item in the list is indented and prefixed with a bullet (normally, a black dot). In the HTML world, a bulleted list is an *unordered list*.

Making a normal unordered list

To create a bulleted list, you use the `ul` and `li` elements. The `ul` element defines an unordered list, and its start and end tags enclose the items on the list. The `li` element is used to define each item in the list. Here's a simple example:

```
<ul>
<li>Patriots</li>
<li>Jets</li>
<li>Bills</li>
<li>Dolphins</li>
</ul>
```

Figure 3-1 shows the result in the browser.

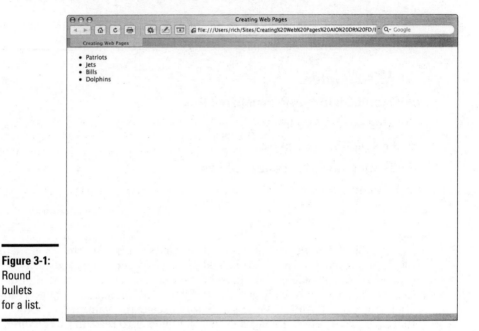

Figure 3-1:
Round
bullets
for a list.

Using alternative bullets

When you use HTML by itself, your bullet choices are limited. However, if you add just a bit of CSS, you can customize the look of the bullets themselves. (See Book V for full details on what CSS is and how it works.)

The `list-style-type` CSS property is used to set the type of list item marker. When working with unordered lists, you can use `square`, `circle` (a doughnut-like circle), `disc` (the default black circle), or `none`. For example, to use square bullets for a simple list, you can add a `style` attribute to the list definition:

```
<ul style="list-style-type:square">
<li>Patriots</li>
<li>Jets</li>
<li>Bills</li>
<li>Dolphins</li>
</ul>
```

Alternatively, if you want to change the style of all unordered lists on your page, you can add the following property definition to a `style` element in the page's document head:

```
<style>
ul { list-style-type: square }
</style>
```

Using images for bullets

Although CSS provides some alternative bullet styles with its `list-style-type` property, images can be the best way to go when you want to use a unique bullet style or specific color that complements your overall Web page design.

To create an image-based bullet list, turn to CSS (again). Although you have a couple of ways to create the list, the best method to ensure consistent results is to use the `background-image` property for the image and then tweak the padding and margin settings for the `ul` and `li` elements.

For this example, the HTML for the list is the same as in the example used throughout this section:

```
<ul>
<li>Patriots</li>
<li>Jets</li>
<li>Bills</li>
<li>Dolphins</li>
</ul>
```

The following CSS rules are added to the document head in a `style` element. The padding and margin rules push the content to the right, to ensure that the text doesn't overlap the background image:

```
<style>
ul {
    list-style-type: none;
    padding-left: 0;
    margin-left: 0;
}
li {
    padding-left: 1.2em;
    background-image: url('images/square.png');
    background-repeat: no-repeat;
    background-position: 0 .1em;
}
</style>
```

Figure 3-2 shows the results in a browser.

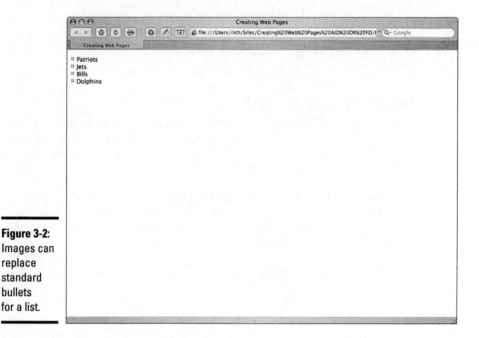

Figure 3-2:
Images can
replace
standard
bullets
for a list.

Creating a Numbered List

HTML also allows you to create numbered lists with the `ol` element.
Numbered (or ordered) lists enclose the list with an `<ol>` start tag and
`</ol>` end tag, and use the `li` elements for each numbered list item.
Here's an example:

```
<ol>
<li>Get up at 6:00am.</li>
<li>Take a shower.</li>
<li>Eat breakfast.</li>
<li>Drive to work.</li>
</ol>
```

The result is a numbered list of items:

1. Get up at 6:00am.

2. Take a shower.

3. Eat breakfast.

4. Drive to work.

As with unordered lists, you can use `list-style-type` to change the numbering style for ordered lists. Here are some of the possible values you can use in Table 3-1.

Table 3-1	Common Number-Related Values for `list-style-type`
Value	*Numbering Styles*
`decimal`	1, 2, 3, 4, 5
`decimal-leading-zero`	01, 02, 03, 04, 05
`lower-roman`	i, ii, iii, iv, v
`upper-roman`	I, II, III, IV, V
`lower-alpha`	a, b, c, d, e
`upper-alpha`	A, B, C, D, E

For example, to change the numbering to lowercase roman numerals, you can add a style attribute to the `ol` list:

```
<ol style="list-style-type:lower-roman">
<li>Get up at 6:00am.</li>
<li>Take a shower.</li>
<li>Eat breakfast.</li>
<li>Drive to work.</li>
</ol>
```

The result looks like this:

i.   Get up at 6:00am.

ii. Take a shower.

iii. Eat breakfast.

iv. Drive to work.

Working with Nested Lists

You can nest ordered and unordered lists, and intermix them as necessary to produce the desired results. Here's an ordered list with three bulleted lists nested inside:

```
<ol>
<li>Europe
 <ul>
  <li>United Kingdom</li>
  <li>France</li>
  <li>Netherlands</li>
 </ul>
</li>
<li>North America
 <ul>
  <li>Canada</li>
  <li>United States</li>
 </ul>
</li>
<li>South America<ul>
  <li>Brazil</li>
  <li>Peru</li> </ul>
</li>
</ol>
```

Working with Tables

Since the early days of the Web, HTML tables have had a tough life. The `table` element was created as a way to organize tabular data into rows and columns. However, as page design became more important, HTML tables were initially the only way to structure a sophisticated page design because only this method enabled you to position elements at specific locations on the page. But, as time went on and designs became more and more sophisticated, the shortcomings of the `table` element as a layout tool became painfully evident.

Fortunately, innovations such as CSS (refer to Book V) and `div` elements (see Chapter 5 in this minibook) have replaced the need to use HTML tables to structure and organize the layout of your entire page. As a result, the `table` element is free to return to its original purpose: organizing tabular data.

Four main elements are used when creating an HTML table. These elements are shown in Table 3-2.

Table 3-2	Principal Elements of HTML Tables
Element	*What It Does*
table	Defines a table and encloses all table-related elements and content
tr	Serves as a table row

Element	What It Does
td	Serves as a table cell
th	Identifies headings

The following steps show you how to create a table in HTML, such as this one, with four columns and five rows:

Team	Wins	Losses	GB
Browns	7	0	--
Giants	5	2	2
Colts	5	2	2
Bills	4	3	3

Here's what you do:

1. **Type the text of the table in your document, and separate the columns with a space:**

```
Team Wins Losses GB
Browns 7 0 --
Giants 5 2 2
Colts 5 2 2
Bills 4 3 3
```

2. **Enclose the table text with `<table>` tags:**

```
<table>
Team Wins Losses GB
Browns 7 0 --
Giants 5 2 2
Colts 5 2 2
Bills 4 3 3
</table>
```

3. **Enclose each of the rows with `<tr>` tags:**

```
<table>
<tr>Team Wins Losses GB</tr>
<tr>Browns 7 0 --</tr>
<tr>Giants 5 2 2</tr>
<tr>Colts 5 2 2</tr>
<tr>Bills 4 3 3</tr>
</table>
```

***4.* Surround header text for each cell with `<th>` tags.**

To make the code easier to read, you're formatting the text in a more hierarchical format, using new lines and indentations:

```
<table>
<tr>
 <th>Team</th>
 <th>Wins</th>
 <th>Loses</th>
 <th>GB</th>
</tr>
<tr>Browns 7 0 --</tr>
<tr>Giants 5 2 2</tr>
<tr>Colts 5 2 2</tr>
<tr>Bills 4 3 3</tr>
</table>
```

***5.* Surround the text of your table cells with `<td>` tags.**

If a cell has no content, place   in the cell, which is a special HTML code indicating a nonbreaking space. For example, if you want to use an empty cell rather than the double hyphen in the last column of the Browns row, you can substitute   instead:

```
<table>
<tr>
 <th>Team</th>
 <th>Wins</th>
 <th>Loses</th>
 <th>GB</th>
</tr>
<tr>
 <td>Browns</td>
 <td>7</td>
 <td>0</td>
 <td> </td>
</tr>
<tr>
 <td>Giants</td>
 <td>5</td>
 <td>2</td>
 <td>2</td>
</tr>
<tr>
 <td>Colts</td>
 <td>5</td>
 <td>2</td>
 <td>2</td>
</tr>
```

```
<tr>
 <td>Bills</td>
 <td>4</td>
 <td>3</td>
 <td>3</td>
</tr>
</table>
```

Figure 3-3 shows the result in the browser.

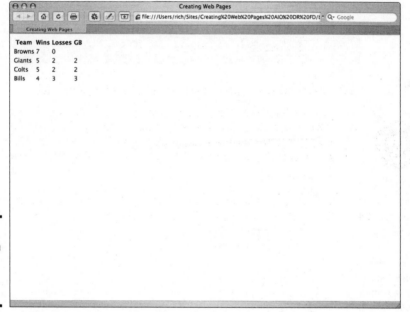

Figure 3-3:
Tabular data
displayed
in an HTML
table.

Adding a border to the table

The table element has a border attribute that allows you to add borders
to your table. The higher the number, the thicker the border. Here's a
minitable with a thin border:

```
<table border="1">
<tr>
 <th>Team</th>
 <th>Wins</th>
 <th>Loses</th>
 <th>GB</th>
</tr>
```

```
<tr>
 <td>Browns</td>
 <td>7</td>
 <td>0</td>
 <td>--</td>
</tr>
</table>
```

Figure 3-4 shows the table defined here.

Removing the `border` attribute is equivalent to `border="0"`.

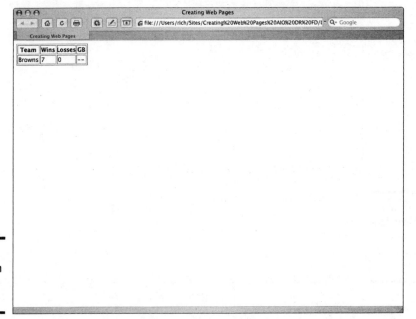

Figure 3-4:
A table with
a defined
border.

You can also use CSS to style your borders. See Book V for more details.

Sizing your table

By default, the width of a table is sized according to its content and the width of the browser window. However, you can set the size of the table by using the `width` attribute. As shown in Figure 3-5, the value of this attribute can be shown either in pixels or as a percentage of the browser window.

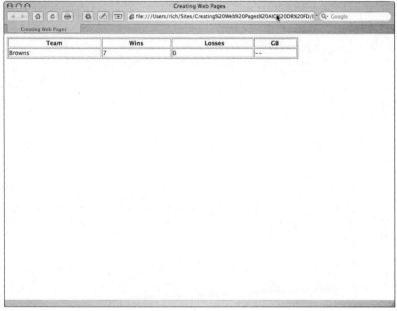

Figure 3-5:
Specifying
the table
width based
on pixels.

Here's an example of a pixel-sized table:

```
<table border="1" width="700px">
<tr>
 <th>Team</th>
 <th>Wins</th>
 <th>Loses</th>
 <th>GB</th>
</tr>
<tr>
 <td>Browns</td>
 <td>7</td>
 <td>0</td>
 <td>--</td>
</tr>
</table>
```

A second example demonstrates a percentage-based table — no matter the
size of the browser window, the table is always 90 percent of the width of the
window:

```
<table border="1" width="90%">
<tr>
 <th>Team</th>
 <th>Wins</th>
 <th>Loses</th>
 <th>GB</th>
</tr>
<tr>
 <td>Browns</td>
 <td>7</td>
 <td>0</td>
 <td>--</td>
</tr>
</table>
```

Figures 3-6 and 3-7 show the table automatically sized according to the changing size of the browser window.

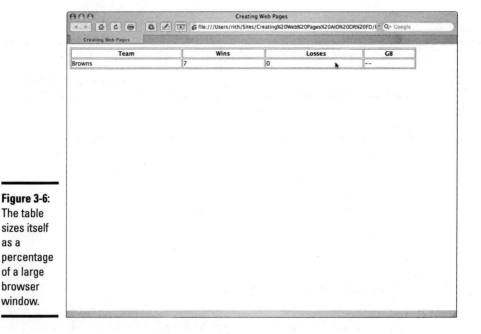

Figure 3-6:
The table sizes itself as a percentage of a large browser window.

Sizing the columns of a table

In addition to being able to adjust the table element, you can adjust the width of each column with the `width` attribute of a `th` or `td` element. The value can be either a pixel value or a percentage of the table width.

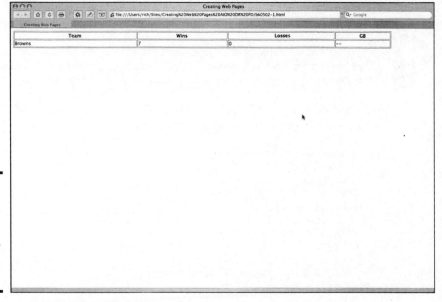

Figure 3-7:
The same
table is
resized as
the browser
window is
resized.

When you adjust one of the cells in a table column, you adjust, in effect, *all* of them. However, the code is often easier to manage if you add the same attribute to each cell of the column.

The following chunk of code widens the first column in the table to 200 pixels:

```
<table border="1" width="90%">
<tr>
 <th width="200px">Team</th>
 <th>Wins</th>
 <th>Loses</th>
 <th>GB</th>
</tr>
<tr>
 <td width="200px">Browns</td>
 <td>7</td>
 <td>0</td>
 <td>--</td>
</tr>
</table>
```

Spacing your table

The table element has two attributes that enable you to space the content inside the table cells: cellspacing and cellpadding. The cellspacing attribute defines the space between cells, and `cellpadding` defines the space between a cell's walls and its content. Both values are in pixels.

When these values aren't specified in the code, most browsers set the value of `cellpadding` to 1 and `cellspacing` to 2. Therefore, if you want to eliminate any spacing between cells, you need to explicitly set them both to 0.

The following chunk of code adds padding and spacing for the table's cells, the results of which are displayed in Figure 3-8:

```
<table width="90%" border="1" cellpadding="2"
    cellspacing="4">
<tr>
 <th width="100px">Team</th>
 <th>Wins</th>
 <th>Loses</th>
 <th>GB</th>
</tr>
<tr>
 <td width="100px">Browns</td>
 <td>7</td>
 <td>0</td>
 <td>--</td>
</tr>
</table>
```

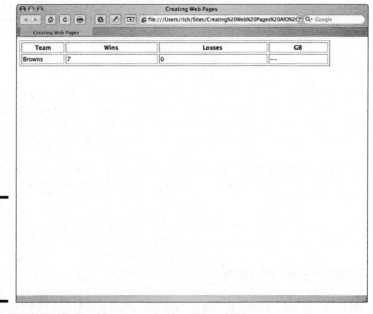

Figure 3-8:
Adjusting the space between cells in a table.

Chapter 4: Adding Images

Many adages stress the importance of visual images over textual information: *Image is everything. A picture equals a thousands words. A photo in hand is worth two documents in the bush.* Okay, we made up that last one, but you get the idea.

Because of the importance of images, you have to be ready to add them to your Web pages. Graphics not only make your site look more attractive, but they also make your documents easier to browse and read.

In this chapter, we show you how to work with images by using HTML. Be sure to check out Book VII for full details about the different types of Web graphics.

Adding an Image

When you add an image to a Web page, you don't embed it into the document, as you do in an application like Microsoft Word. Instead, you link a separate image file into the HTML code. The browser then pulls the image when the page is loaded and displays the image as part of the page.

JPG, GIF, and PNG images are the common types of graphics that you typically add to your pages. (See Book VII for full details about these types of Web graphics.)

The `img` element is used to define an image and has two basic attributes: `src` and `alt`. The basic code looks like this:

```
<img src="http://www.digitalwalk.net/wally.jpg" alt="Portrait
    of Wally"/>
```

The `src` attribute indicates the URL of the image file. The `alt` attribute specifies the text to display if the image isn't displayed.

Always use `alt` (commonly referred to as an "alt tag") when working with images. Alt tags ensure that people using alternative ways of accessing your Web site (screen readers or text-only browsers, for example) can understand the content of the image.

The following chunk of code shows a basic Web page with an image:

```
<!DOCTYPE html PUBLIC "-//W3C//DTD XHTML 1.0 Transitional//
    EN" "http://www.w3.org/TR/xhtml1/DTD/xhtml1-transitional.
    dtd">
<html xmlns="http://www.w3.org/1999/xhtml">
<head>
<meta http-equiv="Content-Type" content="text/html;
    charset=ISO-8859-1" />
<title>HBC Chess Time</title>
</head>
<body>
<p>Chess Time: This Week</p>
<p><img src="images/DSC02669-01.jpg" alt="Justus playing
    chess"/></p>
</body>
</html>
```

Figure 4-1 shows the page displayed in a browser. Figure 4-2 shows the alternative text that's displayed when the image isn't found during the loading of the form.

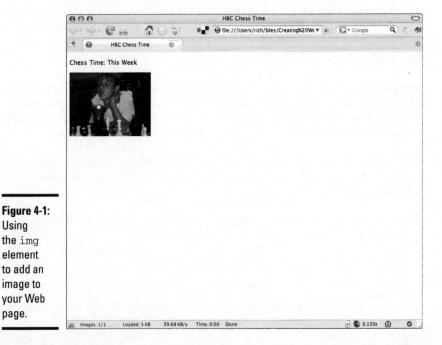

Figure 4-1:
Using the `img` element to add an image to your Web page.

Figure 4-2:
Using
the `img`
element's
`alt`
attribute
to show
alternative
text if the
image isn't
displayed.

Positioning an Image on the Page

When you add an image to your page, it's added *inline:* It's displayed in the document at any location you specify, even in the middle of a line of text. However, you can control the alignment of the image by using CSS styles. (See Book V if you need a primer on CSS.)

In the past, you could control the alignment of the image by using the `img` element's `align` attribute. Because this attribute has been depreciated in the latest HTML and XHTML specifications, however, we recommend that you avoid using it.

Suppose that you want to position a picture alongside the first paragraph of a page. As a result, you place the `img` element just before the paragraph text begins. Here's the code:

```
<!DOCTYPE html PUBLIC "-//W3C//DTD XHTML 1.0 Transitional//
    EN" "http://www.w3.org/TR/xhtml1/DTD/xhtml1-transitional.
    dtd">
<html xmlns="http://www.w3.org/1999/xhtml">
<head>
<meta http-equiv="Content-Type" content="text/html;
    charset=ISO-8859-1" />
<title>War and Peace</title>
```

```
</head>
<body>
<p><img src="images/tolstoy.jpg" alt="Author Leo
   Tolstoy"/>&quot;Well, Prince, so Genoa and Lucca are now
   just family estates of the Buonapartes. But I warn you, if
   you don't tell me that this means war, if you still try to
   defend the infamies and horrors perpetrated by that
   Antichrist--I really believe he is Antichrist--I will have
   nothing more to do with you and you are no longer my
   friend, no longer my 'faithful slave,' as you call
   yourself! But how do you do? I see I have frightened you--
   sit down and tell me all the news.&quot;</p>
<p>It was in July, 1805, and the speaker was the well-known
   Anna Pavlovna Scherer, maid of honor and favorite of the
   Empress Marya Fedorovna. With these words she greeted
   Prince Vasili Kuragin, a man of high rank and importance,
   who was the first to arrive at her reception. Anna
   Pavlovna had had a cough for some days. She was, as she
   said, suffering from la grippe; grippe being then a new
   word in St. Petersburg, used only by the elite.</p>
</body>
</html>
```

The problem is that the img is set inline to the text by default, which extends the text line so that it's the same size as the height of the image. Figure 4-3 shows the result.

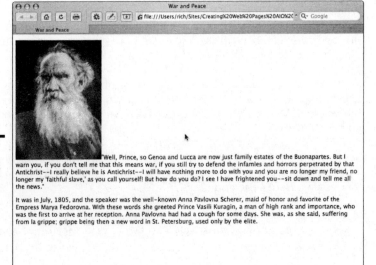

Figure 4-3:
An image is displayed inline with the paragraph text when no align attribute is used.

However, you can use the `float` CSS property to align the image to the left of the text of the paragraph and wrap the text around it. Here's an updated `img` element definition:

```
<img src="images/tolstoy.jpg" alt="Author Leo Tolstoy"
    style="float:left"/>
```

When the updated page is loaded in a browser, the image is left aligned and wraps the text. See Figure 4-4.

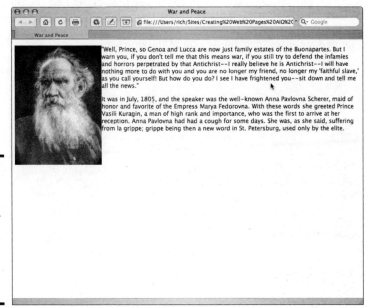

Figure 4-4:
A left-aligned image automatically wraps the text around its dimensions.

Although the image placement looks better using the `float` CSS property, it's still too close to the paragraph text that surrounds it. Therefore, in the next section, we show you how to add padding around the image.

Adding Padding Around Your Image

You typically pad an image with extra spacing to offset it from other visual elements. As you can see in Figure 4-4 (refer to the preceding section), the lack of padding makes the image appear crowded next to the text around it.

The CSS set of `margin` properties comes to the rescue. As Book V explains in greater detail, these properties define the space between an element and the elements around it. The `margin` property sets the margin for all four sides of the element. The `margin-left`, `margin-right`, `margin-top`, and `margin-bottom` properties define the margin for the corresponding side.

In the example earlier in this chapter, you need to offset only the right margin. Therefore, you add a `margin-right` property to the style declaration, to set the value to 15 pixels:

```
<img src="images/tolstoy.jpg" alt="Author Leo Tolstoy"
    style="float:left;margin-right:15px"/>
```

Figure 4-5 shows the results you're looking for.

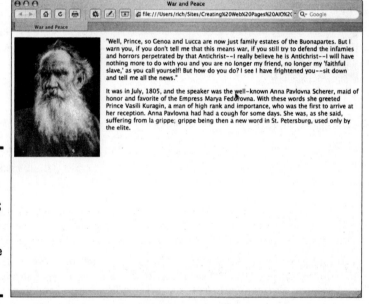

Figure 4-5: Setting the `margin-right` CSS property to add space between the image and the text.

Earlier versions of HTML used `hspace` and `vspace` attributes to provide spacing around an `img` element. However, as with the `align` attribute, these properties have gotten the boot from the newer HTML and XHTML specifications. Use CSS styles instead: They offer much greater control.

Specifying the Dimensions of the Image

The img element also has width and height attributes that you can use to specifically define the dimensions of the image. Modern browsers don't require these attributes because they automatically set the size to be equal to the size of the image itself. But you may want to add height and width information. If you supply them, these dimensions allow the browser to create a placeholder space as it loads the image and the rest of the document, which can result in a faster rendering of the HTML file. Additionally, if you want to enlarge or shrink the size of the image, these attributes can come in handy. Here's an example:

```
<img src="images/tolstoy.jpg" alt="Author Leo Tolstoy"
   width="150" height="300"/>
```

Be careful when you use height and width values that differ from the actual physical size of the image. If you enlarge the values significantly, the image quality is degraded. If you shrink the values significantly, you needlessly add to the size of the Web page. (A better alternative is to shrink the image in an image software program first and then add it to your Web page.) Finally, if you tweak the height and width proportions, the image can become skewed.

Linking Your Image

In Chapter 2 of this minibook, we show you how to create text links to other Web pages by using the anchor (a) element. However, you can use the a element to create clickable images as well.

One handy use for linking images is to display a smaller thumbnail image on your page and allow the user to click it to display a full-size version of the same picture. To create a thumbnail linked image, follow these steps:

1. **Add an img element to your document:**

```
<!DOCTYPE html PUBLIC "-//W3C//DTD XHTML 1.0
   Transitional//EN"
   "http://www.w3.org/TR/xhtml1/DTD/xhtml1-
   transitional.dtd">
<html xmlns="http://www.w3.org/1999/xhtml">
<head>
<meta http-equiv="Content-Type" content="text/html;
   charset=ISO-8859-1" />
```

```
<title>Coming Soon</title>
</head>
<body>
<h2>Coming Soon to a Theater Near You</h2>
<img src="images/cracked_mini.jpg" alt="Thumbnail of
    Cracked poster"/>
<p style="font-style: italic;font-size: x-small">Click
    to view a full-sized image of the movie poster </p>
</body>
</html>
```

2. **Add the `<a>` start and `</a>` end tags before and after the `img` element:**

   ```
   <a><img src="images/cracked_mini.jpg" alt="Thumbnail of Cracked
       poster"/></a>
   ```

   The image should be enclosed in the a element.

3. **Add an `href` attribute that points to the document or file that you want to link to:**

   ```
   <!DOCTYPE html PUBLIC "-//W3C//DTD XHTML 1.0
       Transitional//EN"
       "http://www.w3.org/TR/xhtml1/DTD/xhtml1-
       transitional.dtd">
   <html xmlns="http://www.w3.org/1999/xhtml">
   <head>
   <meta http-equiv="Content-Type" content="text/html;
       charset=ISO-8859-1" />
   <title>Coming Soon</title>
   </head>
   <body>
   <h2>Coming Soon to a Theater Near You</h2>
   <a href="images/cracked_full.jpg"><img
       src="images/cracked_mini.jpg" alt="Thumbnail of
       Cracked poster"/></a>
   <p style="font-style: italic;font-size: x-small">Click
       to view a full-sized image of the movie poster </p>
   </body>
   </html>
   ```

Figure 4-6 displays the page in a browser; Figure 4-7 shows the result when the image thumbnail is clicked.

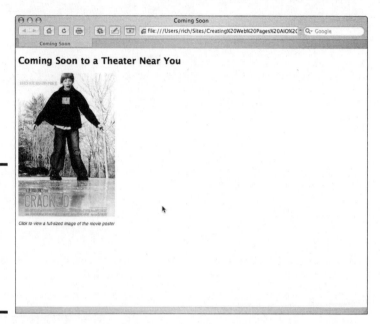

Figure 4-6:
The
thumbnail
image is
linked to a
larger
version of
the same
image.

Figure 4-7:
Clicking the
thumbnail
image
displays the
full-size
version of
the image.

Chapter 5: Divvying Up the Page with DIVs

In This Chapter

✔ Understanding what `div` elements can do

✔ Positioning and sizing a `div` element

✔ Adding border and background settings to a `div` element

✔ Creating a `div`-based page layout

*I*n the early days of the Web, Web pages resembled a typical word processing document — a single-column, text-based layout that flowed from top to bottom and from left to right. An element appeared on the page after the element that came before it. You could shake things up slightly with line breaks and alignment properties, but that was about it.

However, Web designers soon longed to transfer the same kind of sophisticated layouts that they were using for print publications with desktop publishing tools. In other words, the designers wanted to create Web sites that looked Madison Avenue slick, not MIT geek.

To get around this problem of page flow, designers came up with a bandage solution — HTML tables. Although the `table` element was intended as a container for spreadsheet-like data, they found that they could do almost anything with it. A visual Web page may look sleek inside the browser, but viewing its source would reveal the complex grid system of rows and columns, sometimes nested inside each other, to achieve the visual effect. However, these page layouts were a pain to work with and became difficult to manage.

The `div` element was introduced into HTML as a solution to the layout problem. In this chapter, I show you how to use the `div` element as a core element to use as you design your Web site.

Read Book V before you work through this chapter. When you lay out `div` elements on your page, you make heavy use of CSS.

Introducing the div Element

The div element (short for *division*) is a rectangular block used for grouping other HTML elements. By default, a div element occupies 100 percent of the available width of the browser window and adds a line break between other elements. A div element is visible only if you color its borders or background. Otherwise, it's perfectly content to serve as a behind-the-scenes layout device for content contained inside it.

Using CSS, you can position the div element anywhere you want on a page. That flexibility gives the div element its layout power. Here are some elements you can easily create with div elements; without div elements, they're quite difficult to create in HTML:

✦ **A three-column Web page:** Create left, right, and center div elements.

✦ **A text sidebar, alongside the main text:** Float the div element to the side of the main body text.

✦ **A table or set of images:** They appear in the center of the document body, with the text wrapping itself around it.

The div element, by itself, creates a rectangular block where it's positioned on the page. Consider the following bare-bones document:

```
<!DOCTYPE html PUBLIC "-//W3C//DTD XHTML 1.0
    Transitional//EN"
    "http://www.w3.org/TR/xhtml1/DTD/xhtml1-transitional.
    dtd">
<html xmlns="http://www.w3.org/1999/xhtml">
<head>
<title>The Broken Window</title>
</head>
<body>
<p>"I am not troublesome, ma'm," the boy said sturdily. "That
    is, I wouldn't be if they would let me alone; but
    everything that is done bad, they put it down to me."</p>
</body>
</html>
```

Suppose that you enclose the paragraph of content inside a div element, like this:

```
<html xmlns="http://www.w3.org/1999/xhtml">
<head>
<title>The Broken Window</title>
</head>
<body>
<div>
```

```
<p>"I am not troublesome, ma'm," the boy said sturdily. "That
    is, I wouldn't be if they would let me alone; but
    everything that is done bad, they put it down to me."</p>
</div>
</body>
</html>
```

Just adding a `div` element here doesn't do much. In fact, it has no noticeable visual effect on the page, as shown in Figure 5-1.

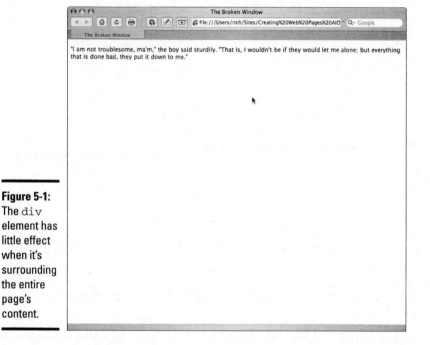

Figure 5-1:
The `div` element has little effect when it's surrounding the entire page's content.

However, suppose that you move the `div` to contain just a portion of the paragraph:

```
<html xmlns="http://www.w3.org/1999/xhtml">
<head>
<title>The Broken Window</title>
</head>
<body>
<p>"I am not troublesome, ma'm," <div>
the boy said sturdily.</div>
  "That is, I wouldn't be if they would let me alone; but
    everything that is done bad, they put it down to me."</p>
</body>
</html>
```

The blockish nature of the `div` element creates a rectangular block around its content, separating it from the other text in the paragraph. A line break is added to separate it from the following element. See Figure 5-2.

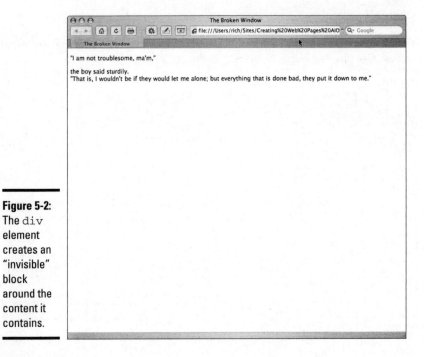

Figure 5-2:
The `div` element creates an "invisible" block around the content it contains.

Positioning and Sizing a div Element on a Page

A `div` element might not look much like a big deal when you're working with plain HTML (as shown in the previous section). However, when you combine it with the positioning capabilities of CSS, you begin to tap into its full potential.

Floating a div element on the page left or right

The CSS property `float` is a handy way to position a `div` block. You can use it to "float" the `div` on the right or left side of the page. Suppose that you want to treat a section of content on your Web page as a sidebar to appear alongside the rest of the document text. The following steps show you how to do it.

In the example, we use the document shown in Figure 5-3. The objective is to take the table of contents out of the flow of the document and move it to a sidebar on the right side of the page.

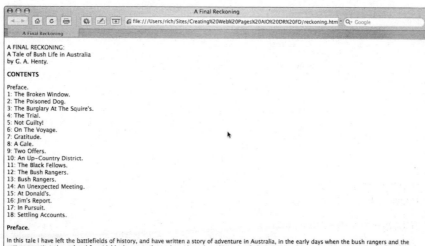

Figure 5-3: Before any changes, the table of contents sits as part of the regular document text.

1. **Open the HTML file you want to modify.**

   Here's the HTML code for the sample document:

   ```
   <!DOCTYPE html PUBLIC "-//W3C//DTD XHTML 1.0 Transitional//EN"
       "http://www.w3.org/TR/xhtml1/DTD/xhtml1-transitional.dtd">
   <html xmlns="http://www.w3.org/1999/xhtml">
   <head>
   <meta http-equiv="Content-Type" content="text/html; charset=ISO-8859-1"
       />
   <title>A Final Reckoning</title>
   </head>
   ```

```
<body>
<p>A FINAL RECKONING:<br />
A Tale of Bush Life in Australia<br />
by G. A. Henty.</p>
<p><strong>CONTENTS</strong></p>
<p>Preface.<br />
  1: The Broken Window.<br />
  2: The Poisoned Dog.<br />
  3: The Burglary At The Squire's.<br />
  4: The Trial.<br />
  5: Not Guilty!<br />
  6: On The Voyage.<br />
  7: Gratitude.<br />
  8: A Gale.<br />
  9: Two Offers.<br />
 10: An Up-Country District.<br />
 11: The Black Fellows.<br />
 12: The Bush Rangers.<br />
 13: Bush Rangers.<br />
 14: An Unexpected Meeting.<br />
 15: At Donald's.<br />
 16: Jim's Report.<br />
 17: In Pursuit.<br />
 18: Settling Accounts.</p>
<p><strong>Preface.</strong></p>
<p>In this tale I have left the battlefields of history, and have written
    a story of adventure in Australia, in the early days when the bush
    rangers and the natives constituted a real and formidable danger to
    the settlers. I have done this, not with the intention of extending
    your knowledge, or even of pointing a moral, although the story is
    not without one; but simply for a change--a change both for you and
    myself, but frankly, more for myself than for you. You know the old
    story of the boy who bothered his brains with Euclid, until he came
    to dream regularly that he was an equilateral triangle enclosed in a
    circle. Well, I feel that unless I break away sometimes from
    history, I shall be haunted day and night by visions of men in
    armour, and soldiers of all ages and times.</p>
<p>If, when I am away on a holiday I come across the ruins of a castle, I
    find myself at once wondering how it could best have been attacked,
    and defended. If I stroll down to the Thames, I begin to plan
    schemes of crossing it in the face of an enemy; and if matters go
    on, who can say but that I may find myself, some day, arrested on
    the charge of surreptitiously entering the Tower of London, or
    effecting an escalade of the keep of Windsor Castle! To avoid such a
    misfortune--which would entail a total cessation of my stories, for
    a term of years--I have turned to a new subject, which I can only
    hope that you will find as interesting, if not as instructive, as
    the other books which I have written.</p>
<p>G. A. Henty.</p>
<p><strong>Chapter 1: The Broken Window.</strong></p>
<p>&quot;You are the most troublesome boy in the village, Reuben Whitney,
    and you will come to a bad end.&quot;</p>
<p>The words followed a shower of cuts with the cane. The speaker was an
    elderly man, the master of the village school of Tipping, near
    Lewes, in Sussex; and the words were elicited, in no small degree,
    by the vexation of the speaker at his inability to wring a cry from
    the boy whom he was striking. He was a lad of some thirteen years of
    age, with a face naturally bright and intelligent; but at present
    quivering with anger.</p>
<p><a href="page2.html">Continue on text page >></a></p>
</body>
</html>
```

2. Enclose the sidebar content inside a `div` element. Add an `id` attribute with a value of `sidebar`:

```
<div id="sidebar">
<p><strong>CONTENTS</strong></p>
<p>Preface.<br />
  1: The Broken Window.<br />
  2: The Poisoned Dog.<br />
  3: The Burglary At The Squire's.<br />
  4: The Trial.<br />
  5: Not Guilty!<br />
  6: On The Voyage.<br />
  7: Gratitude.<br />
  8: A Gale.<br />
  9: Two Offers.<br />
  10: An Up-Country District.<br />
  11: The Black Fellows.<br />
  12: The Bush Rangers.<br />
  13: Bush Rangers.<br />
  14: An Unexpected Meeting.<br />
  15: At Donald's.<br />
  16: Jim's Report.<br />
  17: In Pursuit.<br />
  18: Settling Accounts.</p>
</div>
```

3. Add a `style` element to the document head:

```
<head>
<meta http-equiv="Content-Type" content="text/html; charset=ISO-8859-1"
  />
<title>A Final Reckoning</title>
<style>
</style>
</head>
```

4. Add a CSS `id` selector for the sidebar `div`, and set the `float` style to `right`.

An `id` selector contains a # symbol followed by the `id` value of the `div`. This type of CSS selector specifies the formatting for an element with the associated `id` value. The `float` property moves the `div` element to the side of the page, forcing the content of the page to wrap around it:

```
<style>
div#sidebar { float: right; }
</style>
```

5. Add spacing between the sidebar and the document body by setting the `margin-left` style to `10px`:

```
<style>
div#sidebar { float: right; margin-left: 10px; }
</style>
```

6. **Adjust the width of the sidebar by setting the width sidebar to 200px:**

```
<style>
div#sidebar { float: right; margin-left: 10px; width: 220px; }
</style>
```

7. **Save your HTML file.**

Figure 5-4 shows the newly created sidebar in a browser.

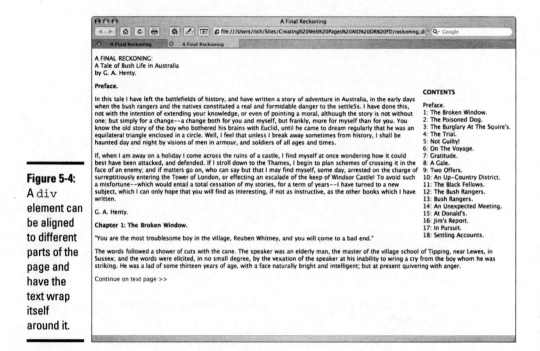

Figure 5-4:
A div
element can
be aligned
to different
parts of the
page and
have the
text wrap
itself
around it.

Centering a div element on the page

Although you can use the float property to align to the left or right of a page, you can't center a div horizontally on a page by using this technique. To center align a div block, you need to set the text-align:center property of the body (or the element container):

```
body {
margin: 0px;
padding: 0px;
text-align:center;
}
```

Note that if you center the text in the body, you need to add `text-align:left` in the `div` elements in the page to left align your text.

Positioning the div element in an absolute position

The example in the earlier section "Floating a div element on the page left or right" shows you one way to position a `div` element by using `float`. However, you can also use the CSS property `position` to set absolute positioning. For example, you might want to change the CSS style from the previous example to

```
div#sidebar { position: absolute; top: 50px; right: 40px; }
```

When you specify `position: absolute`, the `div` element appears at a specific location indicated by the `top` and `right` properties. However (and it's a *big* however!), the document body no longer wraps around the `div` element. As a result, absolute positioning of `div` content isn't nearly as useful for most designers, except for graphical content that you want to place in the background.

Formatting a div Element

Because a `div` element is used as a container for other content, it doesn't have any visible properties by default. However, you can use CSS to format the rectangular shape of the `div`. Typically, you format the border or background.

Adding a border

To add a CSS border to your `div`, use the `border` property (or its related properties — `border-style`, `border-width`, and `border-color`). If you want to add a 1-pixel black border to the sidebar, you add the `border` property to the style definition:

```
div#sidebar { float: right; width: 220px; margin-left: 10px;
    border: 1px black solid; }
```

Figure 5-5 shows the border around the sidebar.

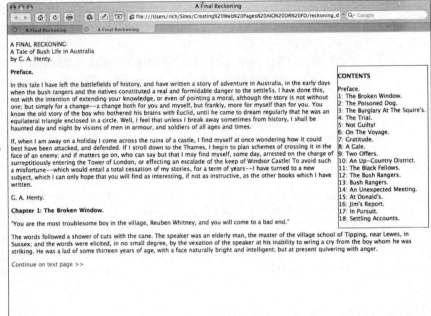

Figure 5-5:
A black border can add tremendous "resale" value to an otherwise nondescript div element.

The problem is that the border is too close to the content inside the sidebar. As a result, you need to add padding around the div content by using the CSS property `padding` (see Figure 5-6):

```
div#sidebar { float: right; width: 220px; margin-left: 10px;
    border: 1px black solid; padding: 7px; }
```

Adding a background

Adding a shaded background or background image to your div involves working with the background properties, usually `background-color` or `background-image`. Here's the code for adding a blue background:

```
div#sidebar { float: right; width: 220px; margin-left: 10px;
    border: 1px black solid; padding: 7px; background-color:
    #99CCFF }
```

Figure 5-7 shows the completed sidebar, now with a border and colored background.

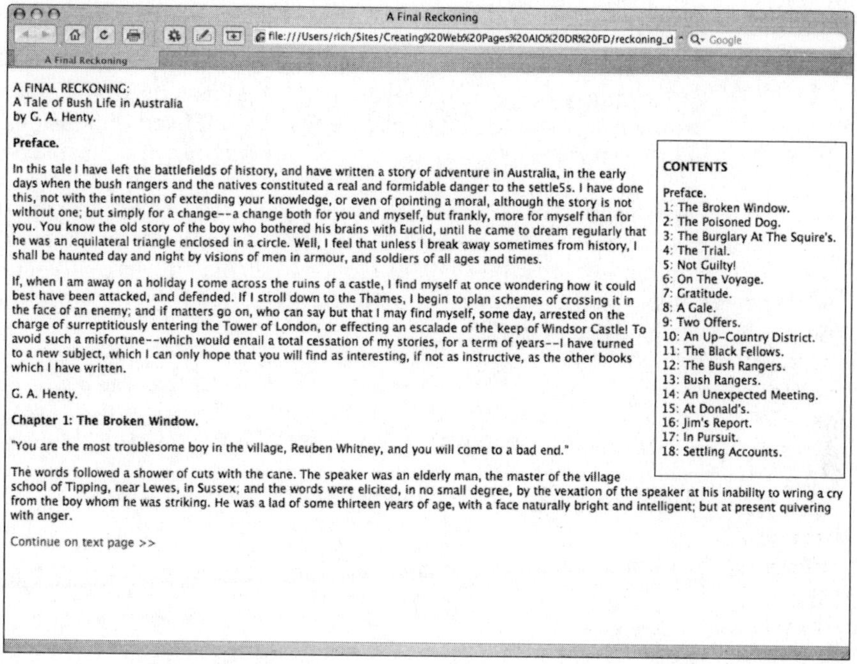

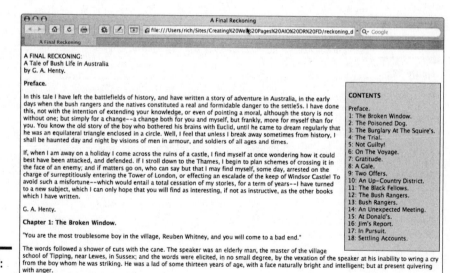

Figure 5-6:
Adding padding to the sidebar to separate the div content from the border.

Figure 5-7:
The sidebar with a colored background.

Creating a scrollable div

By default, a `div` adjusts its height based on its content. If you specify the CSS property `height`, however, the `div` adjusts its size to this value. The problem is that if the content extends beyond fixed dimensions of the `div`, some content is left "out in the cold" and unable to be displayed on the page.

Once again, CSS comes to the rescue with its `overview` property. When `overview: auto` is added to the style definition, scrollbars are added if the content exceeds the available space to display it. Here's the code for the sidebar in the example (note the newly added `height` property to fix the vertical size of the `div`):

```
div#sidebar { float: right; width: 220px; margin-left: 10px;
    border: 1px black solid; padding: 5px; background-color:
    #99CCFF; height: 150px; overflow: auto;}
```

Figure 5-8 shows the result in a browser.

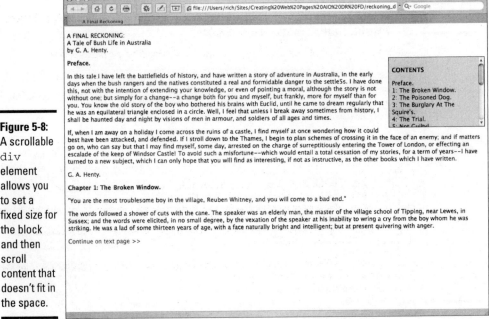

Figure 5-8:
A scrollable `div` element allows you to set a fixed size for the block and then scroll content that doesn't fit in the space.

Structuring a Basic Two Column Page Layout

The div is the primary building block for page layout because it allows you to carve up the page into different regions yet format and work with each of them independently of each other.

Here's how to set up a fixed-width div-based layout, using the popular two-column layout:

1. **Create a new HTML document with a skeleton page structure.**

```
<!DOCTYPE html PUBLIC "-//W3C//DTD XHTML 1.0 Transitional//EN"
   "http://www.w3.org/TR/xhtml1/DTD/xhtml1-transitional.dtd">
<html xmlns="http://www.w3.org/1999/xhtml">
<head>
<meta http-equiv="Content-Type" content="text/html; charset=UTF-8" />
<title>Two Column Layout</title>
</head>
<body>

</body>
</html>
```

**Book VI
Chapter 5**

**Divvying Up the
Page with DIVs**

2. **Add div elements to represent the major regions of a typical layout — header, body, sidebar, and footer.**

Use a container div element to enclose the body and sidebar.

Use descriptive id attributes to identify each element:

```
<!DOCTYPE html PUBLIC "-//W3C//DTD XHTML 1.0 Transitional//EN"
    "http://www.w3.org/TR/xhtml1/DTD/xhtml1-transitional.dtd">
<html xmlns="http://www.w3.org/1999/xhtml">
<head>
<meta http-equiv="Content-Type" content="text/html; charset=UTF-8" />
<title>Two Column Layout</title>
</head>
<body>
<div id="header">Don't play head games with the header content.</div>
<div id="container">
<div id="sidecolumn">This is the side column. It can go on the right or
    left and still be happy. </div>
<div id="bodytext">This section contains of the main body text of the
    document.</div>
</div>
<div id="footer">Not to be stepped upon, the footer content goes inside
    of this element.</div>
</body>
</html>
```

As you can see, we placed dummy text in the `div` elements for this example.

3. Add a `style` element to the document head.

To simplify this example, we're adding the CSS rules in the document head of this file. However, if you're using the same style settings for multiple pages, we recommend using an external style sheet (see Book V for more on this subject):

```
<head>
<meta http-equiv="Content-Type" content="text/html; charset=UTF-8" />
<title>Two Column Layout</title>
<style>
</style>
</head>
```

4. Enter the style definition for the `header div`.

Set the header to a variable width of 90 percent of the browser window and a fixed height of 80 pixels. The left margin is set to 20 pixels, ensuring spacing between the browser's window and the left side of the page:

```
#header {
    width: 90%;
    height: 80px;
    margin-left: 20px;
}
```

5. Add the style information for the `container` element.

The `container` element allows you to work with the main part of the document as one unit rather than always as two pieces (body text and sidebar):

```
#container {
    width: 90%;
    margin-left: 20px;
    min-height: 600px;
}
```

6. Add the `sidecolumn` element's style definition.

The `sidecolumn` element sets the `float` property to the right side. The width should be set to 150 pixels so that it's large enough to contain content yet small enough to work well as a sidebar for normal Web pages. The `margin` and `padding` properties are also set:

```
#sidecolumn {
    float: right;
    width: 150px;
    margin: 20px 0 0 0;
    padding: 1em;
    min-height: 570px;
}
```

7. Add the style information for the `bodytext` `div` element.

Padding is added around the document body text and adds a right margin of 175 pixels. The right margin is needed to ensure that there's ample padding around the `bodytext` content and that the document body never intrudes on the `sidecolumn` "column," even if the document body has a greater height than the sidebar:

```
#bodytext {
    padding: 1em;
    margin-right: 175px;
}
```

8. Add the `footer` style information:

```
#footer {
    width: 90%;
    height: 60px;
    margin-left: 20px;
}
```

9. Save your HTML document.

You now have a basic two-column layout in which you can begin to enter content into each of the `div` elements.

For demonstration purposes, we add a `border: 1px red solid` rule to each of the CSS selectors for the `div` elements. The results are shown in Figure 5-9.

Because the `sidecolumn` div has no fixed height, it's only as large as the content inside it. However, because of the margin settings of the `bodytext` `div`, the two-column look of the page is maintained, regardless of the height of the page.

The `div`-based layout is extremely flexible. For example, you can easily switch the `sidecolumn` div to the left side by modifying the `float` and `margin` properties of `sidecolumn` and the `margin` rules of `bodytext`.

In addition, if you want to transform the two-column layout into three columns (`bodytext`, `rightcolumn`, `leftcolumn`), you need to simply add a new `div` and set the `float` and `margin` properties for each one accordingly.

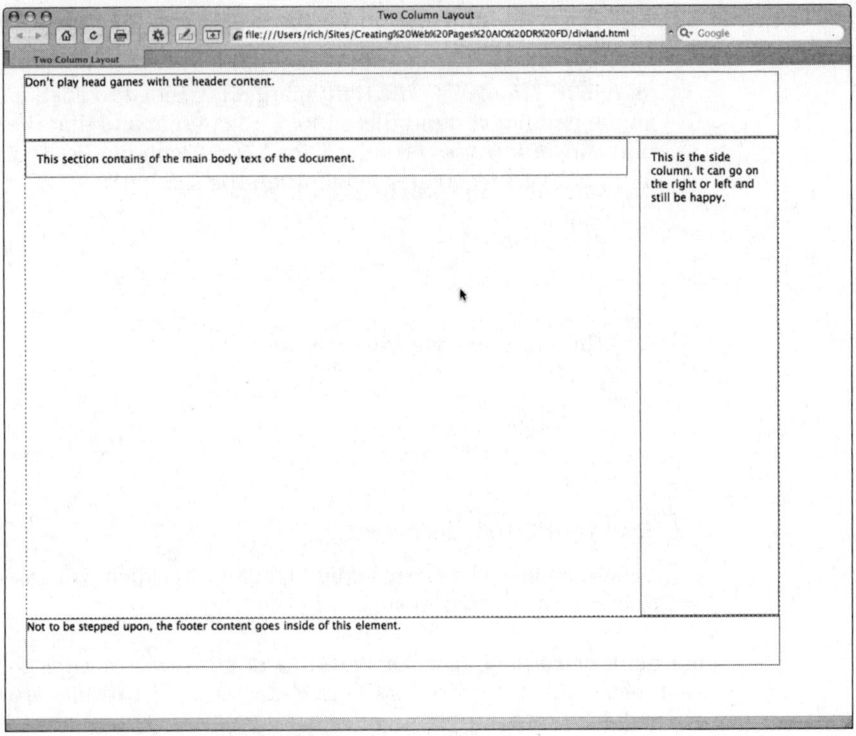

Figure 5-9: A basic `div`-based page layout with two columns.

Chapter 6: Creating Forms

In This Chapter

✓ Understanding the way forms work

✓ Creating a form

✓ Working with text boxes

✓ Adding check boxes, radio buttons, and drop-down lists

✓ Passing hidden values to the server

*M*any activities that people conduct on the Web can be considered passive: surfing, scanning, and reading content and clicking links. Forms provide a means for visitors to interact with Web sites. The familiar Google search box, the Amazon shopping cart, and any site's feedback form are all examples of HTML forms.

In this chapter, you're introduced to creating and working with HTML forms.

How Forms Work

A *form* on a Web page is used to collect information entered by the user into its controls and to pass it along to a program on the Web server for processing. The server-based program is responsible for working with the data passed by the form and then pointing the browser to an updated URL for the user to view. Figure 6-1 illustrates the process.

The `form` element is at the heart of forms processing in HTML. By itself, the `form` element is rather limited. It simply serves as a container for the form's controls and declares how the Web server will process the data that's collected. When a Submit button inside the form is clicked, all the contents of the form are submitted to a Web server for processing.

Most of the form's controls are `input` elements. Each has a `name` attribute that is passed along with its value (entered by the user) in the form of a name-value pair.

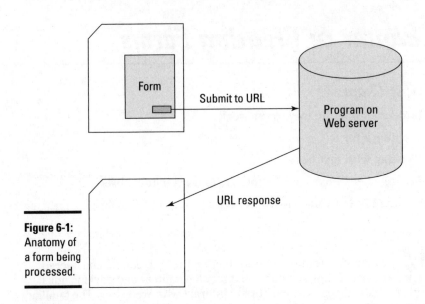

Figure 6-1:
Anatomy of
a form being
processed.

You can't just create an HTML form and expect it to work. It needs to work with a process on the Web server. Check with your ISP to find out which form processing modules are available for you. Typical applications include guest books, form submissions to your e-mail address, and feedback forms.

Creating a Form

The form element houses all the controls in a form, including edit controls, push buttons, and any text or images you want to include. The two common attributes of the form element that you work with are action and method:

✦ **action attribute:** Points to a URL on the Web server that receives the data when the form is submitted. The server must be set up in advance by the server administrator or ISP to provide this functionality.

✦ **method attribute:** Also used to specify how the data is delivered. Possible values are get and post. The default value, get, is the most commonly used method. It places the form's data inside the URL that's sent to the server. However, because data is being placed inside the URL, the get method has size restrictions. The post method involves transmitting the data in a message to the server. Check the instructions in the program being used on the server to determine the value for your form.

Here's the basic `form` element syntax:

```
<form name="order" action="../cgi-bin/processfrm.cgi"
   method="get">
 Form controls go here.
</form>
```

Adding Form Elements

After you define the form container, you're ready to add controls, such as edit boxes or drop-down lists, to your form that will collect the kinds of data you want to pass on to the server for processing. HTML uses the `input` element to define all but one of these form controls (`textarea` is the lone exception). The key attribute for `input` is its `type` attribute, which specifies one of ten possible values. Table 6-1 lists these form controls.

Table 6-1	Common Form Controls	
Control	*Type*	*What It Creates*
`<input type="text"/>`	Data entry	A one-line text box
`<input type="checkbox"/>`	Data entry	A check box control
`<input type="radio"/>`	Data entry	A radio button control
`<select></select>`	Data entry	A drop-down list control
`<select multiple="multiple></select>`	Data entry	A multi-select list box
`<textarea>Content<./textarea>`	Data entry	A multi-line text box
`<input type="password"/>`	Data entry	A one-line text box that masks the text that's entered by displaying another character (such as an asterisk) in its place
`<input type="hidden"/>`	Data entry	An invisible control that you can use to transmit data that you don't want displayed on-screen
`<input type="submit"/>`	Button	A button that users click to submit the form
`<input type="reset"/>`	Button	A button that clears data entered by users and returns it to its original state

Because the `input` element contains only attributes and not any content inside the start and end tags, you can, for example, shorten `<input type="submit"></input>` to simply `<input type="submit"/>`.

Powering your form with buttons

No matter which type of controls you use for data entry, your form is merely eye candy useless you add buttons to process the information you're collecting. Therefore, you should add a Submit button to every form you create. You use the `<input type="submit"/>` element for this purpose:

```
<form name="order" action="process.cgi" method="get">
<input type="submit"/>
</form>
```

A push button labeled with the word *Submit* is added to the form. However, if you want to customize the text, you can add a `value` attribute. For example, if you want to change the text to *Send My Order,* use the following code:

```
<input type="submit" value="Send My Order"/>
```

You can also add a Reset button to give users a quick way to clear the data they entered:

```
<form name="order" action="process.cgi" method="get">
<input type="reset"/>
<input type="submit"/>
</form>
```

As with the Submit button, you can add your own text by using the `value` attribute.

Be careful where you place the Reset button — don't put it where users would naturally expect to find a Submit button. More than once, I absent-mindedly clicked a button (usually in the lower-right corner of the page) that I thought would submit the form, only to discover that all my values were cleared. Not fun!

Working with form labels

In the early days of the Web, form labels were nothing more than ordinary text placed beside form controls. For example, check out the following label (in bolded text) before a text box control:

```
<form name="order" action="process.cgi" method="get">
Name: <input type="text" name="customer_name"/><br/>
<input type="submit" value="Submit"/>
</form>
```

This approach has a couple of problems:

✦ **The form is less accessible for people using screen readers.** A screen reader wouldn't recognize the text as the element name.

✦ **You cannot easily assign a common style to all the labels in the form.** For example, you might have ten labels provided in this manner alongside other text inside the form.

You can use the `label` element, which was recently introduced as a way to work around this problem, to associate a label with any kind of form control. It not only offsets the problems we already discussed but also provides additional control inside the form. For example, when a label is associated with a check box, users can click the label to select the check box.

You can add labels to your form in one of these two ways:

✦ **As a container:** A `label` element can contain the `input` element it's associated with, as shown in this example:

```
<form name="order" action="process.cgi" method="get">
<label>Name: <input type="text"
    name="customer_name"/></label><br/>
<input type="submit" value="Submit"/>
</form>
```

✦ **Linked with the `for` attribute:** A label element can also be associated with an input element, by specifying the `id` attribute value of an `input` element in the `for` attribute, as shown in this example:

```
<form name="order" action="process.cgi" method="get">
<label for="custname">Name: </label>
<input type="text" name="customer_name"
    id="custname"/><br/>
<input type="submit" value="Submit"/>
</form>
```

When you're using the `for` attribute, the placement of the `label` element relative to its associated `input` element is important. Place the `label` element in front of the `input` element for the label to be displayed before the control on the page. Place it after the `input` element code definition if you want the label to follow the control.

Although you can continue to use ordinary text to label your controls, the best practice is to use `label` elements to produce more accessible Web pages for all potential visitors to your Web site.

Adding a text box

A text box is the most common form control. To add a text box to a form, add a `label` element and then embed an `input type="text"` element inside it (or link to a `label` using the `for` method, described earlier in this chapter, in the "Working with form labels" section). For example, to add first and last name fields to a blank form, use this bit of code:

```
<form name="order" action="process.cgi" method="get">
<label>First name: <input type="text"
    name="first_name"/></label><br/>
<label>Last name: <input type="text"
    name="last_name"/></label><br/>
<input type="submit" value="Submit"/>
</form>
```

The `name` attribute is required and is used when sending data to the server for processing.

Four other attributes are commonly used with text boxes:

✦ `maxlength`: Defines a maximum number of characters allowed in the control; for example, `maxlength="30"`

✦ `size`: Defines the width (number of characters) of the text box; for example, `size="20"` (You can also set the width by using CSS.)

✦ `readonly`: Prevents the control from being modified, as shown in this example: `readonly="readonly"`

✦ `value`: Provides a default value for the field; for example, `value="Indiana"`

The password text box (`<input type="password"/>`) is nearly identical in function to the standard text box. However, as is the norm, the on-screen characters are replaced with asterisks. Note that when the form is submitted, the text (not the asterisks) that the user enters is treated as the element's value.

Adding a check box

A check box is used to indicate a true/false value and can be used for a single option on your form. Or, you can list a series of unrelated check boxes in which users can select one, many, or even none of these options.

You can create a check box with the `<input type="checkbox"/>` element. The following chunk of code shows a check box added to a basic submission form:

```
<form name="order" action="process.cgi" method="get">
<label>Name: <input type="text"
    name="cust_name"/></label><br/>
<label>Email: <input type="text" name="email"/></label><br/>
<label>Add me to your mailing list: <input type="checkbox"
    checked="checked" value="SubscribeToList"/></label><br/>
<input type="submit" value="Submit"/>
</form>
```

In this example, notice the following two optional attributes, which are often used with check boxes:

✦ `checked` attribute: Can be used to specify the checked state of the box when the form initially loads.

✦ `value` attribute: Indicates the value (true or false) that's sent to the Web server when the check box is selected.

Adding a set of radio buttons

Although check boxes are independent of each other, radio buttons are always grouped together as mutually exclusive options (you know, kind of like a multiple choice question on a high school history test). When a user selects one radio button, any radio button that was previously selected is automatically deselected.

The `<input type="radio" />` element is used to define each of the radio controls. This sample form uses four radio buttons:

```
<form name="order" action="process.cgi" method="get">
<p>Which team will go undefeated this year? </p>
<label><input name="poll" type="radio" value="patriots"/>
    Patriots</label><br/>
<label><input name="poll" type="radio" value="colts" />
    Colts</label><br/>
<label><input name="poll" type="radio" value="chargers" />
    Chargers</label><br/>
<label><input name="poll" type="radio" value="saints" />
    Saints</label><br/>
</form>
```

The `name` attribute is different for radio buttons than for other form controls. Its value (`poll`) is the same for each of the four radio buttons in the group. However, the `value` attribute is unique for each radio button. This value is sent to the server when it's selected by the user.

Like the check box, the radio button supports the optional `checked` attribute to indicate an initial On state for one of the buttons, as shown in this example:

```
<label><input name="poll" type="radio" value="patriots"
   checked="checked"/> Patriots</label><br/>
```

Adding a multi-line text box

Although the text box (`<input type="text"/>`) is effective in capturing ordinary text that users enter, it's practical only for relatively short entries (fewer than 30 characters). You can use the `textarea` element when you need to capture multiple lines of text from users. The basic structure of a `textarea` element is shown in the following example:

```
<form name="order" action="process.cgi" method="get">
<label>Enter your life story in the space provided:<br/>
<textarea name="life_story" rows="10"
   cols="40"></textarea></label>
</form>
```

The `rows` attribute indicates the number of rows visible in the `textarea` box. The `cols` attribute specifies the number of columns visible in the box. The `textarea` element also supports the optional `readonly` attribute.

If you want to place default text in the text box when the form loads, enter this content between the `textarea` start and end tags.

Adding a drop-down list or multi-select list

Another form control that's loosely related to the "multiple choice" aspect of the radio button is the `select` element. It's usually used to create a drop-down list of items from which users can choose. Each item in the list is defined with an `option` element. This simple example shows you how a drop-down list works:

```
<form name="order" action="process.cgi" method="get">
<label>Select your state:
<select name="cust_state">
   <option value="ma">MA</option>
   <option value="me">ME</option>
   <option value="nh">NH</option>
```

```
        <option value="vt">VT</option>
</select>
</label>
</form>
```

As you can see, the `select` element contains the `option` elements that are included in its list. The text between the start and end tags of the `option` elements are displayed to users as the item's text. However, the form sends the text inside the selected item's `value` attribute to the server when the form is processed.

You can also use the `select` element to create a multi-select list box. Suppose that you tweak your form to ask users to select each New England state they have visited. Here's the new code:

```
<form name="order" action="process.cgi" method="get">
<label>Select each of the states you have visited:
<select name="cust_state" multiple="multiple" size="4">
   <option value="ma">MA</option>
   <option value="me">ME</option>
   <option value="nh">NH</option>
   <option value="vt">VT</option>
</select>
</label>
<p>To select multiple states, hold the Ctrl or Command key
    while you click the items with your mouse.</p>
</form>
```

The `multiple` attribute allows users to select multiple items. (Standard browsers allow users to select multiple entries by clicking the items while they hold down the Ctrl key [in Windows] or the Command key [on the Mac]).

The `size` attribute is optional, but useful, when working with multi-select list boxes. It enables you to specify how many items should be visible in the list box. Scroll bars are automatically added to the list box as necessary.

An `option` element has an optional `selected` attribute. If `selected="true"`, the item is preselected by the document.

Adding a hidden field

Hidden input controls allow you to pass information from the page to the form processor without displaying the data on the form. Suppose that you have a form processor that automatically e-mails the results of the form to your e-mail address. Rather than be forced to display your e-mail address on the form itself, you can pass this information to the form processor by using a hidden field, as shown in this example:

```
<form name="order" action="process.cgi" method="get">
<label>Name: <input type="text"
    name="cust_name"/></label><br/>
<label>Email: <input type="text" name="email"/></label><br/>
<label>Add me to your mailing list: <input type="checkbox"
    checked="checked" value="SubscribeToList"/></label><br/>
<input type="hidden" name="mailto" value="info@ofniq.net"/>
<input type="submit" value="Submit"/>
</form>
```

Because the value of the hidden field is never displayed on-screen, you don't want to add a label for the hidden field.

Although hidden fields are invisible on the Web page, users can plainly see them if they view the HTML source of your document in their browsers.

Book VII

Graphics & Multimedia

The 5th Wave   By Rich Tennant

"How's it going? You get a handle on that Lasso function yet?"

Contents at a Glance

Chapter 1: Understanding Web Graphics

In This Chapter

✔ Obtaining quality graphics for your site

✔ Knowing what graphics to avoid

✔ Looking at graphics software options

✔ Exploring graphical design trends

The Web is a visual medium of communication. If you're going to create a Web site, therefore, where people will want to visit and spend some time, you must know how to work with graphics. A well-designed site effectively and efficiently uses photos and other images. A poorly designed site, on the other hand, is cheapened and weighed down by them. Your success depends on what images you use, how they fit into your page, and how fast they download over the Web.

In this chapter, we get you started with Web graphics, by showing you how to obtain quality images for your site and understand what kinds of tools you can use to edit and optimize them, and then we give you some graphical design tips to consider.

It's a Rasterized World: Exploring the Two Types of Graphics

The world of graphics has two basic types of graphics: *raster* (or bitmap) and *vector:*

✦ **Raster graphics** are composed of tiny pixels that are structured as a rectangle. Each of these pixels has a different color value (or, in some cases, transparency or opaque value). Because raster graphics are pixel based, they're dependent on the resolution. Therefore, you can't resize (and, especially, enlarge) a raster graphic without hurting its image quality. Examples of raster file formats are JPEG, GIF, and PNG, each of which is explored in Chapter 2 of this minibook. Photos and typical Web graphics are examples of raster images.

✦ **Vector graphics**, in contrast, are geometric shapes composed of angles, curves, and lines. Because vector graphics are based on mathematical calculation, you can scale them up or down without hurting their quality. The best known vector graphic format for the Web is Adobe Flash SWF. (However, keep in mind that a Flash movie can contain raster images.) SVG is another, lesser known vector format for the Web. Finally, EPS and AI (Adobe Illustrator) are vector formats that aren't supported by browsers.

The Web is now essentially a rasterized world because the vast majority of non-Flash images are raster graphics (JPEG, GIF, or PNG).

It's All about Quality: Finding Good Graphics

We can talk to you until we run out of pages in this book about how to optimize and manage your graphics. But if the quality of the graphics you're using is bad, our advice doesn't do you much good. Therefore, your first stop along the way is to the supply store:

✦ **DIY (Do-It-Yourself):** If you have a digital camera and an eye for taking a good picture, you already have the most hassle-free way to add graphics to your Web site. However, if your snapshots are filled with cut-off portraits, red-eyed people, and boring scenery, perhaps you should turn to other options on the list.

✦ **Free stock art:** A few years ago, if you wanted to find free graphics online, you were forced to visit tacky-looking sites filled with banner ads that offered cheesy clip art. Fortunately, free stock photography sites now rival commercial sites for the average person's needs.

Two in particular that we recommend are stock.xchng (www.sxc.hu), shown in Figure 1-1, and morguefile.com. However, note that these sites focus on photographic images and offer much less in illustrations.

✦ **Commercial stock art:** If you have a specific need and can't shoot it yourself or find a good free solution, you have to step up to commercial stock-art sites. These sites typically have royalty-free photos at a moderate price and often have both photos and illustrations.

Getty Image's Photodisc (www.photodisc.com) is our favorite commercial site, particularly if you need professional-looking illustrations. Another option is Photos.com, which offers unlimited downloads through a subscription service.

Figure 1-1:
The stock.xchng site offers professional-quality photographic images at no cost.

Avoiding Graphics That Lead to No Good

We strongly recommend that you avoid two kinds of graphics at all costs. One can get you into trouble with the law, and the other gets you a visit from the tacky police:

✦ **Copyrighted images:** Many legal issues surround the use of copyrighted images. Therefore, avoid going to another Web site and downloading an image for your own use unless you explicitly know that you have the right to use it. Even some of the lesser-quality, free sites have copyrighted material on them. Be wise in the images you use for your site.

✦ **Clip art:** Clip art is material for school newsletters and kids' birthday cards. However, it isn't something you should consider using for your Web site. Given all the other preferable graphics supply options now available, clip art looks amateurish and just plain tacky.

Choosing a Graphics Editor

Although the latest versions of the Windows and Mac operating systems provide the basic ability to crop and resize raster graphics, you quickly outgrow these very limited solutions when you begin working with graphics for your Web site. Here are some options to consider:

✦ **Web site software:** You can't edit your graphics, but some Web site software tools offer the modest ability to modify and tweak your images. Dreamweaver, for example, allows you to optimize, crop, resample, adjust brightness and contrast, and sharpen an image — without ever needing to leave the Dreamweaver environment. See Figure 1-2 for a look at Dreamweaver's Image Properties inspector.

Figure 1-2:
Use the Dreamweaver Image Properties inspector to tweak your images.

Even Dreamweaver, however, doesn't allow you to edit your graphics inside its environment. For editing, you need something more advanced.

✦ **Adobe Photoshop:** If price isn't an issue, hop on over to your favorite software-buying Web site or store and pick up a copy of Photoshop. It is, by far, the industry standard image-editing software for Windows and the Mac. When you first start out with it, you'll probably use only a fraction of its total capabilities. However, as you continue to use it, you gradually discover more and more of its power.

As a more casual — although economical alternative — Adobe also offers Adobe Photoshop Elements, which is a trimmed-down version of Photoshop.

Go to `www.adobe.com/products/photoshop/photoshop` for details.

✦ **Other commercial products:** In addition to Photoshop, you can consider other commercially available products. Microsoft has traditionally never been competitive in the graphics market, but its new Microsoft Expression Design is the company's best offering to date. It serves as a graphics-editing companion to Expression Web (see Book III for more on Expression Web). Go to `www.microsoft.com/products/expression` for more information.

Corel's Paint Shop Pro (`www.corel.com`) is another option to consider.

✦ **Gimp, the open source alternative:** If you're on a shoestring budget, you can check out Gimp to see whether t meets your needs. Gimp is open source software, so you're free to use it. And, it has versions for Windows, Mac, and Linux. Some users swear by Gimp, whereas others just swear at it. Given its price, it's probably worth your while to check it out. Go to `www.gimp.org` to download.

Following Contemporary Design Trends

If you spend any amount of time on the Web, you doubtless find some sites comfortable and attractive and other sites annoying and ugly. Book I covers quite a few design rules that you might find helpful. In this chapter, however, we want to touch on some important concepts of contemporary graphical design.

**Book VII
Chapter 1**

Understanding
Web Graphics

"Off with their heads": Cropping creatively

Never feel compelled to include the entire subject in an image. Take a look at Nordstrom.com. As you can see in Figure 1-3, two of the three models' heads are chopped off, and parts of their legs are missing. Cutting the size of photos is *cropping,* and every graphics application has a cropping tool. Creative cropping provides excitement, grabs the visitor's attention, and can even give a sense of motion by not showing the *entire* subject within your photo.

Avoiding symmetry

You often want to avoid symmetry in your graphics — that is, placing elements smack dab in the middle of images and Web pages. Consider, for example, the Nordstrom Web site shown in Figure 1-3. Suppose that you draw two lines to subdivide the main home page image into four quadrants.

As Figure 1-4 indicates, nothing is centered within these squares or positioned on the lines. Instead, the Web designer arranged the main focal points at almost random parts of the page.

Figure 1-3:
Near-sighted photographer or well-designed site?

Remembering the rule of thirds

Consider employing the rule of thirds to help you avoid symmetrical positioning. To use this rule, you draw imaginary lines to divide your photo or page into thirds, as shown in Figure 1-5.

In fact, you frequently find the element that the designer wants to emphasize most placed at the conjunction of thirds lines. For example, in Figure 1-5, check out the placement of the Full-On Fall headline.

The Tiffany & Co. Web site, shown in Figures 1-6 and 1-7, also follows this design principle. Notice how several key focal points for the two images align with the division of thirds.

Figure 1-4:
Dividing a Web page into quadrants illustrates how designers generally avoid symmetry.

Figure 1-5:
Notice how some important elements of this page align with the rule of thirds.

Figure 1-6:
The Tiffany
Web site
aligns with
the division
of thirds.

Figure 1-7:
Is the
placement
of the watch
on this
Tiffany
Web page
accidental
or by
design?

Chapter 2: Optimizing Your Graphics

In This Chapter

✔ **Optimizing graphics design**

✔ **Choosing the right graphics format**

✔ **Improving graphics download speed**

*E*verything has a trade-off, or so it seems. In Chapter 1 of this minibook, we discuss how to obtain and work with great-looking graphics for your Web site. However, if the graphics you add are roly-poly, megahuge bandwidth hogs, visitors to your Web will leave your site before you can say "Photoshop."

With the widespread use of broadband connectivity to the Internet, image size is less of an issue than it was a decade ago. At the same time, you should continue to pay attention to minimizing the overall size of your graphics — especially for visitors who access your site from dial-up modems.

In this chapter, you explore optimization techniques you can use to minimize the size of your graphics. We begin, however, by showing you the different types of Web formats you can use and when you should use each type.

Determining Which Graphics File Type to Use

Web browsers support three popular types of graphics formats:

✦ JPG/JPEG (`.jpg` or `.jpeg` files)

✦ GIF (`.gif` files)

✦ PNG (`.png` files)

Each of these types supports compression, making them preferred over other image formats, such as RAW or TIFF. For example, a 15 megabyte TIFF image can be shrunk to as little as 50 kilobytes using JPEG format.

These three formats have their own strengths and weaknesses. In the following sections, we fill you in on the details of each of the three main file types.

JPEG: A great all-around format

JPEG (short for Joint Photographic Experts Group and pronounced "jaypeg") format is your best all-around image format, useful for high-resolution digital photos (up to 16.7 million colors) and normal Web graphics. JPEG uses the *lossy compression* technique for compressing color and grayscale continuous tone images, which means that it tosses out colors that aren't easily seen by the human eye.

In general, the more complex the image, the better JPEG performs. It doesn't do well with simple graphics, line drawings, or text lettering. Also, unlike GIF and PNG, JPEG doesn't support transparency, so every pixel of a JPEG image must have a color.

One of the most powerful aspects of JPEG images is your ability to precisely control the level of optimization that you want to use for a given image. Image editing software enables you to specify the quality level of the JPEG image (on a scale of 0 to 100, where 0 is most compressed [smaller file] and 100 is no compression [larger file]). Figure 2-1 shows you the JPEG options that are available when you save an image in Adobe Photoshop. As you adjust the Quality value, Photoshop simultaneously updates graphic and file size — enabling you to determine where the "sweet spot" is between size and image quality.

In most cases, you should use a quality level of 30–75, depending on the image. We usually find a sweet spot for our images in the 40–60 range. Lower than 30–35, most images show noticeable degradation. Above 75, you don't get much difference in overall quality, even though the file size jumps significantly.

With small images, there isn't much visible difference between a heavily compressed JPEG image and one that's barely compressed. However, if you're displaying a larger photo (that occupies more than 20 percent of your Web page), you might want to back off on the compression because visitors will notice the difference.

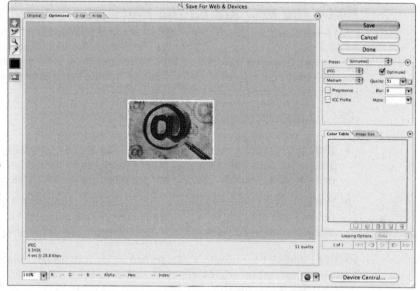

Figure 2-1:
JPEG format
allows you
to determine
the level of
compression
you want.

GIF: Great for text and transparencies

GIF (short for Graphics Interchange Format and pronounced "jif") was the
standard image format in the early days of the Web and still remains popular.
GIF supports only 256 colors, so it isn't a viable alternative for high resolution photos. However, its *lossless compression* technique is designed to work
extremely well with text, lines, and simple graphics in which only a few
colors are being used. (Lossless compression doesn't throw out information
to shrink the size.)

GIF also supports *transparency*, enabling you to designate the image's background as transparent. Transparency allows you to get away from simply
using rectangular images and create rounded corners, different shapes, and
so on. Finally, it's the only one of the three graphics formats that supports
animation.

Until recently, the biggest problem with GIF wasn't its technology, but,
rather, its legal handcuffs. For decades, Unisys had a patent on the GIF compression algorithm, and companies that used the algorithm in their software
were required to license the technology. Although that situation never
affected those of us creating Web sites, it did affect software makers like
Adobe and Microsoft. As a result, PNG (discussed in the next section) was
developed as an open source alternative to GIF. Fortunately, the legal claims
surrounding GIF have recently expired.

PNG: The new kid on the block

PNG (short for Portable Network Graphics and pronounced "ping") is the newest graphics format available for the Web. All modern browsers support the format, however, so you can now safely use it on your pages. As we mention earlier, PNG was developed as an open source alternative to the proprietary GIF format.

PNG comes in two versions:

+ **PNG-8:** The PNG-8 version is similar to GIF in 256-color support and simple transparency. You can often get better compression ratios by using PNG-8 over GIF, making it a great option for small, simple graphics.

+ **PNG-24:** The PNG-24 version supports 24-bit colors (that's millions of colors) and opacity. However, because PNG uses lossless compression, high-resolution PNG images are much larger than JPEG images.

PNG-24's support for *opacity* (also known as *smooth transparency*) is a step beyond simple on-off transparency in that it enables you to specify the level of transparency or opaqueness (on a scale from 0 to 255) for any pixel in the image. Using opacity, you can create translucent effects for your images, allowing the background to show through non-opaque pixels. (Note that earlier versions of Internet Explorer don't support opacity.)

Table 2-1 compares each of the three Web graphic formats.

Table 2-1	Comparing Web Graphic Formats			
Format	*Best Use*	*Worst Use*	*Transparency Support?*	*Animation Support?*
JPEG	Photos, continuous color and grayscale images	Simple graphics, images with sharp edges and lines	No	No
GIF	Text, sharp-edged art, line drawings	Continuous color images, photos, images with more than 256 colors	Yes	Yes
PNG-8	Text, sharp-edged drawings, clip art	Continuous color images, photos, images with more than 256 colors	Yes	No
PNG-24	Photos (although much larger than the JPEG equivalent), translucent images	Continuous color photos when file size is important	Yes (support for full opacity blending)	No

Avoiding Graphic Violence: Speed Up Your Web Graphics

Although 56K modem connections aren't the norm they once were, visitors from various parts of the country or world still don't have access to broadband. Don't laugh. Rich's hometown (which he regarded for years as the "black hole of the Internet") only recently offered a high-speed solution for its residents. What's more, as handheld devices like smart phones and cellular phones are increasingly used to access the Web, you still need to keep the overall size of your graphics in mind as you design your pages.

In fact, some visitors consider it criminal to leave unoptimized graphics on your site and express their frustration by leaving. To help you avoid the "graphic violence" of a slow page load, we have some suggestions for you. If you put these tips to good use, we may be able to make your graphics download quicker than you can say "Speedy Gonzales."

To ensure that slow connections display your pages rapidly, just reduce the size of your graphics files. You can do this in four ways:

✦ Reduce the file size.

✦ Reduce the dimensions of the graphical image.

✦ Give the appearance of quick performance.

✦ Define the image size accurately in the Web page.

We discuss each option in the following sections.

A great way to check your page speed is to use the freely available Web Developer extension in Firefox. From the Web Developer toolbar menu, choose Tools⇨View Speed Report. The page is submitted to Weboptimization.com, which provides a detailed performance report.

Reducing the file size

Consider the following tips as you work to reduce the file size of your image:

✦ **JPEG files:** The first place to optimize your Web graphics is to open these files in an image editor, such as Photoshop, and reduce their quality level. Start at a low value (as low as 5 to 10 on small images) and incrementally work your way upward until the image quality becomes acceptable. The moment the quality looks good, save the new file.

✦ **PNG-24:** If you're working with high-color PNG-24 images, save them as JPEG files instead.

✦ **GIF files:** If you're trying to reduce the size of a GIF file, check out the number of colors you're using. If it's more than 200, JPEG becomes a strong option to consider. If the file uses only a few colors, try PNG-8.

Cropping and shrinking the image

You can also reduce the size of a graphics file by *cropping* (lopping off parts of the picture that aren't important to what you want to show). Almost every graphics application has a *crop* tool, and you can experiment with it to see whether you can shave off some of the non-essential parts of the image.

Or, if you don't want to crop your picture, you can reduce its overall dimensions by resizing it.

A graphics application also has an *image size* tool, which you can use to specify either an absolute size (in pixels or inches) or a percentage, whichever is easier.

When you shrink an image to an absolute size, the graphics software often increases the pixels-per-inch (PPI) setting. When this happens, resample the image to 72 or 96 pixels per inch. However, you can avoid this issue by resizing with percentages.

Using percentages is easy because you just specify "Shrink the image 20 percent," and — wham! — it shrinks (automatically maintaining the original pixels-per-inch resolution). If you're clever with math, you immediately see that when an image is reduced to 20 percent of its original size, it loads five times faster.

Suppose that you want to display on a blog the photo of a deer shown in Figure 2-2. The deer, found roaming on our property, was photographed with an 8-megapixel camera. This photo, which is much larger than most monitors, measures 15 x 20 inches and obviously should be shrunk. Its file size is 4.66MB even when it's a compressed JPEG file.

To fix the problem, you resize. Click the drop-down list to change the current *inches* measurement to *percent*. Change the width to 15 percent. The height automatically changes to 14.98 to maintain the aspect ratio (the correct, original shape of the photo). Click OK and you see the result, shown in Figure 2-3.

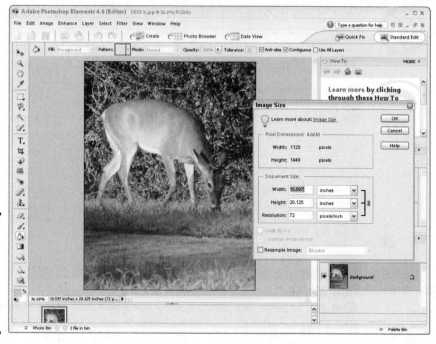

Figure 2-2:
This photo is larger than most monitors and must be shrunk.

Figure 2-3:
The newly resized photo is much more workable on a Web page.

Don't shrink an image too much, or else you lose quality. Shrink it to only the dimensions in which you will display it on the Web page.

Making the image download "seem" faster

The final technique you can use to optimize your Web graphics is to make the page *seem* to load faster than it really is. The way to do this is to explicitly define the `height` and `width` attributes in the `img` element; for example:

```
<img src="deer.jpg" width="239" height="148" alt="Bambi's
    return"/>
```

When you specify the dimensions of your image, the browser displays an empty frame as a placeholder *while the text of the page loads first*. As a result, the user can browse the page while waiting for images to be downloaded from the Web server.

Ensuring accurate image dimensions

Most Web site software tools, such as Dreamweaver and Expression Web, allow you to place any image in your document and resize it manually with your mouse. Although resizing an image in this way is handy, avoid doing so. Most tools don't resize the *image* — they simply adjust the `height` and `width` attributes of the `img` element. Therefore, if you shrink an image by performing this action, you shrink only the display dimensions, not the file size of the image.

For example, we recently troubleshot a friend's slow home page. When we investigated, we discovered that he was shrinking a very large (more than 3MB!) photo measuring 1266 x 815 pixels inside a relatively small `img` element of 383 x 214 pixels. Because the image looked small to him, he didn't realize the hidden weight behind it.

Therefore, as a general rule, when you need to resize images, use an image editor. Don't let the browser do the work for you.

Chapter 3: Hotspots and Image Maps

*I*magine that you're designing a Web site for a restaurant chain and you need to offer a restaurant-locator utility. You can offer a list of text links for each state. However, you much prefer a visual solution — displaying a clickable map of the United States. A visitor can click the state in which to locate the restaurant. The map image is then designed to respond to the click and send the visitor to the correct link.

In this chapter, we explore how you can transform ordinary graphics into clickable links for your Web site.

Understanding Graphical Links

As you can explore in Book VI, a hyperlink in an HTML document is defined with an a element, such as in this example:

```
<a href="http://www.cnet.com">Visit CNET</a>
```

When the browser displays the link, it normally appears as underlined text. You can use CSS to add text styles to links through pseudo-classes (see Book V). However, as nice as CSS styles can be, occasionally text alone isn't enough. In that cases, you need to use a graphical image as a link.

You can easily enough define a graphic as a normal hyperlink by simply enclosing the img element in the a link; for example:

```
<a href="http://www.cnet.com"><img src="cnet_logo.png"
    alt="Visit CNET"/></a>
```

What's more, if you're using Dreamweaver or Expression Web, you can work with graphical links much like you would work with text links.

Understanding Hotspots and Image Maps

Sometimes, a normal graphical link doesn't work. In the United States map example we discuss at the beginning of this chapter, a single link on the map image gets you nowhere. You need, therefore, to begin working with hotspots.

A *hotspot* is an invisible area within a graphical image that, when clicked, behaves like a regular hyperlink. An image that contains clickable hotspots is an *image map*.

Any JPEG, GIF, or PNG image can be used as an image map. In fact, the image itself isn't directly involved in the mapping. The hotspots are defined within the HTML code by specifying locations (x,y coordinates) inside the image.

The map element is used to represent the image map, and multiple area elements are defined inside the map element for each hotspot. The map is linked to the image by adding a usemap attribute to the img element. Here's an example:

```
<html>
<head></head>
<body>

<img src="countrymap.gif" usemap="#sweden">

<map name="sweden">
<area shape="polygon" coords="19,44,45,11,87,37,82,76,49,98"
   href="east.html">
<area shape="rect" coords="128,132,241,179"
   href="southern.html">
<area shape="circle" coords="68,211,35"
   href="stockholm.html">
</map>

</body>
</html>
```

In this example, the image is linked to the sweden map through usemap. (Notice in the code that the map name is prefixed with a pound sign.)

The `map` element serves as a container for the three `area` elements that define the hotspots. The `area` element has a `shape` attribute that specifies whether the shape of the hotspot is a rectangle, polygon, or circle. The `coords` attribute is used to define the pixel coordinates for the area. When the browser renders the image map, it connects the pixel values provided in the shape specified in a geeky game of connect-the-dots.

You can create image maps by using HTML code in this way, but using the correct pixel coordinates is a tricky process when you're doing it by hand. At a minimum, you need to open the image in an image editor and do a lot of homework on the pixel locations of your hotspot.

Despite this challenge, an image map is, quite frankly, an element you *really* should use in a tool like Expression Web, Dreamweaver, and even Photoshop. Visual tools like these enable you to easily define hotspots with your mouse.

Creating an Image Map by Using Expression Web

We show you how to create an image map in HTML, but doing it in a Web site builder is much easier. In this section, we walk you through the steps of using Expression Web. If you're using Dreamweaver, just flip to Book IV for instructions.

Book VII
Chapter 3

Here's how to create an image map in Expression Web:

1. **In Expression Web, open the HTML document that contains the image you want to work with.**

2. **While in Design view, click the picture to select it.**

The text *img* appears in the upper-left corner of the picture, and a resize frame surrounds the picture.

3. **Choose View➪Toolbars➪Picture.**

The Picture toolbar appears, as shown in Figure 3-1. You can add a rectangular, circular, or polygonal hotspot to an image.

Figure 3-1:
The Picture
toolbar.

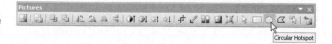

4. **Click the circular or rectangular hotspot button on the Picture toolbar.**

5. **Drag your mouse over the area that you want to become a hotspot (so that users can click it).**

6. **Release the mouse button after dragging the hotspot.**

   The Insert Hyperlink dialog box appears, as shown in Figure 3-2.

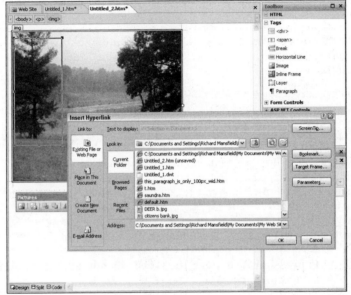

Figure 3-2:
Use this
dialog box
to specify
the action
that should
occur when
a user clicks
this hotspot.

7. **Choose from the Link To list the type of link that you want to add.**

8. **Click OK to close the dialog box.**

   If you look at the underlying code, you see that some code, similar to the following example, has been added to your HTML code:

```html
<p>
<map name="FPMap0" id="FPMap0">
<area href="default.htm" shape="rect" coords="2, 14,
    120, 265" />
</map>

<img alt="my modest home" src="file:///C:/backyard.jpg"
    width="407" height="346" usemap="#FPMap0" />
</p>
```

9. **Repeat Steps 3 through 8 to create other, additional hotspots in your image.**

The purpose of your image map will differ from the one in our example because we're pretending to build a tree-identification site. A user who clicks the tree shown on the left in Figure 3-2 is sent to a Web page describing pine trees. A user who clicks the tree on the right triggers a link to a page describing pear trees.

10. **Choose File⇨Save to save your document.**

11. **Press F12 to look at your Web page in a browser.**

When your browser opens, you might see a security warning (because of the image map). If so, make sure that you allow the block content to be displayed.

The image map is displayed in the browser, as shown in Figure 3-3. Notice that when the mouse pointer hovers over one of the hotspots, it changes from the usual arrow to a white hand, indicating that the user can click this spot.

Book VII
Chapter 3

Hotspots and
Image Maps

Figure 3-3:
Here's your
page!

12. **Click one of the hotspots.**

You jump to the destination of the hyperlink you previously defined.

Chapter 4: Image Rollovers

A rollover is a visual effect that you can add to your Web page. When a mouse pointer hovers over an image, the rollover changes the appearance of the graphical image.

Rollovers are the most popular image effect on the Web, and with good reason. They're relatively easily to create but make your site feel more responsive. They also add visual flavor without going over the top and looking tacky.

Rollovers can't be created by using HTML alone. Instead, you need to use JavaScript or CSS to create a rollover effect. Or, even easier, if you're using Expression Web or Dreamweaver, you can create rollovers without even having to write any code.

In this chapter, we show you how to create rollovers by using CSS. We then walk you through the process of creating them in Expression Web.

Creating Rollovers by Using CSS

Rollovers have traditionally been written using JavaScript. A script is set to swap the normal image with another when the mouse hovers over it. The images usually have text on them, to identify the link destination.

You can, however, use CSS to create a rollover. And, unless you're letting a tool like Dreamweaver do all the work for you, the CSS option is much easier — you don't need to write *any* scripting code. Additionally, CSS rollovers are more flexible and extensible — you don't need to create individual graphical buttons for each rollover link you're creating. In fact, all you need to do is create two generic buttons (without text) to represent the normal and hover states of the rollover. The text is added on top of the button by using CSS.

To show you how to create rollovers, we walk you through the creation of a navigation menu bar. (Or, if you need only a single rollover rather than a complete set, you can still follow along.) Here's how:

1. **Obtain or create two images that will serve as your rollover images.**

Use two nearly identical images — one for when the button is in its default state and another when the button is in a hover state. Make sure that no text is on the image itself.

We're using the two button graphics shown in Figure 4-1.

Figure 4-1:
These
buttons will
serve as
our pair of
rollover
images.

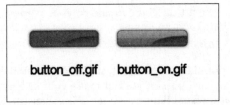

button_off.gif   button_on.gif

2. **Copy these images files into the root or images folder of your local Web site.**

We placed our two files (`button_on.gif` and `button_off.gif`) into the root.

3. **In your Web page editor, open the HTML document in which you want to add the navigation bar.**

4. **In your document source, add a `div` element at the location where you want to place to navigation bar.**

The code should look like this:

```
<div class="navmenu">
</div>
```

5. **Inside `navmenu div`, add a new `div` element for each of the buttons you want to add to your navigation menu.**

Here's the code we used for the four menu buttons:

```
<div class="navmenu">
<div class="menuitem"</div>
<div class="menuitem"</div>
<div class="menuitem"</div>
<div class="menuitem"</div>
</div>
```

6. **Add an a link for each of your buttons, too add a URL that will be accessed when the button is clicked.**

The following code shows what we did:

```
<div class="navmenu">
<div class="menuitem"><a href="index.html"></a></div>
<div class="menuitem"><a href="products.html"></a></div>
<div class="menuitem"><a href="services.html"></a></div>
<div class="menuitem"><a href="aboutus.html"></a></div>
</div>
```

7. **Add an img element inside each of the links, each referencing the default-state button.**

Our default-state button is named `button_off.gif`. The following code shows the navigation bar we're creating:

```
<div class="navmenu">
<div class="menuitem"<a href="index.html"><img src="button_off.gif"
    alt="Home" /></a></div>
<div class="menuitem"><a href="products.html"><img src="button_off.gif"
    alt="Products" /></a></div>
<div class="menuitem"><a href="services.html"><img src="button_off.gif"
    alt="Services" /></a></div>
<div class="menuitem"><a href="aboutus.html"><img src="button_off.gif"
    alt="About Us" /></a></div>
</div>
```

8. **Add a span element inside each the links, adding the text that you want to appear on the label.**

The navigation bar displays the span text on top of the button image.

Here's our code:

```
<div class="navmenu">
<div class="menuitem"><a href="index.html"><img src="button_off.gif"
    alt="Home" /><span>Home</span></a></div>
<div class="menuitem"><a href="products.html"><img src="button_off.gif"
    alt="Products" /><span>Products</span></a></div>
<div class="menuitem"><a href="services.html"><img src="button_off.gif"
    alt="Services" /><span>Services</span></a></div>
<div class="menuitem"><a href="aboutus.html"><img src="button_off.gif"
    alt="About Us" /><span>About Us</span></a></div>
</div>
```

Your HTML code is now complete. You can always add or remove buttons by repeating Steps 5 through 8.

You're ready to attach CSS styles to the navigation bar.

**Book VII
Chapter 4**

Image Rollovers

9. Copy the `navmenu.css` file (located on this book's CD) into the root or styles folder of your local Web site.

   We placed this file into the root folder.

   If you don't have access to this book's CD, you can re-create the CSS style sheet by entering the CSS code shown in Listing 4-1 and saving it as `navmenu.css`.

10. Open the `navmenu.css` in your Web site software or in a text editor.

    You need to tweak some of the settings to work with your navigation menu and buttons.

11. Update the lines marked with BUTTON WIDTH and BUTTON HEIGHT to match the sizes of your button images.

    As you can see in Listing 4-1, you need to modify the `div.navmenu`, `div.menuitem`, and `div.menuitem img` selectors.

12. Adjust the `width` property of the `div.navmenu` selector to fit the size of your navigation menu bar.

    Make sure that the width you define is equal to or greater than the number of buttons you're using multiplied by the button image width.

13. Optionally, adjust the font, font size, and text color properties in the style sheet.

    We identified these properties in the code to make them easier to find.

14. Choose File⇨Save to save the changes to your style sheet.

15. Back in your HTML document, add a `link` element to the `head` to attach the `navmenu.css` style sheet.

    The code is shown here:

    ```
    <head>
    <link href="navmenu.css" rel="stylesheet" type="text/css">
    </head>
    ```

16. Choose File⇨Save to save your document.

17. Open the document in your default browser, to check out the final results.

    Figure 4-2 displays our navigation menu.

18. Move your mouse over the buttons to display the rollover effect.

    Figure 4-3 shows off our rollover in action.

Figure 4-2:
A CSS
navigation
bar in its
default
state.

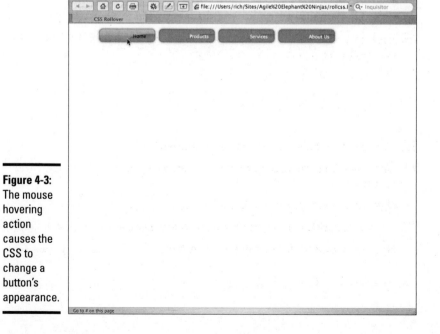

Figure 4-3:
The mouse
hovering
action
causes the
CSS to
change a
button's
appearance.

Listing 4-1   navmenu.css

```
/* Horizontal Navigation Menu Container */
div.navmenu {
    width: 700px; /* <-- OVERALL LENGTH OF MENU */
    height: 39px;  /* <-- BUTTON HEIGHT */
    margin: 0 auto; /* optional: centers navigation menu in its container */
}

/* Navigation Menu Item */
div.menuitem       {
    font: 11px "Lucida Grande", Helvetica, Arial, sans-serif; /* <-- DEFAULT
    FONT/SIZE */
    background: url( "button_on.gif" ) no-repeat; /* <--  ROLLOVER HOVER IMAGE */
    width: 144px; /* <-- BUTTON WIDTH */
    height: 39px; /* <-- BUTTON HEIGHT */
    position:relative;
    float: left;
    margin: 0;
    padding: 0;
    overflow:hidden;
}

/* Menu Link */
div.menuitem a {
    color: ffffff; /* <-- DEFAULT TEXT COLOR */
    display: block;
  text-decoration: none;  /* disables any normal link styles you have set */
    overflow:hidden;
}

/* Menu Text */
div.menuitem span {
    position: absolute;
    width: 144px;
    top: 14px; /* adjust vertical positioning of label text */
    left: 30px; /* adjust horizontal positioning of label text */
    text-align: center;
    cursor: pointer;
}

/* Menu Link: Hover */
div.menuitem a:hover {
  color: #000000; /* <-- DEFAULT HOVER TEXT COLOR */
}

/* Menu Image */
div.menuitem img {
  width: 144px; /* <-- BUTTON WIDTH */
  height: 39px;  /* <-- BUTTON HEIGHT */
  border: 0;
 }

/* Menu Link: Hover Image */
div.menuitem a:hover img { visibility: hidden; }  /* hides default button image
    during hover */

* html a:hover { visibility: visible; }
```

Creating a Rollover with Expression Web

As we mention earlier in this chapter, Web site builders such as Expression Web and Dreamweaver have built-in features that can make rollovers even easier. You don't even have to mess around with JavaScript or CSS because you let your design application do that work for you.

In this section, we demonstrate how to add a rollover in Expression Web. The following example shows you how to display a message when the user's mouse pointer moves over a photograph:

1. **Choose File➪New➪HTML in Expression.**

A blank HTML Web page is created for you. If you aren't in Design mode, click the Design tab, at the bottom of the main workspace.

2. **Choose Insert➪Picture➪From File.**

A file browser opens.

3. **Locate a .jpg picture, and then click OK to insert the picture into your Web page.**

4. **Click the picture to ensure that it has the focus (it has a drag frame around it, and the word *img* appears in its upper left corner).**

5. **Choose Format➪Behaviors.**

The Behaviors pane appears in the workspace, as shown in Figure 4-4. You use this pane to create and manage rollovers in Expression Web.

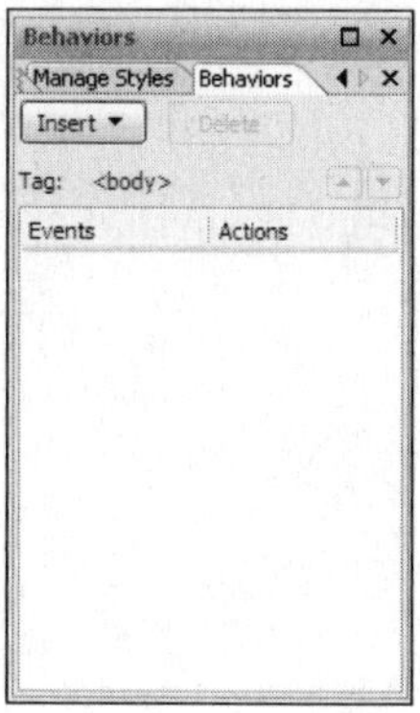

Figure 4-4:
Creating
and
managing
rollovers in
Expression
Web.

6. **Click the Insert button in the Behaviors pane.**

A menu of behaviors, or actions, appears, as shown in Figure 4-5.

Figure 4-5:
Choose
from one
of these
behaviors
for your
rollover.

7. **Click the Popup Message option.**

A dialog box appears, where you type the message that appears during the rollover, as shown in Figure 4-6.

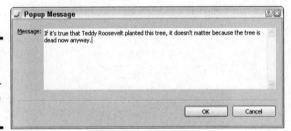

Figure 4-6:
Type your
special pop-
up message
here.

8. **Type a message, and then click OK.**

The dialog box closes, and you see that two items have been added to the Behaviors pane: `onclick` (in the Events column) and `Popup Message` (in the Actions column).

When the user clicks this image, the pop-up message appears. (That isn't what you want.) Although a click event is often the default setting for various page elements, you can change the event.

9. **Move the mouse pointer over the word `onclick`.**

A drop-down arrow appears, indicating that a list box can be revealed.

10. **Open the list box by clicking the down-arrow button next to `onclick`.**

A menu of options opens, consisting of all the actions you can select from to trigger the pop-up message, as shown in Figure 4-7.

Figure 4-7:
Any of these events can trigger a pop-up message.

11. **Click `onmouseover` to select that event as the message trigger.**

Now, things should work as you want them to.

12. **Press F12 to test your new rollover technique.**

You may see some dialog boxes asking whether you want to save your page and image. (You do, so click OK.) Eventually, your browser opens and displays the image.

13. **Move the mouse pointer over the picture.**

There it is! The pop-up message appears whenever a user rolls the mouse over the picture, as shown in Figure 4-8.

Book VII
Chapter 4

Image Rollovers

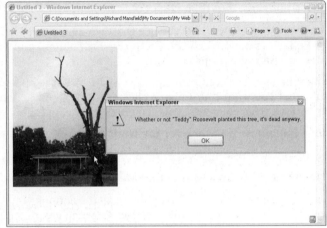

Figure 4-8:
The rollover is working. Your message appears whenever the mouse pointer moves onto this image.

By peeking under the hood of the document, you can see the code that Expression Web added for you. To do so, click the Code tab at the bottom of the workspace, and you see some code that looks something like this:

```
<!DOCTYPE html PUBLIC "-//W3C//DTD XHTML 1.0 Transitional//
    EN" "http://www.w3.org/TR/xhtml1/DTD/xhtml1-transitional.
    dtd">
<html xmlns="http://www.w3.org/1999/xhtml">

<head>
<meta http-equiv="Content-Type" content="text/html;
    charset=utf-8" />
<title>Expression Web Rollover</title>

<script type="text/javascript">
<!--
function FP_popUpMsg(msg) {//v1.0
 alert(msg);
}
// -->
</script>

</head>

<body>

<p>
```

```
<img alt="Mr. Roosevelts Tree" src="teddytree.jpg"
    width="255" height="325" onmouseover="FP_popUpMsg('Whether
    or not &quot;Teddy&quot; Roosevelt planted this tree,
    it\'s dead anyway.')" /></p>

</body>

</html>
```

Book VIII describes scripting in depth; for now, however, notice the connection between the *function* (the behavior that's carried out) and the *trigger* (the onmouseover event that triggers the function). The img element defines a message that is "passed" (because it's in parentheses following FP_popUpMsg, which is the name of the function). This message is passed to the function whenever the mouse pointer moves into the photo. The function then uses that passed message (which is identified as msg in the function) and displays it by using the built-in alert behavior (which display a message box with an exclamation point inside a yellow triangle).

Book VIII

Scripting

The 5th Wave   By Rich Tennant

© RICHTENNANT

F. MUTT

"Ms. Lamont, how long have you been sending out
bills listing charges for 'Freight,' 'Handling,'
and 'Sales Tax,' as 'This,' 'That,' and
'The Other Thing?'"

Contents at a Glance

Chapter 1: Understanding How Scripting Works

In This Chapter

✔ Working with the `script` element

✔ Connecting a script with an HTML element

✔ Understanding how JavaScript can add content to your document

✔ Triggering a script with event handlers

✔ Adding a ready-made script to your Web page

In this chapter, we don't dive into the details of JavaScript programming yet. Instead, we introduce you to how JavaScript works, how it's added to a Web page, and how it's called when a certain event occurs.

Surveying the JavaScript Scripting Language

Because HTML is a markup language, it contains a set of tags that are placed around blocks of content that categorize it or describe how to display it in a browser. However, when an HTML document is sent by a Web server for display in a browser, the document can't change.

JavaScript, on the other hand, is a scripting language that works with your HTML document to create interactive Web pages, such as image rollovers, self-validating forms, and dynamic visual effects. By itself, an HTML document is much like an inanimate statue. JavaScript "code" transforms this statue into a full-fledged moving robot.

In contrast to HTML, JavaScript is more like a traditional programming language, such as C++ or Java. However, JavaScript is easier to use and designed for specific tasks specifically inside Web pages.

JavaScript allows you to access different parts of a Web page, such as a form, an image, the entire document, or even the browser window. These objects are known as the *document object model (DOM)*, which we discuss more fully in Chapter 3 of this minibook. As you work with JavaScript, you create *scripts* — or mini-programs — that can control, modify, and transform various objects on your page.

JavaScript is universally supported by all major Web browsers, including Internet Explorer, Firefox, and Safari. The DOM is standardized by the W3C standards body, but not all browsers (particularly older versions) are fully compliant with it. Therefore, as you work with JavaScript, you should regularly test your work across multiple browsers to ensure that the functionality works as you intend.

Although it's not normally an issue, users can disable JavaScript in their browsers. Be sure, therefore, that your Web site doesn't depend entirely on scripts to let users function on the site.

Working with the script Element

JavaScript code can exist inside an HTML document in two locations: in a `script` element and inside the event handlers of HTML elements.

The `script` element serves as a container for JavaScript code that you want to execute. A `script` element is normally placed inside the document head, although in certain instances you place it inside the body. It has one required attribute, `type`, which indicates the MIME type (`text/javascript`) of the script:

```
<script type="text/javascript">
</script>
```

In older versions of HTML, the `script` element sported a `language` attribute to indicate the version of JavaScript. However, this attribute has been depreciated in newer specifications. Therefore, avoid using it.

Executing JavaScript automatically on load

JavaScript code is inserted as content in the `script` element, as shown in this example:

```
<script type="text/javascript">
alert( 'Welcome to the world of scripting.' );
</script>
```

This script displays an alert message box. JavaScript commands, such as `alert()`, inside a `script` element are processed when the script is loaded by the browser. In this case, the browser displays the alert message box to the user when the page is opened.

If the code inside the script element makes no sense, flip to Chapters 2 and 3 in this minibook, which deal with the basics of writing a JavaScript script.

Executing JavaScript on demand

Not all code is executed when the script is loaded. If JavaScript code is placed inside a function, the function must be specifically called by name to execute. A *function* is a block of code that begins with the keyword `function` and has the following structure:

```
function functionname() {
 // code goes here
}
```

For example, consider the following HTML file:

```
<!DOCTYPE html PUBLIC "-//W3C//DTD XHTML 1.0 Transitional//
    EN" "http://www.w3.org/TR/xhtml1/DTD/xhtml1-transitional.
    dtd">
<html xmlns="http://www.w3.org/1999/xhtml">
<head>
<meta http-equiv="Content-Type" content="text/html;
    charset=UTF-8" />
<title>Scripting test</title>
<script type="text/javascript">
alert( 'I show up when this script loads' );

function alertOnDemand() {
 alert( 'I show up only when I am triggered.' );
}
</script>
</head>
<body>
</body>
</html>
```

In this example, the first `alert()` command is triggered when the document head loads (see Figure 1-1). However, because the `alertOnDemand()` function is never explicitly called, the second alert message box isn't displayed to the user.

Figure 1-1:
A Java-
Script
message
box is
displayed
when the
script is
processed.

Therefore, although a `script` element contains the JavaScript code, you often want to trigger it from other HTML elements on the page.

Enabling JavaScript with an Event Handler

An *event,* which is at the heart of scripting in Web pages, is anything that happens to any object in the DOM — including all HTML elements, the document, and even the browser window. The page's loading — that's an event. So too is a button being clicked by a user or a user moving the mouse on top of a button.

JavaScript and HTML allow you to assign a piece of JavaScript code to execute when a particular event occurs in your Web page. The event-driven nature of JavaScript gives the scripting language its ability to dynamically interact with the user.

To connect the pieces, HTML elements have event handler attributes that essentially bridge the HTML world with the JavaScript world. For example, an `img` element has an `onclick` handler:

```
<img src="images/suki.jpg" onclick="openPreview()"/>
```

The image is displayed as normal, but when a user clicks the image with the mouse, the `openPreview()` function is called, which is a piece of code you can write to display an enlarged view of the picture in a special preview window.

The code inside an event handler doesn't need to consist only of calls to functions you have created in a script elsewhere in the document. You can also call any kind of JavaScript calls in there. If you want to display an alert message box when a user clicks an image, you can write this bit of code:

```
<img src="images/jboys.jpg" onclick="alert('J-boys love
    eating macaroni and cheese.')"/>
```

Figure 1-2 displays the results.

Figure 1-2:
This message box is displayed from a JavaScript command inside the `onclick` handler.

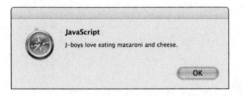

See Chapter 4 in this minibook for complete details on working with event handlers.

Embedding Ready-Made Scripts into Your Web Pages

As you're getting up to speed with JavaScript, be sure to check out several Web sites that provide ready-made JavaScript scripts that you can quickly copy and paste into your pages. These sites, however, are more than just useful for people who don't know how to use JavaScript. They're also excellent resources for even advanced scripters who don't want to reinvent the wheel on popular scripting techniques.

You can find a variety of JavaScript scripting repository sites, but many are dated and not well maintained. Two that do a good job of keeping current are Dynamic Drive (`www.dynamicdrive.com`) and dhtmlgoodies.com (`www.dhtmlgoodies.com`).

Chapter 2: Programming in JavaScript

In This Chapter

✔ Dissecting a script

✔ Knowing the basic syntax rules of JavaScript

✔ Discovering what variables are

✔ Exploring conditional expressions and loops

✔ Working with functions and operators

*I*f you're new to scripting, looking at JavaScript code can resemble trying to find an exit door in a dark room: It's confusing. It's hard to take even a step without bumping something or knocking it over. However, as your eyes slowly begin to adjust to the dark surroundings, you can start to discern the vague outline of an obstacle right in front of you.

As you begin to work with JavaScript, making sense of a script can seem daunting. However, as you begin to let your eyes adjust to your new environs, you begin to gradually see the shadows and outlines of the obstacles.

In this chapter, we help light your path through those dark alleys and cracks of JavaScript. After an introduction to object-based programming, you take a close look at a script and dissect the pieces of it. As you do so, you pick up on the key syntax rules of JavaScript and then can read about and better understand the code you're working with. We then talk about key programming constructs, including variables, conditional expressions, and loops.

It's All about Objects

When you write scripts, you work primarily with different objects in an HTML document and in the JavaScript language. An object in the real world is anything you see lying around your office or house: a desk, a cup of coffee, or a cat, for example.

In the same way, an *object* in a script is any element that might be found inside a Web page, such as a `table` element, a collection of a links, or even the document itself. In general, you can work with two groups of objects:

✦ **DOM objects:** The scripting equivalents of HTML elements and other parts of a Web page. When an HTML element is created by the browser, a corresponding DOM object is created at the same time. As a result, you don't need to do anything explicitly to create the DOM objects in your script before using them.

You're likely to spend most of your scripting time working with DOM objects. That's why you want to be sure to thumb over to Chapter 3 in this minibook for full details on how to work with the DOM.

✦ **Built-in JavaScript objects:** A set of objects that don't directly relate to an HTML document. These objects are used for working with data types (such as strings and dates) or for performing certain utility functions, like math calculations. Unlike DOM objects, built-in JavaScript objects aren't created by default. Therefore, you need to create them by using the `new` operator.

For full information on built-in objects, see the online JavaScript Reference at Mozilla.org: `http://developer.mozilla.org/en/docs/JavaScript`.

An object in JavaScript contains both properties and methods:

✦ **Property:** An attribute associated with an object that helps describe it. For example, the `document` object has a `url` property that specifies the location of the Web page.

✦ **Method:** An action or behavior that can be performed by the object. The `document` object has a `getElementById` method that retrieves a reference to the first element that has a specific `id` value.

Making Sense of JavaScript Syntax

As you begin, we want to avoid immediately explaining how a script code works. (The rest of this book does that!) Instead, begin by looking at the following code in the script:

```
<script type="text/javascript">

/* getParaCount()
Last modified: 3/29/07
Developer:          R. Wagner
Purpose:            Counts the total number of paragraphs in the document
                    and displays the results in a message box.
*/
```

```
function getParaCount()
{
  var paraCollection = document.getElementsByTagName( 'p' );
  var paracollection = 'dummy variable';
  var count = paraCollection.length;
  // If we find a match, then display count and then the first paragraph
  if ( count > 0 ) {
      alert("There are exactly " + count + " paragraphs in this HTML document.");
    alert( 'In fact, just for fun, here is first one: ' +
    paraCollection[0].childNodes[0].nodeValue );
  }
  // Otherwise...
  else {
      alert( 'Sorry, no paragraphs were found. Try writing one first!' );
  }
}

</script>
```

If this code sample looks terribly confusing, don't worry. In this section, we dissect various aspects of the script as we explain some basic "rules of the road" for JavaScript programming. Read this section to understand how to read the script for yourself.

Case is all important

Just like XHTML, JavaScript is case sensitive. The `paraCollection` variable is a different variable from the dummy variable that has all lowercase letters (`paracollection`). In addition, `var` is a valid keyword for defining a variable, and using `VAR` gives you a syntax error.

Semicolons mark the end of a statement

A normal statement in JavaScript can be almost any command, expression, or assignment operation. Take a look at the code and you can see each of the normal statements ending with the most neglected punctuation mark: the semicolon. Truth be told, JavaScript is flexible and doesn't force you to use semicolons (as long as each new statement is on a new line). However, it's considered good programming practice to include the semicolon.

Objects do dots

In the scripting code, JavaScript uses the syntax convention *dot notation* when working with objects and its properties and methods. In dot notation, the object name is listed first, followed by a dot, and the name of the property or method is separated with a period. For example, the following code snippet shows how the `document` object's `url` property and `getElementById` method are written:

```
var myUrl = document.url;
var myLink = document.getElementById( 'newslink' );
```

A second example is taken from the sample script. Check out this code snippet:

```
document.getElementsByTagName( 'p' );
```

`getElementsByTagName()` is a method of the `document` object that returns a collection of all the specified elements in the current Web page.

Curly braces are used to enclose blocks of code

In JavaScript, curly braces are used as containers for sections of a script. A function (for now, think of a function as a module of code with a unique name) uses them to define its starting and ending points. The `getParaCount()` function, for example, contains all its code inside the `{ }` braces. Curly braces are also used by various JavaScript statements (such as `if...else` in the example) to separate code in different branches.

Scripters often debate whether the first brace should be on the same line as the beginning of the statement or on a separate line. In this book, we prefer to keep it on the same line as the first code segment, but it makes no difference to the interpreter.

Collections and arrays are zero based

A collection and an array are special kinds of objects that can contain multiple items. For example, the `document.all` DOM object is a collection that contains all the HTML elements in a document. An *array* is a type of variable that can also store multiple items. In each case, you can access a particular member of the collection or array by an index number. However, in order to access the first item, you use 0, not 1. That's because collections and arrays are zero based, meaning that you start counting at 0 rather than at 1. For example, the following line of code that we use in the sample script returns the content of the first paragraph in the `paraCollection` collection:

```
paraCollection[0].childNodes[0].nodeValue;
```

Also, keep in mind that the last item in the collection or array will have an index value of one less than the total number of elements in an array.

White space doesn't matter

The spacing of the code matters to you only as a scripter, not as the JavaScript interpreter. Therefore, you can add as much white space as you want (by using tabs, spaces, and even blank lines) between parts of the code. Notice that one of us has the habit of adding a space after his parenthesis marks.

Helpful comments are encouraged

Comments are helpful to describe what a script or a specific line in it does. You can add your own comments to your scripts in two ways:

✦ **Single-line comment:** Add two slashes (//) to a line. Anything on the rest of the line is considered a comment and is ignored by the interpreter. In the example, we use slash marks to comment on the `if..else` statement.

✦ **Multi-line comment:** If you want to add a comment that spans multiple lines, enclose it inside /* and */ marks. The comment at the top describing the `getParaCount()` function shows you how this works.

Quotation marks come in a variety pack

You can use both single quote and double quote marks to indicate a string literal. As long as both sides of a pair match, it doesn't matter which kind you use. In the sample code, for example, we use double quotes in the first `alert()` command and then single quotes for the remaining two.

makeSureYouUnderstandHungarian NamingConventions

The JavaScript naming convention is popularly known as *Hungarian*. (No, you don't need to travel to Budapest to use it.) The Hungarian convention calls for a name to begin with a lowercase letter, and the first letter of each subsequent new word in a "compound word" should be uppercase with all other letters lowercase. With a couple of exceptions, the core JavaScript language and DOM uses this convention throughout.

For example, check out the following line of code from the example:

```
var paraCollection = document.getElementsByTagName( 'p' );
```

`document` is the object name for the HTML document and is in all lowercase letters. Its method, `getElementsByTagName`, is a compound word that gets elements by the specified tag name. Note that the remaining new words in the method name are capitalized.

We follow this convention in our variable names (`paraCollection`, `count`) for consistency's sake, even though it isn't required.

Book VIII Chapter 2

Programming in JavaScript

Avoid reserved words

JavaScript has a set of reserved words that are core parts of the language. You can't use these words when you name variables and functions, for example. Following is a list of all JavaScript reserved words:

abstract	final	public
boolean	finally	return
break	float	short
byte	for	static
case	function	super
catch	goto	switch
char	if	synchronized
class	implements	this
const	import	throw
continue	in	throws
debugger	instanceof	transient
default	int	true
delete	interface	try
do	long	typeof
double	native	var
else	new	void
enum	null	volatile
export	package	while
extends	private	with
false	protected	

Different types of data

In a script, you can work with a variety of basic data types, including string literals, numbers, and Boolean (true/false) values.

Strings

A *string literal* is a string of characters enclosed in single or double quotation marks. The following examples show string literals in the sample script:

```
'p'
'dummy variable'
"There are exactly "
" paragraphs in this HTML document."
'In fact, just for fun, here is first one: '
'Sorry, no paragraphs were found. Try writing one first!'
```

Although you normally want to work with strings as literals, JavaScript also allows you to work with strings as objects. This capability can be helpful when you want to perform certain processes on a string. Check out this example:

```
var str = new String( 'my life as a bus boy' );
alert( 'Original string is ' + str );
str.toUpperCase();
alert( 'Updated string is ' + str );
```

In this example, we declared `str` as a new String object by using the `new` operator and assigning it the value of `dummy`. Its original value is shown to the user, and then its `toUpperCase()` method is called. The `toUpperCase()` method converts the string to uppercase text. The updated text is then shown in the `alert` message.

Numbers

A number can be either an integer or a floating point number. You can even get fancy and use scientific notation, hexadecimal, and octal numbers. The script uses the numeric value 0 for a variety of purposes.

JavaScript supports a Number object. Again, although you normally prefer the simplicity of working with plain number values, a Number object is helpful when you need to convert it to different notations, such as exponential or precision.

Boolean values

A Boolean value is either true or false and is often used to determine whether a condition is true. Here's an example of testing the value of a variable named `confirm`:

```
if ( confirm == true ) {
    alert( 'You have been confirmed. Do not back out now!' );
}
```

JavaScript also provides a built-in Boolean object type, although it's rarely used by most scripters.

Arrays

An *array* is a collection of items that are indexed. The items can be a variety of data types, such as strings, numbers, or even objects. You can even mix and match data types within a single array. An array is defined with the `new` operator:

```
var states = new Array();
```

You can define the items in the array when you create the array by passing the values in as parameters:

```
var states = new Array( 'MA', 'ME', 'RI', 'VT' );
```

Alternatively, you can add items by listing them by their index value, or the order in which they appear in the list. The index value is designated by a zero-based value within brackets, such as

```
states[0]= 'MA';
states[1] = 'ME';
states[2] = 'RI';
states[3] = 'VT';
```

You can then access any value in the array according to its index. For example, to display the fourth item in the array in an alert box, you can use the following line of code:

```
alert( 'Customer is from ' + states[3] );
```

Working with Variables

Remember the television series *Alias?* Sydney Bristow was a secret agent and master of disguise who dressed herself up in a variety of costumes each week to defeat her evil enemies. JavaScript may not have the same intrigue, tropical locales, and plot twists as the television show, but it does have its own sort of master of disguise: the variable.

A variable is an "alias" for values you want to work with in your JavaScript scripts. In other words, a *variable* is a word that stores another value. For example, you can declare a variable named `myName` to be equal to the value of `Rich`. Then, everywhere that you want to use the word `Rich` in your script, you can use `myName` instead.

Why go to all the trouble? Why not just use the literal string `Rich` throughout? As you see throughout this book, a variety of programming tasks require variables. But, perhaps most noteworthy is that just like Sydney Bristow might wear multiple costumes in an episode, so too a variable can change its values multiple times during the course of a script. As a result, variables enable you to create dynamic scripts rather than have everything defined up front.

Declaring and assigning a variable

To use a variable in your script, you declare it. A variable is formally defined by using the keyword `var`:

```
var myVariable
```

The `var` keyword essentially says, "Hey, the word that follows will be a variable in this script." The variable name that follows needs to begin with either a letter or an underscore (although you can include a number elsewhere in the word).

In traditional programming languages, like C++ or Java, you have to declare the type of data that's stored in the variable: a number, character string, or Boolean (true or false), for example. The *interpreter,* a program that processes the code, needs to know that sort of thing. However, JavaScript is more flexible, which means that you don't need to specify the type of value that the variable will hold.

After the variable is defined, the variable can receive a value. For example, if you want to assign the value `Rich` to `myName`, here's the code snippet:

```
var myName;
myName = "Rich";
```

Didn't we say that JavaScript is flexible? Rather than declare the variable in one step and then assign it a value in another, you can combine them into a single line of code:

```
var myName = "Rich";
```

As the infomercials say, "Wait — there's more!" JavaScript allows you to use shortcut notation and declare a variable and then assign an initial value without using the keyword `var`:

```
myName = "Rich";
```

TIP

Although you can use this shorthand notation, the use of the keyword `var` can make your code more readable and easier to understand as you work with it.

Accessing a variable

After a variable is defined, you can reference the variable in your code, and its current value is used. Check out the code in the following brief script. The value of `currentName` starts out as `"Rich"` but is then reassigned to a value that the user enters in a prompt dialog box:

```
var currentName = "Rich";
alert( "Hello, my name is" + currentName );
currentName = prompt( "Please enter your name.", "Jimmy
    Crackcorn" );
alert( "Hello, " + currentName + ". That is a really nice
    name. And I don't say that to just anyone." );
```

Scoping out variable scope and lifetime

A variable can have either a global or local scope. Any variable that's defined outside of a function is a *global variable* — you can access it from any other part of the document. A variable declared inside a function (a *local variable*) is accessible only to the function itself and is destroyed when the function is done processing.

In addition, the location in which a variable is defined matters. A variable is accessible only after it's declared. Therefore, you generally want to make sure that all global variables are defined at the start of the first `script` element in the document head.

The following code provides a good illustration of the scope of variables:

```
<!DOCTYPE html PUBLIC "-//W3C//DTD XHTML 1.0 Transitional//EN"
    "http://www.w3.org/TR/xhtml1/DTD/xhtml1-transitional.dtd">
<html xmlns="http://www.w3.org/1999/xhtml">
<head>
<meta http-equiv="Content-Type" content="text/html; charset=UTF-8" />
<title>Scoping out Variables</title>
<script type="text/javascript">
// Global variable
var quote = 'Think global.';

// Function
function quoteme() {
    // Local variable
    var quote = 'Act local.'
    alert( quote );
}
```

```
alert( quote ); // called when document opens
</script>
</head>

<body>

<form id="form1" name="form1" method="post" action="">
  <input type="button" name="localvar" value="Local" onclick="quoteme();"/>
  <input type="button" name="globalvar" value="Global" onclick="alert( quote
    );"/>
</form>

<script type="text/javascript">
// Global variable
var quote = 'Think globally with a twist. ';
</script>

</body>
</html>
```

The variable `quote` is defined three different times:

✦ As a global variable in the top `script` element

✦ As a local variable in the `quoteme()` function

✦ As a global variable in a `script` element that's placed at the bottom of the document body.

When the document loads, the `alert()` command (the final line of the first `script` element) is called and displays the current value of `quote`, which is `'Think global.'` When the Local button is clicked, it calls the `quoteme()` function, which displays the value of the local version of the `quote` variable, `'Act local.'` Finally, when the Global button is clicked, it displays "Think globally with a twist" because the global variable `quote` was reassigned a new value when the bottom `script` element was processed (on document load).

Working with constants

Not all variables need to change values during the processing of the script. Sometimes, a variable is simply a handy way to refer to another value. Many programming languages, in fact, have *constants*, which are essentially variables that don't change values.

JavaScript doesn't have the concept of a constant built into the language. Don't let that stop you. You can create a constant as a normal variable but use a special naming convention to make constants and variables easy to distinguish from each other. To follow the conventions of traditional languages, use all uppercase words and separate different words with underscores:

```
var COUNTY = "United States of America";
var PI = 3.14159;
var VERSION_NUMBER = "8.02";
```

You can use a constant value in the same manner as you use a variable in your code (which is good because it really is a variable with an uppercase name).

Basic Conditional Expressions

"That depends." How often do you find yourself using that expression during the day? Suppose that the bartender asks, "Would you like another beer?" You look at the friend you drove to the bar with and say, "That depends. Am I driving, or are you?"

JavaScript also allows you to perform conditional logic in your scripts with three types of statements:

✦ if

✦ if...else

✦ switch

The if statement

The if statement is used when you want to run a portion of code if the expression you're testing is true. The basic structure looks like this:

```
if ( condition ) {
    // code to execute if condition is true
}
```

For example, consider the following code snippet:

```
secretcode = prompt( "Enter the secret code.", "" );
if ( secretcode == "moops" ) {
    alert( "You won the contest." );
}
```

A prompt dialog box is displayed to the user when the script is executed. The secretcode variable stores the value given by the user. The if statement then evaluates whether secretcode is equal to "moops". If so, a message box is displayed. Otherwise, the alert() command is bypassed.

Let us mention that the double equal sign in the conditional expression isn't a typo. A single equal sign (=) is used to assign a value to a variable, and a double equal sign (==) is used to compare one side of an expression with another.

The if...else statement

The `if...else` statement is similar to the `if` statement, except that you can also run code only if the expression evaluates to false:

```
if ( condition ) {
    // code to execute if condition is true
}
else {
    // code to execute if condition is false
}
```

Here's an example of the `if...else` statement in action:

```
if ( document.title == 'Home page' ) {
    alert( "Welcome home" );
}
else {
    alert( "Here's where you are instead " + document.title
    );
}
```

The switch statement

The `if` and `if..else` statements are ideal for evaluating for a single value, but suppose that you want to check for multiple values. The `switch` statement comes in handy for exactly this reason. Its basic structure is shown here:

```
switch ( expression ) {
case label1:
  // code to be executed if expression equals label1
  break;
case label2:
  //code to be executed if expression equals label2
  break;
default:
  // code to be executed if expression is different
  // from both label1 and label2
}
```

The `switch` evaluates the condition and looks to see whether the result equals the first `case` value. If so, the program performs the code inside the `case` statement. The `break` statement is used to stop the flow of the `switch` statement from continuing its evaluation in the `case` statements that follow. The `default` statement is executed if no matches are found.

Here's an example that uses the `switch` statement to evaluate the current time by using the built-in `Date()` object:

```
var d = new Date()
var hr = d.getHours()

switch ( hr ) {
case 8 :
   document.write( "Good morning sunshine." );
   break;
case 12 :
   document.write( "Lunch time!" );
   break;
case 15 :
   document.write( "Afternoon tea with the queen." );
   break;
case 22 :
   document.write( "Time to hit the sack." );
   break;
default
   document.write( "Come back later." );
}
```

The `hr` variable is assigned the current hour by using the `getHours()` method. The `switch` statement evaluates `hr`, by looking at each of the `case` statements in sequence. If it finds a match, the code inside is executed. Otherwise, the `default` statement is executed.

Getting Loopy: Working with Looping Constructs

A common need when you develop in JavaScript is the ability to loop through a task a number of times or until a specific condition changes. JavaScript provides two programming constructs that allow you to "get loopy": `for` and `while`. The `for` loop cycles through a block of code a specific number of times. The `while` loop loops through a program block as long as a specific condition is true.

The for loop

A `for` loop can look rather intimidating for new scripters because the construct looks much like gibberish. After you understand the pieces, though, it becomes a rather straightforward tool to add to your scripting tool belt. Here's an example of a loop cycling through ten times:

```
for ( var i=1;i<=10;i++) {
    document.write( "Pass number " + i + "<br/>" );
}
```

- ✦ **Initialization statement:** The `var i=1` is the initializing piece, indicating that the loop declares and then uses a counter variable named `i`, which has a starting value of `1`. (The variable `i` is the standard name for most JavaScript loop counters.)

- ✦ **Condition:** The `i<=10` indicates the condition that's evaluated each time the loop is cycled through. The condition returns true as long as the `i` value is less than or equal to 10.

- ✦ **Update statement:** The `i++` is the update statement that's processed after each time through the loop. In this case, the shortcut expression `++` increments the value by 1.

This `for` loop repeats the code block inside the brackets ten times. After the loop evaluates to false on the 11th pass, the script goes on to the next line of code. The output for the script is shown here:

```
Pass number 1
Pass number 2
Pass number 3
Pass number 4
Pass number 5
Pass number 6
Pass number 7
Pass number 8
Pass number 9
Pass number 10
```

For the most part, you can copy and paste a `for` loop construct into your script. For most purposes, you need to update only two values (the counter number and the code to process), which we indicate by bolding in this example:

```
for ( var i=1;i<=10;i++) {
    // code
}
```

However, you don't always need to use a number. Here's an example of a loop based on the total number of links in the current document:

```
for ( var i=0;i<document.links.length;i++ ) {
    processLink( document.links[i] );
}
```

The while loop

Like a `for` loop, a `while` loop cycles through a block of code multiple times. However, although `for` loops through a specific number of times, `while` executes a block of code as long as a condition evaluates to true. Its generic form is simpler than the `for` loop:

```
while( condition ) {
  // code to process when condition is true
}
```

Here's an example:

```
while( items > 10 ) {
    document.writeln( "Current item count is " + items );
    processOrder( items ); // Fictional custom function
    items++;
}
```

In this example, the code block loops through as long as the `items` variable is less than 10. Inside the block, the current item count is written, followed by a call to a fictional function named `processOrder()`, which can be used to act on the current state of the order. Finally, the value of the `items` variable is incremented by 1 by `items++`.

Working with Functions

A *function* is a named group of JavaScript commands and statements that has to be explicitly called by an event or your script before it's executed. Suppose that you have a miniscript that performs a validity check on a form text field. You can create a function to handle this process and then call the function by name every time the user leaves any text field in your form.

You can think of a function as a factory that processes stuff. A real world factory receives raw material (such as steel), does something to it inside the factory (molds the steel into components, for example), and then sends out a finished product (such as a car). In the same way, a function can accept optional input values (called *arguments* or *parameters*), performs a specific process, and can optionally send back a *return value* to whichever event handler or line of code called it.

To define a function, you use the following structure:

```
function myFunctionName( [param1,param2...] ) {
    // Function code goes here
}
```

To illustrate, here's a function for creating a cookie. The function is named `addCookie()` and accepts three arguments, the last of which is optional:

```
function addCookie( cookieName, cookieValue, days ) {
    if ( days ) {
        var dt = new Date();
        dt.setTime( dt.getTime()+ ( days*24*60*60*1000 ) );
        var expdate = "; expires=" + date.toGMTString();
    }
    else {
var expdate = "";
    }
    document.cookie = cookieName + "=" + cookieValue +
    expdate + "; path=/";
}
```

To call this function, here's what the statement looks like:

```
addCookie( 'username', 'rayman', 90 );
```

The `addCookie()` function processes its code based on the arguments that are supplied and creates a cookie. In this example, no result is sent back to the statement that called the code. Instead, `addCookie()` simply performs its job and then quits.

A second example demonstrates how a value is returned to the calling statement by using the `return` command:

```
function calcTotal( netTotal ) {
   var t = ( netTotal * .05 );
   return t;
}
```

**Book VIII
Chapter 2**

**Programming
in JavaScript**

Note: This bit of code is expanded for clarity. You can combine the two into a single line: `return ( netTotal * .05 );`.

When the `return` command is encountered, the function stops executing and returns program control to the statement that called the function. Therefore, if you place statements after the `return` command, the interpreter ignores them.

A method of an object is basically the same thing as a function. The only difference is that a method is designed to perform an action on its associated object, and a function is a more generic piece of code that you can create to do anything you please.

Operators Are Standing By: Connecting with JavaScript Operators

In this digital age, the role of the telephone operator is long forgotten for all except special needs. However, if you think back to the early years of the telephone, the operator played an important role in connecting the caller to another phone line. A JavaScript operator acts something like the old phone operator, by connecting different JavaScript pieces of code. You use operators to add numbers, connect two strings, assign values to variables, or evaluate expressions, for example.

Postmodern JavaScript

In the early days of JavaScript, scripters needed to account for browsers that didn't support scripting. Therefore, to prevent JavaScript code from screwing up an older browser's processing of the document, a common practice was to enclose all the scripting code with HTML comments:

```
<script>
<!--
    // JavaScript code
-->
</script>
```

All browsers now deal with the `script` element. What's more, using HTML comments inside a `script` tag violates XHTML standards. Avoid this practice when you're writing your own JavaScript.

Tables 2-1, 2-2, 2-3, and 2-4 list the major operators in JavaScript. The ones you most often use are shown in bold.

Table 2-1		Assignment Operators
Operator	*Example*	*Description*
=	**x=y**	**The value of y is assigned to x**
+=	**x+=y**	**Same as x=x+y**
−=	x−=y	Same as x=x-y
*=	x*=y	Same as x=x*y
/=	x/=y	Same as x=x/y
%=	x%=y	Same as x=x%y (modulus)

Table 2-2		Comparison Operators
Operator	*Example*	*Description*
==	**x==y**	**x is equal to y**
!=	**x!=y**	**x is not equal to y**
===	x===y	Evaluates both for value and data type (for example, if x = "5" and y = 5, then x==y is true, but x===y is false)
<	**x<y**	**x is less than y**
<=	**x<=y**	**x is less than or equal to y**
>	**x>y**	**x is greater than y**
>=	**x>=y**	**x is greater than or equal to y**
?:	x=(y<5) ? -5 : y	If y is less than 5, then assign -5 to x; otherwise, assign y to x (known as the conditional operator)

Table 2-3		Logical Operators
Operator	*Example*	*Description*
&&	**if (x > 3 && y=0)**	**logical and**
||	if (x>3 || y=0)	logical or
!	if !(x=y)	not

Table 2-4		Mathematical Operators
Operator	*Example*	*Description*
+	x+2	**Addition**
–	x-3	**Subtraction**
*	x*2	Multiplication
/	x/2	Division
%	x%2	Modulus (division remainder)
++	x++	**Increment (same as x=x+1)**
--	x--	**Decrement (same as x=x–1)**

Chapter 3: Understanding the Document Object Model

In This Chapter

✓ Understanding the DOM

✓ Accessing objects in the DOM

✓ Working with properties and methods

✓ Adding and removing DOM objects

✓ Exploring DOM objects

As we start introducing scripting to you, we dance around the Document Object Model (DOM) in two chapters. We allude to it. We used it in some scripting examples, but now we dive head first into the DOM, which is the heart of scripting Web pages.

In this chapter, you explore the DOM and how to work with it to create interactive scripts for your Web pages.

What Is the DOM?

The *Document Object Model (DOM)* is a scripting interface to HTML and XML documents. That's a geeky way of saying that the DOM allows you to access, tap into, and even modify the structure of your Web page by using scripting. As its name suggests, the DOM is a modeled structure that describes the relationships of all elements on a document through a hierarchy. The DOM also defines which properties, methods, and events are available for each of its objects.

The DOM is a standard set by the W3C, the Web standards body. All newer browsers (Internet Explorer, Firefox, Safari, and Opera, for example) support the Level 1 and Level 2 versions of the DOM. (Level 1 focused on HTML, and Level 2 refined the standard to support XML and XHTML documents.)

The cross-browser support of the DOM that you can now enjoy is a relatively new phenomenon. When the DOM was introduced in the late 1990s, different browsers provided various levels of support and often had their own idiosyncratic additions to the standard. Fortunately, these problems have largely disappeared in newer generations of browsers.

Think of the DOM as a tree-like structure that organizes the parts of the HTML document as a hierarchy of object nodes. A *node* can be an element, an attribute, some content, or any part of a Web page. A node can contain other nodes. The DOM uses family terminology to describe the relationships of these nodes. A parent contains child nodes, and two nodes on the same hierarchical level are considered siblings.

The `document` object serves as the "trunk" of this document tree. Because this object has no HTML element equivalent, you can think of it as a "super-object" of sorts, as it contains every document element, including `html`, `head`, and `body`. All remaining elements and other parts of the Web page are descendent nodes of `document`.

For most common purposes, you work exclusively with HTML elements in the DOM. But, technically speaking, the nodes in a document tree consist of elements and content. (The content of an element is a child node of the container element.) Attributes aren't considered part of the document tree, but are accessed as properties of the element object.

Consider, for example, the following code snippet for a basic Web page:

```
<html>
<head>
<title>Great Novelists Online</title>
</head>
<body>
<h1>Best Opening Lines</h1>
<p id="p1">It was the best of times. It was the worst of
    times.</p>
</body>
</html>
```

Figure 3-1 shows what this HTML code looks like as a DOM document tree.

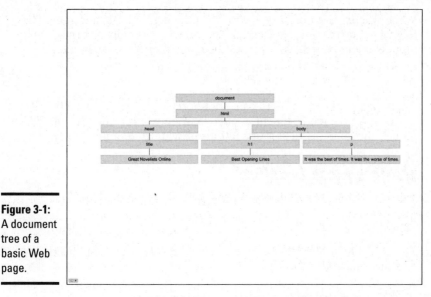

Figure 3-1:
A document
tree of a
basic Web
page.

Accessing DOM Objects

As you work with DOM objects in your scripts, one of the most important tasks is being able to access the particular object or collection of objects that you want to manipulate. The DOM provides several ways to reference a particular DOM object.

Using dot notation

To access a particular object, you need to refer to it in your code relative to the document's object hierarchy by using dot notation. Consider the following HTML snippet:

```
<form id="shippingForm" method="post" action="">
<input type="text" id="firstName" />
</form>
```

To reference the text input element inside the form and assign it to a variable, you use this line:

```
var fn = document.shippingForm.firstName;
```

When you use dot notation, be aware of the document's hierarchy. The following line of code, for example, doesn't successfully return the text input element because we left out the containing form reference:

```
var fn = document.firstName; // Doesn't work
```

A significant shortcoming to using dot notation is that because the object name is "hard coded," it cannot change when you run your script. The techniques shown in the next four sections provide greater flexibility.

Using square brackets

You can also access an object by using square brackets instead:

```
document.shippingForm['firstName']
```

The object identifier (the input element's `id` value) is placed inside brackets and surrounded by quotes.

Using DOM arrays

You can reference several built-in collections of objects. Perhaps the most notable is `document.forms`, which returns a collection of `form` elements from the document. You can access it by index (the order in which it occurs in the source). For example, to access the first form in a page, you use this line:

```
document.forms[0]
```

However, this technique is problematic because moving forms around on a page ruins your script. A much better practice is to reference the form's `id` (or `name`) attribute instead:

```
var cf = document.forms['customer_form'];
```

Similarly, to access a form element, you can use the `elements` collection:

```
var ln = document.form['customer_form'].elements['last_name'].value;
```

Accessing an element by its id value

The `document` object's `getElementById()` method retrieves the element that has a specific `id` attribute value. It eliminates the need to worry about hierarchy and get straight to it:

```
document.getElementById("elementID")
```

Suppose that you have the following line of HTML:

```
<div id="main_text"></div>
```

You can access the `div` by using the following line of code:

```
var main = document.getElementById( 'main_text' );
```

The main variable now references the `main_text` div. You can now use `main` to access its properties and perform methods on it.

Accessing an element by its tag name

The `getElementById()` is ideal to use if the element you're trying to retrieve has an `id` value that's defined in the HTML code. However, when an `id` doesn't exist or you need to access multiple elements of the same kind, you can use `document.getElementByTagName()`.

The `document` object's `getElementByTagName()` method allows you to return all elements with a particular tag name as a collection (officially, a *nodeList*). For example, to retrieve all `div` elements in your document, you can use this command:

```
var divList = document.getElementByTagName( 'div' );
```

After you have the collection of elements, you can access a particular `div` in the list by using its index number. For example, to access the first `div` in the document, write this line:

```
var div1 = divList[0];
```

Alternatively, if you don't need to work with the collection, you can simply combine the two lines of code into one:

```
var div1 = document.getElementByTagName('elementId')[0];
```

If you want to retrieve a collection of all elements in a document, you can use an asterisk in place of a tag name:

```
var allElements = document.getElementsByTagName('*');
```

The `allElements` variable references all elements in the order in which they occur in the HTML source. However, note that this technique isn't supported by Internet Explorer 5.5 and earlier.

Accessing and Modifying Properties

As we discuss in Chapter 2 in this minibook, a *property* is an attribute associated with an object that helps describe it. Many common properties of a DOM object correspond to an HTML element's attributes. For instance, bgColor is a property of the body object, and action is a property of form.

JavaScript gives you access to those properties in your scripts. Suppose that you define the following img element:

```
<img id="houseImage" alt="Your future home"
    src="images/default.jpg">
```

You can change the src value of this image in JavaScript by using the following code:

```
document.getElementById( 'everestImage').src =
    "images/Colonial22.jpg";
```

Alternatively, you can also use the setAttribute() method for any DOM object to perform the same task. For example, consider the following line of HTML code:

```
<p id="intro">This is a test</p>
```

You can set the align attribute to the right by using either of the following commands:

```
// Set property by calling a method
document.getElementById( 'intro' ).setAttribute('align', 'right');
// Set a property through direct access
document.getElementById( 'intro' ).align = 'right';
```

Calling Object Methods

A method defines an action or a behavior of an object. A method's name is an action-oriented word that indicates what happens when it's called. For example, the submit() method triggers a form to be submitted to the server for processing, and the write() method of the document enables you to "write" new content to the Web page.

Again, use dot notation syntax to reference the object you want to work with. Here are a few examples:

```
document.write( 'I am adding new text from my script.' );
document.forms['form1'].submit();
document.forms['form1'.elements['moreButton'].click();
```

Adding and Removing Nodes from the DOM

The DOM provides the ability to add and remove elements and content from JavaScript.

Adding new nodes

Each HTML element in the DOM has `appendChild()` and `insertBefore()` methods that can be used for adding new elements into the document tree. Consider the following HTML snippet:

```
<h1>Welcome to World@Large</h1>
<div id="sidebar"></div>
```

Suppose that you want to add a new paragraph inside the `div` and a new paragraph just above it. Here's the code you use to perform this function:

```
// Create p node (we'll put it in the right place later)
var p1 = document.createElement( 'p' );
// Assign an id attribute
p1.setAttribute( 'id', 'insideDiv' );
// Create a text node for the paragraph content
var p1_content = document.createTextNode( 'This web site is
    used for...' );
// Add content to the paragraph
p1.appendChild( p1_content );
// Add paragraph as a child node under the sidebar div
document.getElementById( 'sidebar' ).appendChild( p1 );
```

Next, to add that second paragraph before the `div` element, do this:

```
var p2 = document.createElement( 'p' );
p2.setAttribute( 'id', 'subheading' );
var p2_content = document.createTextNode( 'We hope you enjoy
    your stay' );
p2.appendChild( p2_content );
document.getElementById( 'sidebar' ).insertBefore( p2 );
```

Removing a DOM object

You can remove a DOM object by referencing an element's parentNode property and calling its removeChild() method. For example, to remove a paragraph with an id="intro", you can use the following code snippet:

```
var para = document.getElementById( 'intro' );
para.parentNode.removeChild( para );
```

In this example, the para variable references the intro paragraph. You then need to work with its parent by using the parentNode property. After you reference the parent, you call its removeChild() method, specifying para as the node to remove. The paragraph is then removed from the DOM (and the live version of the Web page inside the browser).

You can remove all child nodes of an element by looping through all the child nodes and deleting them one at a time:

```
while ( div_content.childNodes[0] ) {
  div_content.removeChild( div_content.childNodes[0];
}
```

Or, much like Indiana Jones simply shooting the fierce swordsman rather than sword-fighting him, you can simply get the big guns out and clear all the HTML by using the innerHTML property instead:

```
div_content.innerHTML = '';
```

Note, however, that innerHTML isn't part of the W3C DOM standard (although it's generally supported in the major browsers).

Exploring the DOM

An unabridged, get-every-last-bit-and-byte DOM reference is a rather formidable beast. You just have to consider so many variables when working with the DOM, including the ones in this list:

✦ Two W3C standards (Level 1 and Level 2), one designed chiefly for HTML documents and the other intended for XML (XHTML) documents

✦ Some objects, properties, or methods introduced only in Internet Explorer or Mozilla or Firefox, and not the others

✦ Some objects, properties, or methods implemented across all the major browsers, but not officially part of the W3C standard

✦ Parts supported in the latest browsers, but not in older versions

This section, therefore, focuses on the parts of the DOM that are used mainly by Web page designers, like yourself, to create scripts that work in all the major browsers. To get additional details online, check out these three sources:

✦ **Mozilla.org (Firefox) DOM Reference:** http://developer.mozilla. org/en/docs/Gecko_DOM_Reference

✦ **Microsoft DHTML Reference:** http://msdn.microsoft.com/library/default.asp?url=/work shop/author/dhtml/reference/dhtml_reference_entry.asp

✦ **JavaScript Kit DOM Reference:** www.javascriptkit.com/domref/index.shtml

✦ **Quirksmode.org:** www.quirksmode.org/dom/contents.html

Note: For information on events, be sure to check out Chapter 4 in this minibook.

HTML elements

Every HTML element in the DOM has properties that correspond to the element's attributes. For example, the body element in the DOM has alink and bgColor properties, and an a element has href and target properties. However, all the HTML elements have a set of common properties, methods, and events, as shown in Tables 3-1, 3-2, and 3-3, respectively. *Note:* The events listed in Table 3-3 are defined in Chapter 4 of this minibook (which covers event handlers).

Table 3-1	HTML Element DOM Properties
Property Name	*Applies To*
attributes	All attributes of element (read-only)
childNodes	All child nodes of element (read-only)
className	Element's class
clientHeight	Inner height of element (read-only)

(continued)

Table 3-1 *(continued)*

Property Name	Applies To
clientWidth	Inner width of element (read-only)
dir	Directionality of element
firstChild	First direct child node (read-only)
id	id attribute
innerHTML	Markup and content of element
lang	Language of element's attributes, text, and element contents
lastChild	Last direct child node (read-only)
localName	Local part of qualified element name (read-only)
name	Name attribute
namespaceURI	Namespace URI of this node (read-only)
nextSibling	Node immediately following the given one in the tree (read-only)
nodeName	Name of the node
nodeType	Number representing node type — 1 for elements (read-only)
nodeValue	Value of node; null for elements (read-only)
offsetHeight	Height of element (read-only)
offsetLeft	Distance from element's left border to its offsetParent's left border (read-only)
offsetParent	Element from which all offset calculations are calculated (read-only)
offsetTop	Distance from element's top border to its offsetParent's top border (read-only)
offsetWidth	Width of element (read-only)
ownerDocument	Document that this node is in (read-only)
parentNode	Parent element (read-only)
prefix	Namespace prefix of node (read-only)
previousSibling	Node immediately before element in tree (read-only)
scrollHeight	Scroll view height (read-only)
scrollLeft	Left scroll offset of element
scrollTop	Top scroll offset of element
scrollWidth	Scroll view width of element (read-only)
style	Style attributes (read-only)
tabIndex	Position of element in tab order
tagName	Name of tag for element (read-only)
textContent	Text content of element (and descendants)

Table 3-2	HTML Element DOM Methods
Method Name	*What It Does*
addEventListener(type, handler, bubble)	Register a special event handler
appendChild(appendedNode)	Insert a node as the element's last child node (returns a Node)
blur()	Remove keyboard focus from the element
click()	Simulate a click
cloneNode(deep)	Clone a node (and all of its contents if deep = true) (returns a Node)
dispatchEvent(event)	Dispatch an event to this node (returns a Boolean)
getAttribute(name)	Get the value of an attribute (returns an Object)
getAttributeNS(namespace, name)	Get the value of an attribute with the specified name and namespace (returns an Object)
getAttributeNode(name)	Get the node of the named attribute (returns an Attr)
getAttributeNodeNS (namespace, name)	Get the node representation of the attribute with the specified name and namespace (returns an Attr)
getElementsByTagName (name)	Get a set of all descendant elements of a specific tag name (returns a NodeSet)
getElementsByTagNameNS (namespace, name)	Get a set of all descendant elements of a specific tag name and namespace (returns a NodeSet)
hasAttribute(name)	Check if the current element has the specified attribute (returns a Boolean)
hasAttributeNS(namespace, name)	Check if the current element has the specified attribute in the specified namespace (returns a Boolean)
hasAttributes()	Check if the current element has any attributes (returns a Boolean)
hasChildNodes()	Check if the current element has any child nodes (returns a Boolean)
insertBefore(insertedNode, adjacentNode)	Insert the first node before the second node (returns a Node)
normalize()	Clean up all the text nodes contained by element (combine adjacent, remove empty)

(continued)

Table 3-2 *(continued)*

Method Name	What It Does
removeAttribute(name)	Remove the named attribute
removeAttributeNS(namespace, name)	Remove the attribute with the specified name and namespace
removeAttributeNode(name)	Remove the node representation of the named attribute
removeChild(removedNode)	Remove a child node (returns a Node)
removeEventListener(type, handler)	Remove an event listener
replaceChild(insertedNode, replacedNode)	Replace a child node with another (returns a Node)
scrollIntoView (alignWithTop)	Scroll the document until the current element gets into the view
setAttribute(name, value)	Set the value of the specified attribute
setAttributeNS(namespace, name, value)	Set the value of the specified attribute with the name and namespace provided
setAttributeNode(name, attrNode)	Set the node representation of the named attribute
setAttributeNodeNS(namespace, name, attrNode)	Set the node representation of the attribute with the specified name and namespace

Table 3-3   **HTML Element DOM Events**

Event Name
onblur
onchange
onclick
ondblclick
onfocus
onkeydown
onkeypress
onkeyup
onmousedown
onmousemove
onmouseout
onmouseover
onmouseup
onresize

The document object

The document is the root node of the DOM tree and has no corresponding HTML element — for example, the html, head, and body elements are all contained by document. It serves as the chief controller of everything related to the HTML document. Tables 3-4 and 3-5 describe its properties and methods, respectively.

Table 3-4	document Properties
Property Name	*Applies To*
alinkColor	Color of active links (depreciated)
anchors	List of anchors in document
applets	Ordered list of applets in document
bgColor	Background color (depreciated)
body	A reference to body element (read-only)
contentType	Content-Type from the MIME header
cookie	Semicolon-separated list of cookies
defaultView	Reference to the window object
doctype	Document Type Definition (DTD) of current document (read-only)
documentElement	Element that is a direct child of the document — the html element (read-only)
domain	Domain of current document
embeds	List of embedded objects within document
fgColor	Foreground or text color (depreciated)
firstChild	First node in list of children
forms	List of form elements within document
images	List of images in document
lastModified	Date that document was last modified
linkColor	Color of hyperlinks (depreciated)
links	List of hyperlinks in document
plugins	List of available plug-ins
referrer	URI of page that linked to this document
styleSheets	List of stylesheets associated with document
title	Title of current document
URL	URL of current document
vlinkColor	Color of visited hyperlinks (depreciated)

Table 3-5	document Methods
Method Name	*What It Does*
close()	Closes document stream (after writing)
createAttribute()	Creates new attribute
createDocumentFragment()	Creates new document fragment
createElement(tagName)	Creates new element with supplied tag name
createEvent()	Creates event
createRange()	Creates Range object
createTextNode()	Creates text node
getElementById()	Returns reference to specified element
getElementsByName()	Returns list of elements with the given name
getElementsByTagName()	Returns list of elements with specified tag name
importNode()	Returns a clone of a node from an external document
write()	Writes text to document
writeln()	Writes a line of text to document

The window object

The window object is the controller for working with the browser window rather than with the document inside the window. Because the window doesn't interact with documents, the W3C has shied away from adding the window object into its standards. Although various browsers provide individually supported properties, methods, and events, Tables 3-6, 3-7, and 3-8 list which ones generally work across all the major browsers.

Table 3-6	window Properties
Property Name	*Applies To*
defaultStatus	Status bar text for window
document	Reference to associated document
frames	Array of frames in window
history	Reference to history object
length	Number of frames in window
location	URL of window

Property Name	Applies To
name	Name of window
navigator	Reference to navigator object
opener	Reference to window that opened current window
parent	Reference to parent of current window (or subframe)
self	Reference to window object (itself)
status	Text in status bar at bottom of browser
top	Reference to topmost window in window hierarchy
window	Reference to current window

Table 3-7	window Methods
Method Name	What It Does
alert()	Displays an alert dialog box
blur()	Sets focus away from window
clearInterval()	Cancels repeated execution set when using setInterval()
clearTimeout()	Ends previously set delay
close()	Closes window
confirm()	Displays message box that user needs to respond to
focus()	Sets focus on window
moveBy()	Moves window by specified amount
moveTo()	Moves window to specified coordinates
open()	Opens new window
openDialog()	Opens new dialog window
print()	Displays Print dialog box to print document
prompt()	Displays dialog box and then returns text entered by user
resizeBy()	Resizes current window by specified amount
resizeTo()	Resizes window
scroll()	Scrolls window to specific place in the document
scrollBy()	Scrolls document in window by specified amount
scrollTo()	Scrolls to specific set of coordinates in document
setInterval()	Executes function to occur each xx milliseconds.
setTimeout()	Specifies delay for executing function

Table 3-8	window Events
Event Name	
onblur	
onerror	
onfocus	
onload	
onresize	
onunload	

The form object

The form object is the scripting equivalent of the form element. You use a form to obtain information from users and submit the data to the Web server for processing. Tables 3-9 and 3-10 list its properties and methods, respectively.

Table 3-9	form Properties
Property Name	*Applies To*
elements	List of form controls contained in form element (read-only)
length	Number of controls in form element (read-only)
name	Name of current form element
acceptCharset	List of supported character sets for current form
action	Action of form element
enctype	Content type of form element
encoding	Content type of form element
method	HTTP method used to submit form
target	Target of the action

Table 3-10	form Methods
Method Name	*What It Does*
submit()	Submits form
reset()	Resets form

The table object

The `table` object is the scripting interface to a `table` element. You can use the DOM interface to add and remove parts of the table. Tables 3-11 and 3-12 show the supported properties and methods, respectively.

Table 3-11	table Properties
Property Name	*Applies To*
`align`	Alignment of table
`bgColor`	Background color (depreciated)
`border`	Border of table
`caption`	Table caption (read-only)
`cellPadding`	Cell padding
`cellSpacing`	Spacing
`rows`	A collection of the rows in the table (read-only)
`summary`	Table summary (read-only)
`tBodies`	A collection of table bodies (read-only)
`tFoot`	Table footer (read-only)
`tHead`	Table head (read-only)
`width`	Width of table

Table 3-12	table Methods
Method Name	*What It Does*
`createCaption()`	Creates new caption for table
`createTFoot()`	Creates table footer
`createTHead()`	Creates table header
`deleteCaption()`	Removes table caption
`deleteRow()`	Removes a row
`deleteTFoot()`	Removes table footer
`deleteTHead()`	Removes table header
`insertRow()`	Inserts new row

Inspecting Your DOM

One of the best ways to get a handle on the DOM is to use the DOM Inspector, available in any version of Firefox (see Figure 3-2). You can access the DOM Inspector by looking on the Tools⇨Web Developer menu. The downside is that you can feel like it provides information overload and gives you far more information than what most developers really want to see.

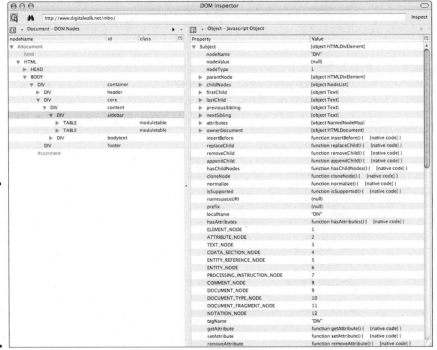

Figure 3-2:
The Firefox
DOM
Inspector
provides an
advanced
look into
the object
model of a
document.

A second live DOM Inspector is available at www.brainjar.com. This site provides a JavaScript script that you can download or use to display DOM information, as shown in Figure 3-3. The script also is a bit more user friendly in displaying just the node-related info of the DOM.

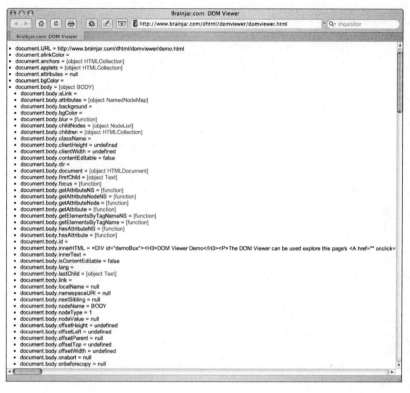

Figure 3-3:
Brainjar.com
provides a
DOM
Inspector
written in
JavaScript.

Chapter 4: Adding Event Handlers to Your Web Page

*I*n Chapter 1 of this minibook, we say that scripting is useful because it enables you to create dynamic, interactive pages. However, scripting can do this because it's driven by events that take place inside the browser window: A mouse moves. A key is pressed. A document loads. A form value changes. JavaScript can trap for each of these events and then allow you to perform any script you want when these events occur.

In this chapter, you discover how to assign a script-based event handler to a document event. You also survey the variety of events available in JavaScript.

Assigning Event Handlers

Event handlers in JavaScript can be defined in two different ways:

✦ **From an HTML element:** Link a JavaScript function or expression with the event handling attribute of an HTML element.

✦ **In JavaScript code:** Assign a JavaScript function to an event handler in your script.

We go into more detail on each of these strategies in the following sections.

Linking from an HTML element

Many elements in HTML have events that are associated with them. The `img` element, for example, has an `onmouseover` event. The `a` link element has an `onclick` event. You can tell the browser to run a piece of script code whenever one of these events occurs. To do so, you add an attribute (the event name) to an element. The value of the attribute is a call to a JavaScript function or a snippet of JavaScript code:

```
<element onevent="myFunction()" />
```

or

```
<element onevent="alert( 'event fired' )" />
```

For example, the `body` element supports the `onload` attribute, and the `form` element supports the `onsubmit` attribute. If you want to trigger actions based on these events, here's how you can connect the two HTML elements with JavaScript code:

```
<head>
<script type="text/javascript">
function init() {
  // Initialize something
}

function checkFormValues() {
  // Check form values
}
</script>
</head>
<body onload="init()">
<form id="myform" onsubmit="checkFormValues()">
</form>
</body>
```

When the document body loads, the `init()` function is called. Then when the form is submitted by the user, the `checkFormValues()` function is also executed.

A second example uses JavaScript statements inside the event handlers:

```
<span onmouseover="this.style.backgroundColor='yellow';this.style.border='2px
    solid black';"
    onmouseout="this.style.backgroundColor='white';this.style.border='none';">"W
    hy do you suppose it was Reuben?" Mrs. Ellison asked the master.
</span>
```

When a mouse hovers over the span element, the background turns yellow and a border is displayed. When the mouse exits the area of the span element, the styling returns to normal. The this keyword refers to the object that triggered the event, which in this case is the span element.

Connecting an event handler in code

You can also assign a function to be the event handler of an event in the code itself. For example, rather than add an onload attribute to the body and an onsubmit attribute to the form element, like we did earlier, you can add the following snippet of code instead inside your script:

```
<head>
<script type="text/javascript">
function init() {
  // Initialize something
}
function checkFormValues() {
  // Check form values
}

window.onload = init;
var iform = document.getElementById( 'myform');
iform.onsubmit = checkFormValues;
</script>
</head>
<body>
</body>
```

The window.onload event is assigned the init() function. However, notice that when you assign an event handler in code, you don't add the closing parentheses. The form follows in the same manner.

When you assign an event handler by linking it to an HTML element, you can add JavaScript statements directly inside the handler (as shown in the preceding example). However, when you assign event handlers inside your code, you must assign the event to a function name.

Surveying the Events

You can work with a variety of different events in JavaScript. Tables 4-1, 4-2, 4-3, 4-4, and 4-5 list these events in five separate categories.

Table 4-1	**User Interface Events**	
Event	*Occurs When*	*Applies To*
onload	Document has been fully loaded (including images and other external content)	window
onunload	Document has been unloaded (for example, going to another page or closing the browser window)	window
onresize	Browser window has been resized	window
onscroll	Page or any element with the CSS property overview:flow is being scrolled	document and any element that can have scroll bars (div, for example)
onblur	Object loses input focus	window, form elements, any element with a tab index attribute, link (some browsers)
onfocus	Object receives input focus	window, form elements, any element with a tab index attribute, and link (some browsers)
oncontextmenu	User triggers the right-click pop-up menu	document and all visible elements (not supported in all browsers)

Table 4-2	**Mouse Events**	
Event	*Occurs When*	*Applies To*
onmousedown	User depresses the mouse button on an element	Any visible element
onmouseup	User releases the mouse button on an element	Any visible element
onclick	Both a mouse-down and mouse-up action occur on the same element (triggers after mousedown and mouseup events)	Any visible element
ondblclick	Mouse button is rapidly clicked twice on an element	Any visible element
onmousemove	User rolls the mouse over an element (fires repeatedly)	Any visible element

Event	Occurs When	Applies To
onmouseover	User first moves the mouse inside the area of an element (fires once)	Any visible element
onmouseout	User moves the mouse outside the border of an element	Any visible element

Table 4-3   **Keyboard Events**

Event	Occurs When	Applies To
onkeydown	User presses a key	window, document, and all visible elements that can receive focus
onkeyup	User releases a key	window, document, and all visible elements that can receive focus
onkeypress	User both presses and releases a key (triggers *after* keydown and keyup events)	document and all visible elements that can receive focus

Table 4-4   **Form Events**

Event	Occurs When	Applies To
onchange	A form element loses focus and its value has changed	Text-based input, textarea, select elements
onselect	User selects text in a text field	onmouseup fired when selection action completed Text-based input, textarea
onsubmit	User submits the form (by clicking a Submit button); not triggered when submit is done through a scripting call	form
onreset	User or script resets the form	form

Table 4-5	Other Events	
Event	*Occurs When*	*Applies To*
error	An image isn't loaded properly or a script error occurs	window, img
abort	A page loading is stopped before an image has finished loading (little practical use of this event)	img, object

Chapter 5: Useful Things to Know When Scripting

In This Chapter

✔ **Reusing scripts across your site with** `.js` **files**

✔ **Opening browser windows from a script**

✔ **Executing a script from a link**

✔ **Updating a Web page on the fly**

✔ **Validating form values**

✔ **Scrambling e-mail addresses to avoid spam**

✔ **Testing for features, not for browser type**

*A*fter you have a basic introduction to JavaScript, it's time to get practical and apply some of that newfound knowledge to developing scripts for your Web site. As you do so, you'll encounter some common tasks that you want to perform using JavaScript. Use this chapter as a helpful guide to find helpful tips and techniques as you work on your scripts.

Storing Scripts in an External Script File

You can place all your scripting code for a document inside a `script` element. And, until now in this minibook, that's what we showed you for all the examples. However, the `script` element has an optional `src` attribute that can reference an external `.js` file. A *.js* file is simply a plain-text file that houses JavaScript code. Here's a reference to a `.js` file that contains general validity-checking routines for forms:

```
<script type="text/javascript" src="valform.js"></script>
```

When the `src` attribute is present, any code placed between the start and end tags of the `script` element is ignored.

The biggest advantage of placing your script code in .js files is that you can then easily reuse the same routines throughout your Web site. Suppose that you have a script for creating rollover buttons. You can either copy and paste the code throughout your pages or create the code in a single .js file and then simply point to the code by using a `<script src=""/>` reference.

The contents of the .js file are pure JavaScript. Just as you cannot place HTML elements inside a `script` tag, you cannot add any markup in an external script file.

Creating a New Browser Window

You may occasionally need to open a new browser window when the user enters your site or performs a specific action. You can use JavaScript to create a new browser window by using the `window` object's `open()` method. The syntax is

```
window.open( 'url', 'windowName' [, 'featuresList'] )
```

The `url` argument is a string specifying the URL to point to. The `windowName` argument is a string literal that is the name to give to the new window. You can reference this name elsewhere in your code. Here's a basic call to open a new window:

```
window.open( 'http://www.digitalwalk.net/more.html',
    'moreWin' );
```

The `open()` method has a return value that references the new `window` object that's created. Although you don't have to explicitly do anything to the return value, we strongly recommend it. Doing so enables you to properly handle references to the new window. For example, the following snippet opens a new window and then performs a `document.write` command in the new window:

```
var moreWindow = window.open(
    'http://www.digitalwalk.net/more.html', 'moreWin' );
moreWindow.document.write( 'Peek-a-boo. I am writing this
    from a different window' );
```

Never leave the `windowName` argument as an empty string because different browsers give you different results.

However, if you're just opening a new, ordinary window, you can just as easily do that without scripting by using a `target="_blank"` attribute on an a link. That's why the real power of `window.open()` lies in its optional list of features. With this argument, you can specify how the new browser window will look like when it opens. The argument is a comma-delimited string literal that contains name-value pairs for some or all of the features shown in Table 5-1.

Table 5-1	Features for `window.open()`
Argument	*What It Does*
`status`	Shows or hides the status bar at the bottom of the window
`toolbar`	Shows or hides the standard browser toolbar (with Back and Forward buttons, for example)
`location`	Shows or hides the Address/URL box
`menubar`	Shows or hides the menu bar
`directories`	Shows or hides the standard browser directory buttons
`resizable`	Allows or prevents the user from resizing the window
`scrollbars`	Enables or disables the scrollbars if the document is bigger than the window
`height`	Specifies the height of the window in pixels
`width`	Specifies the width of the window in pixels
`top`	Specifies the Y coordinate of the upper-left corner of the window
`left`	Specifies the X coordinate of the upper-left corner of the window

The `height, width, top,` and `left` arguments are assigned a pixel value. The remaining arguments are assigned a value of `1` to explicitly enable or show the feature and `0` to specifically disable or hide the feature. Here's an example:

```
var myWin = window.open( 'second.html', 'secWin', 'left=20,
    top=10,width=400,
       height=250,toolbar=1,resizable=0,menubar=0,location=0' );
```

Attaching a Script to a Link

One of the confusing tasks that many scripters struggle with is attaching a script to the clicking of an a link. After all, HTML allows you to place a JavaScript command as the `href` attribute value by using the `javascript:` protocol (`<a href="javascript:alert('click')">Click me</a>`). However, a much better practice is to use the `onclick` event handler instead.

Here are a couple of scenarios. First, suppose that you want to use the capability of an a link to kick off a script but you don't really want to send the user to another page. To execute a JavaScript statement and prevent the normal link functionality, add an `onclick` handler that calls the function or statement that you want to perform, and add a `return false` statement at the end to tell the browser to ignore the `href` value. Then you can assign a # as the `href` value. Here's what it looks like:

```
<a href="#" onclick="checkPage();return false">Check now</a>
```

A second scenario is when you want to perform a conditional check when the link is clicked. If the check passes, the browser continues to the supplied `href` value. If not, the user remains on the current page. The a element code looks something like this:

```
<a href="continue.html" onclick="checkPage();">Continue</a>
```

The `checkPage()` function that's called performs validity checking on the page. If the test passes, a true value is returned from `checkPage()`. If something needs user attention before continuing, a false value is returned. The false value causes the `href` value to be ignored.

Modifying a Web Page on the Fly

In addition to reacting to existing HTML elements on a page, JavaScript allows you to add your own content on the fly — without having to go to the Web server for a page refresh. In Chapter 3, I show you how to do this by using DOM methods, such as `createElement()` or `appendChild()`. However, you also have an easier way to add content, by using the `innerHTML` property. The `innerHTML` property isn't endorsed by W3C, the Web's standards body, but it's still supported widely enough in all modern browsers that make this a viable alternative (even if purists disagree).

The `innerHTML` property allows you to set and retrieve the HTML content between the start and end tags of a given element. You can also work with either text content or markup.

Suppose that you want to update the contents of a div, span, p, or other element without refreshing the entire page. A simple call to `innerHTML` does the trick. Consider the simple page shown in Figure 5-1.

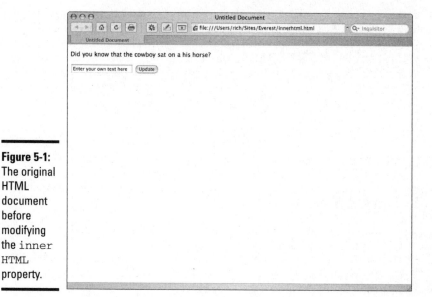

Figure 5-1:
The original
HTML
document
before
modifying
the inner
HTML
property.

When you look at the document source, you see that the span element is
updated based on the text that the user enters in the text box. Check out
the code:

```html
<html>
<head>
<script type="text/javascript">
function refreshText(){
    var txt = document.getElementById( 'userText' ).value;
    document.getElementById('ontheflyupdate').innerHTML = txt;
}
</script>
</head>
<body>
<p>Did you know that the <span id='ontheflyupdate'>cowboy sat
    on a his horse</span>?</p>
<input type='text' id='userText' value='Enter your own text
    here' />
<input type='button' onclick='refreshText()' value='Update'/>

</body>
</html>
```

Therefore, whenever you enter new text, the span content is updated when
you click the Update button. The results are shown in Figure 5-2.

**Book VIII
Chapter 5**

**Useful Things
to Know When
Scripting**

Figure 5-2:
Updating
the HTML
document
by using
the `inner`
`HTML`
property.

Don't use `innerHTML` for tables. Instead, use the DOM methods discussed in Chapter 4 in this minibook to add rows and other table parts.

Validating Forms

Data validation has always been one of JavaScript's most useful capabilities within an HTML document. Using JavaScript, you can check the quality of the data to be submitted by the user before sending it over the Internet for processing. You might want to perform various types of validation:

✦ Check for values in required fields.

✦ Check for numeric values for number fields (for example, age or 5-digit ZIP code).

✦ Check to ensure entry matches a certain format (for example, e-mail address or telephone number).

Some techniques that scripters have implemented for validation have been frustrating for users filling out the form. Figure 5-3 shows you one technique you can use to display error information (rather than annoying alert message boxes) to the user in a `span` element beside the text box.

Note: Before beginning this process, place the `validate.js` file (located on the CD in the back of this book) in the same folder as your HTML page.

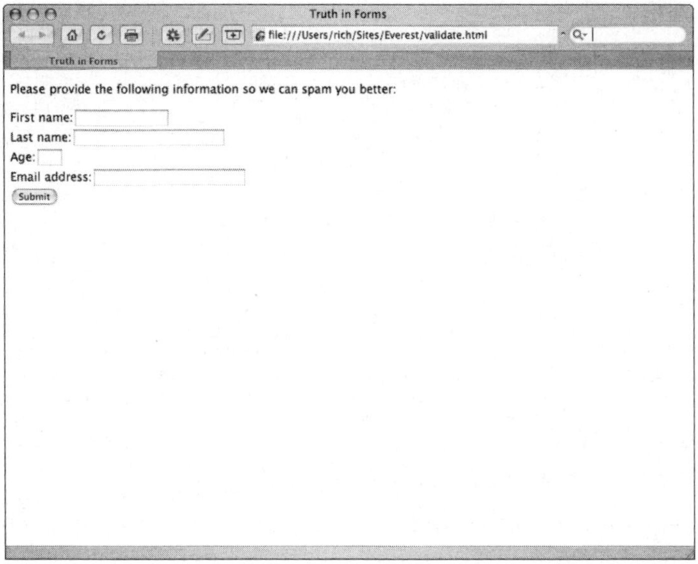

Figure 5-3:
This basic form is in dire need of validation help.

1. **Open a Web page in your editor that contains form fields to which you want to add validation.**

2. **Add a reference to the `escrambler.js` file in the document head:**

```
<script src="validate.js"
    type="text/javascript"></script>
```

This instruction loads the `validate.js` routines into the Web page. Here's the source code for the script file:

```
MSG_REQUIRED_ERROR = 'Value is required';
MSG_INVALID_NUMBER_ERROR = 'Invalid number entered. Please try again.';
MSG_INVALID_EMAIL_ERROR = 'Invalid email address. Please try again.';

function checkRequired( valField, displayID ) {
  var displayHandler = document.getElementById( displayID );

  if ( valField.value == null || valField.value == '' ) {
    displayHandler.innerHTML = MSG_REQUIRED_ERROR;
    valField.focus();
    return false;
  }
```

```
    else {
      displayHandler.innerHTML = '';
      return true;
    }
  }

  function isValidNumber( valField, displayID )  {
    var displayHandler = document.getElementById( displayID );
    if ( isNaN( valField.value ) ) {
      displayHandler.innerHTML = MSG_INVALID_NUMBER_ERROR;
      valField.focus();
      return false;
    }
    else {
      displayHandler.innerHTML = '';
      return true;
    }
  }

  function checkEmail( valField, displayID ) {
    var displayHandler = document.getElementById( displayID );
    var emailFormat = /^[^@]+@[^@.]+\.[^@]*\w\w$/; // Regular Expression
      string
    var emailStr = valField.value;
    if ( !emailFormat.test( emailStr ) ) {
      displayHandler.innerHTML = MSG_INVALID_EMAIL_ERROR;
      valField.focus();
      return false;
    }
    else {
      displayHandler.innerHTML = '';
      return true;
    }
  }
```

3. **In the document head, add a style element. Inside it, add a class selector named `.msg_container`.**

This style rule is applied to your error message containers:

```
<style>
  .msg_container { color: #FF0000 }
</style>
```

4. **Next to each field you're validating, add an empty `span` element.**

Be sure to give each `span` element a unique `id` value and add `class="msg_container"` to associate the CSS class selector that you defined in Step 3.

Here's how the form looks with the `span` elements added:

```
<div style="width:500px">
<p>Please provide the following information so we can spam you
    better:</p>
<form id="customer_form" name="customer_form" method="post" action="">
  <label>First name:<input  type="text" name="first_name" id="first_name"
    size="15"/></label>
```

```
        <span class="msg_container" id="first_name_msg"> </span><br/>
      <label>Last name:<input type="text" name="last_name" id="last_name"
        size="25"/></label>
        <span class="msg_container" id="last_name_msg"> </span><br/>
      <label>Age:<input type="text" name="age" id="age" size="3"/></label>
        <span class="msg_container" id="age_msg"> </span><br/>
      <label>Email address:<input type="text" name="email" id="email"
        size="25"/></label>
        <span class="msg_container" id="email_msg"> </span><br/>
      <input name="submit" type="submit"/>
    </form>
    </div>
```

These span elements are used to provide error feedback to the user as needed.

5. For every field that you want to require, add an `onblur` handler that attaches to the `checkRequired()` function.

The checkRequired() function requires two arguments:

- The keyword this, which points to the calling object (the input field itself)

- A string literal that provides the id value of the error message container

We added this check on the first name and last name fields for the form:

```
<div style="width:500px">
<p>Please provide the following information so we can spam you
  better:</p>
<form id="customer_form" name="customer_form" method="post" action="">
  <label>First name:<input  type="text" name="first_name" id="first_name"
    size="15" onblur="checkRequired( this, 'first_name_msg' )"/></label>
    <span class="msg_container" id="first_name_msg"> </span><br/>
  <label>Last name:<input type="text" name="last_name" id="last_name"
    size="25" onblur="checkRequired( this, 'last_name_msg' )"/></label>
    <span class="msg_container" id="last_name_msg"> </span><br/>
  <label>Age:<input type="text" name="age" id="age" size="3"/></label>
    <span class="msg_container" id="age_msg"> </span><br/>
  <label>Email address:<input type="text" name="email" id="email"
    size="25"/></label>
    <span class="msg_container" id="email_msg"> </span><br/>
  <input name="submit" type="submit"/>
</form>
</div>
```

6. For every field you want to check for valid numbers, add an `onblur` handler that attaches to the `isValidNumber()` function.

Like the checkRequired() function, isValidNumber() also requires two arguments: this and a string of the id value of the error message container.

For this example, we added this validity check for the age field:

```
<div style="width:500px">
<p>Please provide the following information so we can spam you
    better:</p>
<form id="customer_form" name="customer_form" method="post" action="">
  <label>First name:<input  type="text" name="first_name" id="first_name"
    size="15" onblur="checkRequired( this, 'first_name_msg' )"/></label>
      <span class="msg_container" id="first_name_msg"> </span><br/>
  <label>Last name:<input type="text" name="last_name" id="last_name"
    size="25" onblur="checkRequired( this, 'last_name_msg' )"/></label>
      <span class="msg_container" id="last_name_msg"> </span><br/>
  <label>Age:<input type="text" name="age" id="age" size="3"
    onblur="isValidNumber( this, 'age_msg' )"/></label>
      <span class="msg_container" id="age_msg"> </span><br/>
  <label>Email address:<input type="text" name="email" id="email"
    size="25"/></label>
      <span class="msg_container" id="email_msg"> </span><br/>
  <input name="submit" type="submit"/>
</form>
</div>
```

7. **For e-mail address fields, add an `onblur` handler that attaches to the `checkEmail()` function.**

   The `checkEmail()` function uses the same two arguments as the other two validity check routines. Here's the code:

```
<div style="width:500px">
<p>Please provide the following information so we can spam you
    better:</p>
<form id="customer_form" name="customer_form" method="post" action="">
  <label>First name:<input  type="text" name="first_name" id="first_name"
    size="15" onblur="checkRequired( this, 'first_name_msg' )"/></label>
      <span class="msg_container" id="first_name_msg"> </span><br/>
  <label>Last name:<input type="text" name="last_name" id="last_name"
    size="25" onblur="checkRequired( this, 'last_name_msg' )"/></label>
      <span class="msg_container" id="last_name_msg"> </span><br/>
  <label>Age:<input type="text" name="age" id="age" size="3"
    onblur="isValidNumber( this, 'age_msg' )"/></label>
      <span class="msg_container" id="age_msg"> </span><br/>
  <label>Email address:<input type="text" name="email" id="email"
    size="25" onblur="checkEmail( this, 'email_msg' )"/></label>
      <span class="msg_container" id="email_msg"> </span><br/>
  <input name="submit" type="submit"/>
</form>
</div>
```

8. **Save your HTML document and test the results in a browser.**

   You can load the Web page in a browser and check out the validation routines. Figures 5-4 and 5-5 show the results.

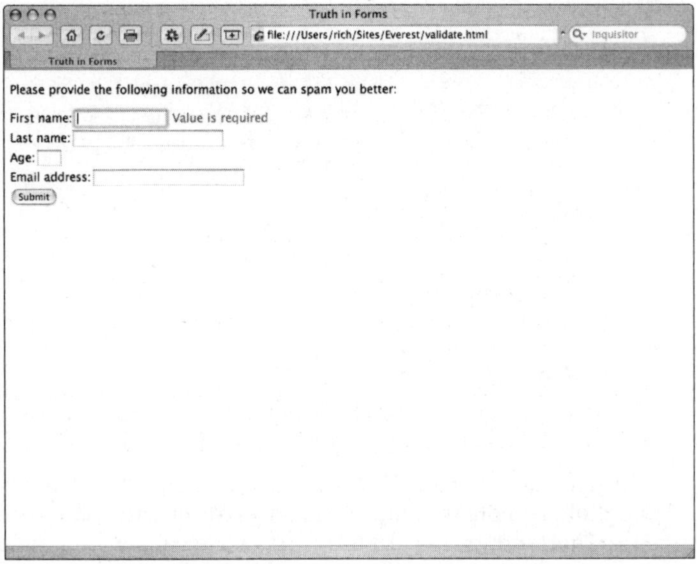

Figure 5-4:
The user is flagged when no value is entered in a required field.

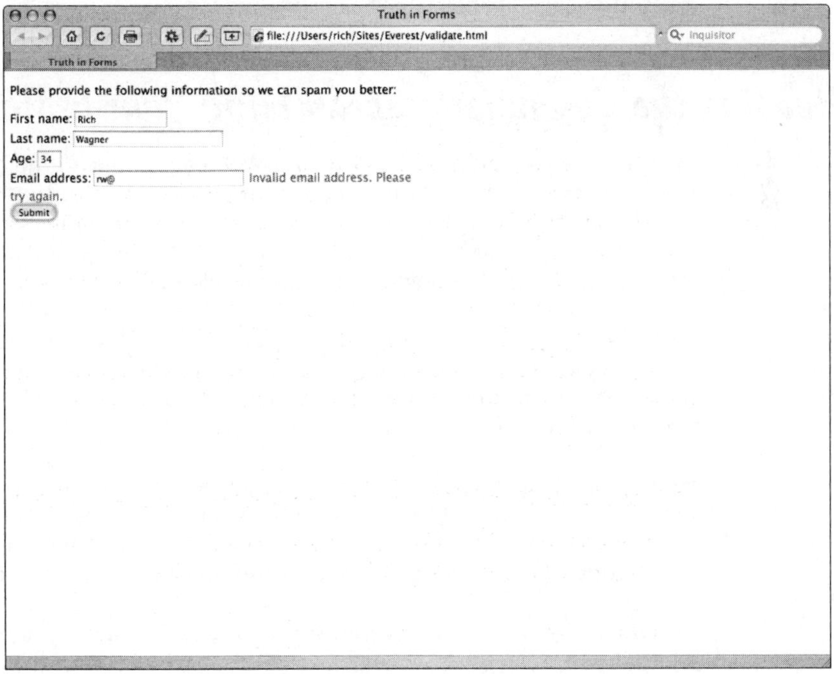

Figure 5-5:
The user is prompted when an invalid address is entered.

A closer look at the routines is helpful in understanding how the validation works. The `checkRequired()` function is an example:

```
function checkRequired( valField, displayID ) {
   var displayHandler = document.getElementById( displayID );

   if ( valField.value == null || valField.value == '' ) {
      displayHandler.innerHTML = MSG_REQUIRED_ERROR;
      valField.focus();
      return false;
   }
   else {
      displayHandler.innerHTML = '';
      return true;
   }
}
```

The `displayHandler` variable is defined and references the element with an `id` value that equals the `displayID` value.

The value of the `valField` argument is then evaluated to see whether it's a blank value. If yes, an error message is assigned to `displayHandler.innerHTML`. After the calling input field then receives focus, the function ends with a false return value. If no, the `displayHandler.innerHTML` is cleared out and control is returned to the calling field.

Beating the Spammers: Scrambling Your E-Mail Links

A `mailto:` e-mail address link on your Web page is one of the handiest and most effective ways to communicate with people you're trying to reach. Unfortunately, it comes at a significant cost: spam. Spammers scour the Web to look for defenseless e-mail addresses to add to their evil databases. You can fight back with the newest tool in your arsenal: JavaScript.

We show you how to add standard and maximum protection. Standard protection is easier to work with, but spammers might potentially account for it in their Web scouring. Although maximum protection is a pain to work with, spammers almost certainly cannot circumvent it.

Note: Before beginning this process, place the `escrambler.js` file (located on the CD in the back of this book) in the same directory as your HTML page.

Follow these steps to scramble your e-mail links with a JavaScript routine:

1. **Open a Web page in your editor that contains one or more e-mail links that you want to scramble.**

2. **For each address, replace the normal e-mail address with a scrambled version.**

For standard protection, all you need to do is to replace the @ sign with
_at_ — for example, steve@acmeinc.com becomes steve_at_
acmeinc.com.

If you want to add maximum protection, replace the @ sign with a !a!,
the dot with a !d!, and the domain suffix with a !ds!. For example,
steve@acmeinc.com now becomes a bulletproof but confusing-looking
steve!a!acmeinc!d!!ds!.

3. **Add a reference to the `escrambler.js` file in your document head:**

```
<script src="escrambler.js" type="text/javascript"></script>
```

This instruction loads the escrambler.js scrambling routines into the
Web page. Here's the source code for the script file:

```
// Iterate through each link
function hrefReplacer( origStr, newStr ) {
    for ( i=0; i<=(document.links.length-1 ); i++ ) {
            if ( document.links[i].href.indexOf( origStr )!=-1 )
                document.links[i].href=
    document.links[i].href.split( origStr )[0] + newStr +
                document.links[i].href.split( origStr )[1]
    }
}


// ***********************************************************
// unscramble( securityLevel, [domainSuffix] )
//          securityLevel: 0 = Minimal, 1 = Maximum
//          domainSuffix : suffix, if not com
// ***********************************************************
function unscramble( securityLevel, domainSuffix ) {
    // Standard format: me_at_mydomain.com
    if ( securityLevel == 0 ) {
            var separator = '_at_';
            hrefReplacer( separator, '@' );
    }
    // Maximum format: me!a!mydomain!dt!!ds!
    else {
            var separator    = '!a!';
            var dot          = '!dt!';
            var suffix          = '!ds!';
            if ( domainSuffix == '' ) domainSuffix = 'com';
            hrefReplacer( separator, '@' );
            hrefReplacer( dot, '.' );
            hrefReplacer( suffix, domainSuffix );
    }
}
```

4. **Add a new `script` element to the bottom of your page, just above
the `</body>` end tag.**

In this script, you call the unscramble() function that's located in the
escrambler.js file. It syntax is shown here:

```
unscramble( securityLevel [, domainSuffix] )
```

where `securityLevel` is 0 for standard and 1 for maximum protection. If you're using maximum, supply a domain suffix if your domain is different from `com`.

For standard protection, use the following code:

```
<script type="text/javascript">
unscramble( 0 );
</script>
```

For maximum protection with a `com` suffix, use the following code:

```
<script type="text/javascript">
unscramble( 1 );
</script>
```

For maximum protection with an alternative suffix, add it as the second parameter, as shown in this example:

```
<script type="text/javascript">
unscramble( 1, 'org' );
</script>
```

5. **Save your file and test the results in a browser.**

You can load the Web page in a browser and ensure that your e-mail addresses are now properly formatted in your live HTML source, as shown in Figure 5-6.

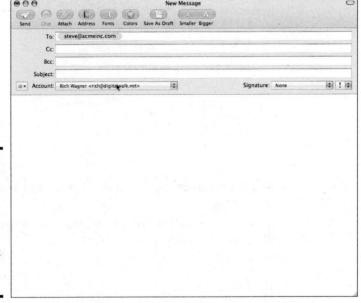

Figure 5-6:
After the scrambler processes the page, the e-mail address link works for the user.

Testing for Features, Not for Browser Type

In the early days of the Web, it was considered a good programming practice to detect the browser type and version before running a script. Because JavaScript implementation differed strongly back then, a browser detector could reroute your script before it tried doing something that a nonsupporting browser couldn't handle.

To borrow from S.E. Hinton, "That was then, this is now." Nowadays, there's little or no reason to test for a specific browser type. Instead, your best bet, if you're concerned about browser support for a script you want to perform, is to test by feature.

For example, if you want to check to ensure that the browser supports the getElementById() method before performing a process that relied on a feature, you can perform a conditional check first:

```
if ( document.getElementById ) {
    // Code relying on getElementById goes here
}
```

If the getElementById() method is unsupported, the conditional statement returns a null value to the if statement. Otherwise, the code is executed.

You can also perform this test on an object or a property. For example, to test whether the browser supports the images collection object (an object often used in rollovers), you can test by using the following statement:

```
if ( document.images ) {
  // Code relying on images collection goes here
}
```

Book IX

Flash

The 5th Wave   By Rich Tennant

"Don't be silly - of course my passwords are safe. I keep them written on my window, but then I pull the shade if anyone walks in the room."

Contents at a Glance

Chapter 1: Getting to Know Adobe Flash

In This Chapter

✔ Understanding how Flash differs from other Web technologies

✔ Exploring the Flash environment

✔ Introducing Flash tools

✔ Exploring the Properties inspector and panels

✔ Customizing your Flash workspace

*V*ive la différence! That's the expression that Web site designers and users have long used about Adobe Flash (formerly Macromedia Flash). In an environment in which standards-based solutions (HTML, CSS, and JavaScript, for example) have long been insisted on and proprietary technologies have been shunned, Flash stands alone. It's proprietary. It doesn't do much with HTML or JavaScript or CSS. Yet, because of its ability to play multimedia over the Web and provide a great user experience, Flash movies are as much a part of the Web as HTML is.

It's time, therefore, for you to jump on board and embrace Flash to help you create your Web site. You can use this chapter as a jumping-off point. We start by taking you on a guided tour through the various parts of the Flash development environment.

Like Dreamweaver (see Book IV), Flash is available for both the Microsoft Windows and Mac OS X platforms. The screen shots in this book are from the Mac version, but all the instructions are for both operating systems.

A Matter of Timing: Making the Mind Shift to Flash

The expression *Vive la différence!* is not only appropriate for Web site visitors but also suitable for you as you design and create Web sites. Flash is definitely much different from the other technologies you explore in this book.

HTML is designed to display content on the Web. CSS comes alongside and helps you present that content in a user-friendly manner. Enter JavaScript. It can be used to perform certain interactive actions when an event on the page is triggered. However, even though each of these technologies, when added together, form a more complex solution, they are all fairly linear in how you create them.

Flash, however, introduces you to the added dimension of time. Everything in a Flash movie that you work with is coordinated with time. Animations, movie loops, sound effects — each of these elements is introduced in a Flash movie based on a timeline you manipulate.

Much like a motion picture, a Flash movie is a series of frames that are displayed rapidly in succession (often, 12 frames per second), giving the appearance of animation or motion. Suppose that you place an image in a different position for each frame of a movie. When the movie is played back, the image gives the illusion of being in motion.

This added element of time is a factor that you need to wrap your mind around as you begin to work with Flash. For many people, this concept takes some getting used to.

Introducing the Flash Workspace

When you first launch Flash, you see a Welcome screen, like the one shown in Figure 1-1. From this screen, you can get started in creating a new Flash file, opening an existing file, or creating a new file based on a sample.

By default, the Welcome screen appears every time you start Flash. To bypass this window, however, select the Don't Show Again check box before proceeding.

Click either the Flash File (ActionScript 3.0) button under the Create New section or any other option you want to select. The new file is created inside the Flash workspace (see Figure 1-2).

You compose and design layers for your Flash movie by drawing or inserting objects into the Stage, which is a drawing area. (See Chapter 2 in this mini-book for more on the Stage.) These layers are then added to the Timeline as frames. Each panel that surrounds the Stage window is used in the development of your movies.

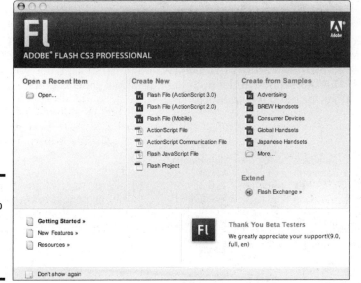

Figure 1-1:
Welcome to
Flash. We
hope you
enjoy your
stay.

Layers window   Panels

Tools   Timeline

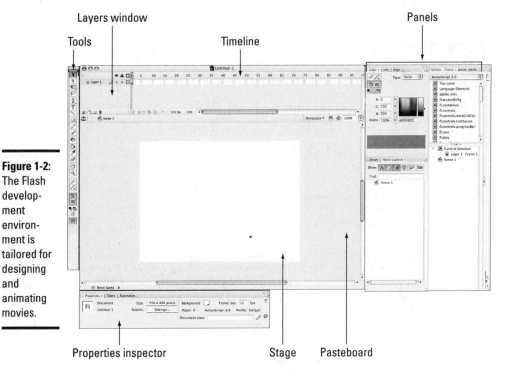

Figure 1-2:
The Flash
develop-
ment
environ-
ment is
tailored for
designing
and
animating
movies.

Properties inspector   Stage   Pasteboard

Exploring the Flash Drawing Tools

To create or modify drawings, images, and text in the Stage, you work with the drawing tools in the Tools panel (shown in Figure 1-3). Some buttons have drop-down arrows that display additional tools. When you select a tool, the Options section at the bottom of the Tools panel is updated to provide options for the selected tool.

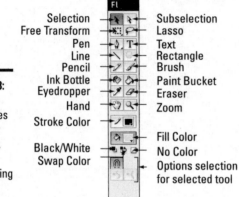

Figure 1-3: The Tools panel gives you many selection, painting, and drawing tools.

Selection — Subselection
Free Transform — Lasso
Pen — Text
Line — Rectangle
Pencil — Brush
Ink Bottle — Paint Bucket
Eyedropper — Eraser
Hand — Zoom
Stroke Color

Black/White — Fill Color
Swap Color — No Color
— Options selection for selected tool

TIP

Table 1-1 lists the available tools and describes what they do.

If you have worked with Adobe Photoshop, you have a head start. Many Flash tools are similar to what you've already used in Photoshop.

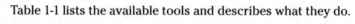

Table 1-1	Flash Tools
Tool	*What You Use It For*
Selection	Select an object in the Stage.
Subselection	Select, drag, and reshape an object by using anchor points and handles.
Free Transform	Transform (scale, rotate, skew, or distort) an object.
Gradient Transform	Transform a gradient or bitmap fill object.
Lasso	Select an object by drawing a lasso around it.
Pen	Draw straight lines and curves.
Add Anchor Point	Add an anchor point for drawing.
Delete Anchor Point	Remove an anchor point.

Tool	What You Use It For
Convert Anchor Point	Convert an anchor point for drawing.
Text	Create text.
Line	Draw straight lines.
Rectangle	Draw rectangles.
Oval	Draw ovals.
Rectangle Primitive	Draw primitive rectangles.
Oval Primitive	Draw primitive ovals.
Polystar	Draw a polygon or a star.
Pencil	Draw lines and shapes.
Brush	Paint brush strokes.
Ink Bottle	Change the color, width, or style of lines or shape outlines.
Paint Bucket	Fill a closed shape with a solid color or gradient.
Eye dropper	Copy the color of an object and apply it to another one.
Eraser	Erase strokes, lines, and fills.
Hand	Move the entire movie area in the Paste board.
Zoom	Change the magnification level of the Stage.

Exploring the Properties Inspector

The Properties inspector, shown in Figure 1-4, displays the properties of the document or the selected object in the Stage. The Properties inspector contains these three tabs:

✦ **The Properties tab** sets the commonly accessed properties of the selected object.

✦ **The Filters tab** is used for applying special-effect filters to text, movie clips, and buttons.

✦ **The Parameters tab** is used only when working with components.

Figure 1-4:
The
Properties
inspector.

Exploring the Flash Panels

Surrounding the Stage and Timeline window are several panels that are used for a variety of tasks in the movie creation process. These panels can be displayed in their own floating windows or grouped together into panel groups. A panel that's docked with a group appears as a tab inside the panel group window. You can access each of these panels from the Window menu.

Each panel has a drop-down menu on its right side that displays various available commands related to the panel.

Flash has more panels than you can shake a stick at. The following sections describe the ones you most commonly work with, organized by purpose.

Media components and elements panels

The three panels used for working with assets of a movie are described in this list:

✦ **Components:** The Components panel (shown in Figure 1-5) is used to add various user interface, multimedia, or data controls to your movie.

Figure 1-5:
Drag and
drop your
component
onto the
Stage.

✦ **Movie Explorer:** The Movie Explorer (see Figure 1-6) provides a visual hierarchical tree display of your movie showing the various elements (text, buttons, movie clips, and graphics, for example) that are in use. The Movie Explorer can be a handy way to take a big-picture look at a Flash movie (to see all the elements included in it) or as a way to search for a particular element.

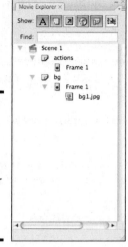

Figure 1-6:
The Movie
Explorer
gives you a
big-picture
view of your
movie
compo-
nents.

✦ **Library:** The Library (see Figure 1-7) contains media assets (movie clips,
sounds, graphics) that you either create or import. It can also contain
symbols, which are graphics, buttons, or movie clips that you create
once and then reuse. You can use the Library to manage the assets.

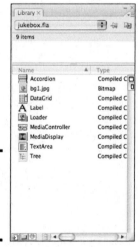

Figure 1-7:
The Library
stores your
media
assets.

Design panels

Five main panels are used as aids in the design process (see Figure 1-8):

✦ **Color:** The Color panel is used for setting the Stroke or Fill color.

✦ **Info:** The Info panel provides size and x,y position information about the selected object.

✦ **Swatches:** The Swatches panel helps you manage color sets.

✦ **Align:** The Align panel is used to align, distribute, and match the size and spacing of selected groups of objects.

✦ **Transform:** The Transform panel is used for rotating, skewing, or scaling the selected object.

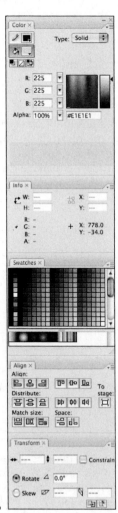

Figure 1-8:
Design panels help you as you're creating your movies.

Scripting panels

Two panels are related to scripting your movie:

✦ **Actions:** The Actions panel (shown in Figure 1-9) is used for working with ActionScript scripts within a movie.

✦ **Behaviors:** The Behaviors panel contains predefined scripts that you can use to add animation to your movie.

Figure 1-9:
ActionScript
can add
power and
interactivity
to your
Flash movie.

Customizing Your Workspace

The sheer number of various panels and windows that you can work with in Flash can make your workspace difficult to manage. However, like Dreamweaver (discussed in Book IV), you can use Flash to customize your working environment to position windows just the way you like and then to save your workspace for future use.

Showing and hiding a panel

You can access all the panels from the Window menu. You can show or hide a panel by selecting its menu item from a list. You can also hide a panel that's open by clicking its Close button.

TIP

Pressing F4 toggles the visibility of all panels and inspectors. This shortcut is useful when you want to eliminate distractions as you create, test, or preview your Flash movie.

Adding a panel to (or removing a panel from) a panel group

Each panel can be combined with others to form a panel group. A panel group can be arranged as tabs, such as the panel group shown in Figure 1-10. To add a panel as a tab, simply drag the panel on top of another panel. When you release the mouse, Flash adds the panel as a new tab.

Figure 1-10:
Use panels arranged as tabs you minimize screen real estate.

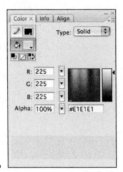

Alternatively, you can arrange panels on top of each other (such as the design panels shown in Figure 1-8). To add a panel above or below another panel, drag a panel onto the second panel's top or bottom border. When you release the mouse button, the panel is docked in the new position.

To move a panel from a panel group, drag the panel's tab and drop it in a new location.

Undocking and docking a panel group

In the Mac version of Flash, panel groups always float. However, in the Windows version, panel groups are normally docked at one side of the application window. To undock and create a floating panel group, simply drag the group into the Document window. The panel group undocks and floats on top of the workspace.

To redock the panel group, drag it to the side of the application window that you want to dock. Flash then redocks it.

Saving a workspace layout

After you arrange the workspace the way you want, choose Window⇨ Workspace⇨Save Current from the menu. In the Save Workspace Layout dialog box, give your new, customized workspace a name and click OK. The new layout is added to the Workspace list.

To use a workspace, choose Window⇨Workspace and select a layout from the list.

Chapter 2: Working with the Stage and Layers

Because Flash is used to create movies, the tool also uses, appropriately, movie-oriented terminology inside the workspace — stages, scenes, frames, temperamental actors, and needless violence. Okay, we made up the last two, but you get the idea that Flash introduces a whole new vocabulary to us non-Hollywood types.

In this chapter, you get started by focusing on perhaps the most important of these movie-sounding terms: the Stage. As you do so, you also explore how to work with layers that are placed on top of it.

Exploring the Stage

The *Stage* is the rectangular design canvas on which you create a Flash movie. The Stage, which is shown in Figure 2-1, looks just like the familiar rectangular shape of a Flash movie file that you see embedded inside a Web page.

You can work with several design aids in the Stage, all available from the View menu:

✦ **Ruler:** Used, as you might expect, for measuring in pixels, inches, or other units

✦ **Grid:** Displays an overlay grid on the Stage

✦ **Guide:** A horizontal or vertical line that you can drag from the ruler to the Stage

✦ **Snapping:** Options that allow you to snap to grids, guides, pixels, or objects

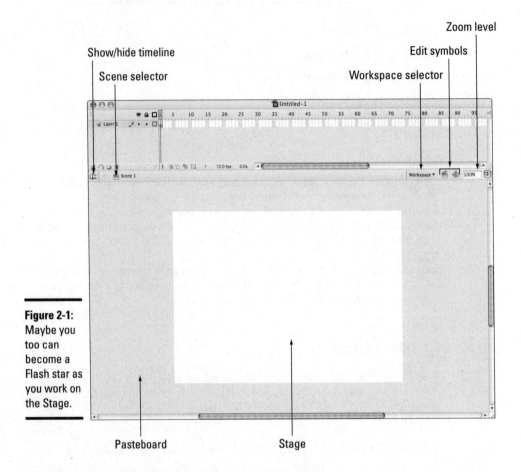

Zoom level

Show/hide timeline

Edit symbols

Scene selector

Workspace selector

Pasteboard

Stage

Figure 2-1:
Maybe you too can become a Flash star as you work on the Stage.

Exploring the Timeline and Layers

The *Timeline* is the filmstrip-like panel that's displayed above the Stage. In the Timeline (see Figure 2-2), you work with layers and frames. The Timeline consists of the Layers pane on the left side and the Frame timeline on the right.

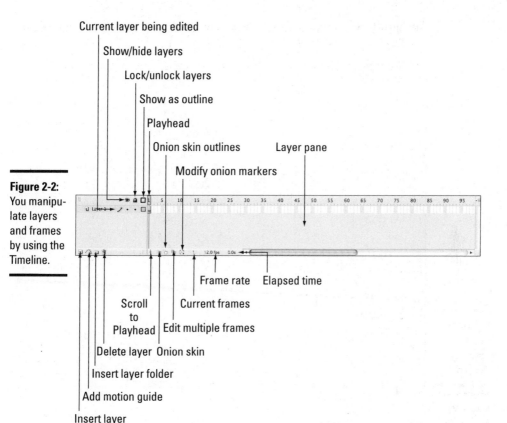

Figure 2-2:
You manipulate layers and frames by using the Timeline.

Current layer being edited
Show/hide layers
Lock/unlock layers
Show as outline
Playhead
Onion skin outlines
Modify onion markers
Layer pane
Frame rate
Elapsed time
Current frames
Scroll to Playhead
Edit multiple frames
Delete layer
Onion skin
Insert layer folder
Add motion guide
Insert layer

A *frame* is the basic unit of time inside a Flash movie. It's just like the individual frames in a long strip of film stock. A *layer* is a transparent sheet, displayed on the Stage, that contains elements. A Flash movie can (and usually does) contain multiple layers of content. The advantage of working with layers rather than placing everything on one canvas is that you can hide, show, and animate individual layers at various times inside a movie.

If you have worked with Photoshop, you're already familiar with the concept of layers. You work with Flash layers in much the same way.

Creating a layer

To create a layer, click the Insert Layer button in the lower left corner of the Timeline window (refer to Figure 2-2). Or, you can choose Insert➪Timeline➪ Layer from the menu.

The new layer is displayed on top of the previous one (as shown in Figure 2-3) and becomes the active layer.

Figure 2-3:
Creating a
new layer in
the Timeline.

Working with layers

The only disadvantage to using layers is that they take some time to get used to. Because elements you place on different layers all appear in the Stage area at the same time, you can become confused about which layer's element you're manipulating. Therefore, the Layers pane is your handy window because it always tells you which layer is active when the Pencil icon appears next to the layer name. (When the pencil icon has a slash through it, the layer is active but can't be edited — usually when the layer has been locked.)

Here are some common tasks that you perform with layers:

✦ **Select a layer:** You can select a layer by using one of these methods:

  • Click an object on the stage. The layer that contains the object is automatically selected.

  • Click the layer in the Layers pane.

  • Click in a frame of the Timeline on the layer row.

+ **Change the order of a layer:** The order in which the layers appear in the Layers pane indicates their display order. In other words, the top layer is shown on top of all other layers, and the bottom layer is on the bottom of the pecking order. You can change a layer by selecting it with your mouse and then dragging it to a new location in the list.

+ **Show or hide a layer:** In the Layers pane, you can toggle the visibility of a layer by clicking the dot under the Eye icon. Or, to show or hide all layers at one time, click the Eye icon.

+ **Lock or unlock a layer:** When you lock a layer, you prevent any editing from taking place in the Stage. To lock a layer, click the dot under the Padlock icon. You can lock all layers at one time by clicking the Padlock icon.

+ **View a layer as an outline:** Click the colored box beside the layer name to view the layer as an outline in the Stage. You can set the outline color by double-clicking the colored box and setting a new color in the Layer Properties dialog box.

+ **Rename a layer:** You can rename a layer by double-clicking its name in the Layers pane. After the name is selected, enter a new name.

+ **Delete a layer:** You can delete a layer by selecting it in the Layers pane and then dragging it on top of the garbage can icon.

Using guide layers

In addition to the design aids discussed in the section "Exploring the Stage," earlier in this chapter, you can define *guide layers* in Flash to help you position or size elements on the Stage. Guide layers are for design-time only and aren't included in the published movie.

To create a guide layer, follow these steps:

1. **Click the Insert Layer button to add a new layer to the movie.**

2. **Right-click the new layer and choose Guide from the pop-up menu.**

   The page icon in the Layers pane beside the layer is replaced with a ruler icon.

A *motion guide layer* is a special type of guide layer that you use to define a path for motion-tweened animations.

Adding Movie Elements to the Stage

You can add artwork, text, graphics, components, and symbols to the Stage for use in your movie. Each time you add an element, you add to the active layer. The following sections describe some of the ways in which you can add content.

Adding lines, shapes, and text from the Tools panel

The Tools panel, discussed in Chapter 1 of this minibook, has several tools for adding text, shapes, and lines to a layer. For example, by using the Text Tool, you can add text to a layer, as shown in Figure 2-4.

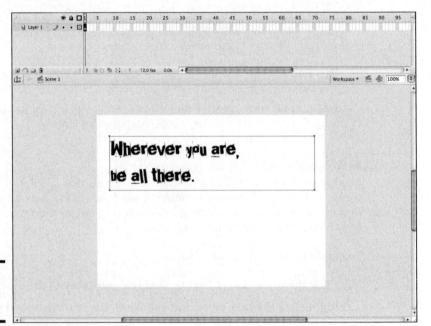

Figure 2-4:
Adding text
to a movie.

Inserting external graphics and media

You can insert video files, bitmapped graphics (such as JPG, PNG, GIF, and Photoshop PSD files), and vector graphics (such as Adobe Illustrator files) into Flash. You can either import the file directly onto the Stage or into the Library.

You can add external media into Flash in three different ways:

✦ Use the File➪Import commands.

✦ Drag and drop an image or media file from an Explorer (Windows) or Finder (Mac) window.

✦ Paste from the Clipboard by choosing the Edit➪Paste in Center Menu command.

Adding user interface and video components

Flash comes with a variety of components that you can add to your Stage, including user interface components, such as push buttons, edit boxes, drop-down list boxes, and other data entry controls. It also has video control components, such as a volume bar and forward and backward buttons. You can add these components from the Components panel, which you access by choosing Window➪Components.

Figure 2-5 shows user interface components added to the Stage.

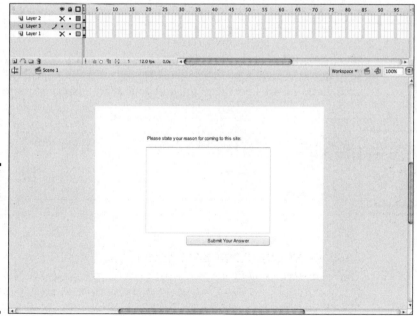

Figure 2-5:
Components
have built-in
capabilities
that you
can easily
configure
for use in
your movies.

Adding symbols

A symbol is an image, button, or movie clip that you create inside Flash and then insert instances of onto the Stage. Symbols are an important topic, however, so we save that discussion for Chapter 3 in this minibook.

Working with Movie Elements

When you draw or add a movie element onto the Stage, you can use the Selection tool to select and move the element. When an element is selected, its properties are displayed in the Properties inspector. For example, Figure 2-6 shows the properties of a text element.

Figure 2-6:
Working hand in hand with the selected element.

If you're working with a component from the Components panel, you work with the Parameters panel, shown in Figure 2-7. All the properties you can configure that are specific to the component are displayed there.

Figure 2-7:
The Parameters panel.

Chapter 3: Working with Symbols

In this chapter, you discover how to use symbols. No, we're sorry, you don't get to learn how to play in the percussion section of the band. That's what *Cymbals For Dummies* would talk about. We're talking about Flash symbols, which are handy thingamajigs that you frequently use as you author Flash movies. In this chapter, you see how to create and work with symbols, instances of symbols, and the Library.

Understanding Symbols and Instances

As we mention in Chapter 1 of this minibook, *symbols* are graphical images, buttons, or movie clips that you create once and then reuse in your movie file. An *instance* is a "copy" of the symbol that's added to the Stage.

Symbols are important because they have a major effect on the overall size of your Flash movie file. Let us explain. Suppose that you have a 70K graphic that you're using in a Flash file that you want to put into 100 frames in a movie — which is a common scenario when you're animating an element. Without symbols, you need 7MB of disk space to store all that graphical data. When you use symbols, however, Flash stores the 70K file just once and then references it for each instance used on the Stage.

Much like when you use a template, when you edit a symbol in Flash, all instances of that symbol are automatically updated. Although an instance is a "copy" of the symbol, however, you can set properties that are specific to that particular instance.

Symbols are normally added to the Library of the active Flash movie file. However, Flash supports shared symbols in its Shared Library.

Flash has three main types of symbols:

✦ **Graphics:** A graphical symbol is used for still-image graphics and works inside the main timeline of the Flash movie.

✦ **Movie clips:** A movie clip symbol is used for reusing an animation clip, video, or audio clip. However, a movie clip has its own mini-timeline that's independent of the main Flash movie Timeline. You can also insert a movie clip inside a button symbol (explained in the following bullet) to create an animated button.

✦ **Buttons:** A button symbol is used to create "rollover-like" buttons that interact with the mouse. You can define various graphics associated with the four main button states (mouse up, mouse over, mouse down, and mouse hit). A button also has its own mini-timeline, consisting of four frames (one for each of the button states). You can then attach code to the button to respond to the button when it's clicked.

Creating a New Symbol

You can create a symbol by either converting an existing media element into a symbol or creating one from scratch.

Creating a symbol from an existing element

To convert an existing element, follow these steps:

1. **Import a graphical image or other media element onto your Stage.**

A quick way is to drag a media file from Explorer (Windows) or Finder (Mac) onto the Stage.

Figure 3-1 shows a JPG image added to the Stage. Notice how the Properties inspector treats the image as an instance of the `.jpg` file.

2. **After the element is selected, choose Modify➪Convert to Symbol from the menu.**

The Convert to Symbol dialog box (shown in Figure 3-2) opens.

3. **Enter a name for the symbol in the Name field.**

We named our symbol `Box`.

4. **Select a symbol type: movie clip, graphic, or button.**

5. **If needed, adjust the registration point for the symbol.**

The *registration point* is the index point that's used when you're rotating or transforming an element. You might want to add it to the center of the symbol rather than to the upper left corner.

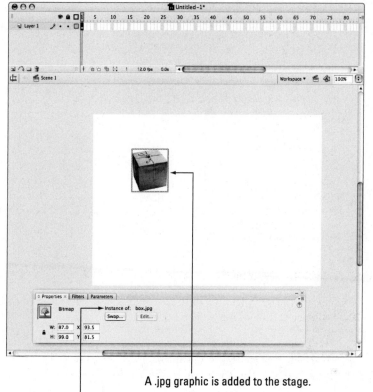

Figure 3-1:
Dropping an
image onto
the Stage.

A .jpg graphic is added to the stage.

The graphic is treated as an instance of the .jpg file.

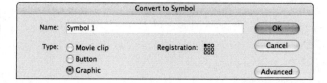

Figure 3-2:
Converting
an image
into a
symbol.

6. **Click OK.**

The symbol is added to the movie file's library (see Figure 3-3), and the
element on the Stage is automatically converted to an instance of the
new symbol (see Figure 3-4).

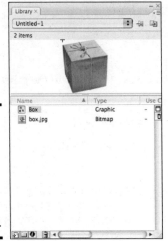

Figure 3-3:
If you're
looking for
a symbol,
go to your
friendly
neighbor-
hood library.

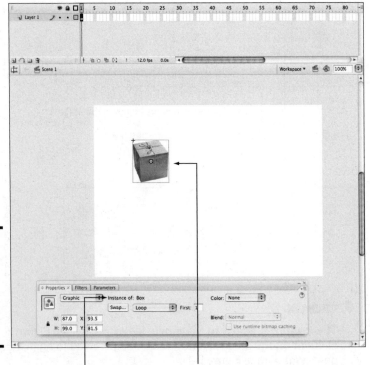

Figure 3-4:
The box
image is
now an
instance of
the new
symbol.

The element is now an instance of the new symbol.

The Instance Of area

Creating a symbol from scratch

To create a new symbol from scratch, follow these steps:

1. **Choose Insert⇨New Symbol.**

You can also click the Create New Symbol button in the Library panel.

The Create New Symbol dialog box is displayed.

2. **Enter a name for the symbol in the Name field.**

3. **Select a symbol type: movie clip, graphic, or button.**

4. **Click OK.**

The symbol is added to the Library, and then something unexpected happens on the Stage: The normal document-editing mode gives way to symbol-editing mode with an empty Stage. In the example, we named the symbol MyFileFolder (see Figure 3-5).

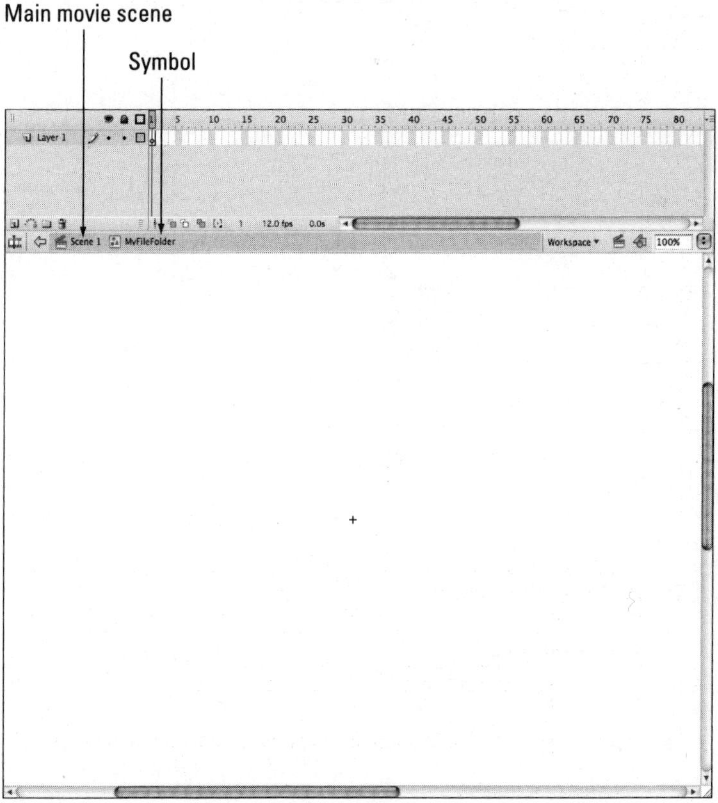

Main movie scene

Symbol

Figure 3-5:
Editing a
symbol on
the Stage.

The crosshairs in the middle of the window comprise the registration point for the symbol.

5. **Draw content in, or add content to, the symbol in the Symbol Editor.**

   You can, for example, drag a graphics file to the Symbol Editor.

6. **When you finish editing the symbol, click the name of the main scene (Scene1 in the example) at the top of the Stage window.**

   You can also choose Edit↪Edit Document.

   The normal document-editing Stage is displayed again.

Working with Symbols in the Library

The Library panel displays the symbols that have been added to the current Flash document (see Figure 3-6). The preview pane at the top displays the selected item in the Library.

Preview pane

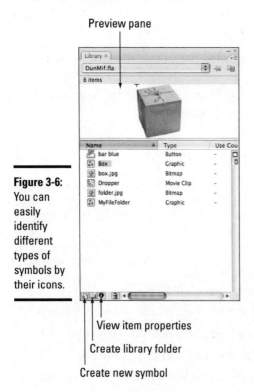

Figure 3-6: You can easily identify different types of symbols by their icons.

View item properties

Create library folder

Create new symbol

To create a new instance of the symbol:

1. **Select the symbol from the Library.**

2. **Drag the symbol to the Stage with your mouse.**

The instance is added to the active layer in the Timeline.

To edit the contents of the symbol, follow these steps:

1. **Double-click the symbol in the Library panel.**

The Stage area displays the symbol inside symbol-editing mode.

2. **Modify the symbol the way you want.**

Although you can modify the properties of symbol instances, you might sometimes want to duplicate a symbol and make changes to it. To duplicate a symbol, follow these steps:

1. **Right-click the symbol in the Library panel, and choose Duplicate from the pop-up menu.**

The Duplicate Symbol dialog box appears.

2. **In the Duplicate Symbol dialog box, provide a name for the new symbol and click OK.**

The newly cloned symbol has no linkage to the symbol it originated from.

Working with Common Library Buttons

Even though you can create your own button symbols, Flash comes with a set of button symbols as part of the Common Libraries. You might find that these buttons provide exactly what you need in order to use inside your Flash files.

To add a button symbol from the Common Libraries, follow these steps:

1. **Choose Window⇨Common Libraries⇨Buttons.**

A special, common Library panel is displayed, as shown in Figure 3-7.

2. **Expand the folder of the button symbol set that interests you.**

In the example, we clicked the `buttons rect flat` folder.

3. **Select the button symbol you want from the folder and drag it to the Stage.**

We selected the `rectangle flat grey` button (see Figure 3-8). A new instance of it is added to the Stage.

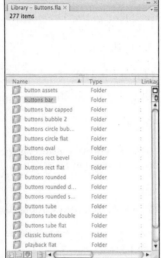

Figure 3-7: Flash features a common library packed with more buttons than a political convention.

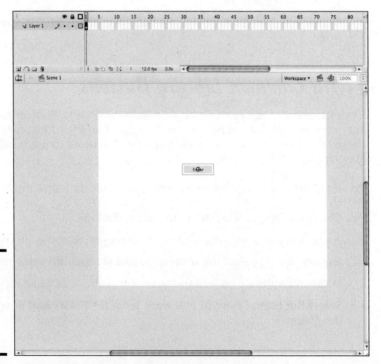

Figure 3-8: Dropping a common library button on the Stage.

A button isn't useful unless it *does* something when you click it, so we show you one way to add functionality to it. However, before doing so, you need to make a change in your Flash publish settings.

4. **Choose File⇨Publish Settings.**

The Publish Settings dialog box is displayed.

5. **Click the Flash tab.**

6. **Choose ActionScript 2.0 from the ActionScript version drop-down list.**

Note: ActionScript 3.0 doesn't support behaviors, which we use in this example.

7. **Click OK.**

8. **Choose Window⇨Behaviors to display the Behaviors panel.**

9. **After the button instance is selected, click the Add Behavior drop-down button.**

A menu of behaviors is displayed.

10. **Choose Web⇨Go to Web Page from the drop-down menu.**

This behavior causes the browser to go to a specified URL.

The Go to URL dialog box is displayed (see Figure 3-9).

Figure 3-9:
Jumping
to the
specified
URL.

11. **Type a Web address to go to in the URL box.**

12. **Click OK.**

The behavior is added to the button and is displayed in the Behaviors panel (see Figure 3-10).

13. **Choose Control⇨Test Movie.**

Flash compiles the movie and displays it in a Flash window (see Figure 3-11).

14. **Test the button functionality when the mouse moves over the button.**

Figure 3-10:
The Behaviors panel displays behaviors defined for the selected element on the Stage.

Figure 3-11:
Testing the button.

15. **Click the button to jump to the URL in your browser.**

16. **Close the test window to return to the Flash authoring environment.**

You can double-click a button to enter symbol-editing mode, as shown in Figure 3-12. The button symbol has a Timeline of four keyframes: Up, Over, Down, and Hit.

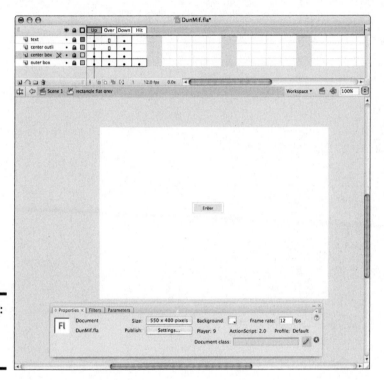

Figure 3-12:
Editing a
button
symbol.

Chapter 4: Making Movies

In This Chapter

✔ Exploring Flash animation

✔ Creating frame-by-frame animations

✔ Creating tweened motion and shape animations

✔ Introducing behaviors and actions

✔ Adding sounds to your movies and buttons

*I*n the first three chapters of this minibook, we show you how to work with the Stage, layers on the Stage, and media elements and symbols inside the layers. However, we saved one key aspect of the Flash authoring environment for this chapter: the Timeline. The Timeline is at the heart of any Flash movie. As you begin to master working with frames inside the Timeline, you can create animations and interactive Flash movies.

Creating Animations in Your Movie

You can use two types of animation techniques in Flash:

✦ **Frame-by-frame animation** adjusts the contents of the Stage for every individual frame. This type of animation is much like a children's flip book. When you flip the pages, the effect is an animation. (It's also the way that the first animated films, like the early Disney films, were made, except that the "flipping" was done on reels of film rather than on pages of a book.)

✦ In **tweened animation,** you define an element (or group of elements) in a starting frame and then make changes to it (for example, a different location or properties) in the ending frame. Flash then automatically generates all the frames between these two points.

The changes you make in an animation are made in special frames called *keyframes.* Each frame in a frame-by-frame animation is a keyframe. In tweened animation, however, you define keyframes only in the frames in which something changes (at least the starting and ending frames) in the Timeline.

Frame-by-frame animation

When you create frame-by-frame animation, the Stage changes in every frame. Frame-by-frame animation works well for highly detailed animations, but it increases the file size because Flash has to store data for every frame of the animation.

To create a frame-by-frame animation of a layer you already created, follow these steps:

1. **Select a layer from the Layers pane of the Timeline (see Figure 4-1).**

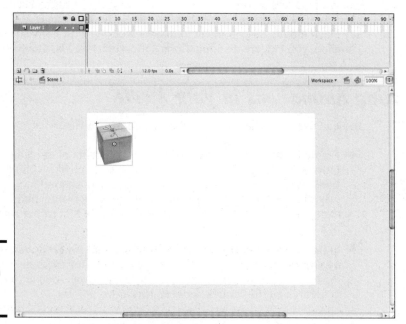

Figure 4-1:
Selecting a
layer to
animate.

2. **Add to the Stage the content that you want to animate.**

We recommend using symbols (see Chapter 3 in this minibook) to minimize storage space.

3. **In the Timeline, right-click the frame in which you want to start the animation.**

The pop-up menu appears.

4. **Choose Insert Keyframe from the pop-up menu.**

A round dot is added to the frame, to represent the keyframe (see Figure 4-2).

Keyframe

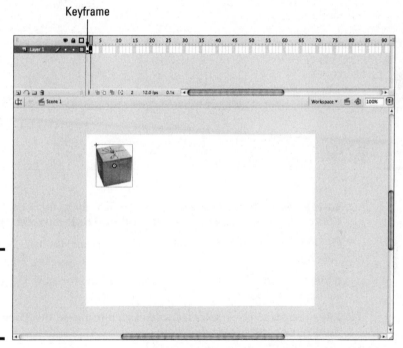

Figure 4-2:
The key-frame is shown with a black dot.

5. **Select the second frame in the Timeline, and right-click it to display its pop-up menu.**

6. **Choose Insert Keyframe from the pop-up menu.**

7. **Edit the contents of the Stage slightly as the first step in the animation.**

8. **Repeat Steps 4 through 6 as needed until you finish your animation.**

Figure 4-3 shows the final keyframe of a 12-framed animation.

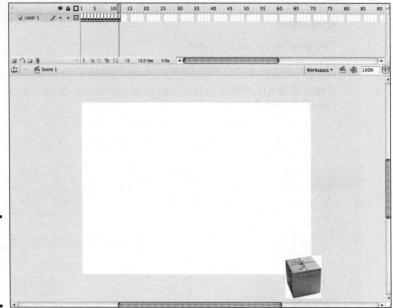

Figure 4-3:
A 12-framed
frame-by-
frame
animation.

9. **Test the animation in the authoring environment by choosing Control⇨Play or pressing Enter (Windows) or Return (Mac).**

   Or, to see the animation in the compiled version, choose Control⇨ Test Movie.

   If you're satisfied with the animation, you can stop now. Or, if you want to make tweaks, continue.

10. **Keep the same layer selected and click a frame in the Timeline to modify its contents on the Stage.**

11. **Adjust the contents of the Stage as needed to improve the animation effect.**

12. **Test the animation again by choosing Control⇨Play.**

Tweened animation

Flash has two types of tweened animation:

✦ **Motion tweening:** Deals with changing the properties or location of an element from start to finish.

✦ **Shape tweening:** Focuses on a starting shape and then a different finishing shape. Flash creates the gradual transformation in the frames between them, thus giving the appearance of animation.

Motion tweens

To create a motion-tweened animation, follow these steps:

1. **Select a layer from the Layers pane of the Timeline.**

2. **If it isn't already selected, click the first frame in the Timeline.**

3. **Add to the Stage the content that you want to animate.**

Be sure to convert your artwork to a symbol (see Chapter 3 in this minibook) by choosing Modify➪Convert to Symbol. Symbols are required for creating a motion tween.

Figure 4-4 shows a nifty little box on the Stage.

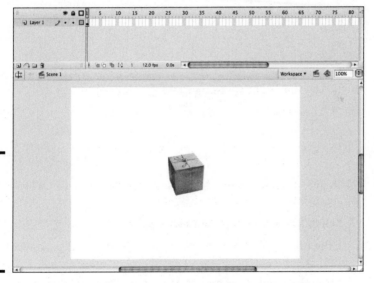

Figure 4-4:
The beginning point of a motion tween animation.

4. **Select the frame in the Timeline in which you want the animation to end.**

In honor of Jack Bauer, we chose the 24th frame.

5. **Right-click the frame and choose Insert Keyframe from its pop-up menu.**

   Pressing F6 is a handy shortcut for inserting a keyframe.

6. **Change the content of the Stage in the ending keyframe.**

   You can relocate the element to another location in the Stage. Or, you can change its size, rotation, skew, or other visual property.

   In the example, we enlarged the box (by using Free Transform from the symbol's pop-up menu) and then set its brightness level to 82 percent (see Figure 4-5).

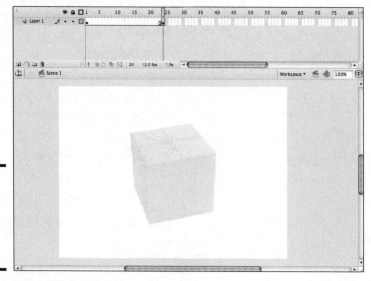

Figure 4-5:
The ending point of a motion tween animation.

7. **Select the layer from the Layers pane.**

   If the Properties inspector isn't already visible, choose Windows➪ Properties.

8. **From the Properties inspector, choose Motion from the Tween drop-down list.**

   Several new Motion properties are displayed, as shown in Figure 4-6.

9. **If the size of the animated element changed, check the Scale box.**

10. **Choose a rotation option from the Rotate drop-down list.**

Figure 4-6:
The
beginning
point of a
motion
tween
animation.

11. **Set an ease value by using the Ease slider.**

The 0 default setting causes the motion to be constant. A positive value (1 through 100) begins the tweened animation quickly and slows it as it nears the end. A negative value (–1 through –100) begins the tween slowly and speeds it up toward the end.

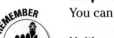

If you want to get fancy, you can click the Edit button beside the Ease box to customize the ease value even further.

12. **Select the Sync check box to match the frame count of the animation with the number of frames of the instance in the movie.**

13. **Choose Control⇨Play to test the animation.**

Shape tweens

You can use shape tweens to morph one shape into another.

Unlike motion tweens, the elements you morph *cannot* be symbols.

Here's how to set up a shape tween animation:

1. **Select a layer from the Layers pane of the Timeline.**

2. **If the first frame in the Timeline isn't already selected, click it.**

3. **Add to the Stage the shape that you want to animate by using the drawing tools from the Tools panel.**

Figure 4-7 shows a rectangular shape in the keyframe.

4. **Select the frame in the Timeline in which you want the morphing to end.**

We chose the 24th frame.

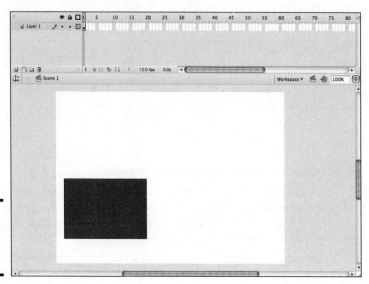

Figure 4-7:
It all started
with a
rectangle.

5. **Right-click the frame and choose Insert Keyframe from its pop-up menu.**

6. **Delete the artwork that you previously added in the first keyframe.**

7. **Create a new object in the Stage in the ending keyframe.**

   In the example, we created an oval shape (see Figure 4-8).

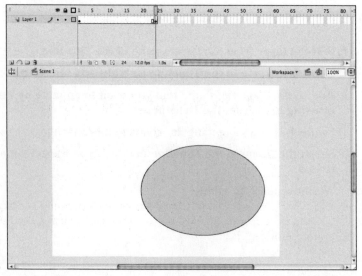

Figure 4-8:
And it ended
with an oval.

8. **Select the layer from the Layers pane.**

   If the Properties inspector isn't already visible, choose Windows⇨Properties.

9. **From the Properties inspector, choose Shape from the Tween drop-down list.**

   Several new Shape properties are displayed, as shown in Figure 4-9.

Figure 4-9:
Shape
tweens
have
several
options.

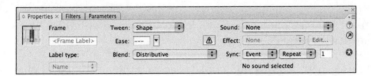

10. **Select the blending option from the Blend drop-down list.**

    The Distributive option better smoothes the intermediate shapes. Angular better sharpens the intermediate shapes.

11. **Choose a rotation option from the Rotate drop-down list.**

12. **As you did with the motion tween, set an ease value by using the Ease slider.**

    The 0 default setting causes the motion to be constant. A positive value (1 through 100) begins the tweened animation quickly and slows it as it nears the end. A negative value (–1 through –100) begins the tween slowly and speeds it up toward the end.

13. **Choose Control⇨Play to test the movie.**

Involving the User: Interactive Flash Movies

Flash movies aren't meant as just gizmos for users to watch. You can add interactivity to them, such as going to a URL when a user clicks a button or moving an element when the user's mouse hovers over it. You can add interactivity to your Flash movie by using behaviors and actions:

✦ **Behaviors:** You can attach these easy-to-use predefined scripts to objects in your movie. You access behaviors by using the Behaviors panel (Window⇨Behaviors).

✦ **Actions:** These programming scripts are for more advanced users. The code is written in ActionScript, the Flash scripting language; it looks similar to JavaScript. You can work with actions in the Actions panel (Window➪Actions).

Behaviors aren't compatible with ActionScript 3.0, which is the Flash scripting language. Therefore, if you plan to use Behaviors in your Flash movie, you need to specify ActionScript 2.0 (or ActionScript 1.0) as your ActionScript version. This setting is on the Flash tab of the Publish Settings dialog box. (Choose File➪Publish Settings.)

When you're beginning to work with Flash interactivity, behaviors are a good place to start. Then, when you feel comfortable with them, you can begin to work with actions.

See Chapter 3 in this minibook for an example of adding a behavior to a button symbol.

Adding sound to your movie

In addition to being able to add graphics and video clips, you can add sound effects or sound clips into your movie in Flash. You can add audio in two different ways. For short sound effects, such as a blip sound when a button is pressed, you can download the entire audio clip before it's played. Or, for large audio files, you can stream them. When you stream an audio file, Flash downloads the beginning of the song or audio clip and then begins playing in synch with the Timeline of the movie.

Importing an audio file

Before you can work with an audio file, you must add it to your Flash library by choosing the File➪Import➪Import to Library command. In the dialog box that appears, add one or more sound files and click the Import to Library button. Go to the Library panel for your movie; the files are displayed there.

Flash supports AIFF, MP3, and WAV sound files.

Adding an audio clip to your movie

To add a soundtrack or audio clip to your movie, follow these steps:

1. **Import an audio file into Flash by following the instructions in the preceding section.**

2. **Insert a new layer in the Timeline by clicking the Insert Layer button at the bottom of the Timeline window (or by choosing Insert Timeline➪Layer).**

3. **From the Library panel, drag the sound file you want to include and drop it on top of the layer name in the Layers pane of the Timeline.**

   The audio clip is added, as shown in Figure 4-10.

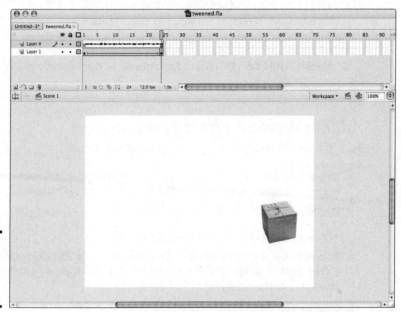

Figure 4-10:
The audio file is added in a layer.

4. **You can optionally add an effect (such as a fade-in) by selecting an option from the Effect drop-down list in the layer's Properties inspector.**

   If you want to get fancy, click the Edit button to customize the sound wave.

5. **Pick a synchronization option from the Sync drop-down list:**

   - *Event:* Synchronizes the sound to an event
   - *Start:* Begins playing the sound (like Event), except that if the sound is already playing, it doesn't start again
   - *Stop:* Halts playing the sound
   - *Stream:* Ensures that the animation of the movie is in synch with streamed audio

6. **Determine the number of times the sound should loop or whether it should be continuous. Use the Repeat drop-down list and the box beside it to specify your response.**

   If you want the sound to play throughout the entire animation, be sure to enter a value large enough to last the length of your movie.

   You can have multiple sounds per film. Therefore, if you want to have additional sounds (overlapping each other), repeat Steps 1 through 6.

7. **Choose Edit⇨Edit Document to return to document-editing mode.**

8. **Choose Control⇨Test Movie to test your new sound.**

Adding a sound effect to a button

To add a sound effect to a button, follow these steps:

1. **Import an audio file into Flash by following the instructions in the section "Importing an audio file," earlier in this chapter.**

2. **Double-click the button on the Stage to enter symbol-editing mode.**

   The four-frame button Timeline appears.

3. **Insert a new layer in the button's Timeline by clicking the Insert Layer button at the bottom of the Timeline window (or choosing Insert Timeline⇨Layer).**

4. **Double-click the layer name and rename it as** Sound.

5. **In the Timeline, click the sound layer's frame under the button state you want to assign the sound to: Up, Over, Down, or Hit.**

6. **Insert a keyframe by pressing F6 (or right-clicking the frame and choosing Insert Keyframe from the pop-up menu).**

7. **After the new keyframe is selected, view the Properties inspector.**

8. **Select the sound clip you want to attach from the Sound drop-down list.**

9. **If you want, add an effect from the Effect drop-down list.**

10. **Pick a synchronization option from the Sync drop-down list:**

    - *Event:* Synchronizes the sound to an event.

    - *Start:* Begins playing the sound (like Event), except that if the sound is already playing, it doesn't start again.

- *Stop:* Halts playing the sound.

- *Stream:* Ensures that the animation of the movie is in synch with streamed audio.

11. **Determine the number of times the sound should loop or whether it should be continuous. Use the Repeat drop-down list and the box beside it to specify your response.**

12. **Choose Edit⇨Edit Document to return to document-editing mode.**

13. **Choose Control⇨Test Movie to check out your new sound-enabled button.**

Chapter 5: Publishing Your Movie

In This Chapter

✔ Optimizing the size of your movie file

✔ Profiling download performance

✔ Publishing your movie in Flash format for the Web

After you create and test your Flash movie, you're ready to go live with it. Before doing so, you first need to publish the movie so that it can be viewed inside browsers. In this chapter, we begin by showing you how to optimize your movie to decrease its file size. After that, we show you how to publish the movie. Finally, you explore how to export your movie file to different formats.

For Best Results: Optimizing Your Movie

As you create your Flash movie, be mindful of the size of the movie you're creating. Even with broadband connections, visitors still get impatient and frustrated with your Web site if they have to wait awhile for a Flash movie to download.

Optimization tips

Here are several tips to keep in mind to optimize your movie:

✦ **Use symbols.** If you have an element, such as a video clip or graphic, that appears more than once in the movie, be sure to use a symbol for it. When you use symbols, elements are stored once and Flash uses instances of those elements every time they occur in the movie.

✦ **Use tweened animation.** Tweened animation occupies much less space than does frame-by-frame animation. Flash needs to store information for only the two keyframes rather than for every frame.

✦ **Optimize curves.** Curves that you create with the pencil and other tools are stored as miniature line segments. You can optimize the number of line segments used by Flash by choosing Modify⇨Shape⇨Optimize. The Smoothing slider determines how much the shape is smoothed.

✦ **Optimize text.** When you work with fonts, you can use either device fonts or embedded fonts. If you use a device font, Flash looks for the closest matching font installed on the user's system, much like a browser does when displaying a Web page. An embedded font, on the other hand, is stored as part of the Flash file. The font takes up more space but ensures that the text looks exactly as you intended. The decision about whether to use embedded fonts is ultimately a cost-benefit issue on design versus download speed.

✦ **Draw and paint wisely.** Although optimization issues shouldn't limit your creativity, keep in mind how your artwork can affect file size. Pencil strokes take less space than brush strokes. Solid lines are smaller than dotted and dashed lines. Grouped elements take up less space than ungrouped ones.

✦ **Compress the movie and embedded bitmapped graphics when you publish.** Flash provides several optimization settings that further compress the movie when you publish. See the section "Outputting Your Movie for the Web," a little later in this chapter, for more information.

Profiling download performance

As you're testing your movie (choose Control➪Test Movie), you can test the download performance and even profile the specific frames of the animation that cause the greatest download delays. Follow these steps:

1. **Choose View➪Bandwidth Profiler from the test mode's menu.**

If you don't see this menu item on the View menu, choose Control➪ Test Movie and then continue.

2. **Choose View➪Download Settings to specify the simulated download rate to use in the testing.**

3. **Turn on the View➪Simulate Download setting to perform a simulated download based on the download speed you set before the movie runs.**

The Bandwidth Profiler is displayed on top of the Flash movie window (see Figure 5-1). As the movie is played, Flash performs a performance test on it.

The left side of the profiler displays overall statistics about the movie, including its size and the length of time it took to download before playing.

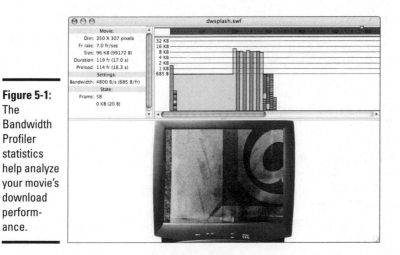

Figure 5-1:
The Bandwidth Profiler statistics help analyze your movie's download performance.

The right side displays a timeline and graph. The graph can display either streaming data (choose View⇨Streaming Graph) or a frame-by-frame look (choose View⇨Frame-By-Frame Graph). The Streaming Graph displays all frames that cause slowdowns. The Frame-By-Frame Graph displays the size of every frame in the movie. Frames that are above the red line cause the movie to load more slowly, making them good targets for optimization. Click the bar to view the specific frame.

Outputting Your Movie for the Web

When you create, design, and test a Web page in Dreamweaver, Expression Web, or another software tool, you're working with the HTML files that you will publish to your remote server. So, when you speak of "publishing a Web page," that term is roughly synonymous with "uploading." However, Flash is a different story.

When you create a Flash movie inside the Flash environment, you're working with an editable `.fla` file. However, `.fla` files need to be transformed into a different non-editable file format before they can be played back over the Web in a browser. This conversion process is known as *publishing*.

To publish a Flash movie that's opened inside the Flash design environment, follow these steps:

***1.* Choose File⇨Publish Settings.**

The Publish Settings dialog box is displayed, as shown in Figure 5-2.

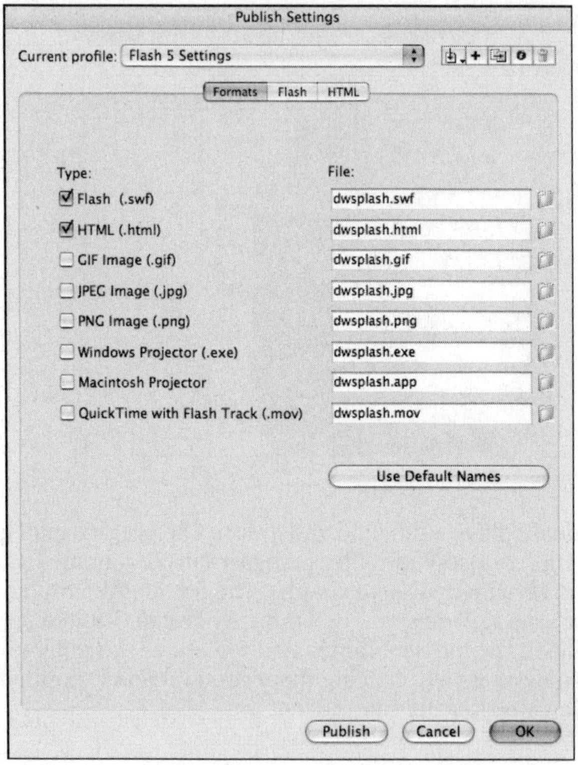

Publish Settings

Current profile: Flash 5 Settings

Formats   Flash   HTML

Type: File:
☑ Flash (.swf)   dwsplash.swf
☑ HTML (.html)   dwsplash.html
☐ GIF Image (.gif)   dwsplash.gif
☐ JPEG Image (.jpg)   dwsplash.jpg
☐ PNG Image (.png)   dwsplash.png
☐ Windows Projector (.exe)   dwsplash.exe
☐ Macintosh Projector   dwsplash.app
☐ QuickTime with Flash Track (.mov)   dwsplash.mov

Use Default Names

Publish   Cancel   OK

Figure 5-2:
Specifying
in which
types of
formats the
movie
should be
published.

2. **If you need to, click the Formats tab and select all the file formats that you want to publish (Flash (.swf) and HTML (.html) are selected by default):**

   • *Flash:* The actual movie file; required for viewing inside a browser over the Web.

   • *HTML:* Creates an HTML document with the .swf file already embedded into it. If you plan to insert your Flash movie inside a Web page you already built, you can deselect this option.

   Because you're likely to insert the Flash file you created into a Web page you previously built, you may be tempted to simply discard this option. However, by enabling this option and working with the HTML publish settings, you can see all the tasks that are possible when adding a Flash movie to a Web page.

   • *GIF Image, JPEG Image, PNG Image:* Create a single image version of your movie clip.

- *Windows Projector, Macintosh Projector:* Create a standalone application that can be run on a local Windows or Mac computer outside a browser.

- *QuickTime with Flash Track:* Creates a QuickTime movie.

Note that for every file format that you enable, a new tab is added to the dialog box for publishing settings.

3. **In the File section, specify a filename for each of the file formats you selected.**

   Use the Browse button beside the filename box to navigate to a specific output folder. Otherwise, the file is published in the same location as the `.fla` file.

4. **Click the Flash tab (see Figure 5-3) and specify the publish settings for the Flash movie.**

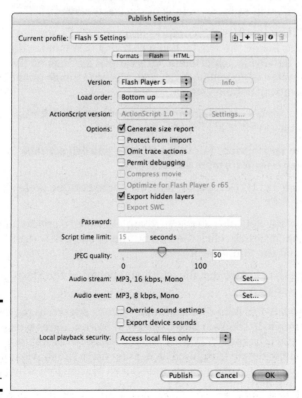

Figure 5-3:
Setting
Flash
publishing
preferences.

Some of the more noteworthy options are described in this list:

- *Version:* Sets playback for older Flash players.

- *Load Order:* Indicates how the first frame is displayed when the movie downloads.

- *Generate Size Report:* Helpful in determining movie download performance and even tracking down specific frames that are causing slowdowns. The report is generated in the same location as the `.swf` file.

- *Protect From Import:* Ensures that no one can import your `.swf` file into the Flash environment and edit it.

- *Omit Trace Actions:* Should be checked when you have a final movie ready to go. Trace actions are used in debugging ActionScript.

- *Compress Movie:* Reduces file size, but then the `.swf` output cannot be played in earlier versions of the Flash player.

- *JPEG Quality:* Sets the compression ratio that's applied to bitmapped images inside the movie. If you're trying to minimize the size of your movie file, experiment with various settings on the slider to determine which value gives you adequate image quality while maximizing compression.

- *Audio Stream, Audio Event:* Set the sound quality for streams and events.

5. Click the appropriate tab to specify the publish settings for HTML and any other output formats you selected.

If you checked HTML output, here are some notable preferences (shown in Figure 5-4):

- *Template:* Specifies a specific template used to create the document. For each setting, click the Info button to see a description summary of what the template provides.

- *Dimensions:* Specifies the width and height of the Flash object inside the Web page.

- *Playback:* Provides four common options related to the playback of the movie in the Web page. *Paused at Start* requires a user to manually start the movie. *Display Menu* displays the Flash pop-up menu when the movie is right-clicked. *Loop* plays the movie continually. *Device Font* substitutes an anti-aliased system font when it can't locate a particular font on the computer.

- *Quality:* Specifies the amount of anti-aliasing applied to the movie.

- *HTML Alignment, Flash Alignment:* Specify the positioning of the control inside the document body.

The File⊃Publish Preview command is helpful when you're testing different publish settings for any of the formats.

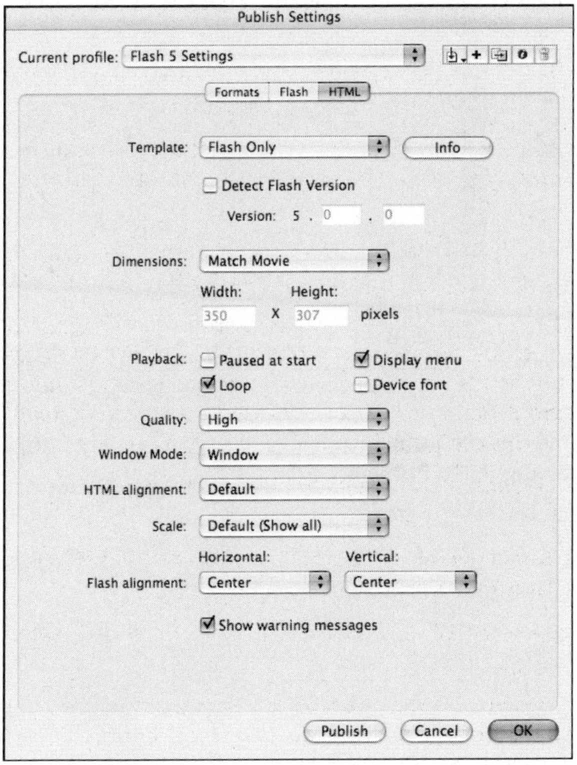

Figure 5-4:
You have a variety of options for displaying a Flash movie inside an HTML document.

6. Click the Publish button to publish the movie.

Flash generates output files for each of the file formats specified on the Formats tab.

If you selected the option to generate a report, you can display the results inside Flash (see Figure 5-5) by double-clicking the file in an Explorer (Windows) or Finder (Mac) window.

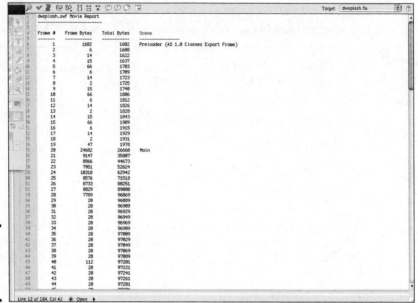

Figure 5-5:
Viewing the report of a Flash movie.

After you configure the publish settings, you can quickly publish a Flash movie by choosing File➪Publish.

Appendix: About the CD-ROM

In This Appendix

✓ System requirements

✓ Using the CD with Windows and the Mac

✓ What you'll find on the CD

✓ Troubleshooting

*T*he CD-ROM that accompanies this book contains several software programs, tools, and utilities that will help you as you create Web sites. In this appendix, we talk you through what you need to know to install these tools on your system.

System Requirements

Make sure that your computer meets the minimum system requirements shown in the following list. If your computer doesn't match up with most of these requirements, you may have problems using the software and files on the CD. For the latest and greatest information, please refer to the ReadMe file located at the root of the CD-ROM.

✦ A PC running Windows Vista, Windows XP, Windows NT4 (with SP4 or later), or Windows 2000

✦ A Macintosh running Apple OS X or later

✦ An Internet connection (for accessing Web-based content)

✦ A CD-ROM drive

If you need more information on the basics, check out these books published by Wiley Publishing, Inc.: *PCs For Dummies,* by Dan Gookin; *Macs For Dummies,* by David Pogue; *iMacs For Dummies,* by David Pogue; *Windows Vista For Dummies* and *Windows 2000 Professional For Dummies,* both by Andy Rathbone.

Using the CD

To install the items from the CD to your hard drive, follow these steps:

1. **Insert the CD into your computer's CD-ROM drive.**

The license agreement appears.

Note to Windows users: The interface doesn't launch if Autorun is disabled. In that case, choose Start⇨Run. (In Windows Vista, choose Start⇨ All Programs⇨Accessories⇨Run.) In the dialog box that appears, type **D:\Start.exe**. (Replace D with the proper letter if your CD drive uses a different letter. If you don't know the letter, see how your CD drive is listed under My Computer.) Click OK.

Note for Mac Users: The CD icon appears on your desktop. Double-click the icon to open the CD and double-click the Start icon.

2. **Read through the license agreement and then click the Accept button if you want to use the CD.**

After you click Accept, the License Agreement window doesn't appear again.

The CD interface appears. The interface allows you to install the programs and run the demos with just a click of a button (or two).

What You'll Find on the CD

The following sections are arranged by category and provide a summary of the software and other goodies you'll find on the CD. If you need help with installing the items provided on the CD, refer to the installation instructions in the preceding section.

Shareware programs are fully functional, free, trial versions of copyrighted programs. If you like particular programs, register with their authors for a nominal fee and receive licenses, enhanced versions, and technical support.

Freeware programs are free, copyrighted games, applications, and utilities. You can copy them to as many PCs as you like — for free — but they offer no technical support.

GNU software is governed by its own license, which is included inside the folder of the GNU software. There are no restrictions on distribution of GNU software. See the GNU license at the root of the CD for more details.

Trial, demo, or *evaluation* versions of software are usually limited by either time or functionality (such as not letting you save a project after you create it).

Author-created material

The CD contains `navmenu.css`, a CSS style sheet used in Book VII, Chapter 4. This file works under Windows or Mac OS X.

CSSEdit

Trial version.

For Mac OS. CSSEdit, by MacRabbit, has rapidly become our favorite tool for working with style sheets. Its visual editor lets you create and edit your styles and instantly see a "live" preview of your CSS code. Check out `macrabbit.com/cssedit` for full details.

CSS Tab Designer

Freeware version.

For Windows. From OverZone Software, a visual tool for designing CSS-based lists and tabs visually and without any programming knowledge required. You can check out its home page at `www.highdots.com/css-tab-designer`.

Cyberduck

Open source, GNU version.

For Mac OS. A Mac-based open source FTP client for uploading and downloading files from an FTP server. Check out `cyberduck.ch` for more info.

FileZilla

Open source, GNU version.

For Windows. An open source FTP client for uploading and downloading files from an FTP server. Check out `sourceforge.net/projects/filezilla` on the World Wide Web for a full description.

GIMP

GNU version.

For Windows and Mac OS. An open source image editor for photo retouching, image composition, and image authoring. For more information, visit `www.gimp.org`.

Notepad2

Freeware version.

For Windows. A freeware text editor for Windows that you can use for editing Web files, including HTML, CSS, and JavaScript files. For more information, check out `www.flos-freeware.ch/notepad2.html`.

Nvu

Open Source, GNU version.

For Windows and Mac OS. An open source Web site builder for creating pages and managing your Web site. NVU stands for "new view." Visit `www.nvu.org` for full details.

TextWrangler

Freeware version.

For Mac OS. A freeware text editor for Mac, created by BareBones Software. Use it for editing HTML, CSS, and JavaScript files. For more information, check out `www.barebones.com/products/textwrangler`.

Web Links

Links to free Web services and trial software versions.

The Web Links section provides links to a host of free Web-based services and tools (such as free stock art, open source templates, a color scheme selector, and a font comparison tool) that are invaluable tools for creating your Web site. This section also provides instant access to the latest trial versions of the most popular Web tools now available, including

✦ **Adobe Dreamweaver CS3:** The most popular Web site building and management tool for Windows and Mac OS X. It enables users to efficiently design, develop, and maintain standards-based Web sites and applications. Dreamweaver is covered fully in Book IV.

✦ **Adobe Flash CS3:** The authoring environment for creating Flash media, interactive Web sites, digital experiences, and mobile content. It's available on the Windows and Mac OS X platforms. See Book IX for more on Flash.

✦ **Adobe Photoshop CS3:** The industry standard image editor that's available for Windows and Mac OS X.

✦ **Microsoft Expression Web:** The premier Web site design tool from Microsoft for creating modern, standards-based sites that deliver superior quality on the Web. It's the successor to Microsoft FrontPage. Book III shows you how to use Expression Web for creating Web pages.

Troubleshooting

We tried our best to compile programs that work on most computers with the minimum system requirements. Alas, your computer may differ, and some programs may not work properly for some reason.

The two likeliest problems are that you don't have enough memory (RAM) for the programs you want to use, or you have other programs running that are affecting installation or running of a program. If you get an error message such as `Not enough memory` or `Setup cannot continue`, try one or more of the following suggestions and then try using the software again:

✦ **Turn off any antivirus software running on your computer.** Installation programs sometimes mimic virus activity and may make your computer incorrectly believe that it's being infected by a virus.

✦ **Close all running programs.** The more programs you have running, the less memory is available to other programs. Installation programs typically update files and programs, so if you keep other programs running, installation may not work properly.

✦ **Have your local computer store add more RAM to your computer.** This is, admittedly, a drastic and somewhat expensive step. However, adding more memory can really help the speed of your computer and allow more programs to run at the same time.

If you have trouble with the CD-ROM, please call the Wiley Product Technical Support phone number at (800) 762-2974. Outside the United States, call 1(317) 572-3994. You can also contact Wiley Product Technical Support at `http://support.wiley.com`. John Wiley & Sons provides technical support only for installation and other general quality-control items. For technical support on the applications themselves, consult the program's vendor or author.

To place additional orders or to request information about other Wiley products, please call (877) 762-2974.

Index

rules (CSS)
creating, 255–257
declaration, 293
defined, 293
editing, 257
font size, 311–312
fonts, 309–311
hierarchy of selectors, 305–306
pseudo-classes, 307
pseudo-elements, 308
selectors, 293, 301–308
syntax, 293–294
text formatting, 309–311
rules (horizontal lines), 362–363
Rules pane (CSS Styles panel), 253

S

Safari browser, 14
safety of MySpace, 42
Sample Style Sheets dialog box (Adobe Dreamweaver CS3), 261
sans serif fonts, 309
saving
CSS (Cascading Style Sheet), 258
Dynamic Web Templates, 170–171
Web pages, 200
workspace layout (Adobe Dreamweaver CS3), 191
workspace layout (Adobe Flash CS3), 543
scope of variables, 478–479

scrambling e-mail links, 526–528
`script` element, 464–466, 515
scripts
alert message box, 465–466
attaching script to a link, 517–518
defined, 464
dhtmlgoodies.com Web site, 467
Dynamic Drive Web site, 467
`escrambler.js` file, 526–528
events, 466–467
executing automatically on load, 464–465
executing on demand, 465
finding, 467
functions, 465
`innerHTML` property, 518–520
`.js` filename extension, 515–516
objects, 469–470
`script` element, 515
sources of, 467
storing, 515–516
testing browser support for features, 529
scrollable `div` element, 410
search engines
`meta` element, 356–357
meta keywords, 357
`title` element, 356
searching blogs, 91
security, 31

Select Image Source dialog box (Adobe Dreamweaver CS3), 208–209
selecting layers, 547
Selection tool (Adobe Flash CS3), 536, 552
selectors (CSS rules)
adjacent sibling selectors, 305–306
attribute selectors, 307
child selectors, 305–306
class selectors, 302–303
combining, 303–304
defined, 293
descendant selectors, 305–306
hierarchy, 305
id selectors, 304
multiple selectors, 305
pseudo-classes, 307
pseudo-elements, 308
syntax, 293
type selectors, 301–302
universal selectors, 304–305
self-linking pages, 30
seller's account (eBay), 106–108
selling items at eBay
categories of items, 108–109
listing page, 109–114
payment methods, 112–113
PayPal, 113
pictures of items, 106, 110–111, 114–116
seller's account, 105–108
shipping costs, 113
writing tips, 114

templates
  blogs, 83–84, 92–95
  Dreamweaver templates, 263–271
  Dynamic Web Templates, 167–174
  MySpace profile, 53–54
testing
  browser display of Web pages, 14
  browser support for features, 529
  Flash movies, 580
testing server, 276
text. *See also* content
  aligning, 74, 318, 342
  alternative text, 149, 209, 352
  baseline, 342
  blinking, 314–315
  bold, 74, 314, 364
  colors, 74, 317–318, 368–369
  Flash movies, 580
  Flash text, 224–226
  forms, 242–243
  GIFs, 437
  Google Page Creator, 59, 74
  grouping inline text, 363–364
  I-beam text selection cursor, 332
  indentation, 294, 319
  inserting, 203
  italics, 74, 314, 364
  justification, 294
  line-height, 319
  line-through, 314–315
  lowercase, 315
  overlining, 314
  paragraphs, 359–360

small caps, 315
spacing, 316
strikethrough, 314–315
superscripting, 343
underlining, 314
uppercase, 315
wrapping text around images, 152
text attribute, 354
text boxes (forms), 420, 422
text editors
  Notepad, 11, 292
  Notepad2, 589
  TextWrangler, 590
text formatting
  Adobe Dreamweaver CS3, 204–207
  CSS rules, 309–311
  CSS styles, 145–148, 204, 207, 309
  div element, 161–163
  Google Page Creator, 74
  HTML, 144–145, 204–207
  Microsoft Web Expression, 144–148
Text tool (Adobe Flash CS3), 537
text-align CSS property
  block level elements, 318
  div element, 406–407
  positioning, 334
text-decoration CSS property, 314–315
text-indent CSS property, 319
text-transform CSS property, 315
th element, 381
this keyword, 511
this reserved word, 474
three-column layout, 413

throw reserved word, 474
throws reserved word, 474
thumbnails of images, 153, 395–396
TIFF file format, 436
Tiffany & Co. Web site, 432, 434
Timeline (Adobe Flash CS3), 546–547
title element, 356, 358
titles
  adding, 136
  blogs, 81
  Google Page Creator, 59
  HTML documents, 356
tone of Web sites, 14
toolbars (Adobe Dreamweaver CS3)
  Document toolbar, 184, 281–282
  Insert bar, 182–184
  Standard toolbar, 184–185
  Style Rendering toolbar, 185
toolbars (Microsoft Expression Web)
  Common toolbar, 144–145, 154
  Pictures toolbar, 153, 155
  Positioning toolbar, 161
Toolbox task pane (Microsoft Expression Web), 126–127
tools (Adobe Flash CS3)
  Add Anchor Point tool, 536
  Convert Anchor Point tool, 537
  Delete Anchor Point tool, 536

Notes

Notes

Notes

Notes

Wiley Publishing, Inc.
End-User License Agreement

READ THIS. You should carefully read these terms and conditions before opening the software packet(s) included with this book "Book". This is a license agreement "Agreement" between you and Wiley Publishing, Inc. "WPI". By opening the accompanying software packet(s), you acknowledge that you have read and accept the following terms and conditions. If you do not agree and do not want to be bound by such terms and conditions, promptly return the Book and the unopened software packet(s) to the place you obtained them for a full refund.

1. **License Grant.** WPI grants to you (either an individual or entity) a nonexclusive license to use one copy of the enclosed software program(s) (collectively, the "Software") solely for your own personal or business purposes on a single computer (whether a standard computer or a workstation component of a multi-user network). The Software is in use on a computer when it is loaded into temporary memory (RAM) or installed into permanent memory (hard disk, CD-ROM, or other storage device). WPI reserves all rights not expressly granted herein.

2. **Ownership.** WPI is the owner of all right, title, and interest, including copyright, in and to the compilation of the Software recorded on the physical packet included with this Book "Software Media". Copyright to the individual programs recorded on the Software Media is owned by the author or other authorized copyright owner of each program. Ownership of the Software and all proprietary rights relating thereto remain with WPI and its licensers.

3. **Restrictions on Use and Transfer.**

    (a) You may only (i) make one copy of the Software for backup or archival purposes, or (ii) transfer the Software to a single hard disk, provided that you keep the original for backup or archival purposes. You may not (i) rent or lease the Software, (ii) copy or reproduce the Software through a LAN or other network system or through any computer subscriber system or bulletin-board system, or (iii) modify, adapt, or create derivative works based on the Software.

    (b) You may not reverse engineer, decompile, or disassemble the Software. You may transfer the Software and user documentation on a permanent basis, provided that the transferee agrees to accept the terms and conditions of this Agreement and you retain no copies. If the Software is an update or has been updated, any transfer must include the most recent update and all prior versions.

4. **Restrictions on Use of Individual Programs.** You must follow the individual requirements and restrictions detailed for each individual program in the "About the CD" appendix of this Book or on the Software Media. These limitations are also contained in the individual license agreements recorded on the Software Media. These limitations may include a requirement that after using the program for a specified period of time, the user must pay a registration fee or discontinue use. By opening the Software packet(s), you agree to abide by the licenses and restrictions for these individual programs that are detailed in the "About the CD" appendix and/or on the Software Media. None of the material on this Software Media or listed in this Book may ever be redistributed, in original or modified form, for commercial purposes.

5. **Limited Warranty.**

   (a) WPI warrants that the Software and Software Media are free from defects in materials and workmanship under normal use for a period of sixty (60) days from the date of purchase of this Book. If WPI receives notification within the warranty period of defects in materials or workmanship, WPI will replace the defective Software Media.

   (b) **WPI AND THE AUTHOR(S) OF THE BOOK DISCLAIM ALL OTHER WARRANTIES, EXPRESS OR IMPLIED, INCLUDING WITHOUT LIMITATION IMPLIED WARRANTIES OF MERCHANTABILITY AND FITNESS FOR A PARTICULAR PURPOSE, WITH RESPECT TO THE SOFTWARE, THE PROGRAMS, THE SOURCE CODE CONTAINED THEREIN, AND/OR THE TECHNIQUES DESCRIBED IN THIS BOOK. WPI DOES NOT WARRANT THAT THE FUNCTIONS CONTAINED IN THE SOFTWARE WILL MEET YOUR REQUIREMENTS OR THAT THE OPERATION OF THE SOFTWARE WILL BE ERROR FREE.**

   (c) This limited warranty gives you specific legal rights, and you may have other rights that vary from jurisdiction to jurisdiction.

6. **Remedies.**

   (a) WPI's entire liability and your exclusive remedy for defects in materials and workmanship shall be limited to replacement of the Software Media, which may be returned to WPI with a copy of your receipt at the following address: Software Media Fulfillment Department, Attn.: *Creating Web Pages All-in-One Desk Reference For Dummies, 3rd Edition*, Wiley Publishing, Inc., 10475 Crosspoint Blvd., Indianapolis, IN 46256, or call 1-800-762-2974. Please allow four to six weeks for delivery. This Limited Warranty is void if failure of the Software Media has resulted from accident, abuse, or misapplication. Any replacement Software Media will be warranted for the remainder of the original warranty period or thirty (30) days, whichever is longer.

   (b) In no event shall WPI or the author be liable for any damages whatsoever (including without limitation damages for loss of business profits, business interruption, loss of business information, or any other pecuniary loss) arising from the use of or inability to use the Book or the Software, even if WPI has been advised of the possibility of such damages.

   (c) Because some jurisdictions do not allow the exclusion or limitation of liability for consequential or incidental damages, the above limitation or exclusion may not apply to you.

7. **U.S. Government Restricted Rights.** Use, duplication, or disclosure of the Software for or on behalf of the United States of America, its agencies and/or instrumentalities "U.S. Government" is subject to restrictions as stated in paragraph (c)(1)(ii) of the Rights in Technical Data and Computer Software clause of DFARS 252.227-7013, or subparagraphs (c) (1) and (2) of the Commercial Computer Software - Restricted Rights clause at FAR 52.227-19, and in similar clauses in the NASA FAR supplement, as applicable.

8. **General.** This Agreement constitutes the entire understanding of the parties and revokes and supersedes all prior agreements, oral or written, between them and may not be modified or amended except in a writing signed by both parties hereto that specifically refers to this Agreement. This Agreement shall take precedence over any other documents that may be in conflict herewith. If any one or more provisions contained in this Agreement are held by any court or tribunal to be invalid, illegal, or otherwise unenforceable, each and every other provision shall remain in full force and effect.

USINESS, CAREERS & PERSONAL FINANCE

0-7645-9847-3

0-7645-2431-3

Also available:
- Business Plans Kit For Dummies
  0-7645-9794-9
- Economics For Dummies
  0-7645-5726-2
- Grant Writing For Dummies
  0-7645-8416-2
- Home Buying For Dummies
  0-7645-5331-3
- Managing For Dummies
  0-7645-1771-6
- Marketing For Dummies
  0-7645-5600-2

- Personal Finance For Dummies
  0-7645-2590-5*
- Resumes For Dummies
  0-7645-5471-9
- Selling For Dummies
  0-7645-5363-1
- Six Sigma For Dummies
  0-7645-6798-5
- Small Business Kit For Dummies
  0-7645-5984-2
- Starting an eBay Business For Dummies
  0-7645-6924-4
- Your Dream Career For Dummies
  0-7645-9795-7

ME & BUSINESS COMPUTER BASICS

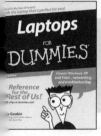

0-470-05432-8

0-471-75421-8

Also available:
- Cleaning Windows Vista For Dummies
  0-471-78293-9
- Excel 2007 For Dummies
  0-470-03737-7
- Mac OS X Tiger For Dummies
  0-7645-7675-5
- MacBook For Dummies
  0-470-04859-X
- Macs For Dummies
  0-470-04849-2
- Office 2007 For Dummies
  0-470-00923-3

- Outlook 2007 For Dummies
  0-470-03830-6
- PCs For Dummies
  0-7645-8958-X
- Salesforce.com For Dummies
  0-470-04893-X
- Upgrading & Fixing Laptops For Dummies
  0-7645-8959-8
- Word 2007 For Dummies
  0-470-03658-3
- Quicken 2007 For Dummies
  0-470-04600-7

OD, HOME, GARDEN, HOBBIES, MUSIC & PETS

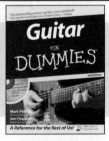

0-7645-8404-9

0-7645-9904-6

Also available:
- Candy Making For Dummies
  0-7645-9734-5
- Card Games For Dummies
  0-7645-9910-0
- Crocheting For Dummies
  0-7645-4151-X
- Dog Training For Dummies
  0-7645-8418-9
- Healthy Carb Cookbook For Dummies
  0-7645-8476-6
- Home Maintenance For Dummies
  0-7645-5215-5

- Horses For Dummies
  0-7645-9797-3
- Jewelry Making & Beading For Dummies
  0-7645-2571-9
- Orchids For Dummies
  0-7645-6759-4
- Puppies For Dummies
  0-7645-5255-4
- Rock Guitar For Dummies
  0-7645-5356-9
- Sewing For Dummies
  0-7645-6847-7
- Singing For Dummies
  0-7645-2475-5

ERNET & DIGITAL MEDIA

0-470-04529-9

0-470-04894-8

Also available:
- Blogging For Dummies
  0-471-77084-1
- Digital Photography For Dummies
  0-7645-9802-3
- Digital Photography All-in-One Desk Reference For Dummies
  0-470-03743-1
- Digital SLR Cameras and Photography For Dummies
  0-7645-9803-1
- eBay Business All-in-One Desk Reference For Dummies
  0-7645-8438-3
- HDTV For Dummies
  0-470-09673-X

- Home Entertainment PCs For Dummies
  0-470-05523-5
- MySpace For Dummies
  0-470-09529-6
- Search Engine Optimization For Dummies
  0-471-97998-8
- Skype For Dummies
  0-470-04891-3
- The Internet For Dummies
  0-7645-8996-2
- Wiring Your Digital Home For Dummies
  0-471-91830-X

te Canadian edition also available

te U.K. edition also available

wherever books are sold. For more information or to order direct: U.S. customers visit www.dummies.com or call 1-877-762-2974.
mers visit www.wileyeurope.com or call 0800 243407. Canadian customers visit www.wiley.ca or call 1-800-567-4797.

SPORTS, FITNESS, PARENTING, RELIGION & SPIRITUALITY

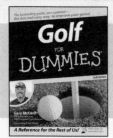

0-471-76871-5

0-7645-7841-3

Also available:

- Catholicism For Dummies
  0-7645-5391-7
- Exercise Balls For Dummies
  0-7645-5623-1
- Fitness For Dummies
  0-7645-7851-0
- Football For Dummies
  0-7645-3936-1
- Judaism For Dummies
  0-7645-5299-6
- Potty Training For Dummies
  0-7645-5417-4
- Buddhism For Dummies
  0-7645-5359-3

- Pregnancy For Dummies
  0-7645-4483-7 †
- Ten Minute Tone-Ups For Dummies
  0-7645-7207-5
- NASCAR For Dummies
  0-7645-7681-X
- Religion For Dummies
  0-7645-5264-3
- Soccer For Dummies
  0-7645-5229-5
- Women in the Bible For Dummies
  0-7645-8475-8

TRAVEL

0-7645-7749-2

0-7645-6945-7

Also available:

- Alaska For Dummies
  0-7645-7746-8
- Cruise Vacations For Dummies
  0-7645-6941-4
- England For Dummies
  0-7645-4276-1
- Europe For Dummies
  0-7645-7529-5
- Germany For Dummies
  0-7645-7823-5
- Hawaii For Dummies
  0-7645-7402-7

- Italy For Dummies
  0-7645-7386-1
- Las Vegas For Dummies
  0-7645-7382-9
- London For Dummies
  0-7645-4277-X
- Paris For Dummies
  0-7645-7630-5
- RV Vacations For Dummies
  0-7645-4442-X
- Walt Disney World & Orlando
  For Dummies
  0-7645-9660-8

GRAPHICS, DESIGN & WEB DEVELOPMENT

0-7645-8815-X

0-7645-9571-7

Also available:

- 3D Game Animation For Dummies
  0-7645-8789-7
- AutoCAD 2006 For Dummies
  0-7645-8925-3
- Building a Web Site For Dummies
  0-7645-7144-3
- Creating Web Pages For Dummies
  0-470-08030-2
- Creating Web Pages All-in-One Desk
  Reference For Dummies
  0-7645-4345-8
- Dreamweaver 8 For Dummies
  0-7645-9649-7

- InDesign CS2 For Dummies
  0-7645-9572-5
- Macromedia Flash 8 For Dummie
  0-7645-9691-8
- Photoshop CS2 and Digital
  Photography For Dummies
  0-7645-9580-6
- Photoshop Elements 4 For Dumm
  0-471-77483-9
- Syndicating Web Sites with RSS F
  For Dummies
  0-7645-8848-6
- Yahoo! SiteBuilder For Dummies
  0-7645-9800-7

NETWORKING, SECURITY, PROGRAMMING & DATABASES

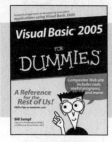

0-7645-7728-X

0-471-74940-0

Also available:

- Access 2007 For Dummies
  0-470-04612-0
- ASP.NET 2 For Dummies
  0-7645-7907-X
- C# 2005 For Dummies
  0-7645-9704-3
- Hacking For Dummies
  0-470-05235-X
- Hacking Wireless Networks
  For Dummies
  0-7645-9730-2
- Java For Dummies
  0-470-08716-1

- Microsoft SQL Server 2005 For Du
  0-7645-7755-7
- Networking All-in-One Desk Ref
  For Dummies
  0-7645-9939-9
- Preventing Identity Theft For Dun
  0-7645-7336-5
- Telecom For Dummies
  0-471-77085-X
- Visual Studio 2005 All-in-One D
  Reference For Dummies
  0-7645-9775-2
- XML For Dummies
  0-7645-8845-1

EALTH & SELF-HELP

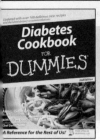

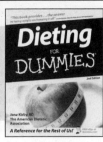

0-7645-8450-2   0-7645-4149-8

Also available:

✔ Bipolar Disorder For Dummies
0-7645-8451-0
✔ Chemotherapy and Radiation
For Dummies
0-7645-7832-4
✔ Controlling Cholesterol For Dummies
0-7645-5440-9
✔ Diabetes For Dummies
0-7645-6820-5* †
✔ Divorce For Dummies
0-7645-8417-0 †

✔ Fibromyalgia For Dummies
0-7645-5441-7
✔ Low-Calorie Dieting For Dummies
0-7645-9905-4
✔ Meditation For Dummies
0-471-77774-9
✔ Osteoporosis For Dummies
0-7645-7621-6
✔ Overcoming Anxiety For Dummies
0-7645-5447-6
✔ Reiki For Dummies
0-7645-9907-0
✔ Stress Management For Dummies
0-7645-5144-2

UCATION, HISTORY, REFERENCE & TEST PREPARATION

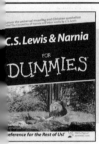

0-7645-8381-6   0-7645-9554-7

Also available:

✔ The ACT For Dummies
0-7645-9652-7
✔ Algebra For Dummies
0-7645-5325-9
✔ Algebra Workbook For Dummies
0-7645-8467-7
✔ Astronomy For Dummies
0-7645-8465-0
✔ Calculus For Dummies
0-7645-2498-4
✔ Chemistry For Dummies
0-7645-5430-1
✔ Forensics For Dummies
0-7645-5580-4

✔ Freemasons For Dummies
0-7645-9796-5
✔ French For Dummies
0-7645-5193-0
✔ Geometry For Dummies
0-7645-5324-0
✔ Organic Chemistry I For Dummies
0-7645-6902-3
✔ The SAT I For Dummies
0-7645-7193-1
✔ Spanish For Dummies
0-7645-5194-9
✔ Statistics For Dummies
0-7645-5423-9

Get smart @ dummies.com®

- **Find a full list of Dummies titles**
- **Look into loads of FREE on-site articles**
- **Sign up for FREE eTips e-mailed to you weekly**
- **See what other products carry the Dummies name**
- **Shop directly from the Dummies bookstore**
- **Enter to win new prizes every month!**

ate Canadian edition also available
ate U.K. edition also available

wherever books are sold. For more information or to order direct: U.S. customers visit www.dummies.com or call 1-877-762-2974.
mers visit www.wileyeurope.com or call 0800 243407. Canadian customers visit www.wiley.ca or call 1-800-567-4797.

Do More with Dummies

Tickle my ribs!

Grilling FOR DUMMIES

12" x 12" kit
Scrapbooking Basics FOR DUMMIES

Quilting Notions FOR DUMMIES

Sewing Patt FOR DUMMIE

Cocktail Kit FOR DUMMIES

Poker FOR DUMMIES

Golf FOR DUMMIES

Pilates Workout FOR DUMMIES

'80s Pop Music FOR DUMMIES

'70s Soul Mu FOR DUMMIES

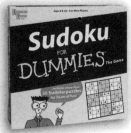

Tarot Deck & Book Set FOR DUMMIES

Sudoku FOR DUMMIES The Game

Texas Hold 'em FOR DUMMIES

**Instructional DVDs • Music Compilations
Games & Novelties • Culinary Kits
Crafts & Sewing Patterns
Home Improvement/DIY Kits • and more!**

Check out the Dummies Specialty Shop at www.dummies.com for more information!

 WIL